Reading in the Composition Classroom: Second Language Perspectives

Joan G. Carson
Georgia State University

Ilona Leki
University of Tennessee

Editors

HEINLE AND HEINLE PUBLISHERS
A Division of Wadsworth, Inc.
Boston, Massachusetts 02116 U.S.A.

Dedication

ཤ

To J.K.R.
To K.D.T.

Publisher: Stanley J. Galek
Editorial Director: David C. Lee
Assistant Editor: Ken Mattsson
Editorial Production Manager: Elizabeth Holthaus
Production Editor: Kristin Thalheimer
Manufacturing Coordinator: Jerry Christopher
Interior Design and Composition: Greg Johnson
Cover Design: Hannus Design Associates

Library of Congress Cataloging-in-Publication Data

Reading in the composition classroom: second language perspectives /
    Joan Carson, Ilona Leki, editors.
      p.   cm.
   ISBN 0-8384-3972-1
   1. English language—Study and teaching—Foreign speakers.
  2. English language—Composition and exercises—Study and teaching.
  3. Reading (Adult education)   I. Carson, Joan, 1944– . II. Leki,
Ilona.
PE1128.A2R265   1993
428'.007—dc20   92-31766
                                              CIP

Heinle & Heinle Publishers is a division of Wadsworth, Inc.

Manufactured in the United States of America

10 9 8 7 6 5 4 3 2

Contents

Reading in the Composition Classroom: Second Language Perspectives

SECTION I

INTRODUCTION

Joan G. Carson and Ilona Leki, *Editors*

The ESL teaching profession is on the brink of an important new understanding of the connections between reading and writing. For many years reading and writing in ESL classrooms were taught separately and as technical skills. Reflecting audiolingual methodology, these two language acts were thought of as consisting of component language subskills that could be taught one by one until the student had mastered all the pieces and, consequently, reading and writing. In this formulation, reading was rightly understood as a process distinct from writing, but the distinction was too sharply drawn and failed to recognize that the two skills share similar cognitive processes of meaning construction. In the second language composition classroom reading typically played no more than a secondary role, serving mainly as linguistic model for rhetorical patterns and as content material for writing assignments.

Over the last 10 years ESL writing classrooms have changed dramatically, focusing on writing as a communicative act and emphasizing students' writing processes and communicative intentions. Along with this change has come recognition of the extent to which reading can be, and in academic settings nearly always is, the basis for writing. Recent research has also called into question the traditional narrow view of the function of reading in the teaching of writing. Goodman (1986) argues for a "whole language" approach to literacy development. In this view, reading and writing develop together, confirming what first and second language researchers (Belanger, 1987; Krashen, 1984; Stotsky, 1983) have claimed and what language teachers intuitively know: Reading and writing abilities are inextricably linked.

Reading in the Composition Classroom: Second Language Perspectives examines the importance and potential impact of second language reading on second language writing. The chapters of this book focus both on cognitive perspectives—how individual learners process text—as well as on social perspectives—how cultural background and literacy contexts affect reading/writing understanding and performance. Because much work on reading/writing relationships has been confined to cognitive

1

issues, the inclusion of papers with a social perspective provides the balance that is needed for a more holistic approach to second language literacy development. The practical chapters of the book provide illustrations and discussions of ways in which a reading/writing perspective can inform composition classroom practices. Other chapters extend this inquiry beyond pedagogy, to a wide range of theoretical and research issues. Thus both teachers and researchers have access to in-depth examinations of how second language reading and writing interact from separate and overlapping cognitive and social perspectives, since, as Flower (1989) has claimed, it is individual cognition and sociocultural contexts that are the motive forces in literacy acts.

To provide this depth of coverage, we have focused most closely on the role of reading in the writing classroom rather than on writing in the reading classroom. It is chiefly in the thousands of L2 writing classrooms that the question of how reading and writing may interact specifically arises. Nevertheless, we fully recognize and acknowledge the reciprocity of the effects of L2 reading and writing in academic contexts, in literacy training, and in research settings (see Chapter 1). Writing provides a way into reading, extends reading, and consolidates understanding of a text just as reading sustains writing and furnishes, for the writer, the counterpoint of another voice. The ways in which writing enhances the interpretation of texts are implied in several chapters of this book (see, for example, chapters by Blanton and Spack), which also suggest further directions for exploration of the interrelationship between reading and writing.[1]

The overall structure of *Reading in the Composition Classroom: Second Language Perspectives* consists of three primary sections and an epilogue. Section I is an overview. Section II presents issues relating to the cognitive perspective on reading in the composition classroom. Section III covers issues relating to the social perspective on reading in the composition classroom. An epilogue summarizes the papers and discusses the relationship between these two perspectives. In this way, theoretical issues and practical applications are presented within a single perspective, either cognitive or social.

SECTION I: OVERVIEW

Section I provides relevant background information as well as a general introduction to the issues discussed in the book. In Chapter 1, "Reciprocal Themes in ESL Reading and Writing," Ilona Leki establishes the focus for the book by introducing current issues in L2 writing and reading. She maintains that recent empirical and classroom experiments

---

[1]See Zamel (1992) for a fuller discussion of the effect of writing on reading.

with reading and writing place ESL practitioners at the beginning of a new, major shift in perspective similar to the one that occurred in the teaching of ESL composition during the 1980s. In Chapter 2, Joy Reid examines the historical trajectory of this emerging shift. "Historical Perspectives on Writing and Reading in the ESL Classroom" explores the roles of three major components of reading/writing classrooms—author, text, and reader. Reid describes traditional and typical uses of text in writing classrooms and their theoretical bases. Her paper includes a discussion of how current classroom practices are being informed and reformed by recent theories of the reading/writing relationship.

Chapter 3, "Teaching Writing IS Teaching Reading: Training the New Teacher of ESL Composition," by Barbara Kroll, orients both teacher trainees and experienced teachers to the relationship between the production and interpretation of texts. Kroll notes that ESL writing teachers need to know the basics of reading theory before they can successfully teach writing. It is this knowledge, she claims, that focuses teachers' attention on the relevant and necessary connections between production (writing) and interpretation (reading) of texts. Together, these three articles examine the broad issues of the reading/writing relationship from the composition classroom perspective.

SECTION II: COGNITIVE PERSPECTIVES

Section II focuses on cognitive perspectives of the reading/writing relationship. Chapter 4, Joan Carson's "Reading for Writing: Cognitive Dimensions," presents a theoretical overview of this relationship, examining current research and relevant literature in both L1 and L2. Focusing on psycholinguistic aspects of literacy development, she considers cognitive dimensions of meaning construction in writing that results from reading, as well as meaning construction in reading that is driven by writing tasks. In Chapter 5, "The Role of Metacognition in Second Language Reading and Writing," Joanne Devine provides a review of recent research on metacognition and focuses on important aspects of commonality between reading and writing. She examines knowledge of cognition and self-regulating mechanisms as well as significant differences in metacognitive operations involved in reading and writing, especially those involving cognitive monitoring and repair.

The next three chapters present research studies that explore how the cognitive dimension of reading affects writing. Chapter 6, Douglas Flahive and Nathalie Bailey's "Exploring Reading/Writing Relationships in Adult Second Language Learners," is a study of the reading/writing relationship that tests three specific generalizations derived from L1 studies. The first generalization tested is that subjects who read more write better. The second is that subjects who read better write better. And the third is that subjects who read more and read better write more complex, more grammatically correct prose.

In Chapter 7, Ulla Connor and Patricia Carrell investigate the importance of reading in the assessment of writing. Their paper, "The Interpretation of Tasks by Writers and Readers in Holistically Rated Direct Assessment of Writing" examines how reader/raters interpret the prompt and rate the essay, using the Test of Written English scoring guide. The study explores the varying perspectives of the two groups regarding the task, the prompt itself, and the final product in order to better understand the reading/writing connections operating in ESL testing situations.

In Chapter 8, Gissi Sarig's "Composing a Study–Summary: A Reading/Writing Encounter" investigates (1) the processes involved in writing an L1 study–summary for L1 and L2 texts and (2) the relation between processes and products when composing a study–summary from texts in L1 as opposed to texts in L2. Her results show that summarization is an intricate process, resulting from a cyclical interaction between planning and assessing on one hand, and performing, facilitating, clarifying, linking, transforming, and revising on the other. Furthermore, she finds evidence that summarization skills transfer from L1 to L2 and makes suggestions for classroom applications based on her study.

The last two papers in this section focus on ways in which the cognitive perspective on the reading/writing relationship can inform classroom practices. In Chapter 9, "Student Meets Text, Text Meets Student: Finding a Way into Academic Discourse," Ruth Spack argues for an undergraduate ESL composition program of reading and writing that "bridges the gap between what students bring to the academy and what the academy will ultimately expect of them." Writing and discussion facilitate the students' encounter with complex academic readings and help them explore the readings' "personal relevance and larger implications."

In Chapter 10, Linda Gajdusek and Deborah vanDommelen describe classroom practices designed to foster the kind of critical thinking that characterizes Western academic writing and that is essential to the completion of academic writing tasks facing many ESL students. They argue that interactive classroom work with a literary text can provide the intellectual and affective motivation for genuinely engaging student writers in the writing topic. The authors of "Literature and Critical Thinking in the Composition Classroom" work with a specific example—a modern American short story—to demonstrate an approach to reading and working with literature in the composition classroom so that teachers can model critical thinking procedures and thus encourage students not only to use them in their own writing, but also to transfer the same techniques to the reading and writing tasks of other disciplines and genres.

SECTION III: SOCIAL PERSPECTIVES

While the examination of the cognitive processes of L2 readers and writers provides insight into individual L2 development, reading and writing as meaning-making acts take place within a social context. Section III of the book focuses on social perspectives of the reading/writing relationship. David Eskey's overview paper in Chapter 11, "Reading and Writing as Both Cognitive Process and Social Behavior," claims that literacy development must be understood as a process that is not only cognitive but social as well. Because human languages are social constructs, he argues, they involve sets of rules and conventions that can be learned only by participating in the kinds of social activities that the construct serves to facilitate. Using Frank Smith's metaphor of a literacy club, Eskey discusses the importance to second language teachers and learners of the rules, conventions, and traditions of the many literacy clubs that constitute the universe of texts in English and that result in a fruitful interaction between the language and the various societies that have used it. Eskey urges a sociolinguistic exploration of this literacy club, particularly in the L2 context, in order to better understand who it includes and what must be done to join.

The next five chapters illustrate ways of inviting L2 students to join the literacy club Eskey describes. In Chapter 12, Linda Blanton explores reading and writing as social acts of performance in "Reading as Performance: Reframing the Function of Reading." Like Eskey, she notes that although her ESL students had trouble reading, they were literate; the problem was that they had not joined Smith's literacy club. She highlights the importance of students' interaction with text as the means for transforming them into academically/cognitively proficient readers and writers. Complementing Spack's and Gajdusek & vanDommelen's papers (Chapters 9 and 10) on the cognitive development of critical thinking skills through reading, Blanton argues for a reader-based pedagogy as a way of initiating students into reader–writer roles through academic/intellectual/linguistic socialization.

In Chapter 13, "ESL Authors: Reading and Writing Critical Autobiographies," Sarah Benesch describes another approach to student empowerment through extended reading and writing. Benesch's students write full-length autobiographies reflecting on their experiences as members of their particular social milieu and on the positive and negative forces that act upon them in those contexts. Using a student-as-author approach, Benesch examines how reading and writing extended prose allows students to internalize the structure and style of good writing. The full range of writing abilities is best developed when students can complete the "authoring cycle," taking their work from initial ideas to final publication. Most importantly, when students discuss the texts they have read and then write their own texts, the processes of reading, composing, and publishing are demystified.

In Chapter 14, "Reading for Composing: Connecting Processes to Advancing ESL Literacies," Fran Filipek Collignon uses Vygotskyan and Freirean frameworks to focus on the composing process of one learner. Collignon describes a course designed for Southeast Asian refugees employed as bilingual/bicultural workers in human services, health care, and education, jobs for which writing is a necessary skill. In this course, instructors collaborate with students in selecting and completing job-related writing assignments as well as in finding ways to address a variety of other learning needs. The course highlights the significance of the instructor's incorporating authentic reading into the interactive strategies encouraged among course participants. Collignon shows how this broader approach to literacy development is useful for those second language learners minimally schooled in their countries of origin and/or lacking native language literacy.

In Chapter 15, "Reading and Writing Tasks in English for Academic Purposes Classes: Products, Processes, and Resources," Ann Johns focuses on aspects of the reading/writing relationship that are issues in English for Academic Purposes classes. Johns argues that these EAP classes must utilize a task-based syllabus that takes into account the academic context, the learners and their processes, and the available resources.

Specifically applying the issues raised in Johns' discussion of EAP, Lynn Goldstein describes in Chapter 16 the structure of a graduate course for non-native speakers adjuncted to a course in second language acquisition. In "Becoming a Member of the 'Teaching Foreign Languages' Community: Integrating Reading and Writing Through an Adjunct/ Content Course," Goldstein argues that writing and reading need to be integrated in adjunct courses so that these skills enhance each other and hence improve, and so that students more easily learn the content of their academic courses.

While these chapters focus on the nature of the invitation we offer L2 students to join the literacy club, the final chapter in Section III approaches the notion of the literacy club from the point of view of those who are invited to join. In Chapter 17, "Cross-Cultural Perspectives on Task Representation in Reading to Write," Charlotte Basham, Ruth Ray, and Elizabeth Whalley investigate how students represent to themselves the literacy tasks we set for them in reading/writing classrooms, noting that part of the social context for reading and writing is established by students' varying cultural backgrounds. Their research is designed to explore the cultural assumptions about reading, authorship, and task representation that emerged in a study of summary writing done by Alaska Native, Hispanic, and Asian students. Complementing Sarig's work (Chapter 8) on cognitive processes in summary writing, echoing Blanton's concern (Chapter 12) about the effects of culture on literacy development, and taking up Spack's focus (Chapter 9) on how teachers can help students access a text, this chapter examines how students do in fact access texts and how cultural differences among students influence the process of "reading-when-you-intend-to-write" and the texts that result from such reading.

SECTION IV: EPILOGUE

Chapter 18 is the epilogue, "Reading and Writing: Integrating Cognitive and Social Dimensions." In this paper, Gayle Nelson examines literacy as both an individual and a social act occurring in the context of different cultures and subcultures. Summarizing and integrating the other papers in the volume, Nelson presents a coherent picture of the social dimensions of both student interaction and culture, showing how the cognitive processes of reading and writing are affected by each.

As ESL researchers and classroom teachers, we are beginning to realize the importance of integrating views of L2 writing and reading. *Reading in the Composition Classroom: Second Language Perspectives* provides a wide-ranging overview of current thinking, research, and course development in this area, recognizing reading and writing as both cognitive and social acts that link individual reading and writing behaviors with the broader social context in which literacy exists and literate populations function.

REFERENCES

Belanger, J. (1987). Theory and research into reading and writing connections: A critical review. *Reading-Canada-Lecture, 5,* 10–18.

Flower, L. (1989). Cognition, context, and theory building. *College Composition and Communication, 40,* 282–311.

Goodman, K. (1986). *What's whole in whole language?* Portsmouth, NH: Heinemann.

Krashen, S. (1984). *Writing: Research, theory, and applications.* Oxford: Pergamon Institute of English.

Stotsky, S. (1983). Research on reading/writing relationships: A synthesis and suggested directions. *Language Arts, 60,* 627–642.

Zamel, V. (1992). Writing one's way into reading. *TESOL Quarterly, 26,* 463–485.

CHAPTER 1

Reciprocal Themes in ESL Reading and Writing

Ilona Leki

University of Tennessee

> Reading, like writing, begins in confusion, anxiety and uncertainty. . . it is driven by chance and intuition as well as by deliberate strategy and conscious intent . . . certainty and authority are postures, features of a performance that is achieved through an act of writing, not qualities of vision that precede such a performance. (Bartholomae & Petrosky, 1986, p. 21)

Over the last 10 to 20 years, research in L2 reading and writing has progressed almost entirely independently, yet their findings echo each other. Relying heavily on insights from L1 research and on psycholinguistic studies of reading and composing processes, L2 researchers have made extensive use of miscue, protocol, and think-aloud analyses of the reading and writing of proficient and less skilled L2 readers and writers. As a result of these studies, we have some idea of where L2 readers focus their attention as they try to make sense of a text—to what extent they predict upcoming text, what they do with unknown vocabulary, how they try to process incoming text and relate it to what they have already read (Carrell, 1983b; Clarke, 1979; Cziko, 1978; Devine, 1988; Hudson, 1982; Rigg, 1977). We also have an idea of what goes on in the minds of experienced and inexperienced L2 writers as they compose—how much they plan, how much they translate from their L1, where they focus their attention, how they handle vocabulary problems (see Krapels, 1990 for an overview of L2 writing research; Arndt, 1987; Cumming, 1989; Hall, 1990; Jones & Tetroe, 1987; Raimes, 1985; Zamel, 1983).

Often (but not always—see Raimes 1985) these studies reveal that less skilled readers and writers both appear to attend to the same thing, to the text on the page rather than to the meaning potential of that text, to the forms of the letters and words rather than to the overarching connections between them. Inefficient L2 readers read too locally (Cohen, *et al.*, 1979), failing to link incoming text with previous text, and because they are unskilled in rapid text processing in L2, depend too heavily on bottom-up strategies to decode or extract the message assumed to exist in the text (Carrell, 1988b; Hosenfeld, 1984; McLaughlin, 1987; Stanovich,

1980).[1] Poor L2 writers focus excessively on word- and sentence-level grammatical and print code concerns (Arndt, 1987; Hatch, Polin, & Part, 1970; Silva, 1990).[2] All of this is to the detriment of meaning. Good readers and writers, on the other hand, are better able to focus on broader concerns related to communication.

Further parallels between cognitive research in reading and in writing indicate that proficient L2 readers and writers use strategies not hierarchically or linearly, but interactively in reading and recursively in writing (Carrell, 1983b; Zamel, 1983). The unifying characteristic of good readers and good writers seems to be flexibility, the ability to use and reuse different strategies as the moment calls for them.

The implications of this research have generally discouraged teachers from our previous focus on subskills of reading and writing, such as grammar and vocabulary, and encouraged us to focus on cognitive strategies that imitate those of proficient L1 readers and writers. Classrooms have turned toward teaching the processes of reading and writing.

Yet, oddly enough, until recently little in the L2 research literature has addressed reading and writing together, and despite the parallels between research findings in these domains and despite commonsense views that reading and writing have a reciprocal effect on each other, including the notion that good writers learn to write well in part by reading a great deal (see, however, Flahive & Bailey, this volume), adult ESL classrooms are only beginning to consider how to effectively integrate both reading and writing. We know that reading builds knowledge of various kinds to use in writing and that writing consolidates knowledge in a way that builds schemata to read with (Bereiter & Scardamalia, 1987; Sternglass, 1988). We also know that, for example, biology professors learn to write articles the way biology professors do by reading articles that biology professors have written. We do not have courses that teach biology professors to write like biology professors. Yet we continue to separate ESL reading courses from ESL writing courses.

This anomaly probably results from several causes. First, reading researchers themselves have urged that reading be taught in its own right and not be thought of as merely a skill in support of other language skills (Grabe, 1986). That is, reading should be thought of as more than merely a prompt for discussion or writing.

Second, writing pedagogy of the 1980s has also made the role of reading material in the ESL classroom unclear. In the past, readings that

---

[1]Evidence from studies of inefficient L1 readers also shows the opposite tendency, excessive and inaccurate guessing about the meaning of a text without enough bottom-up information (Kimmel & MacGinitie, 1984).

[2]The picture is actually more complex than this. L1 studies consistently show this pattern of allotting attention (Bereiter & Scardamalia, 1987; Perl, 1979), but at least one L2 study shows that even less-proficient writers also attend to meaning (Raimes, 1985).

appeared in ESL writing textbooks were used as model texts; classes ana-lyzed the structure of these texts, and students were instructed to pattern their own writing after those model structures (Raimes, 1986; Reid, this volume). Influenced by process approaches to writing instruction, teach-ers became reluctant to continue the use of texts as models because of the implication that form pre-exists content, that to write well students need-ed only to pour their content into the model forms exemplified in the reading passages. The role of reading in the writing classroom became somewhat uncertain. Were readings to be used as source material for stu-dent writing, as stimulus for ideas? How were writing teachers to treat those reading texts? Were writing teachers being asked to teach reading at the same time as writing? (See Kroll, this volume, for the argument that L2 writing teachers must also be reading teachers.) No systematic approach or consensus on how to use nonfiction readings in ESL writing classrooms has yet emerged. Up to now, discussion in the literature on using readings in writing classrooms has primarily revolved around mak-ing a case for teaching fiction (Gajdusek, 1988; Mlynarczyk, 1992; Spack, 1985).

A third reason functioning to keep reading instruction out of the advanced ESL writing classroom is related to the structure of higher edu-cation in this country. Although native English speakers take courses in freshman composition (often without readings in support of writing), reading courses are considered remedial for native students (Bartholomae & Petrosky, 1986) and as a result are typically also unavailable for non-natives except in language institutes.[3] It is assumed that ESL students at advanced levels are already reading well independently. (See Blanton, this volume, on the error of this view.) After all, these students are reading a great deal in other content-area classes. But difficulty and inefficiency in reading are easily dissimulated. This effort is hidden from us and from our content-area colleagues. While we see and hear about our students' prob-lems in writing, their reading problems may remain invisible, implying no problem exists.

Finally, however problematic, exit exams in writing are quite com-mon in colleges and universities, prompting the development of writing courses to prepare students for them; this is not the case in reading.[4] As a result, we have advanced ESL writing courses but do not typically teach reading beyond the level of language institutes despite the fact that ESL students report a greater need for proficiency in reading than in any other

---

[3]Among the odd historical divisions within higher education in this country, we might also mention the division in English departments between literature and writing instruction, in certain ways analogous to the division between writing and reading courses: the first in each pair considered more prestigious and more appropriately a concern of higher education.

[4]This is not to suggest in any way that there should be exit exams in reading. The wisdom of exit exams in writing is already questionable enough.

English language skill at the university level (Carrell, 1988a; Christison & Krahnke, 1986).

The unfortunate separation of reading and writing has impoverished instruction in both domains. Without readings in ESL writing classrooms, teachers tend to rely heavily on expressivist writing assignments based on personal experience or previous knowledge (Bazerman, 1980; Horowitz, 1986b; Spack, 1988). While this form of writing is valuable, it is limited and not the type of writing typically required from ESL students in higher education (Horowitz, 1986a; Johns, 1981; Reid, 1987). Reading, a major source of new knowledge, is ignored, and students are not called upon to develop the ability to select and integrate new knowledge with knowledge and information they already possess and with their analyses and reactions to that new knowledge and information. It is this ability to integrate or internalize new information in writing that undergirds the notions both of knowledge-transforming (Bereiter and Scardamalia, 1987) and of critical literacy (Flower *et al.*, 1990) and may in fact be what we actually mean when we speak of comprehension of a text.

Writing pedagogy in the 1980s and 1990s has remained fairly closely in line with writing research, having undergone an enormous change in the 1980s, a virtual paradigm shift, as teachers abandoned remedial models of writing instruction and incorporated research insights into their classroom. While L2 reading research has produced insights as far-reaching as those of writing research, its impact on textbooks and classrooms has been less noticeable (Grabe, 1986). Schema theory and the notion of top-down processing of text did inspire the successful incorporation of pre-reading activities into many reading classrooms (Anderson & Pearson, 1984; Carrell & Eisterhold, 1983; Goodman, 1976). But to judge by textbooks and pedagogical articles on reading in the 1980s, researchers' exploration of the notion of the interactive nature of reading (Rummelhart, 1977; Stanovich, 1980) has had an almost negligible impact (Grabe, 1986). As a result, the unfortunate effect of teaching reading and writing in separate courses has had dramatic consequences on reading instruction, robbing reading of its natural purpose and ignoring its social dimensions. The rest of this chapter will explore the implications of this situation, touching on a number of themes that will be taken up again more specifically in the subsequent chapters of this book.

ISOLATED READING CLASSES: READING FOR NO REAL REASON

The research literature in L2 emphasizes the importance of purpose in both writing and reading (Eskey, 1986; Kroll, 1991). In recent writing instruction, purpose for writing has become a central focus. Many classrooms now include, for example, unevaluated writing journals in which students can freely explore topics of personal interest to them and from which they may select entries to develop into full essays (Blanton, 1987; Spack & Sadow, 1983). Writing on topics selected in this manner goes a long way toward ensuring the kind of internal motivation for writing which presumably results in the commitment to task which, in turn, is thought to help writing and language improve. But the immediate purpose for writing about a particular subject is neither language nor even writing improvement. It is, rather, a more natural purpose, i.e., communication with a reader about something of personal significance to the writer. The emphasis on publishing student writing grows from the same belief in the importance of purpose; if a piece is to be published, a student has far more reason to feel intellectually committed to the writing, to both the content and form of the text. Finally, the entire thrust of writing instruction within an English for Specific Purposes context rests on the belief that students should learn to write what they will need to write and in the way they will need to write within the academic disciplines they have chosen (Horowitz, 1986a; Reid, 1987).

The literature on reading has also pointed out that readers read for different purposes and that those purposes affect what is attended to and with what intensity (Eskey, 1986). This concern with purpose has emerged in the L2 reading classroom most clearly in pre-reading questions intended to lend direction to reading by giving students something to read for. But this understanding of purpose is extremely narrow. Certainly, having a purpose for reading a text should make that text easier to read, but that avoids the real question: Why is this text being read in the first place? While it is axiomatic that our L2 students learn to read by reading, it appears that in L2 reading classes this axiom has been inappropriately reversed: the reason for reading a text is to learn to read. Yet as Flower *et al.* (1990) point out,

> Literacy, as Richardson, Vygotsky, and others have defined it, is not synonymous with the ability to read (decode) or write (transcribe) per se. Rather it is a "goal-directed, context-specific" behavior, which means that a literate person is able to use reading and writing in a transactional sense to achieve some purpose in the world at hand.... (p. 4)

The failure to provide real purposes for reading suggests that in isolated L2 reading classes (i.e., ones in which students are not reading to write), students are not reading but merely practicing reading. This "reading practice" is evident in reading selections and in pedagogical focuses in L2 reading classrooms.

Text Selection

The reading material used in many ESL reading classes both reveals and furthers the distortion of the reading class into the reading practice class.

Since isolated reading classes serve no other purpose than to teach reading, there is no particular reason to read one text rather than another. In line with that reasoning, then, most readings in L2 reading classes are short texts on a variety of topics that are thought to be of high interest to our students: pollution, friendship, language, cultural differences, education, the role of women in various cultures.[5]

Short texts are selected because they conveniently fit into our class periods better than long texts, they take less time to read, and they are thought to be easier to read than longer texts. But short texts are, in fact, likely to be more difficult to read since students never read enough about the subject to build the knowledge about it that would allow them to read with ease and pleasure. (See Sternglass, 1988 on the issue of knowledge building for the purpose of knowledge making.) Like our students, we allow our intuitions to lead us astray—when our students have trouble reading, they slow down and try to decode the text word for word, operating locally, microscopically, and hoping that by simplifying and separating, they will later be able to add up all the pieces and understand. When confronted with students having difficulties reading, we have the same reaction: to break up the reading, go microscopic, and give students shorter, "easier" texts to read (Bartholomae & Petrosky, 1986).

Furthermore, we select a variety of subject matters to maintain student interest and motivation and, ostensibly, to focus attention on content. We hope that by using a shotgun approach to subject matter we will eventually hit upon at least one subject of interest to each of our students. That may or may not happen, but the result of constant shifts in subject matter is once again the same: The texts are harder to read because the students must gear up for a new subject with each reading selection. This approach to reading material also denies our students the eye-opening experience readers have when they return to a text read earlier with new knowledge structures born of reading other texts on the same subject (see Spack, this volume). The original text now literally means something new to the reader; the meaning of sections of text previously blurred by misunderstanding is clarified through the lens of new knowledge. But the possibility for such growth is eliminated by asking students to switch their attention from pollution to animal behavior to education with each new chapter.

Finally, there is the question of high interest. It is possible to argue that the subjects typically covered in ESL readers are of high interest to teachers and textbook writers, but not particularly to L2 students. The topics *might* be of high interest if these students could already read them as easily as *we* read them. But L2 reading is a struggle, and these subjects are unlikely to be of high enough personal interest to our students to compensate for the burden created by asking students to read a hodge-

---

[5]ESP, adjunct, and sheltered writing courses are the exceptions to this pattern.

podge of subjects for no particular reason except to learn to read English better. (See Kroll, this volume, for a glimpse into a classroom using such an approach.) This approach to teaching reading resembles writing classes of ten years ago, when teachers struggled to divine what might be interesting, motivating topics for students to write on and came up with such assignments as "Describe your most embarrassing moment." Even if we locate high interest readings, as Bartholomae & Petrosky (1990) maintain, the issue is less what students read (i.e., the discovery of the perfect text) than what they then *do* with what they read, how we ask them to engage that text.

Pedagogical Practices

One source of the problems in isolated reading classes is confusion about what we can accomplish. If we are convinced by evidence that pleasure reading contributes to L2 reading and writing proficiency (Elley & Mangubhai, 1983; Hafiz & Tudor, 1989; Krashen, 1988, 1984; van Naerssen, 1985), one goal of a reading class might be to promote pleasure reading. Unfortunately, this goal is unrealistic; for all but the most proficient of our students, L2 reading is too difficult a chore to be engaged in simply for pleasure (Janopoulos, 1986), and to build proficiency in reading strictly through pleasure reading takes time our ESL students may not have.

Our goal then becomes to attempt to preempt reading difficulties by teaching generic strategies for reading *any* text. Our teaching strategy has been to examine the cognitive processes of proficient readers, those who presumably do read a great deal for pleasure, to isolate the strategies they use, and to teach these strategies to our students. We find that proficient readers do not read all texts in an invariable, plodding pace from word to word, dictionary in hand, as some of our less proficient students do. Instead, they skim some texts or sections of text, they scan, they read in chunks rather than word for word, they note cohesion markers, they guess vocabulary meaning from context, and they read fast (Grabe, 1986). So we direct our students to imitate these behaviors and practice skimming, scanning, guessing, and chunking texts; we tell them not to use dictionaries; we give them practice recognizing cohesion markers; and we push them to read fast (Eskey & Grabe, 1988).

The problem with teaching these cognitive strategies is that even if our students accomplish these goals, they are still not learning reading; they are learning strategies for reading, which can at best be only imitations of reading behaviors, like children turning the pages of books they cannot yet read. We seem to have assumed that these strategies are the causes of proficiency in reading. But these strategies are the *result* not the cause of reading proficiency; good readers read fast because they can. They are able to comprehend incoming text quickly. If our students use dictionaries and read slowly with an even amount of attention to every word, they do this because this is all they *can* do. They do *not* comprehend; they do not know which words are essential to meaning and which may be passed over.[6] If proficient readers skim some texts, they do so because the text, as they themselves judge it for their own internally motivated purposes, merits no more careful reading. The answer to the question of which texts should be skimmed, which scanned, which words looked up in the dictionary, or which texts abandoned altogether is determined by the reader's purpose in reading. If the purpose in reading is only to practice reading, there can be no internally motivated answers to these questions. With no purpose for reading, then skimming, scanning, or any of the other strategies we teach all become no more than artificial exercises. By taking over control of their reading through post-reading exercises and telling our students which texts to skim, which information to scan for, and how fast to read, we are preventing the very grappling with meaning that would allow students to develop their own strategies for rapid and accurate text processing. (See Devine, this volume, for discussion of the interaction between goal setting, or purpose, and metacognition.)

The problems inherent in teaching strategies to improve reading devoid of any true purpose for reading are exacerbated by textbooks that direct students to practice these techniques thoroughly, that is, with every, or nearly every, text in the book. Despite the research findings that good readers read for varying purposes and with varying degrees of attention, isolated reading courses tend in fact to direct students to do the opposite, to regard each reading selection addressed in class as equally important and eligible for similar analysis. Again we see clear parallels with the kinds of discredited writing instruction practices in which every text students write is taken to be a final draft and then corrected and evaluated.

Another nearly universal pedagogical practice in L2 reading classrooms is post-reading comprehension checks, often aimed, like standardized reading tests, at checking comprehension by asking students to identify the main idea of a text or passage. But this enterprise is problematic. First, knowing the main idea of a text does not mean understanding the text. Second, questioning students about the main idea does absolutely nothing to *show* students how to achieve comprehension, whether or not they can successfully spot the same main idea we spot. Finally, pointing out that our students' version of the main idea is or is not the same as ours, far from helping our students achieve understanding, does not even help our students identify the main idea! It is not clear that we even know exactly how we determine what the main idea of a text is. (See Parry, 1987 for an interesting discussion of factors that may have influenced a group of West African students in their construction of the meaning of a text.) If we do not know how we ourselves recognize the main

---

[6]In the same way, excessive attention to details in inexperienced writers is the symptom, not the cause, of difficulty with the task.

idea of a text, we cannot teach it to our students and end by merely mystifying them. Yet there seems to be almost an obsession with main ideas in reading pedagogy and testing that is reminiscent of the previous exaggerated interest in topic sentences in writing and that represents a reductionist view of reading. By relying so heavily and confidently on comprehension and main idea questions, we seem to be defining—and encourage our students to define—text comprehension as correct responses to comprehension questions. Yet, many would argue that

> the only way to demonstrate comprehension is through extended discourse where readers become writers who articulate their understandings of and connections to the text in their responses. Response is, then, an expression and explanation of comprehension; and comprehension means using writing to explicate the connections between our models of reality—our prior knowledge—and the texts we recreate in light of them. (Petrosky, 1982, pp. 24-25, discussing David Bleich)

Typical comprehension checks also imply that the meaning of a text resides in the text and that the students' goal is to ferret out the meaning the author put there. This implication is out of tune with the notions, so pervasive in current reading research, of reading as the construction, not the deciphering, of meaning and of reading as interaction between reader and text, in which meaning depends as much on what the reader brings to the text as what the text brings to the reader. The usual comprehension check denies the role of the reader in constructing meaning. Yet Tierney & Pearson (1983) assert that "there is no meaning on the page until a reader decides there is" (p. 569).

Furthermore, exactly what do our students gain by correctly identifying the main idea in an ESL textbook article on dreams or friendship? What difference does it make if the student correctly or incorrectly identifies the same main idea as the teacher? In natural reading contexts, proficient and even less skilled readers reading for a real-world purpose not only skim, scan, or chunk for their own purposes, but they also choose to privilege either main ideas or details of a text, again depending on their purpose in reading. In a given text read by a specific reader in a real-world context, the main idea may or may not be significant. The reader may retain only a striking image or line of reasoning, or even, as is often the case with academic readers, only a citation or reference to another text. But if the purpose for reading a text is to practice reading, then students have no basis on which to privilege main ideas or details. By persistently imposing a check for comprehension of main ideas, we may in fact be training our students to read in ways characteristic of poor readers, bound to the text and lacking the purpose that would allow them to skip over information they themselves judge uninteresting or unnecessary.

Thus on one hand, a leveling process takes place such that all the texts read are given equal attention and therefore equal weight, and on the other hand, a selection process occurs whereby someone besides the reader decides what should be salient to the reader. If that which resonates for the student does not match the main idea of the text, the importance of the student's encounter with the text is undermined and the student's reading is dismissed as a failure to understand.

Attempting to Teach What Cannot be Taught

Perhaps one difficulty with the entire enterprise of teaching the construction of meaning, whether in reading or in writing, is that although it can be learned, in some important, very real sense, it cannot be taught (see Eskey, 1986). Perhaps we are unwilling to believe this. Perhaps it is because we feel we need to teach *something* in isolated reading classes that we have typically turned to teaching not reading, not text comprehension or meaning construction, but reading strategies and study skills.

One of the complaints in the early 1980s against traditional approaches to teaching L2 writing was that students were not really writing but rather manipulating language, not using language to communicate but rather to practice grammar or to practice larger components of written texts, such as rhetorical patterns (Kroll, 1991). In traditional approaches to teaching writing, we assumed that by teaching students to write a topic sentence, to select and explain three examples, and to write a conclusion, we had given students all the building blocks necessary to create virtually any expository text (Kroll, 1991).

Don't we see the same kinds of narrowly focused aims in current traditional reading courses, aims of learning vocabulary by studying prefixing and suffixing, aims of identifying main idea and supporting details, aims of recognizing discourse features? Certainly, the ability to recognize discourse features and a large number of vocabulary items helps make reading easier, but if these abilities are set as the goals for the course rather than as a means of facilitating the reading of specific texts selected for a real purpose, we are back to teaching skills. More sophisticated ones, to be sure, but for all their sophistication, they still do not get to the heart of the question of how to help L2 students read.

Ironically, it may be that both proficient and less skilled L2 readers already have and can make use of the entire gamut of skills that we teach in reading classes but use these skills to different degrees in L2 reading (Sarig, 1987). L2 reading classes may not even *need* to teach skills, which L2 readers may already possess, but could provide the opportunity for L2 readers to discover *through meaningful contact with L2 texts* which combination of skills works best for them in L2.

In the 1980s, we recognized that if the purpose of writing in a writing class is to practice writing in order to get ready for "real" assignments, students were being seriously handicapped in the development of their ability to decide what to write and how to write it. As long as reading classes have no other purpose than to develop skills, to practice reading, or to learn language, attempts to get students to read with real direction are similarly doomed. The reading class becomes a hothouse, self-referential and solipsistic, in which students spend all their time rehearsing and never performing, getting ready to read while real reading is deferred. (See Blanton, this volume, on reading as performance.) When we teach a reading or writing course as a skills course, we act as though real reading and writing will come later, once our students know where to look for the main idea of a text or how to write a topic sentence. But it makes no sense to defer real reading and writing until students are adequately prepared, because adequate preparation is itself a result of a purposeful plunge into the struggle with meaning.

Reading researchers, paralleling writing researchers, have for years indicated that reading instruction must be more concerned with meaning and less with skills. For over 20 years in the literature on teaching reading to native speakers, researchers have been calling for a focus on meaning (Goodman, 1976; Smith, 1971); for 10 years in the L2 literature (Carrell, 1983a; Hudson, 1982), researchers have emphasized the importance of text content over reading skills. Yet as lately as the December 1989 *TESOL Quarterly*, Carrell, Pharis, & Liberto must again call for approaches to teaching reading, including semantic mapping and ETR, which will aid students not in developing skills and strategies with which to confront *any* text, but in comprehending specific texts.[7] Hudson (1991) makes a similar plea for ESL reading. Isolated L2 reading classes seem to have allowed us to get lost in details, not of decoding skills as in the past, but of main idea hunting and learning word suffixes and prefixes, and to lose sight of reading as a purposeful, real-world activity.

The benefits of integrating L2 reading and writing in the same classroom thus seem undeniable and, since reading and writing draw upon the same cognitive text world (Carson, this volume; Kucer, 1985), reciprocal. The chapters of this book detail the ways in which reading in the composition classroom sustains writing.

But writing, even beyond providing a purpose for reading, clearly also enhances reading. Anticipating in writing the content of a text, i.e., writing before reading (Spack, 1990), primes schemata and thereby facilitates reading a text. Interacting with the content of a text by annotating and engaging the text in dialogue brings home more clearly the reader's own understanding of the text, for it is often through the pressure of new or opposing ideas that our own ideas may become clear to us, just as it is

---

[7]These techniques have been used for some time to teach reading to native English speaking children. For more information on these techniques, see Heimlich & Pittelman (1986), Stahl & Vancil (1986), and Au (1979).

often by expressing the ideas of others in our own words (in effect, translating them), that these other or new ideas begin to have meaning. Writing is a way of reading better "because it requires the learner to reconstruct the structure and meaning of ideas expressed by another writer. To possess an idea that one is reading about requires competence in regenerating the idea, competence in learning how to write the ideas of another" (Squire, 1983, cited in Sternglass, 1986, p. 2). (See Zamel, 1992, for a further discussion of writing to read.) Furthermore, as a student engages a reading text by responding or reacting to it in writing, in effect communicating with the writer through text, the essentially social nature of literacy becomes unmistakable.

Social Acts of Reading and Writing

Research on cognitive processes has had tremendous influence on reading and writing theory, on writing pedagogy, and to some degree on reading classroom practice. But writing classrooms have counterbalanced this emphasis on cognitive processes with an awareness of the social dimension of writing. Writing classrooms have, for example, been much concerned with audience, the discourse communities into which we hope to initiate our students as writers. The recognition of the social dimension of writing has also become commonplace in writing classrooms in the form of peer responding, which has helped to break down the isolation of the individual author and to work against the very notion of individual authorship (Allaei & Connor, 1990; Leki, 1990b; Mittan, 1989).

Like writing, reading is not only a cognitive process. It is intricately bound up in a social, historical, and cultural network, one we are only beginning to explore (Carson, 1992). As readers, we are members of discourse communities formed primarily through reading the same texts. It is this broad social dimension of reading that allows us teachers and textbook writers to agree on the main idea of a text, for example, and to make assertions about textual misinterpretations we think our students make. If we agree on the main idea of a text, it is not because the main idea mechanically signals itself in the text (it is obviously not always the last sentence of the introduction or the first sentence of some fixed paragraph), but because we share the writer's discourse community. An important key to helping our students read better may also lie in clearer classroom recognition of this social dimension of reading.

But reading is also an essentially social activity in the more immediate sense that the text is where a specific reader and writer meet. Reader response theory describes text as the locus of struggle over meaning, suggesting the importance not of the text (where meaning does *not* reside) but of the encounter between individual human beings mediated through the text (Dasenbrock, 1991; Fish, 1980; Nystrand, 1989; Robinson, 1991; Rubin, 1988). L2 reading research, particularly in an interactive view of reading, also does not locate meaning in the text and has shown us repeatedly that the meaning of a given text depends on who is reading it (Anderson *et al.*, 1977; Carrell, 1983a; Parry, 1987; Steffenson & Joag-Dev, 1984). Each reader's reading of a text is somewhat different. Different readings are created not only by different readers but also over time. Thus the Shakespeare we read today is not and cannot be the same work that people read in Shakespeare's time. (See Dasenbrock, 1991 for the L1 debate about the ontological status of historical texts.) In fact, we count on that very fluidity of meaning over time when we advise students to leave a draft aside for a few days before rereading it for revision.

Yet despite this recognition of the instability of meaning, we often seem to entertain only in theory the idea that meaning does not reside in the text. In practice, our insistent privileging of cognitive strategies betrays our view of the text as a puzzle. If meaning did reside in the text, then well-honed cognitive strategies would be sufficient to unravel meaning. But a text is not a puzzle or a dictator; it is a partner in a dialogue, in a negotiation. Yet little is done to give students practice in negotiating meaning mediated by text or to foster the notion that meaning is created by the interaction of a specific reader and a text. In our reading classes a single, privileged interpretation of a text dominates, as is made clear by post-reading comprehension checks with their predetermined answers, ones that the teacher knows and the students must guess.

Ironically, this cognitive bias may be increased by reading theory's current view of reading as interactive, locating meaning in the interaction between the reader and the text, but with no clear role for the writer. The interactive view does, however, leave room for a social dimension in terms of the individual reader's formation as a social being. Schema theory, on which interactive views of reading are based, clearly views schema formation as the result of individual experience *within* a social context. (See, for instance, Anderson *et al.*, 1977, Flynn, 1983, Kintsch & Greene, 1978, and Steffenson & Joag-Dev, 1984 for descriptions of different stances taken before texts by different genders and sociocultural groups.)

Nevertheless, we seem consistently to ignore the social dimension of reading. The usual practice in our reading classrooms, for example, has worked against the idea of the classroom as an interpretive community and instead often sends our students home to read, alone, already published texts, by authors they do not know, writing about settings with which they are not familiar. Significantly, it is only when they return to class that they learn, from the teacher, how well their personal struggle with the text went. Certainly, the struggle with meaning is internal, and cognitive, but this struggle can also be made external, public, and social. By so doing, we can balance the action of individual cognition with the power of social interaction to shape and restructure meaning.

ON THE BRINK OF A CHANGE:
THE TRANSACTIONAL READING/WRITING CLASSROOM

While the attitudes and activities described above persist in reading class-es, we seem now to be on the brink of a shift in reading pedagogy similar to the one that occurred in writing over the last ten years and at least partly occasioned by the growing interest, of which this volume is evi-dence, in bringing reading systematically into writing classrooms. If we use reading and writing reciprocally in L2 classrooms, focusing less on teaching language, reading, or writing and more on allowing students to engage intellectually with text, this engagement with text fosters a view of reading and writing as active construction of meaning. The text can now legitimately be read with varying degrees of attention since the text has peaks and valleys of importance for the reader; comprehension of each section of the text is no longer necessary; the significance of main ideas and details becomes clearer as the student determines which ones further his or her purposes; structures of knowledge are built that can be used to read/write other texts on the same subject; and the student reader/writer must come to terms with the transformation of old knowledge and incor-poration of new knowledge into existing schemata (Bereiter & Scardamalia, 1987). Most importantly, teaching reading in the composi-tion classroom no longer defers real reading until the future; reading is done for present, legitimate purposes.

Reading in composition classrooms may also give reading a social dimension that we have ignored by operating as though reading can only be individual and by directing our students to read at home alone and then answer questions about the text. Our students' facility in reading need not improve only through reading published texts. By reading each other's texts in a reading/writing class, students directly confront the elu-sive, slippery nature of meaning. A writer intends a meaning; a reader per-ceives something else. When the reader and writer are face to face (especially with the support of a teacher's expert guidance), a real negotia-tion over meaning can take place.

If we are convinced by an interactive view of reading, we need to per-mit and encourage our students to become more active in reading—not merely to be led by the text, but to make it their own by responding to whatever is salient *to them* rather than merely pursuing the writer's meaning. This means that for some texts, the author's main idea may be entirely irrelevant to the reader's purpose and will play no role in the reader's use of the text. In this way we might see the metaphor of interac-tive as extending beyond its cognitive dimension, i.e., beyond the idea that both top-down and bottom-up strategies interact in reading. In a read-ing/writing class, interactive takes on a transactional meaning, implying an essential interface of reading and writing (Sternglass, 1986), by which we understand (1) that reading and writing interact, or function recipro-

cally; (2) that the reader can interact more actively with the text by viewing reading as dialogic and by writing to the text (responding to it, for
example, with notes in the margin or in a reading journal); and (3) that in
reading, the reader is also interacting with a writer who wrote for genuine
purposes of communication.

In many writing classrooms these days, students read each other's
writing and respond to it to help the writer improve that draft. In a read-
ing/writing classroom, this activity can take on a new role, not only the
one of various kinds of text repair or editing but of students using each
other's writing as sources for their own writing, considering and addressing their classmates' points of view, and citing each other, not only published work, in their bibliographies.

Even with published texts, by reading them together in groups and
interpreting as they go, students witness competing meanings and clarify
their own understandings through discussion, debate, and the need to
translate their understandings into their own words. By ultimately forming
joint interpretations of their readings rather than learning from the teacher
what the meaning of a text is, students experience the social dimension
inherent in communicating through a text, a dimension too long neglected
in ESL reading instruction. By making reading social, we externalize the
process and demonstrate, or allow students to demonstrate to each other,
that reading is meaning construction, that competing meanings are generated by texts read by different people or even by the same people at different times. (See Section III of this volume, on Social Perspectives, for
further examples of ESL reading instruction that aims at these goals.)

The notion of meaning as negotiation and text as the locus of struggle
suggests another insight that current views on writing may have to offer
reading specialists. In post-reading comprehension questions, reading
classrooms maintain an emphasis on error that many writing classrooms
have chosen to downplay. Writing research has emphasized the futility
and the negative, stifling effect of marking all the errors L2 students make
in writing (Leki, 1990a; Zamel, 1985). As writing specialists tried to come
to terms with the problem of errors in L2 students' writing, it became
increasingly clear that it makes more sense to focus on what students can
do well, rather than constantly reminding them of what they know they
cannot do well, and to intervene in their writing process to help them do
what they cannot do. In many writing classes these days, students show
their drafts to others, including the teacher, as the drafts are developing in
order to get guidance and feedback on their writing. Most writing teachers
are convinced of the value of that kind of intervention. How might such
an attitude be adopted in reading instruction in order to promote the goals
of helping L2 students learn to read with ease, pleasure, and understanding? How can we intervene in our students' reading processes?

In a first step, again by analogy to procedures in writing classes in
which teachers refuse to appropriate their students' writing, reading

teachers might consider refraining from appropriating the meaning of the texts their students read. In other words, in helping students read, the question should not be "What is the author saying here? What is the author's main idea?" but rather "What did you get out of this? What do you make of this part? How does it happen that different class members understand this text differently?" While students lose little by not getting the main idea of an ESL reading passage about dreams or animal behavior, they gain a great deal if they are able to make some portion of that text their own, linguistically, rhetorically, or conceptually.

A de-emphasis of error also implies our acceptance of the idea that our students cannot understand everything they read and that they do not need to. They need to read actively and selectively, picking out what they can use to advance their own agendas. Furthermore, since any individual act of understanding is a reconstruction and in that sense necessarily a misreading (see Bartholomae, 1986), we must also accept that our students will not interpret texts the same way we do.[8] But negotiating through their understandings of a text with other students requires the struggle with meaning that leads to the ability to engage in constructing meaning with power and confidence.

We can also make our own struggle with meaning visible by letting students see our reading processes. Many writing teachers write with their students and share their drafts to demonstrate their writing processes (Spack, 1984). In teaching reading we might consider doing more reading out loud in our classes and doing so in a way that demonstrates our reading processes, thinking aloud as we read, as subjects are asked to do in protocol analyses (Davey, 1983). Rather than only giving individual students individual exercises in chunking, we might show them by reading out loud how we ourselves chunk groups of words together, how we use intonation to get us through heavy embedding, how we backtrack when we have lost the thread of the text, how we ignore incongruities or puzzling words for as long as possible before interrupting the flow of our reading, and, most importantly, how we work to tie the incoming text to patterns of information we already know. To help our students read faster, instead of timing them and pushing them to read faster individually, by reading out loud we keep them to a brisker pace than they might normally adopt when reading silently, and yet through intonation, pauses, and backtracking we also give them additional cues on how we are interpreting a text. By the same token, like writing conferences, reading conferences in which individual students reveal and demonstrate their

---

[8]It is interesting to note that in certain domains, such as in reading literature, idiosyncratic readings are often prized as more illuminating than pedestrian interpretations of a text. What we admire in the best literary critics and the best scientists is not that they understand texts well but that they extend our understanding of the meaning of a text by moving beyond the standard interpretation rendered by the discourse community for which it is intended.

reading processes to us may also uncover unproductive or self-defeating approaches to reading and allow us to intervene directly in the students' construction of meaning from a text.

CONCLUSION

While the research findings in reading and writing echo each other, teaching practices have not kept pace with each other, especially not in helping advanced ESL students read. The separation of reading from writing may be the result of our natural inclination to divide things up in order to deal with them, or it may be that the inclination to divide language up is a legacy of the ALM days, but, as this volume demonstrates, the time seems to have come for a new reintegration of reading and writing classrooms rather than a division of language into atomized, learnable bits or skills. The fact that reading and writing processes can be isolated does not mean that teaching those isolated processes is the best way to help our students read and write with greater ease. The construction of meaning, whether through reading or writing, is a messy, organic, and holistic task, perhaps less amenable to generic attempts to preempt problems than we once thought. Bringing the world of text together in one classroom gives every promise of enhancing our ESL students' ability to both read and write English through the cross-fertilization of reading and writing pedagogy, research, and theory.

REFERENCES

Allaei, S.K. & Connor, U.M. (1990). Exploring the dynamics of cross-cultural collaboration in writing classrooms. *The Writing Instructor, 10,* 19–28.

Anderson, R.C. & Pearson, P.D. (1984). A schema–theoretic view of basic processes in reading comprehension. In P.D. Pearson (Ed.), *Handbook of reading research* (pp. 255–287). New York: Longman.

Anderson, R.C., Reynolds, R.E., Schallert, D.L., & Goetz, E.T. (1977). Frameworks for comprehending discourse. *American Educational Research Journal, 14,* 367–381.

Arndt, V. (1987). Six writers in search of texts: A protocol-based study of L1 and L2 writing. *ELT Journal, 41,* 257–267.

Au, K.H.-P. (1979). Using the experience–text–relationship method with minority children. *The Reading Teacher, 32,* 677-679.

Bartholomae, D. (1986). Wanderings: Misreadings, miswritings, misunderstandings. In T. Newkirk (Ed.), *Only connect: Uniting reading and writing* (pp. 89–118). Upper Montclair, NJ: Boynton/Cook.

Bartholomae, D. & Petrosky, A., (1990). *Ways of reading.* New York: St. Martin's.

Bartholomae, D. & Petrosky, A., (1986). *Facts, artifacts, and counterfacts: A reading and writing course.* Upper Montclair, NJ: Boynton/Cook.

Bazerman, C. (1980). A relationship between reading and writing: The conversational model. *College English, 41,* 656–661.

Bereiter, C. & Scardamalia, M., (1987). *The psychology of writing composition.* Hillsdale, NJ: Erlbaum.

Blanton, L. (1987). Reshaping students' perceptions of writing. *ELT Journal, 41,* 112–118.

Carrell, P.L. (1988a). Introduction. In P.L. Carrell, J. Devine, & D. Eskey (Eds.), *Interactive approaches to second language reading* (pp. 1–7). New York: Cambridge University Press.

Carrell, P.L. (1988b). Some causes of text-boundedness and schema interference in ESL reading. In P.L. Carrell, J. Devine, & D. Eskey (Eds.), *Interactive approaches to second language reading* (pp. 101–113). New York: Cambridge University Press.

Carrell, P.L. (1983a). Some issues in studying the role of schemata, or background knowledge, in L2 comprehension. *Reading in a Foreign Language, 1,* 81–92.

Carrell, P.L. (1983b). Three components of background knowledge in reading comprehension. *Language Learning, 33,* 183–205.

Carrell, P.L., Devine, J., & Eskey, D.E., (Eds.). (1988). *Interactive approaches to second language reading.* New York: Cambridge University Press.

Carrell, P.L. & Eisterhold, J.C., (1983). Schema theory and ESL reading pedagogy. *TESOL Quarterly, 17,* 553–573.

Carrell, P.L., Pharis, B.G., & Liberto, J.C., (1989). Metacognitive training for ESL reading. *TESOL Quarterly, 23,* 647–678.

Carson, J.G. (1992). Becoming biliterate: First language influences. *Journal of Second Language Writing, 1,* 53–76.

Christison, M.A. & Krahnke, K., (1986). Student perceptions of academic language study. *TESOL Quarterly, 20,* 61–81.

Clarke, M. (1979). Reading in English and Spanish: Evidence from adult ESL students. *Language Learning, 29,* 121–150.

Cohen, A., Glasman, H., Rosenbaum-Cohen, P.R., Ferrara, J., & Fine, J. (1979). Reading for specialized purposes: Discourse analysis and the use of student informants. *TESOL Quarterly, 13,* 551–564.

Cumming, A. (1989). Writing expertise and second language proficiency. *Language Learning, 39,* 83–141.

Cziko, G. (1978). Differences in first- and second-language reading: The use of syntactic, semantic and discourse constraints. *Canadian Modern Language Journal, 34,* 473–489.

Dasenbrock, R.W. (1991). Do we write the text we read? *College English, 53,* 7–18.

Davey, B. (1983). Think-aloud: Modeling the cognitive processes of reading comprehension. *Journal of Reading, 27,* 219–224.

Devine, J. (1988). A case study of two readers: Models of reading and reading performance. In P. Carrell, J. Devine, & D. Eskey (Eds.), *Interactive approaches to second language reading* (pp. 127–139). New York: Cambridge University Press.

Devine, J., Carrell, P.L., & Eskey, D.E., (Eds.). (1987). *Research in reading in English as a second language.* Washington, DC: TESOL.

Dubin, F., Eskey, D.E., & Grabe, W., (Eds.). (1986). *Teaching second language reading for academic purposes.* Reading, MA: Addison-Wesley.

Elley, W.B. & Mangubhai, F., (1983). The effect of reading on second language learning. *Reading Research Quarterly, 19,* 53–67.

Eskey, D.E. (1986). Theoretical foundations. In F. Dubin, D.E. Eskey, & W. Grabe (Eds.), *Teaching second language reading for academic purposes* (pp. 3-21). Reading, MA: Addison-Wesley.

Eskey, D.E. & Grabe, W., (1988). Interactive models of second language reading: Perspectives on instruction. In P.L. Carrell, J. Devine, and D. Eskey (Eds.), *Interactive approaches to second language reading* (pp. 223–238). New York: Cambridge University Press.

Fish, S. (1980). *Is there a text in this class? The authority of interpretive communities.* Cambridge: Harvard University Press.

Flower, L., Stein, V., Ackerman, J., Kantz, M.J., McCormick, K., & Peck, W.C., (1990). *Reading to write: Exploring a cognitive and social process.* New York: Oxford University Press.

Flynn, E.A. (1983). Gender and reading. *College English, 45,* 236–253.

Gajdusek, L. (1988). Toward wider use of literature in ESL: Why and how. *TESOL Quarterly, 22,* 227–257.

Goodman, K. (1976). Reading: A psycholinguistic guessing game. In H. Singer & R. Ruddell (Eds.), *Theoretical models and processes of reading* (2nd ed.) (pp. 497–505). Newark, DE: International Reading Association.

Grabe, W. (1986). The transition from theory to practice in teaching reading. In F. Dubin, D.E. Eskey, & W. Grabe (Eds.), *Teaching second language reading for academic purposes* (pp. 25–48). Reading, MA: Addison-Wesley.

Hafiz, F.M. & Tudor, I., (1989). Extensive reading and the development of language skills. *ELT Journal, 43,* 1–13.

Hall, C. (1990). Managing the complexity of revising across languages. *TESOL Quarterly, 24,* 43-60.

Hatch, E., Polin, P., & Part, S., (1970). Acoustic scanning or syntactic processing. Paper presented at meeting of Western Psychological Association, San Francisco.

Heimlich, J.E. & Pittelman, S.D., (1986). *Semantic mapping: Classroom applications.* Newark, DE: International Reading Association.

Horowitz, D. (1986a). Essay examination prompts and the teaching of academic writing. *English for Specific Purposes, 5,* 107–120.

Horowitz, D. (1986b). Process, not product: Less than meets the eye. *TESOL Quarterly, 20,* 141–144.

Hosenfeld, C. (1984). Case studies of ninth grade readers. In J.C. Alderson & A.H. Urquhart (Eds.), *Reading in a foreign language* (pp. 231–244). New York: Longman.

Hudson, T. (1991). A content comprehension approach to reading English for science and technology. *TESOL Quarterly, 25(1)*, 77–104.

Hudson, T. (1982). The effect of induced schemata on the "shortcircuit" in L2 reading: Non-decoding factors in L2 reading performance. *Language Learning, 32*, 1–31.

Janopoulos, M. (1986). The relationship of pleasure of reading and second language writing proficiency. *TESOL Quarterly, 20*, 763–768.

Johns, A. (1981). Necessary English: A faculty survey. *TESOL Quarterly, 15*, 51–57.

Johnson, D.M. & Roen, D.H., (Eds.). (1989). *Richness in writing: Empowering ESL students.* New York: Longman.

Jones, S. & Tetroe, J., (1987). Composing in a second language. In A. Matsuhashi (Ed.), *Writing in real time* (pp. 34–57). New York: Longman.

Kimmel, S. & MacGinitie, W.H., (1984). Identifying children who use a preservative text processing strategy. *Reading Research Quarterly, 19*, 162–172.

Kintsch, W. & Greene, E., (1978). The role of culture-specific schemata in the comprehension and recall of stories. *Discourse Processes, 1*, 1–13.

Krapels, A. (1990). An overview of second language writing process research. In B. Kroll (Ed.), *Second language writing* (pp. 37–56). New York: Cambridge University Press.

Krashen, S.D. (1988). Do we learn to read by reading? The relationship between free reading and reading ability. In D. Tannen (Ed.), *Linguistics in context: Connecting observation and understanding* (pp. 269–298). Norwood, NJ: Ablex.

Krashen, S.D. (1984). *Writing: Research, theory, and applications.* Oxford: Pergamon.

Kroll, B. (1991). Teaching writing in the ESL context. In M. Celce-Murcia (Ed.), *Teaching English as a second or foreign language* (2nd ed.) (pp. 245–263). New York: Newbury House.

Kroll, B. (Ed.). (1990). *Second language writing.* New York: Cambridge University Press.

Kucer, S. (1985). The making of meaning: Reading and writing as processes. *Written Communication, 2*, 317–336.

Leki, I. (1990a). Coaching from the margins: Issues in written response. In B. Kroll (Ed.), *Second language writing* (pp. 57–68). New York: Cambridge University Press.

Leki, I. (1990b). Potential problems with peer responding in ESL writing classes. *CATESOL Journal, 3*, 5–19.

McLaughlin, B. (1987). Reading in a second language: Studies of adult and child learners. In S.R. Goldman & H.T. Trueba (Eds.), *Becoming literate in English as a second language* (pp. 57–70). Norwood, NJ: Ablex.

Mittan, R. (1989). The peer review process: Harnessing students' communicative power. In D.M. Johnson & D.H. Roen (Eds.), *Richness in writing: Empowering ESL students* (pp. 207–219). New York: Longman.

Mlynarczyk, R. (1992). Student choice: An alternative to teacher-selected reading material. *College ESL, 1*(2), 1–8.

Nystrand, M. (1989). A social-interactive model of writing. *Written Communication, 6*, 66–85.

Parry, K.J. (1987). Reading in a second culture. In J. Devine, P.L. Carrell, & D.E. Eskey (Eds.), *Research in reading in English as a second language* (pp. 59-70). Washington, DC: TESOL.

Perl, S. (1979). The composing processes of unskilled college writers. *Research in the Teaching of English, 13*, 317–336.

Petrosky, A. (1982). From story to essay: Reading and writing. *College Composition and Communication, 33*, 19–37.

Radecki, P.M. & Swales, J.M., (1988). ESL students' reaction to written comments on their written work. *System, 16*, 355–365.

Raimes, A. (1986). Teaching ESL writing: Fitting what we do to what we know. *The Writing Instructor, 5*, 153–166.

Raimes, A. (1985). What unskilled writers do as they write: A classroom study. *TESOL Quarterly, 19*, 229–258.

Reid, J. (1987). ESL Composition: The expectations of the academic audience. *TESOL Newsletter, 21*, 34.

Rigg, P. (1977). The miscue–ESL project. In H.D. Brown, C.A. Yorio, & R.H. Crymes (Eds.), *Teaching and learning ESL: Trends in research and practice. On TESOL '77* (pp. 106–118). Washington, DC: TESOL.

Robinson, D. (1991). Henry James and euphemism. *College English, 53*, 403–427.

Rubin, D.L. (1988). Introduction: Four dimensions of social construction in written communication. In B.A. Rafoth and D.L. Rubin (Eds.), *The social construction of written communication* (pp. 1–33). Norwood, NJ: Ablex.

Rummelhart, D. (1977). Toward an interactive model of reading. In S. Dornic (Ed.), *Attention and performance*, vol. 6 (pp. 573–603). New York: Academic Press.

Sarig, G. (1987). High-level reading and the first and foreign language: some comparative process data. In J. Devine, P.L. Carrell, & D.E. Eskey (Eds.), *Research in reading in English as a second language* (pp. 105–120). Washington, DC: TESOL.

Silva, T. (1990). ESL composition instruction: Development, issues and directions. In B. Kroll (Ed.), *Second language writing* (pp. 11–23). New York: Cambridge University Press.

Smith, F. (1971). *Understanding reading: A psycholinguistic analysis of reading and learning to read*, 1st ed. New York: Holt, Rinehart, and Winston.

Spack, R. (1990). *Guidelines: A cross-cultural reading/writing text.* New York: St. Martin's.

Spack, R. (1988). Initiating ESL students into the academic discourse community: How far should we go? *TESOL Quarterly, 22,* 29–51.

Spack, R. (1985). Literature, reading, writing, and ESL: Bridging the gaps. *TESOL Quarterly, 19,* 703–726.

Spack, R. (1984). Invention strategies and the ESL college composition student. *TESOL Quarterly, 18,* 649–670.

Spack, R. & Sadow, C., (1983). Student-teacher working journals in ESL freshman composition. *TESOL Quarterly, 17,* 575–594.

Stahl, S.A. & Vancil, S.J., (1986). Discussion is what makes semantic maps work in vocabulary instruction. *The Reading Teacher, 40,* 62–67.

Stanovich, K.E. (1980). Toward an interactive–compensatory model of individual differences in the development of reading fluency. *Reading Research Quarterly, 16,* 32–71.

Steffensen, M.S. & Joag-Dev, C., (1984). Cultural knowledge and reading. In J.C. Alderson & A.H. Urquhart (Eds.), *Reading in a foreign language* (pp. 48–61). New York: Longman.

Sternglass, M. (1988). *The presence of thought: Introspective accounts of reading and writing.* Norwood, NJ: Ablex.

Sternglass, M. (1986). Introduction. In B. Petersen (Ed.), *Convergences: Transactions in reading and writing* (pp. 1–11). Urbana, IL: NCTE.

Tierney, R.J. & Pearson, P.D., (1983). Toward a composing model of reading. *Language Arts, 60,* 568–569.

Van Naerssen, M. (1985). Relaxed reading in ESP. *TESOL Newsletter, 19,* 2.

Zamel, V. (1992). Writing one's way into reading. *TESOL Quarterly, 26,* 463–485.

Zamel, V. (1985). Responding to student writing. *TESOL Quarterly, 19,* 79–101.

Zamel, V. (1983). The composing processes of advanced ESL students: Six case studies. *TESOL Quarterly, 17,* 165–187.

CHAPTER 2

Historical Perspectives on Writing and Reading in the ESL Classroom

Joy Reid
University of Wyoming

INTRODUCTION

Reading has always taken place in the ESL writing classroom, even when writing, as we think of it now, was not taking place. However, the amount of reading in the ESL writing classroom, the way we approach reading in the writing classroom, and particularly the relationships among the elements of *writer, text,* and *reader,* have changed—or are changing—dramatically. For example, in describing writing and reading processes, early underlying assumptions hypothesized that both were puzzle-solving activities, that "meaning" flowed directly from writer to reader, and that both making meaning and extracting meaning were functions of the application of microskills (Straw, 1990). Over the last fifty years, reading has gradually become a more important part of the writing class; however, ESL writing teachers and researchers have only recently begun to address the best ways to use reading in the writing classroom.

The reflective retrospection (or Monday morning quarterbacking) that precedes an article like this one delights in patterns of tidy linear progress; however, an analysis and historical overview of the use of reading in the ESL writing classroom is in actuality neither tidy nor linear. Instead, the "periods" discussed below are overlapping, recursive, and in many ways cumulative and interrelated. For the purpose of this analysis, however, each of the periods discussed has been separated from what inevitably is a continuum. In addition, each period is discussed in its essential, pristine state, with minimal reference to the other periods, a perspective that is instructive but rather inauthentic. In reality, of course, students in the grammar–translation ESL writing classes probably talked about the whole passages they were translating, discussing ideas and putting forth opinions; no doubt students in audio-lingual writing classes wrote, perhaps even composed, in their classes; certainly students in pattern–model based ESL writing classes (that is, classes that studied model essays for patterns of communication) practiced pre-writing and composing skills; and students in writing process classes read other sources besides their own work.

DEFINITIONS

Because writers, texts, and readers are produced by history and culture, there is an interdependence among them that has only recently begun to be articulated (Nystrand, 1990). However, some basic definitions of the three elements—writer, text, and reader—do exist. In all of the writing/reading models discussed below, the author is a creator of meaning who chooses to communicate in writing. As Kaplan (1987) has noted, there are multiple kinds of written communication, from grocery lists to movie reviews, term papers to news articles, assembly directions to poetry, research reports to novels. Each has a communicative purpose. That is, each author takes into account social factors—content, situation, and reader—as well as language factors (Peyton, 1990). In order to be successful and effective, the author must communicate in a way that reaches his or her audience.

For the purposes of this overview, text is considered a written product—whether unfinished or finished, original draft or final form, prose or poetry—that is written for a reader. Written text varies in form and function according to its author (and her background knowledge, perception of audience, knowledge of topic, and purpose for communication) and its reader (and her background knowledge, perception of the author, knowledge of topic, and purpose for reading). Kaplan (1983) has suggested a grocery list as an example; a successful grocery list written by a person (a) for herself or (b) for her husband might look like the following:

Written for Self	Written for Husband
PB	PB (large, Jif)
OJ	OJ (3)
ff ranch	Fat Free Ranch Dressing
bagels	bagels (2 dozen)
Rsn Bd/Bn	Raisin Bran
	Raisin Bread (2)
milk	Skim milk (2)
Amer. Dr.	American Dream IC (1)

While the first list would be entirely clear to the writer, another person might find it incomprehensible. The second list is still abbreviated, but the shared knowledge of husband and wife requires only slight elaboration in product names and the addition of quantity. The same list, made for a stranger, would no doubt be considerably more detailed (e.g., Kraft Fat-Free Ranch Style salad dressing, one 8 oz. bottle). Despite the brevity of the grocery lists, they are relatively unambiguous pieces of writing for their respective audiences. However, most written products are subject to more interpretation, and the more ambiguous the written product, the more interpretations exist for both author and reader. Expressive writing, for instance, is considered more intentionally ambiguous than scientific and technical prose (Petersen, 1986); at the far end of the ambiguity continuum is poetry, in which each word has been carefully chosen by the author to extend the possibilities of multiple meanings.

The third element, the reader, is the person who encounters, reads, and responds to the text. Like authors, readers bring purposes to their reading (Nystrand, 1990), and the purposes of readers may change as they return to a text for another reading (Straw & Bogdan, 1990); most generally, readers are searching for information, for pleasure, for meaning. The author, then, writes for a reader who can be the author herself, another person, or a group of people who share the distinctive aims and values of a community. These groups of readers, called "discourse communities" (Bizzell, 1982; Faigley, 1985; Johns, 1991; Spack, 1988) by writing researchers and "interpretive communities" by reading researchers (Dasenbrock, 1991; Fish, 1980) have similar (but not exact) sets of background information and expectations. The discourse of that community operates within conventions defined by the community—ideas, language use, and the organization and presentation of ideas (Swales, 1990).

The relationships between writer, text, and reader and the interactions among these three elements are complex and sophisticated. In the past, ESL classroom practices have not recognized the value of relevant language input through reading in the ESL writing class (Carson Eisterhold, 1990). However, the current focus of writing/reading research demonstrates that meaning is created by the active negotiation between writer, text, and reader. What follows is a brief overview of how reading has been used in the ESL writing classroom, a discussion of how the paradigm changes in the models of reading have been paralleled by substantial changes in the teaching of writing, and a description of current views of the connections between writing and reading.

GRAMMAR–TRANSLATION CLASSROOMS

During the early days of the *grammar–translation approach* to teaching ESL, ESL students were reading texts in the target language and writing translations in their native languages, or vice-versa. In the grammar–translation approach to second-language teaching, writing was a language-based skill that assisted students to learn English; students learned the second language by translating from or into it, vocabulary word by vocabulary word, verb tense by verb tense. Students in grammar–translation classes did not compose; that is, they did not actually write—as authors. They did not share their ideas, their opinions, their discoveries in writing. Rather, they were restricted to learning English through the grammar and the vocabulary gained in the translation process. In the grammar-translation approach, the author of the text to be translated was the ultimate authority; the reader's purpose was to extract—decode—the single, correct message of the writer (Straw & Sadowy, 1990). Schematically, we might display the author–text–reader relationships in the grammar–translation writing classroom in a linear pattern:

AUTHOR ──→ TEXT ──→ Reader

AUDIO-LINGUAL CLASSROOMS

For nearly thirty years (1940–1970), during the introduction and continuation of the extended *audio-lingual period,* writing and even reading were still perceived as support skills for grammar. Language learning was based on behaviorist objectives: Modeling and practicing correct structures were paramount, and error was not tolerated. Reading in the ESL writing classroom followed these premises by confining students to texts that were unambiguous (that is, each text had a single message to transfer to the reader) and grammatically correct. In the reading class, ESL students were taught at the micro-skills level—word recognition, for example—with continuous measurement of rate, vocabulary acquisition, and discrete grammar points (Dubin & Bycina, 1991). Writing was merely a way of practicing grammar, which in turn was a way of achieving oral correctness.

Still, students in audio-lingual writing classes read: They read instructions, discrete point exercises (as they wrote answers in the blanks), and grammar explanations on the chalkboard. They "decoded" material in their textbooks, assignments, and test materials. They also read their "controlled" or "guided" writing exercises and their resulting written products. Yet in terms of the students as writers/authors, actual composing was still not taking place; students were learning English by studying grammar in accurate contexts. Moreover, because reading was considered a "receptive" skill (while speaking and writing were defined as "productive" skills), ESL writing students were expected to extract the "right" meaning from texts they read. Again, as in the grammar–translation classroom, the meaning of a text was thought to reside entirely in the text itself, although the text in the audio-lingual classroom was perhaps more important than the author. Schematically, in the audio-lingual ESL writing classroom, the author-text-reader relationship might be depicted as follows:

Author ──→ TEXT ──→ Reader

PATTERN–MODEL CLASSROOMS

The shift from language-based writing classrooms to the study of composition techniques and strategies was gradual; it began as early as the mid-

1960s with the recognition, by teachers and researchers, of the needs of ESL students in the academic environment, and it grew to dominate ESL writing classrooms well into the 1980s. The recognition of the need to focus on writing as a communicative skill rather than writing as a language skill led teachers to bridge the gap between *language-based* writing classes, which focused on sentence writing, and *writing-based* classes, which focused on creating compositions. ESL writing teachers, influenced by the research in and teaching of native-speaker (NS) composition, began to concentrate on the rhetorical *modes* in academic writing: the organization of paragraphs and essays according to specific forms of development such as comparison/contrast, classification, cause–effect, definition, and process. Using models that contained these modes, teachers asked students to read, analyze, and then imitate the models; they taught the concepts of thesis statements, topic sentences, and techniques of support.

In addition to the shift in ESL writing from language-based to composition-based classrooms, ESL writing students began reading more in their reading classes and, importantly, reading differently. Goodman's psycholinguistic theory of reading posited that reading was a "psycholinguistic guessing game" in which the reader predicts meaning based on what he or she had already read, then confirms or corrects his or her guesses, and thereby reconstructs "a message which has been encoded by a writer" (1967, p. 135). According to this new model, the role of readers was quite active: "[T]hey predict meaning as they read, they take in large chunks of a text at a time, they do not attend to separate letters, rather they match what they already know with the meaning they derive from the text" (Dubin & Bycina, 1991, p. 197). This approach, which was investigated and extended by a host of other researchers (see Coady, 1979; Rumelhart, 1977; Smith, 1971, 1986), was a major shift in reading theory: from the linear transmission models of reading in which text information was said to be transferred directly to the passive, receptive reader, to an active model in which the reader participates by reacting to the text in the making of meaning.

As a result of such seminal research, ESL students were taught to become *active* readers and writers, to derive meaning from a text by approaching the text from individual perspectives, whether that text was a model essay, a draft of their own writing, or the essay of a classmate. Students became authors and author/editors; they read and reread their own writing as they edited drafts. They also read and analyzed professional and student "model texts," paragraphs and essays: They outlined and/or took notes about what they read, and they wrote summaries and paraphrases of their reading. Moreover, the concept of audience was introduced in ESL writing classrooms: In order to communicate something purposefully, appropriately, and therefore successfully, students were taught to consider their audience and to organize their ideas in order to fulfill the expectations of that audience. They read the texts and reflected on the contents of the texts, anticipating, predicting, and constructing the meaning (Haas & Flower, 1988; McCormick, Waller, & Flower, 1987; Swaffar, 1988). The relationship of ESL writing students to the texts they wrote and read included the interaction of readers and their texts; it might be depicted as follows:

$$\text{AUTHOR} \longleftrightarrow \text{TEXT} \longleftrightarrow \text{READER}$$

PROCESS WRITING CLASSROOMS

During the 1980s, *"process writing"* dominated the literature and the classrooms of ESL writing. Students in process classrooms wrote—and read—to "discover" what they wanted to communicate; students were encouraged to explore a topic through writing, sharing drafts with the teachers and their peers, using each draft as a beginning for the next. Much time was spent discussing and practicing "composing strategies"— freewriting, brainstorming, clustering—that would lead students to discover their ideas. Cooperative group work often resulted in collaborative writing—and reading—of student texts. Working in these small groups, students incorporated the skills of speaking and listening as they read and then discussed their writing. In the most pristine process writing classroom, a focus on expressive, personal writing prevailed; student creativity and the development of narrative voice were encouraged in an atmosphere that lowered the anxiety level of student writers. As Zamel (1976) stated, "The act of composing should become the result of a genuine need to express one's personal feeling, experience, or reactions, all within a climate of encouragement" (p. 74). This focus on expressive writing often led to the use of student journals (Blanton, 1987; Peyton, 1990; Peyton & Reed, 1991); in one form of journal writing, the ESL teacher read the journal entries, sometimes daily, and responded to the ideas in writing, providing students with a reading/writing "dialog." Dialog journals allowed ESL writers to "become aware of writing as a way to generate ideas and share them in a non-threatening way" (Spack & Sadow, 1983, p. 575).

Reading was an integral part of the writing process classroom; however, because the focus of that classroom was on expressive writing, much of the reading was of personal, narrative prose—that is, of students reading their own writing and responding to that writing. Flower (1979) called this "writer-based" writing: writing written by and for the writer/author. Student/authors generated text and gained confidence and fluency in various written genres; they expressed concepts that were important to them by writing genuine and meaningful texts (Peyton & Reed, 1991). Such writer-based writing has a unique set of author–text–reader relationships that might be schematically demonstrated as follows:

$$\text{AUTHOR} / \text{READER} \longleftrightarrow \text{TEXT}$$

Some process writing classrooms extended student opportunity and experience by exposing students to writing external to the class. One approach offered students selections from literature (Elliott, 1990; Gajdusek, 1988; McConochie, 1982; McConochie & Sage, 1989; Sage, 1987). ESL students read short stories, poetry, and novels; then they discussed and wrote about characters and themes. Brock (1990) summarized the benefits of teaching literature in the ESL writing classroom: Literature teaches culture, and it provides students with a rich linguistic storehouse; it encourages extensive reading, and it provides a basis for student conversation, group work, and problem-solving activities. In the writing process classroom, the reading of literature was usually linked to "reader response journals," in which students recorded and analyzed their feelings and ideas about the literature they were reading (see Collie & Slater, 1987; Costello, 1990; Povey, 1986; Spack, 1985).

Today, both NS and ESL writing process classrooms continue to flourish, and the focus has expanded to include other reader-based genres. In many process writing classes, students read literature, essays, content-based articles, and/or peer writing. They respond, in their journals, individually and personally to those readings. Reading researchers working with NSs (Berthoff, 1981, 1985; Bleich, 1986; Petrosky, 1986; Spivey, 1990) indicate that written response is "an expression and explanation of comprehension" (Sternglass, 1986a, p. 4). Researchers working with ESL students have found that extensive and intensive reading, and writing about reading, improve general language proficiency (see Brinton, Snow, & Wesche, 1989; Datesman, 1990; Devine, 1987; Hafiz & Tudor, 1989; Krashen, 1984a; 1984b; Robb & Susser, 1989; Shih, 1986; Susser & Robb, 1990).

ESL READING AND SCHEMA THEORY

At about the same time that ESL writing teachers began to concentrate on writing processes, reading researchers were investigating the application of schema theory to reading (Carrell, 1981, 1983a, 1983b; Hamp-Lyons, 1985; James, 1987; Johnson, 1986). Carrell & Eisterhold have defined schema: "[P]reviously acquired knowledge is called the reader's background knowledge, and the previously acquired *background knowledge* structures are called *schemata*" (1983, p. 556). If we think of schemata as databases, the activity of reading consists of inputting (words and sentences about ideas), then searching for and potentially modifying the existing database, depending on the information read (Horowitz, 1988; Kucer, 1985). In applying schema theory to reading, Eskey (1988) explains that readers "reconstruct a plausible meaning for the text by relating what it says to what they already know about its subject matter and the world in general" (p. 96).

Moreover, recent reading research with both NSs and ESL students has demonstrated that reading is more than "active": It is *interactive* (see Carrell, 1990; Eskey & Grabe, 1988; Haas & Flower, 1988; McCormick, Waller, & Flower, 1987; Rosenblatt, 1988; Swaffar, 1988). That is, reading is a dynamic interaction between the writer and the reader in which the reader creates meaning for the text by "retaining newly acquired knowledge, accessing recorded and stored knowledge, and attending to the writer's clues as to the meaning intended for the text" (Cohen, 1990, p. 75). Horowitz describes the interaction as "a continuum of inference and interpretation, at one end of which are those inferences (which generally correspond to lower levels of meaning) on which there will be near unanimity of agreement among some community of readers for whom a given text was intended [e.g., an unambiguous grocery list] and at the other end of which are those inferences (which generally correspond to high levels of meaning) for which disagreement would be the norm [e.g., the intentional ambiguity of a poem]" (1988, p. 95).

Carrell's early research with schema theory and reading (1981, 1983b, 1983c, 1984a, 1984d, 1984e) not only indicated that what students know—their prior knowledge—will influence what and probably how they learn. It also demonstrated that schema is culturally specific: "[T]he implicit cultural content knowledge presupposed by a text interacts with the reader's own cultural background knowledge of the content to make texts whose content is based on one's own culture easier to read and understand than syntactically and rhetorically equivalent texts based on a less familiar, more distant culture" (1983c, p. 81). Carrell's research is supported by other researchers who have worked with ESL students (see Johnson, 1981, 1986; Pritchard, 1990; Steffensen, 1987; Steffensen, Joagdev, & Anderson, 1979). In addition, research with NSs (Clifford, 1991; Hartman *et al.*, 1991; Kirsch, 1991; Purves, 1988b) indicates that both readers and texts are deeply influenced by their sociocultural contexts: "[R]eading has both cognitive and cultural dimensions, that is, it is both an intellectual procedure that requires certain mental strategies and skills, and a cultural procedure, contingent upon your wider beliefs and assumptions" (McCormick, Waller, & Flower, 1987, p. 9). Because all readers bring to their experience of reading a complex (and perhaps never fully analyzable) set of expectations, desires, prejudices, and former experiences, "making meaning" varies from reader to reader.

Carrell (1983c) found it useful to distinguish three forms of schemata: linguistic (or language knowledge), content (knowledge of topic), and formal (background knowledge of the rhetorical structures of different types of texts). Each plays a part in the interaction among writer, text, and reader. First, because the effectiveness of written communication and reader interpretation depends on the successful interaction between writer and reader, language knowledge—linguistic schema—plays an integral part in ESL reading and writing. Grabe (1988) discusses a language "ceiling" or "threshold," which ESL students must surpass if they are to develop fluent reading abilities; without the large vocabulary or basic syntactic structures possessed by NS children who are beginning to read, ESL students will not be able to interact with the text and construct meaning. Second, the background of the reader in the subject of the text—content schema—determines, in part, the comprehension and the interpretation of the text (Brown, 1990; Eskey & Grabe, 1988; Grabe, 1986; Roller, 1990; Steffensen *et al.*, 1979). The closer the match between reader knowledge and text information, the better the comprehension will be. As Goodman (1979) pointed out, "Even highly effective readers are severely limited in comprehension of texts by what they already know before they read" (p. 658). Finally, Meyer (1984) defines knowledge about text structure—formal schema—as "the interrelationships among items of information which compose the text, as well as indicating the subordination and coordination of this information" (p. 187); included are such organizational items as topic sentences, paragraph structures, and transition words that establish logical relationships between and among items.

Carrell's ongoing research (1984b, 1984c, 1985, 1987) went a step further: Results of empirical studies indicated that when language *and* form *and* content are familiar and expected, reading is relatively easy, but when one or the other or all are unfamiliar, efficiency, effectiveness, and success for the writer or the reader can be problematic. In an ESL class, the differences in cultural knowledge can be dramatic; students without appropriate linguistic, content, and/or formal schemata encounter difficulty in relating discrete words and ideas to their own background knowledge. However, acquiring relevant cultural schemata can facilitate the learning process by enabling students to integrate and understand material. Carrell, Pharis, & Liberto (1989) and others (Badrawi, 1992; Carrell, 1985; Harris, 1990; Pritchard, 1990; Scarcella & Oxford, 1992; Shih, 1992; Swales, 1990) therefore suggest that ESL students need explicit strategy training in such areas as guessing from context, inferencing, identifying main ideas, and determining cohesive devices.

THE WRITING–READING CONNECTION

While teachers and researchers in ESL reading examined schema theory and implemented their findings, ESL writing teachers and researchers were working independently in the related area of discourse communities; they were investigating the relationships between writers and readers, the identification of audiences and writing contexts, academic audience needs and expectations, and strategies to fulfill those needs and expectations. For example, reexamination of the writing process approach and of academic expectations (see Constantinides & Hall, 1981; Hamp-Lyons, 1986; Horowitz, 1986b, 1990; Horowitz & McKee, 1984; Johns, 1985; Kaplan,

1990; Swales, 1987) suggests that the pendulum towards expressive and personal writing in the ESL classroom may have swung too far, particularly for ESL students who are neither familiar nor comfortable with the conventions and expectations—the cultural schemata—of narrative and/or expressive writing. Horowitz (1986a) and others (Braine, 1989; Budd, 1989) identified, surveyed, and analyzed university writing requirements, and found that academic writing assignments (a) are usually carefully controlled, both in topic selection and in rhetorical organization, by the instructor; (b) rarely deal with personal or expressive writing; and (c) often call for some kind of research (that is, reading) activity. None of these results precluded process writing; rather, Canesco & Byrd (1989) suggested that "the process approach to writing can occur within the context of the preparation of a rigorously defined academic product—if the process is taken to mean that the writer goes through a process of thinking, selection of evidence, writing, and revisions" (p. 311).

Two areas of text-analysis research furthered the writing/reading connection in the ESL classroom. First, Carrell (1987) discussed the implications of schema theory on composition teaching, suggesting that ESL student writers would benefit from studying texts in English for rhetorical organization and cues (that is, transitional words and phrases) that result in successful communication. Genre analysis, the study of how different kinds of writing are organized and presented for a reader, has been found to help both NSs and ESL students read and write more effectively (Hyland, 1992; Miccinati, 1988; Slater et al., 1988; Swales, 1990a, 1990b). Second, contrastive rhetoricians (see Anderson, 1991; Kaplan, 1987; Ostler, 1987a; 1987b; Purves, 1988a; Reid, 1988; Scollon, 1991) demonstrated that the patterns in which many ESL students choose to present written material vary from culture to culture and can be quite distinct from those in their target language, English. In other words, ESL writers differ substantially in their rhetorical schemata. As a consequence of these differences, the shared interpretive abilities so crucial to the interactive communication of writing and reading may well be incomplete or even missing; texts that should be relatively unambiguous may contain *unintentional* ambiguities for the reader as a result of, for example, poor construction, inadequate cohesive ties, differing rhetorical expectations, and/or differing background information (Horowitz, 1988). Language errors, for instance, may obscure meaning; the content may not fulfill the cultural expectations of the reader; and/or the organization and presentation of ideas may differ rhetorically from reader expectations and so confuse that reader. Using schema theory and contrastive rhetoric research, ESL writing teachers have realized that, as an ESL writer communicates his or her ideas and then a U.S. audience reads them, the relationships among author, text, and reader can be seen as a complex interaction of schema, with (a) the level of *unintentional* ambiguity and (b) the range of interpretation (or the intentional ambiguity) by writer and reader determined, in large part, by the schemata of the writer and the reader. Figure 1 demonstrates the variables.

Because the research in writing and reading progressed so independently for the past twenty years, it is only recently that the interaction between the two has occurred. However, the findings have echoed each other: Both writing and reading are processes of making meaning, both involve similar patterns of thinking and similar linguistic habits, both are multifaceted complex processes that involve many subskills, and both depend on individual past experience (see Carrell, 1988; Horowitz, 1988; Janopoulos, 1986; Rosenblatt, 1988; Sarig, 1988; Sternglass, 1986a, 1986b). Furthermore, both writing and reading activate schemata about the language, content, and form of the topic, and both lead to the exploration of those schemata in discovering meaning (see Leki, this volume). Both writers and readers have "drafts" of meaning in their heads as they begin, and both constantly revise these "drafts" in light of what Straw (1990) calls the emerging text. Moreover, research with both NSs (Flower & Hayes, 1980; Meyer, 1982; Stotsky, 1983; Tierney & Leys, 1986; Tierney & Gee, 1990) and ESL students (Carrell, 1987; Janopoulos, 1986; Johns, 1991; Krashen, 1984a) has shown the reciprocal relationship between reading and writing: Good writers are often good readers. Readers discover ideas and form opinions about their reading, ideas and opinions they can write about. At the same time, they also accumulate schema—often unconsciously—about the formats of English writing and the expectations of the U.S. academic audience. As Krashen states, "It is reading that gives the writer the 'feel' for the look and texture" of prose (1984a, p. 20).

FIGURE 1   Interactive Reading Graphic

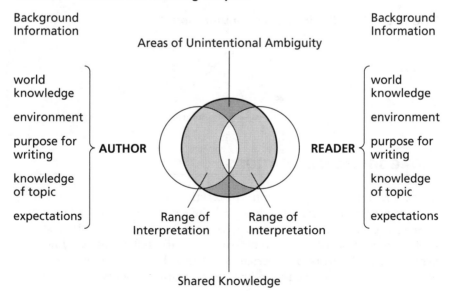

The current paradigm in ESL writing classrooms, then, rests on the balance between process and product, between generating and discovering ideas and identifying and analyzing audience and purpose. Teachers employ a process-oriented pedagogy that, as Zamel puts it, "establishes a supportive environment in which students are acknowledged as writers, encouraged to take risks, and engaged in creating meaning" (1987, p. 697). Students in these ESL writing classes are given opportunities "to explore a variety of systematic methods of discovery while they read, write, and talk to each other" (Raimes, 1987, p. vii). In addition, however, the student/writers must know as much about their readers and about their purposes as possible as they "(1) attempt to reconcile what they want to say with what they think their readers are willing to attend to, and (2) attempt to reconcile how they want to say it with the discoursal demands of the genre in which they are working" (Swales & Horowitz, 1988, p. 91). The successful writer understands the knowledge that potential readers are expected to bring to the text, as well as their expectations about writing conventions, linguistic experience, and social and environmental conditions (Rosenblatt, 1988). ESL writing students are thus becoming more aware of the lines of communication that exist among author, text, and reader. In his widely known research with NS writing, James Moffat (1968) described these lines of communication as a way to "overcome the imbalance of knowledge" as the writer anticipates the needs of the audience and the audience anticipates the ideas of the author—an interactive model of reading and writing. Moffat's diagram (Figure 2) shows the interactive quality of the author–text–reader relationships demonstrated by research that has begun—but just begun—to impact on NS and ESL classes.

FIGURE 2   Moffat's Lines of Communication

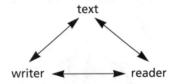

PEDAGOGICAL IMPLICATIONS

In the writing/reading classroom, interactive reading and writing activities can prepare ESL students to fulfill the expectations of academic discourse/interpretive communities (Folman, 1988; Johns, 1991; Swales, 1990). Content-based and/or professionally authored readings allow students to read the work of experienced writers that will act as sources for ideas, as stimuli for discussion and interpretation, and as models of the types of writing students will be expected to produce in order to "build up the schematic knowledge of genre which leads to critical reading, and, in turn, to successful writing" (Horowitz, 1988, p. 99). Hairston (1986) encourages teachers to teach students to read rhetorically, to focus simultaneously on the content of an essay and on the process by which it was written "including the rhetorical situation, i.e., the occasion or demand for writing, the audience to be influenced, and the constraints of the writing task" (p. 181), and to analyze those rhetorical situations in writing. (See Kroll, this volume, for a discussion of rhetorical reading.) Working with NSs in a rhetorical context, Meyer (1982) and her colleagues (Meyer & Freedle, 1984) also suggest that reading and analyzing texts for successful communication patterns—that is, for what makes a passage unified and meaningful for readers in a specific discourse or interpretative community—should help readers plan their own written texts. Similarly, reading and writing researchers working with ESL students (Carrell, 1984c; 1987; Dubin & Bycina, 1991; Lee & Riley, 1990) suggest that explicit teaching of the text structure(s) of academic prose facilitates successful written communication as well as reading comprehension. Kroll (1991) states that "close reading exercises can be done to draw students' attention to particular stylistic choices, grammatical features, methods of development, and so on. Such exercises help to raise student awareness of the choices writers make and the consequences of those choices for the achievement of their communicative goals" (p. 254).

In addition to reading rhetorically, students can write about their reading. For example, "pre-reading writing" about texts (Flynn, 1982, p. 145) serves to explore topics and ideas that can trigger associations and raise students' awareness of those associations; analyzing supporting detail and relevant evidence will help writing students read—and write— to learn. More informal, writer-based prose in journals, daybooks, and learning logs allows students to respond to reading and evaluate those responses, individualizes instruction, and reinforces learning experiences (Benítez, 1990; Ching & Ngooi, 1991; Fulwiler, 1982, 1987; Garner, 1988; Lucas, 1990). Writing can also help students make sense of assignments and tasks; early in the process, they can describe their audience and purpose(s), defend decisions they have made, anticipate problems, and analyze solutions. Furthermore, "the ESL writing class can incorporate lessons which assist students in preparing academic writing assignments by using readings as a basis to practice such skills as summarizing, paraphrasing, interpreting, and synthesizing concepts" (Kroll, 1991, p. 254).

Moreover, ESL writers can be taught to read and reread their own work in ways that will help them revise with their readers in mind. Research with NSs has shown that skilled writers tend to reread their own writing rhetorically—that is, they "monitor the relationship between the emerging draft, the writer's purpose, and the audience's likely reactions" (Grant-Davie, 1989, p. 4). Skilled writers reread to edit, solve problems, confirm or disconfirm their perceptions of the draft, help them find and give shape to their ideas, maintain or regain momentum, and evaluate the sense of the intended audience. Less experienced writers should therefore be taught the strategies of rereading in order to be able to see their texts as others see them, to comment on—and write about—the effectiveness of their writing from the perspective of an audience, and to reread their drafts as part of their writing process, in which they invent, plan, draft, and troubleshoot.

Still another connection between writing and reading reaches beyond the writer: Peer review and discussion of peer texts have been found effective in helping writers at all levels understand their interactive relationship to their readers. As Rosenblatt puts it, "Their fellow students' questions, varied interpretations, and misunderstandings dramatize the necessity of the writers providing verbal signs that will enable readers to draw on their own resources to make the intended meaning. The writer can become aware of the responsibility for providing verbal means that will help readers gain required facts, share relevant sensations or attitudes, or make logical transitions" (1988, p. 27). The concept of audience gained by peer review allows the writer to think not just *about* readers, but *as* a reader, to read the text through the eyes of potential readers, trying to fathom the meaning they would make. Writers begin to identify their audience, to investigate that audience until they have enough information to become authorities about their audience, and to analyze the social context in which their audience—their interpretive community—will read their writing (Kirsch, 1989). They then begin to adopt the perspectives of their audiences and to assess their writing in terms of how their readers may react to or comprehend their text (Beach & Liebman-Kleine, 1986; Scarcella, 1984). Teachers of writing can prepare their students to do this kind of active, adaptive, productive reading and rereading of their own texts and other texts and to see how reading peers' drafts and rereading their own can help with rhetorical and structural problems as well as generative processes.

In short, ESL writers must learn not only linguistic but also rhetorical situations and conventions, and they must learn that they are constrained not only by how much their readers know but also by how much they know about their readers. As they assimilate linguistic, content, and, particularly, formal schemata about academic writing tasks and audiences, ESL student writers can minimize the unintentional ambiguities of their writing for their readers. Using the concentric circle diagram in Figure 1 above, Figures 3, 4, and 5 indicate the levels of unintentional ambiguity and the ranges of interpretation (or intentional ambiguity) for three writing situations. In Figure 3 the grocery list written by the wife for her husband is easily, literally interpreted by the reader because of the cultural, educational, and situational information shared by the couple. The overall purpose of the list is unambiguous; virtually no unintentional ambiguity

FIGURE 3   Diagram: Grocery List

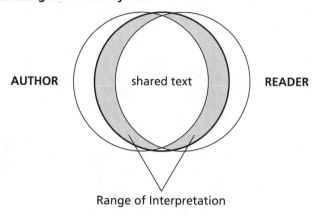

Range of Interpretation

FIGURE 4   Diagram: Poem

Unintentional Ambiguity

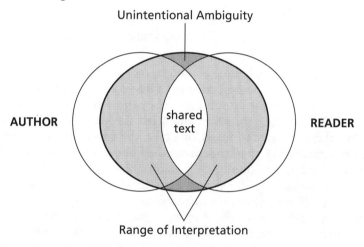

Range of Interpretation

exists, and very little range of interpretation occurs. In the second set of concentric circles, Figure 4, the range of interpretation (or intentional ambiguity) of a poem is greater because while the formal schema (i.e., the structure of the poem) may be well-known to both the writer and the reader (i.e., shared information), the content schema and particularly the linguistic schema (i.e., the words chosen for their ambiguous and/or multiple meanings) may well be interpreted differently by the writer and the reader. So although the reader's interpretation may not correspond to the poet's original intention, both interpretations may be equally valid.

Finally, in Figure 5 the level of unintentional ambiguity and the range of interpretation are great; unfortunately for the student, ambiguity and interpretation are expected to be limited in academic writing. The competent writer in most academic disciplines strives to create a relatively

FIGURE 5   Diagram: ESL Essay Written for U.S. Audience

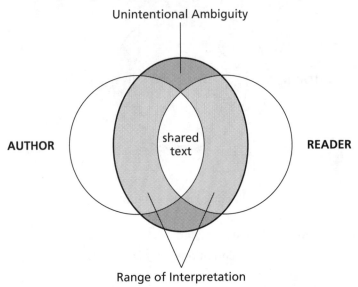

unambiguous text, in which the interpretive processes of the writer and the reader conform to the expectations of his or her community of readers and closely approximate the intentions of the writer (Horowitz, 1988). While the ESL student may have analyzed the writing assignment and identified the audience for the writing task, the paper that he or she turns in demonstrates that the student neither understands nor fulfills the rhetorical and situational expectations of the academic audience. Successful communication has not been achieved. It is also probable that the paper is not representative of the student's native organization and presentation skills; that is, the rhetorical, linguistic, and content schemata demonstrated in the paper may be a kind of "interschema" or "transculture," a paper struggling and not yet succeeding to meet the rhetorical and content demands of U.S. academic prose.

Because there appear to be different rhetorical rules or conventions that govern categories of texts even within a particular language (Brown, 1990; Kaplan, 1990; Scollon, 1991) and because the conventions of academic prose differ among cultures, ESL writing teachers must teach their students ways in which to participate in U.S. academic rhetorical traditions. After all, if NS readers are unable or unwilling to interact with a text as a result of its "foreignness," successful communication will not occur (Kaplan, 1990). Applying schema theory to ESL writing, Carrell (1987) indicates that, by providing necessary cultural information about the rhetorical organization of U.S. expository text and audience expectations of such texts, as well as about the language and content of the text, teachers will help to make ESL writing more effective. Classes should therefore work with authentic text, *reading* and analyzing ideas, structure, and style, *writing* and analyzing purpose and audience in order to develop an awareness for other authors and academic texts (Campbell, 1990). Writing assignments should ask students to read, reread, and write about reading, adding their own schemata to connect and interpret the reading. In short, the study and development of genre-specific schemata empower ESL students, allowing them to explore, reflect upon, and articulate characteristics of particular discourse/interpretive communities (Johns, 1991; Swales, 1990).

CONCLUSION

Effective writing, like successful reading, involves cognitive processes that create meaning by building relations between the text and what we know, believe, and experience. Importantly, communication between writer and reader is most effective when experiences, schemata, and cuing systems are shared. Because, as Kaplan (1990) says, rhetorical conventions within a language are genre specific and change over time, ESL students from different cultural backgrounds who have differing cultural perspectives of texts often write "transculturally." That is, in their attempts to fulfill the expectations of the U.S. academic audience, they write prose that is inappropriate for both their own culture and U.S. culture. The challenge for ESL writing/reading teachers is to provide information about the linguistic and rhetorical schemata of U.S. academic discourse communities and to offer opportunities for practice in identifying and fulfilling U.S. audience expectations. Silva (1990) suggests that ESL teaching focus on a broader conception of what second language writing and reading involve, accounting for the "contributions of the writer, reader, text, and context, as well as their interactions" (p. 20) so that ESL students can be successfully socialized into academic discourse/interpretive communities.

REFERENCES

Anderson, J.W. (1991). A comparison of Arab and American conceptions of effective persuasion. In L.A. Samovar & R.E. Porter (Eds.), *Intercultural communication: A reader* (pp. 96–106). Belmont, CA: Wadsworth.

Badrawi, N. (1992). The reading dilemma: Meeting individual needs. *English Teaching Forum, 30*(3), 16–19, 31, 35.

Beach, R. & Liebman-Kleine, J. (1986). The writing/reading relationship: Becoming one's own best reader. In B.T. Petersen (Ed.), *Convergences: Transactions in reading and writing* (pp. 64–81). Urbana, IL: NCTE.

Benitéz, R. (1990). Using a learning log in an EFL writing class. *English Teaching Forum, 28*(3), 40–41.

Berthoff, A. (1985). How we construe is how we construct. In P.L. Stock (Ed.), *Forum: Essays on theory and practice in the teaching of writing* (pp. 166–170). Upper Montclair, NJ: Boynton/Cook.

Berthoff, A. (1981). *Forming/Thinking/Writing.* Montclair, NJ: Boynton/Cook.

Bizzell, P. (1982). Cognition, convention, and certainty: What we need to know about writing. *PRE/TEXT, 3,* 213–43.

Blanton, L. (1987). Reshaping ESL students' perception of writing. *ELT Journal, 41*(2), 112–118.

Bleich, D. (1986). Cognitive stereoscopy and the study of language and literature. In B.T. Petersen (Ed.), *Convergences: Transactions in reading and writing* (pp. 99–114). Urbana, IL: NCTE.

Braine, G. (1989). Writing in science and technology: An analysis of assignments for ten undergraduate courses. *English for Specific Purposes, 8*(1), 3–15.

Brinton, D.M., Snow, M.A. & Wesche, M.B. (1989). *Content-Based second language instruction.* New York: Newbury House.

Brock, M. (1990). The case for localized literature in the ESL classroom. *English Teaching Forum, 28*(3), 22–25.

Brown, G. (1990). Cultural values: The interpretation of discourse. *ELT Journal, 44*(6), 11–17.

Budd, R. (1989). Simulating academic research: One approach to a study-skills course. *ELT Journal, 43*(1), 30–37.

Campbell, C. (1990). Writing with others' words: Using background reading text in academic compositions. In B. Kroll (Ed.), *Second language writing: Research issues for the classroom* (pp. 211-230). New York: Cambridge University Press.

Canesco, G. & Byrd, P. (1989). Writing required in graduate courses in business administration. *TESOL Quarterly, 23*(2), 305–316.

Carrell, P.L. (1990). Reading in a foreign language: Research and pedagogy. *JALT Journal, 12*(1), 53–74.

Carrell, P.L. (1988). Interactive text processing: Implications for ESL/second language classrooms. In P.L. Carrell, J. Devine & D. Eskey (Eds.), *Interactive approaches to second language reading* (pp. 239–259). Cambridge: Cambridge University Press.

Carrell, P.L. (1987). Text as interaction: Some implications of text analysis and reading research for ESL composition. In U. Connor & R.B. Kaplan (Eds.), *Writing across languages: Analysis of L2 text* (pp. 47–56). Reading, MA: Addison-Wesley.

Carrell, P.L. (1985). Facilitating ESL reading comprehension by teaching text structure. *TESOL Quarterly, 19*(4), 727–752.

Carrell, P.L. (1984a). Inferencing in ESL: Presupposition and implications of factive and implicative predicates. *Language Learning, 34*(1), 1–22.

Carrell, P.L. (1984b). The effects of rhetorical organization on ESL readers. *TESOL Quarterly, 18*(3), 441–469.

Carrell, P.L. (1984c, March). Facilitating reading comprehension by teaching text structure: What the research shows. Paper presented at the International TESOL Convention, Houston.

Carrell, P.L. (1984d). Evidence of formal schema in second language comprehension. *Language Learning, 34*(2), 87–112.

Carrell, P.L. (1984e). Schema theory and ESL reading: Classroom implications and applications. *Modern Language Journal, 68*(4), 332–343.

Carrell, P.L. (1983a). Three components of background knowledge in reading comprehension. *Language Learning, 33*(2), 183–207.

Carrell, P.L. (1983b). Background knowledge in second language comprehension. *Language Learning and Communication, 2*(1), 25–34.

Carrell, P.L. (1983c). Some issues in studying the role of schemata, or background knowledge, in second language comprehension. *Reading in a Foreign Language, 1*(2), 81–92.

Carrell, P.L. (1981). Culture-specific schemata in L2 comprehension. In R. Orem & J. Haskell (Eds.), *Selected papers from the Ninth Illinois TESOL/BE Annual Convention, the First Midwest TESOL Conference* (pp. 123–132). Chicago: Illinois TESOL/BE.

Carrell, P.L. & Eisterhold, J.C. (1983). Schema theory and ESL reading pedagogy. *TESOL Quarterly, 17*(4), 553–574.

Carrell, P.L., Pharis, B.G. & Liberto, J.C. (1989, March). Metacognitive strategy training for ESL reading. Paper presented at the International TESOL Convention, San Antonio.

Carson Eisterhold, J. (1990). Reading–writing connections: Toward a description for second language learners. In B. Kroll (Ed.), *Second language writing: Research issues for the classroom* (pp. 88–101). New York: Cambridge University Press.

Ching, L.P. & Ngooi, A.C. (1991). How journal writing improved our classes. *English Teaching Forum, 29*(3), 43–44.

Clifford, J. (Ed.). (1991). *The experience of reading: Louise Rosenblatt and reader–response theory.* Portsmouth, NH: Boynton/Cook.

Coady, J. (1979). A psycholinguistic model of the ESL reader. In R. Mackay, B. Barkman & R.R. Jordon (Eds.), *Reading in a second language* (pp. 5-12). Rowley, MA: Newbury House.

Cohen, A. (1990). *Second language learning: Insights for teachers, learners, and researchers.* New York: Newbury House/Harper and Row.

Collie, J. & Slater, S. (1987). *Literature in the language classroom: A resource book of ideas.* New York: Cambridge University Press.

Constantinides, J. & Hall, C. (1981). Advanced composition: Beginning at the top. In M. Hines and W. Rutherford (Eds.), *On TESOL '81* (pp. 79–87). Washington, DC: TESOL.

Costello, J. (1990). Promoting literacy through literature: Reading and writing in ESL composition. *Journal of Basic Writing, 9*(1), 20–30.

Dasenbrock, R.W. (1991). Do we read the text we read? *College English, 53*(1), 7–18.

Datesman, M. (1990, March). The interaction between extensive reading and writing. Paper presented at the International TESOL Convention, San Francisco.

Devine, J. (1987). General language competence and adult second language reading. In J. Devine, P.L. Carrell & D. Eskey (Eds.), *Research on reading English as a second language* (pp. 73–85). Washington, DC: TESOL.

Dubin, F. & Bycina, D. (1991). Academic reading and the ESL/EFL teacher. In M. Celce-Murcia (Ed.), *Teaching English as a second or foreign language* (pp. 195–215). New York: Newbury House/HarperCollins.

Elliott, R. (1990). Encouraging reader-response to literature in ESL situations. *ELT Journal, 44*(3), 191–203.

Eskey, D. (1988). Holding the bottom: An interactive approach to the language problems of second language readers. In J. Devine, P.L. Carrell & D. Eskey (Eds.), *Interactive approaches to second language reading* (pp. 93–100). Cambridge: Cambridge University Press.

Eskey, D. & Grabe, W. (1988). Interactive models for second language reading: Perspectives on instruction. In P.L. Carrell, J. Devine & D. Eskey (Eds.), *Interactive approaches to second language reading* (pp. 223–238). Cambridge: Cambridge University Press.

Faigley, L.L. (1985). Non-academic writing: The social perspective. In L. O'Dell & D. Goswami (Eds.), *Writing in non-academic settings* (pp. 231–248). New York and London: Guilford Press.

Fish, S. (1980). *Is there a text in this class? The authority of interpretive communities.* Cambridge, MA: Harvard University Press.

Flower, L. (1979). Writer-based prose: A cognitive basis for problems in writing. *College English, 41*(1), 19–38.

Flower, L. & Hayes, J. (1980). A cognitive process theory of writing. *College Composition and Communication, 31*(4), 365–387.

Flynn, E. (1982). Reconciling readers and texts. In T. Fulwiler and A. Young (Eds.), *Language connections: Writing and reading across the curriculum* (pp. 139–152). Urbana, IL: NCTE.

Folman, S. (1988, March). Towards an EFL reading–writing model of academic learning. Paper presented at the International TESOL Convention, Chicago.

Fulwiler, T. (1987). *The journal book.* Portsmouth, NH: Boynton/Cook.

Fulwiler, T. (1982). The personal connection: Journal writing across the curriculum. In T. Fulwiler & A. Young (Eds.), *Language connections: Writing and reading across the curriculum* (pp. 15–31). Urbana, IL: NCTE.

Gajdusek, L. (1988). Toward wider use of literature in ESL: Why and how. *TESOL Quarterly, 22*(2), 227–257.

Garner, R. (1988). *Metacognition and reading comprehension.* Norwood, NJ: Ablex.

Goodman, K.S. (1979). The know-more and the know-nothing movements in reading: A personal response. *Language Arts, 55*(6), 657–663.

Goodman, K.S. (1967). Reading: A psycholinguistic guessing game. *Journal of the Reading Specialist, 6,* 126–135.

Grabe, W. (1988). Reassessing the term "interactive." In P.L. Carrell, J. Devine & D. E. Eskey (Eds.), *Interactive approaches to second language reading* (pp. 56–70). Cambridge: Cambridge University Press.

Grabe, W. (1986). The transition from theory to practice in teaching reading. In F. Dubin, D. Eskey & W. Grabe (Eds.), *Teaching second language reading for academic purposes* (pp. 25–48). Reading, MA: Addison-Wesley.

Grant-Davie, K. (1989). Rereading in the writing process. *Reader, 21,* 2–21.

Haas, C. & Flower, L. (1988). Rhetorical reading strategies and the construction of meaning. *College Composition and Communication, 39,* 167–183.

Hafiz, F.M. & Tudor, I. (1989). Extensive reading and the development of language skills. *ELT Journal, 43*(1), 4–13.

Hairston, M. (1986). Using nonfiction literature in the composition classroom. In B. Petersen (Ed.), *Convergences: Transactions in reading and writing* (pp. 179–188). Urbana, IL: NCTE.

Hamp-Lyons, L. (1986). No new lamps for old yet, please. *TESOL Quarterly, 20,* 16–27.

Hamp-Lyons, L. (1985). Two approaches to teaching reading: A classroom-based study. *Reading in a Foreign Language, 3*(1), 363–373.

Harris, D. (1990). The use of "organizing sentences" in the structure of paragraphs in science textbooks. In U. Connor & A. Johns (Eds.), *Coherence in writing* (pp. 67–86). Alexandria, VA: TESOL.

Hartman, K., Neuwirth, C., Kiesler, S., Sproull, L., Cochran, C., Palmquist, M., & Zubrow, D. (1991). Patterns of social interaction and learning to write. *Written Communication, 8*(1), 79–113.

Horowitz, D. (1990). Fiction and non-fiction in the ESL/EFL classroom: Does the difference make a difference? *English for Specific Purposes, 9*(2), 161–168.

Horowitz, D. (1988). To see our text as others see it: Toward a social sense of coherence. *JALT Journal, 10*(2), 91–100.

Horowitz, D. (1986a). Process not product: Less than meets the eye. *TESOL Quarterly, 20*(1), 141–144.

Horowitz, D. (1986b). What professors actually require: Academic tasks for the ESL classroom. *TESOL Quarterly, 20*(3), 445–462.

Horowitz, D. & McKee, M. (1984). Methods for teaching academic writing. *English for Specific Purposes, 7*(2), 5–11.

Hyland, K. (1992). Genre analysis: Just another fad? *English Teaching Forum, 30*(2): 14–17, 27.

James, M.O. (1987). ESL reading pedagogy: Implications of a schema-theoretical approach. In J. Devine, P.L. Carrell & D. Eskey (Eds.), *Research in reading in English as a second language* (pp. 177–188). Washington, DC: TESOL.

Janopoulos, M. (1986). The relationship of pleasure reading and second language writing proficiency. *TESOL Quarterly, 20,* 247–265.

Johns, A.M. (1991). Insights into the reading–writing relationship. Paper presented at the California TESOL Conference (CATESOL), Santa Clara.

Johns, A. (1985). Academic writing standards: A questionnaire. *TECFORS, 8,* 11–14.

Johnson, P. (1986). Acquisition of schema for comprehension and communication: A study of the reading-writing relationships in ESL. *RELC Journal, 17*(1), 1–13.

Johnson, P. (1981). Effects on reading comprehension of building background knowledge. *TESOL Quarterly, 15*(2), 169–181.

Kaplan, R.B. (1990). Writing in a multilingual/multicultural context: What's contrastive rhetoric all about? *Writing Instructor, 10*(1), 7–17.

Kaplan, R.B. (1987). Cultural thought patterns revisited. In U. Connor and R.B. Kaplan (Eds.), *Writing across languages: Analysis of L2 texts* (pp. 9–22). Reading, MA: Addison-Wesley.

Kaplan, R.B. (Ed.). (1983). *Annual review of applied linguistics.* Rowley, MA: Newbury House.

Kirsch, G. (1991). Writing up and down the social ladder: A study of experienced writers composing for contrasting audiences. *Research in the Teaching of English, 25*(1), 33–53.

Kirsch, G. (1989). Authority in reading–writing relationships. *Reader, 21,* 56–67.

Krashen, S.D. (1984a). *Writing: Research, theory, and applications.* Oxford: Pergamon Institute of English.

Krashen, S.D. (1984b). Do we learn to read by reading? The relationship between free reading and reading ability. In D. Tannen (Ed.), *Linguistics in context: Connecting observation and understanding* (pp. 269–298). Norwood, NJ: Ablex.

Kroll, B. (1991). Teaching writing in the ESL context. In M. Celce-Murcia (Ed.), *Teaching English as a second or foreign language* (2nd Ed.) (pp. 245–263). New York: Newbury House/HarperCollins.

Kucer, S.L. (1985). The making of meaning: Reading and writing as parallel processes. *Written Communication, 2*(3), 317–336.

Lee, J.F. & Riley, G.L. (1990). The effect of pre-reading rhetorically oriented frameworks on the recall of two structurally different expository tasks. *Studies in Second Language Acquisition, 12*(1), 25–41.

Lucas, T. (1990). Personal journal writing as a classroom genre. In J.K. Peyton (Ed.), *Students and teachers writing together* (pp. 99–124). Alexandria, VA: TESOL.

McConochie, J. (1982). All this fiddle: Enhancing language awareness through poetry. In M. Hines & W. Rutherford (Eds.), *On TESOL '81* (pp. 231–240). Washington, DC: TESOL.

McConochie, J. & Sage, H. (1989). Since feeling is first: Thoughts on sharing poetry in the ESOL classroom. In A. Newton (Ed.), *A forum anthology* (Vol. IV) (pp. 236–239). Washington, DC: USIA.

McCormick, K., Waller, G. & Flower, L. (1987). *Reading Texts: Reading, responding, writing.* Lexington, MA: D.C. Heath.

Meyer, B.J.F. (1984). Organizational aspects of text: Effects of reading comprehension and application for the classroom. In J. Flood (Ed.), *Promoting reading comprehension* (pp. 113–138). Newark, DE: International Reading Association.

Meyer, B.J.F. (1982). Reading research and the composition teacher. *College Composition and Communication, 33*, 37–39.

Meyer, B.J.F. & Freedle, R. (1984). The effects of different discourse types on recall. *American Educational Research Journal, 2*(1), 121–143.

Miccinati, J.L. (1988). Mapping the terrain: Connecting reading with academic writing. *Journal of Reading 31*, 542–552.

Moffat, J. (1968). *Teaching the universe of discourse.* Boston: Houghton.

Nystrand, M. (1990). Sharing words: The effects of readers on developing writers. *Written Communication, 7*(1), 3–24.

Ostler, S. (1987a). English in parallels: A comparison of English and Arabic prose. In U. Connor & R.B. Kaplan (Eds.), *Writing across languages: Analysis of L2 text* (pp. 169–185). Reading, MA: Addison-Wesley.

Ostler, S. (1987b). *A study in the contrastive rhetoric of Arabic, English, Japanese, and Spanish.* Unpublished doctoral dissertation, University of Southern California.

Petersen, B.T. (Ed.). (1986). *Convergences: Transactions in reading and writing.* Urbana, IL: NCTE.

Petrosky, A. (1986). From story to essay: Reading and writing. *College Composition and Communication, 33*, 19–37.

Peyton, J.K. (Ed.). (1990). *Students and teachers writing together.* Alexandria, VA: TESOL.

Peyton, J.K. & Reed, L. (Eds.). (1991). *Dialogue journal writing with nonnative English speakers: A handbook for teachers.* Alexandria, VA: TESOL.

Povey, J.F. (1986). Using literature with ESL students. *ERIC/CALL Bulletin, 10*(1), 3–4.

Pritchard, R.H. (1990). The influence of cultural schemata on processing strategies. *Reading Research Quarterly, 25*(4), 173–293.

Purves, A. (Ed.). (1988a). *Writing across languages and cultures: Issues in contrastive rhetoric.* Newbury Park, CA: Sage.

Purves, A. (1988b). The aesthetic mind of Louise Rosenblatt. *Reader, 20,* 68–76.

Raimes, A. (1987). *Exploring through writing: A process approach to ESL composition.* New York: St. Martin's.

Reid, J. (1988) *Quantitative differences in English prose written by Arabic, Chinese, Spanish, and English students.* Unpublished doctoral dissertation, Colorado State University.

Robb, T. & Susser, B. (1989). Extensive reading vs. skills buildings in an EFL context. *Reading in a Foreign Language, 5*(2), 239–251.

Roller, C.M. (1990). The interaction of knowledge and structure variables in the processing of expository prose. *Reading Research Quarterly, 25*(2), 79–89.

Rosenblatt, L. (1988). Writing and reading: The transactional theory. *Reader, 20,* 7–31.

Rumelhart, D.E. (1977). Toward an interactive model of reading. In S. Dormic (Ed.), *Attention and performance* (pp. 573–603). New York: Academic Press.

Sage, H. (1987). *Incorporating literature in ESL instruction.* Englewood Cliffs, NJ: Prentice-Hall.

Sarig, G. (1988, March). Composing a study–summary: A reading–writing encounter. Paper presented at the International TESOL Convention, Chicago.

Scarcella, R. (1984). How writers orient their readers in expository essays: A comparative study of native and non-native speakers of English writers. *TESOL Quarterly, 18,* 671–688.

Scarcella, R. & Oxford, R. (1992). *The tapestry of language learning: The individual in the communicative classroom*. Boston: Heinle & Heinle.

Scollon, R. (1991) Eight legs and one elbow: Stance and structure in Chinese English compositions. Paper presented at the International Reading Association, Second North American Conference on Adult and Adolescent Literacy, Banff, Canada.

Slater, W.H., Grave, M.F. Scott, S.B. & Redd-Boyd, T.M. (1988). Discourse structure and college freshmen's recall and production of expository text. *Research in the Teaching of English, 22*, 45–61.

Shih, M. (1992). Beyond comprehension exercises in the ESL academic reading class. *TESOL Quarterly, 26* (2), 289–318.

Shih, M. (1986). Content-based approaches to teaching academic writing. *TESOL Quarterly, 20*, 87–103.

Silva, T. (1990). Second language composition instruction: Developments, issues and directions in ESL. In B. Kroll (Ed.), *Second language writing: Research insights for the classroom* (pp. 11–23). New York: Cambridge University Press.

Smith, F. (1986). *Understanding Reading* (3rd ed.). Hillsdale, NJ: Erlbaum.

Smith, F. (1971). *Understanding reading: A psycholinguistic analysis of reading and learning to read*. New York: Holt, Rinehart and Winston.

Spack, R. (1988). Initiating ESL students into the academic discourse community: How far should we go? *TESOL Quarterly, 22*, 29–51.

Spack, R. (1985). Literature, reading, writing and the ESL student. *TESOL Quarterly, 19*, 703–725.

Spack, R. & Sadow, C. (1983). Student-teacher working journals in ESL freshman composition. *TESOL Quarterly, 17*, 575–594.

Spivey, N. (1990). Transforming texts: Construction processes in reading and writing. *Written Communication, 7*, 256–287.

Steffensen, M.S. (1987). The effect of context and culture on children's L2 reading: A review. In J. Devine, P.L. Carrell & D. Eskey (Eds.), *Research on reading English as a second language* (pp. 43–54). Washington, DC: TESOL.

Steffensen, M.S., Joag-dev, C. & Anderson, R.C. (1979). A cross-cultural perspective on reading comprehension. *Reading Research Quarterly, 15*(1), 10–29.

Sternglass, M. (1986a). Introduction. In B.T. Petersen (Ed.), *Convergences: Transactions in reading and writing* (pp. 1–11). Urbana, IL: NCTE.

Sternglass, M. (1986b). Writing based on reading. In B.T. Petersen (Ed.), *Convergences: Transactions in reading and writing* (pp. 151–162). Urbana, IL: NCTE.

Stotsky, S. (1983). Research on reading/writing relationships: A synthesis and suggested directions. *Language Arts, 60,* 627–642.

Straw, S. (1990). Challenging communication. In D. Bogdan & S. Straw (Eds.), *Beyond communication: Reading comprehension and criticism* (pp. 67–89). Portsmouth, NH: Boynton/Cook.

Straw, S. & Bogdan, D. (1990). Introduction. In D. Bogdan & S. Straw (Eds.), *Beyond communication: Reading comprehension and criticism* (pp. 1–18). Portsmouth, NH: Boynton/Cook.

Straw, S. & Sadowy, P. (1990). Dynamics of communication. In D. Bogdan & S. Straw (Eds.), *Beyond communication: Reading comprehension and criticism* (pp. 21–47). Portsmouth, NH: Boynton/Cook.

Susser, B. & Robb, T. (1990). EFL extensive reading instruction: Research and procedure. *JALT Journal, 12*(2), 161–185.

Swaffar, J.K. (1988). Readers, texts, and second languages: The interactive process. *Modern Language Journal, 72*(2), 123–149.

Swales, J. (1990a). *Genre analysis: English in academic and research settings.* New York: Cambridge University Press.

Swales, J. (1990b). Non-native speaker graduate engineering students and their introductions: Global coherence and local management. In U. Conner & A. Johns (Eds.), *Coherence in Writing* (pp. 187–207). Alexandria, VA: TESOL.

Swales, J. (1987). Utilizing the literatures in teaching the research paper. *TESOL Quarterly, 21*(1), 41–68.

Swales, J. & Horowitz, D. (1988, March). A genre-based approach to ESL materials. Paper presented at the International TESOL Convention, Chicago.

Tierney, R. & Leys, M. (1986). What is the value connecting reading and writing? In B. T. Petersen (Ed.), *Convergences: Transactions in reading and writing* (pp. 15–29). Urbana, IL: NCTE.

Tierney, R.J. & Gee, M. (1990). Reading comprehension. In D. Bogdan & S.B. Straw (Eds.), *Beyond communication: Reading comprehension and criticism* (pp. 167–196). Portsmouth, NH: Boynton/Cook and Heinemann.

Zamel, V. (1987). Recent research on writing pedagogy. *TESOL Quarterly, 21,* 697–715.

Zamel, V. (1976). Teaching composition in the ESL classroom: What we can learn from research in the teaching of English. *TESOL Quarterly, 10,* 67–76.

CHAPTER 3

Teaching Writing IS Teaching Reading: Training the New Teacher of ESL Composition

Barbara Kroll
California State University, Northridge

It is the end of an ESL composition class, let us say the freshman composition level. The students are at the most advanced stage of language learning, the point at which they are fully participating as degree seekers in colleges and universities in English-medium institutions. Just as the class ends, the teacher distributes a photocopied text of approximately 1,000 words and says to the students, "Read this article for next time." He is pleased to have found this very engaging reading on the op-ed page of a local newspaper or in a prominent weekly news magazine or in a general interest but intellectually stimulating periodical. The students file the reading with their notebooks and walk out of the room. When the class next meets, the teacher asks the students to take out their copies of the text they have read. He nods approvingly as eager students place their texts on their desks and he sees marginal squiggles that indicate various words have been translated into different languages and yellow highlighter marking a number of passages on their papers; he frowns as some students sheepishly admit they don't have their copy with them and suspects they might never have looked at it. He begins his lesson by asking a variety of questions concerning the content of the reading, checking for presumed comprehension of the text's meaning. Satisfied that the students understand the essence of the text, he selects a range of vocabulary items and conducts a short session on word meanings, urging his students to guess meaning from context and reviewing alternate word forms of the words under scrutiny. If the text is replete with transition words, or examples and illustrations, or citations from sources, or exemplary topic sentences, he will call this to the attention of his students and have them focus on whatever surface rhetorical properties of the text strike him as important for classroom attention. Having thus considered the reading, he asks his students to use the remainder of the lesson to write a first draft of a paper in which they either give their own ideas and opinions about the subject matter presented in the reading or compare and contrast the ideas about subject matter in this particular reading with ideas about the subject matter presented in a previously discussed text. In subsequent classes, the reading passage itself will have been forgotten, focus will shift to the emerging student essays, and the next reading text will be distributed when the writing assignment sequence derived from this particular reading has been completed. The next reading passage will likely be unrelated in content to the previous one and might also be chosen by happenstance, "creating a pinball style classroom that careens madly from one clanging thematic focus to another so that no sustained intellectual engagement is possible" (Schuster, 1991, pp. 38–39).

If this class does not seem familiar to you, let me freely confess that any observer of untold numbers of ESL composition classes that I taught earlier in my career would surely have witnessed such a lesson, one that I believe typifies an attempt to bring together reading and writing. (And part of the reason I have used the pronoun "he" is to distance myself from this demonstration of the reading–writing connection.) But there is so much more to it than that, issues this teacher might never have thought about or been exposed to in his professional training or development, issues I myself was surely unaware of when I began to teach EFL composition in 1970 and ESL composition in 1974.

According to Freeman (1990), many pedagogical choices that a teacher makes evolve from an individual teacher's beliefs, often in the absence of any specific knowledge that might serve to challenge or alter the teacher's beliefs (particularly in a salubrious way). Freeman (1990) further posits that teachers structure classrooms in ways that recreate classrooms in which they themselves have been students, for these earlier experiences form an important building block in the development of belief systems about teaching. Corbett (1990) points out that many college composition teachers who entered the profession without graduate training tend to model their own teaching on that of some teacher they admired, a teacher, I might add, who probably had no true knowledge of reading/writing connections either. Hirsch (1980) warns that there is an "intimate connection between partisan zeal and lack of knowledge" (p. 162), so teachers may feel very strongly about their choices but would be unable to justify them on theoretical or even pedagogical grounds. In fact, Robinson (1991, p. 346) points to a group of newly hired teachers staffing composition classrooms who not only are untrained in composition but who "never exhibit the slightest knowledge of the books and articles that are shaping our field nor the slightest embarrassment about their ignorance." Thus only beliefs can drive their classroom choices.

I think it fair to say that our hypothetical teacher (really the early "me") sincerely *believes* that a lesson such as the one described promotes improvement in writing skills based on reading input, having perhaps participated as a student in similar lessons *and not having any further knowledge* about how to bring together reading and writing. It is also possible that the teacher not only believes that this is a good method for connecting reading and writing, but may also believe that this is the only or the best method.

In fact, the attempt to bring together reading and writing in both the L1 and the L2 writing class has been an ongoing enterprise for decades in one of the following three main instantiations: (1) readings are used to serve as the springboard for a topic to write about (e.g., Read about X's experience with Y and then write about your own experience with Y); (2) readings provide background information and source material for writing about a topic (e.g., Using information from texts X, Y, and Z about Q, write about your own views of Q); and (3) readings are exploited as a model of a particular feature of writing to imitate (e.g., Observe X's incorporation of comparison and contrast in writing about Y, and write about Z using comparison and contrast in the same way). It is the first function that has guided our example lesson, with some overtones of the second function.

However, none of these three ways of incorporating reading in the writing class adequately addresses the concept of reading as a rhetorical activity, a critical component of developing writing skills. Furthermore, texts students produce are also "readings," and writing teachers often remain unaware of how to train their students to view their own developing texts as readings and how awareness of their text as a reading contributes to the improvement in their writing. And until we can train (or retrain) writing teachers to replace the familiar common sequence of activities with ones more likely to promote improved language proficiency skills for ESL students—to replace some of their beliefs with solid knowledge—the classroom described will remain typical of countless ESL composition classrooms where courses are being taught today. And students will leave such classrooms with fewer tools and strategies than they might leave a classroom presided over by a teacher who consciously attends to at least some of the multiplicity of connections between reading and writing.[1]

Let us explore what teacher training looks like and how it might be augmented to provide teachers a larger knowledge base from which to make choices about structuring classrooms in which they exploit at least some of the multilayered connections between reading and writing. To limit the discussion, I shall focus on just two aspects that serve to promote improvement in writing: (1) reading textual material for other than its content and (2) reading one's own texts as a reader rather than as a writer. (Benesch, Blanton, Collignon, Gajdusek & vanDommelen, Goldstein, Johns, and Spack, this volume, address other areas in reading theory that translate into effective writing classroom strategies.)

TEACHER TRAINING

There is little doubt that TESL programs are concerned about training future writing teachers since their future ESL students must demonstrate

---

[1]For openers, Peterson (1989, pp. 251–252) provides a listing of 32 examples of ways to use readings as jumping-off points for writing activities in L1 classrooms.

writing competency in the academic environment (Bridgeman & Carlson, 1983; Jordan, 1989; Reid, 1989; Spack, 1988). All things being equal, we would anticipate (and perhaps insist, if we are on the hiring committee) that teachers of ESL composition have had specific training in the teaching of composition to non-native speakers of English. However, this is not always the case, since there seem to be three pools of candidates from which teachers of ESL composition are drawn. In schools with separate ESL programs (not necessarily departments),[2] teachers hired usually have specialized ESL training but such training may lack depth in the specific area of teaching writing to advanced students. In schools in which ESL composition courses are found within a writing program, teachers may be drawn from the first pool (ESL teachers) or may be either (1) those with experience teaching freshman composition to native speakers or (2) those with experience teaching basic writing students.

ESL Teacher Backgrounds

Some teachers attain the standing of ESL composition teacher through graduate training in ESL teaching in general, with or without a specific course that focuses on the teaching of writing. (Relatively few graduate TESL/applied linguistics programs, it seems, offer such courses [Kroll, 1988], though they certainly exist.) At the minimum, however, such teachers have been introduced to issues in ESL writing through general methodology texts, including such widely used ones as Bowen, Madsen & Hilferty (1985), Celce-Murcia (1991), Harmer (1991), Hubbard et al., (1983), Long & Richards (1987), and Richard-Amato (1988), to name a few that provide prospective teachers theoretical insight into and practical methodologies for the ESL classroom. In addition to "covering" writing in some way, these methodology texts also address issues in reading; they typically compartmentalize the four traditional skills (speaking, listening, reading, and writing), an approach that often promotes skill separation rather than skill integration as a path to language learning.[3] However, since methodology texts encompass approaches to teaching learners at all levels, prospective teachers may not have spent much class time discussing or have read all that much about teaching writing and reading at the most advanced level, let alone exploring ways to connect them.

In this "skill separation" model, some areas we expect that ESL teacher training for prospective writing teachers would at least touch on include how to train students in various stages of the writing process; how to respond to student writing in maximally effective ways; how to

---

[2]Gantzer (1991) provides a discussion of where best to situate an ESL program within an institution.

[3]An extensive review of TESL methodology courses in general is provided by Grosse (1991).

assess, diagnose, and address student error; how to explore the relevancy of contrastive rhetoric; and so on. (More extensive discussion of what the ESL composition teacher needs to know about teaching writing is found in Kroll, 1991, and Reid, in press.) Prospective reading teachers will probably have learned about how to exploit the interactive nature of reading in the classroom, how to expand students' schemata, how to maximize and expand individual reading strategies, how to present texts, and so on. (More extensive discussion of classroom issues in teaching ESL reading is found in Barnett, 1989, while Grellet, 1981, provides abundant exercise materials.) In reality, though, two to four weeks in a methodology class spent on writing and reading does not cover a large knowledge base, let alone make one an authority in the field. To best serve students, Roy (1988, p. 21) points out that "the current strong claim that writing teachers need to know writing from the inside out is as important for teachers of second language students as it is for teachers of native speakers." And even in the best case scenario of specialized graduate training,[4] while knowledge of theoretical work in the field of writing and/or reading coupled with a critical analysis of various pedagogical approaches is necessary, it is not sufficient to equip the teacher to serve his or her students fully without some understanding of the role that the *interaction* of writing and reading plays in literacy events.

Furthermore, presenting separate skills as isolated components, as is typically done in methods training, contributes to the classroom teaching of skills in isolation when trainees "graduate" to the status of teachers. According to Zamel (1991), compartmentalization inhibits rather than assists students in their ultimate language learning goal: full participation in the academy.

> To my way of thinking, skills-based instruction—because it is shaped by reductive and mechanistic assumptions about language and reading and writing development, because it assumes that students need to learn basic or constituent skills (skills that necessarily come prior to reading and writing), and because it presents skills stripped of the very context that gives them meaning and importance—keeps students outside of the academic, content-based conversation they are trying to take part in. (Zamel, 1991, p. 14)

Such sentiments are echoed by ESL students themselves: "[T]he majority [of 80 subjects at 5 separate universities] did not seem to think that instruction in specific skills, such as writing specific rhetorical types or narrowly defined reading skills addressed their later needs [in subject matter courses]" (Christison & Krahnke, 1986, p. 72).

---

[4]A program at the University of Arizona that provides extensive training in ESL composition teaching for its graduate teaching assistants is described in detail by Schlumberger & Clymer (1989).

Freshman Composition Teachers

Still other teachers come to the teaching of ESL composition through experience in teaching composition to native speakers of English, a background that does not necessarily mean they have scholarly preparation in the field of composition. According to Gere, "Most instructors of writing have . . . learned through the informal curriculum of ideas gleaned from self-sponsored reading, orientation sessions, and conversations with other instructors, rather than in graduate classes" (1985, p. 58), though the proliferation of both M.A. and Ph.D. level graduate programs in the field continues. (See Chapman & Tate, 1987, for a review of 53 Ph.D. programs in rhetoric and composition.) Even for those composition teachers who are trained in the field (becoming perhaps "scholars" and "researchers" rather than merely "practitioners" in North's [1987] sense), such a background does not necessarily provide them with specific knowledge about learning to write in a second language. A representative sample of books designed to train native-speaker composition teachers includes several that make no reference to ESL students (Bridges, 1986; Foster, 1983; Hashimoto, 1991; Lindemann, 1987), one that devotes a few pages to issues in teaching non-native English students (Bogel *et al.*, 1988), and only one that provides extensive discussion of issues relating to non-native writers (Williams, 1989). Two widely used sourcebooks (collections of significant articles) for composition teachers, Graves (1990) and Tate and Corbett (1988), include no articles on ESL students. And while there are many similarities between L1 and L2 writers, there are also differences that teachers should be aware of (see, for example, Frankenburg-Garcia, 1990; Krapels, 1990; Raimes 1987; Silva 1991).

In addition to the lack of directly appropriate background credentials for composition-trained teachers in the ESL composition classroom (i.e., they do not have a knowledge base regarding this population of students), it is often the case that such teachers have little or no background in reading theory apart from a literary context. This evolves from the historical separation of what is perceived to be reading skill instruction from instruction in writing. In commenting on the split between writing and reading in terms of the knowledge base common to college professors, Neel (1984) points out that until the 1960's,

> the phenomenon of reading was commonly construed as one person's attempt to extract from a text the meaning another person had put in it. Most literate people were no more concerned with how they read than ambulatory people were with how they walked.... Astonishingly, those working in composition have remained innocent of and uninterested in theories of the reading process, even though the inextricable connection between writing and reading is self-evident. (p. 153)

Basic Writing Teachers

The third pool from which ESL composition teachers may be drawn are teachers of basic writing—either because ESL students are viewed as "basic" (or "developmental" or "remedial") writing students based on their skill level as determined by a particular institution's philosophy or placement testing procedures[5] and are therefore placed in mixed (i.e., native and non-native speaker) basic writing classes or because basic writing teachers are deemed capable of teaching students who have problems in writing and are thus assigned to teach ESL sections. Like "regular" composition teachers, basic writing teachers often have no specific training[6] in either composition studies or in ESL. In the past, they certainly had no training in reading either. Troyka (1986) reports that teaching reading in her basic writing class got her "into some trouble" in the mid-1970's; she was told that because she "had no formal training in reading" (p. 188), she should leave reading instruction to reading teachers.

Leaving aside some early work that focused extensively on the importance of promoting language accuracy (e.g., Gefvert, 1980; Wiener, 1981), the group of composition teachers (and researchers) who have long understood the need to maximize the integration of reading and writing, in fact, are those working in the field of basic writing. In commenting on the reading/writing relationship long before such ideas were common, as they now are in discussions about reading, Shaughnessy (1977), a pioneer in the field of basic writing, pointed out that it is critical for the student to understand the interactive nature of reading and writing. She stated that "the meaning of what [the student] reads or writes resides not in the page nor in the reader but in the encounter between the two." (p. 223).

Other major figures in the development of the field of basic writing studies have commented both on the difficulty of bringing the teaching of reading to the writing classroom and the importance of doing so. Based on her analysis of student progress from an early pilot program in remedial (basic) English that she developed and supervised at Ohio State University, Lunsford (1978) concluded that "the teacher of writing must automatically and always be a teacher of reading as well" (p. 49), a thought echoed in the title of this chapter. Noting that "the contemporary divorce of reading instruction from departments of English is indeed

---

[5]In a survey of basic writing programs throughout the United States, Trimmer (1987, p. 4) reports that "900 respondents reported 700 different ways to identify such [basic writing] students."

[6]In a description of one training course that does exist, Bishop (1990) provides a highly readable ethnographic case study of five experienced teachers enrolled in a summer doctoral seminar titled "Teaching Basic Writing." She focuses on how the teaching seminar influenced the subsequent teaching of subjects who teach basic writing at a variety of institutions in terms of the teachers being relatively open or relatively resistant to change.

lamentable" (p. 51), she goes on to say that "[e]specially in the remedial classroom, the reunion of reading and writing instruction is a consummation devoutly to be wished" (p. 51). Such a consummation was brought about in the work of Bartholomae & Petrosky, whose *Facts, Artifacts and Counterfacts* (1986) presents the detailed syllabus and rationale of a basic reading and writing course taught at the University of Pittsburgh since 1977. They note that part of the initial process of getting their course accepted into the curriculum was convincing the "university administration that reading *could* be taught in an English department" (Bartholomae & Petrosky, 1986, p. 13, emphasis mine).[7]

While examples of success in promoting the reading/writing connection within basic writing programs are encouraging, what remains discouraging is the status of composition teachers in general. The Executive Committee of the Conference on College Composition and Communication (1989), in calling upon institutions to promote quality education in writing as promulgated in the so-called "Wyoming Resolution," referred to teachers of writing as "an enormous academic underclass" (p. 330), with large numbers working on part-time and/or temporary appointments. If this document had addressed the employment of ESL teachers, the comments would have been similar. ESL teachers also tend to be part-time and/or marginalized members of the faculty, a situation that surely does not direct attention to the importance of professional growth and enlargement of one's teaching horizons.

Given this complex picture of teacher training, development, and employment, it is not surprising that what takes place in many ESL composition classrooms fails to reflect the full benefit of either the insights or the pedagogical implications of what we have come to know about writing and reading (see Leki, this volume and Reid, this volume) or about classroom second language learning either (see Chaudron, 1988; Ellis, 1990; Spolsky, 1989; and Tarone & Yule, 1989).

RESTRUCTURING CLASSROOMS

As a way of discussing two critical issues about the connections between writing and reading for ESL composition classroom teachers to familiarize themselves with, let us return to the classroom of our hypothetical teacher and consider his assumptions in structuring the "reading to write" lesson described at the beginning of this chapter. What factors

---

[7]ESL courses, of course, are "housed" in a variety of departments and are not necessarily offered in departments of English. The point is that reading skills (often the purview of a department in a school of education) and writing skills (usually not "housed" in education) should be addressed in the same course, and this would be true for ESL courses regardless of which department bears responsibility for ESL instruction. Again, as in note 2, see Gantzer (1991).

have motivated his pedagogical choices, and what does he need to learn that would alter his belief systems to bring about change in the classroom? In the first place, the teacher has presented the reading in a way that shows no apparent awareness of how to introduce materials to maximize the value of the reading event. He should not feel that time spent in such activities as previewing the reading by discussing its content or style or its potential for use in a writing assignment is anything other than critical for the advancement of writing abilities. Furthermore, our teacher has distributed the reading at the end of a class period to be read for homework so that no class time has been made available for activities to assist the students with schema building. (Benesch, Collignon, and Gajdusek & vanDommelen, this volume, discuss different ways to work toward building schema.) He has supplied no real purpose to direct their reading and no context within which the students might have done their individual and private readings of the text, pedagogical goals a teacher familiar with reading theory would have attended to.

Just as the notion of "purpose" influences to a large extent the shape a written product will take, so too the purpose for which one reads a text will help shape the ways in which one approaches the task of reading. (See Leki, this volume, for further discussion of purpose in reading.) Writing teachers are aware that many students perceive the primary purpose of producing and submitting a written text to be attaining a certain grade from the teacher (either on one particular piece of writing or for the entire course). Therefore, teachers must strive to convince students that "real-world writing" has one of two main purposes: to communicate with a reader (audience-based purpose) or to express oneself in some way (writer-based purpose), including wanting to gain mastery over material (writing for learning, further discussed by Sarig and Goldstein, this volume). In fact, both L1 and L2 composition textbooks often include a chapter or a section directly addressing writing purposes. But "writers at work do not decide on 'their purpose' as the textbooks advise: they create a web of purposes" (Flower, 1988, p. 531). Without understanding "purpose" in its larger sense, writers cannot make informed choices in shaping their developing text. Students must understand that the "purposes" for reading also vary from reading event to reading event; different purposes will lead to differential ways in which the students undertake and complete the reading task.[8]

Because of previous educational experiences, ESL students who have had all or part of their English language instruction in a foreign setting often equate reading with translation, seeing that as its purpose. Thus in the absence of any alternate purpose being specified, the students resort to

---

[8]Flower (1988, pp. 37–38) reviews several experimental studies, for example, that demonstrate how reading with different purposes leads subjects to recall texts differentially.

familiar behavior, treating the text as an exercise and marking down translations of key or difficult words in the margin. Anticipating that they will be asked general comprehension questions, students are also likely to mark passages in the reading that they feel are important; they are unlikely to attend to the reading from the perspective of a writer (to be discussed in the next section). And not knowing what writing activity might follow from classroom consideration of the reading, they are unable to attend to content or features of the text informed by such an awareness.

Furthermore, our hypothetical teacher selected a reading passage based primarily on its "engagement" factor, his motivation probably being to find something interesting for the students and/or for himself. (See Leki, in this volume, for discussion of elements of textbook reading selections.) This shows a certain ambivalence about what a writing class is. To many, the lack of a specific body of subject matter such as is found in a course in economics or biology or physics or psychology makes writing courses seem "content-deprived" (Johns, 1991), and for teachers operating out of this mindset, the subject matter of the readings can transform itself into the content of the course. If, for example, students are reading about the feminization of poverty, it might appear, at least for the day, that the course resembles one in sociology or perhaps women's studies. A danger here, according to Gold (1991), is that such content-driven writing courses become "high level bull sessions" (p. 262). Hairston (1986) points out that when L1 writing teachers use readings to provide content for discussion within the writing class, the "focus of any writing course—the study of the writing process . . . gets lost," (p. 180), and instead much class time is devoted to attending to the substance of reading passages, turning the class into a product-based one instead of a process-based one.

Next, our hypothetical teacher treated the text as something to be "comprehended" and mined for object lessons in vocabulary and surface textual properties, a relatively restricted "bottom-up" approach (see Carrell & Eisterhold, 1983; and Eskey, 1986). Here too Shaughnessy (1977), in writing about the basic writing class, finds such a procedure very product oriented:

> The text stands . . . separate from the reader, impersonal and invulnerable,
> like some ancient tablet that the archeologist struggles to decode. (p. 223)

And "decoding" is exactly what the teacher is asking the students to do in posing comprehension questions—questions that are generated to see if students can prove that they are processing the text in a way that the teacher finds acceptable. Writing about lessons in L1 composition classrooms that focus on comprehending the content of typical texts, Comley (1986) also refers to the importance of code:

> And how does the teacher appear? As keeper of the code, mantled in mysterious and powerful authority as she or he withholds the meaning—the
> One Right Reading—of the text, and interpretation becomes a classroom
> guessing game. (p. 51)

What our hypothetical teacher failed to provide was a context for the "read–discuss–write" sequence, a viable reading lesson, or a framework for the writing. While it is not necessary to abandon the traditional read–then discuss–then write progression within a writing class, it is necessary to embed it within a purposeful context (Flower, 1988; Flower *et al.*, 1990; Kantz, 1990; Spivey, 1990). Perhaps what would help this teacher is to work backwards from the final goal he has in mind for his students. Let us take an example where the goal is for students to prepare an essay in which they write about how they would resolve a particular problem that their institution is facing. The teacher would look for a reading (and preferably several readings) that directly or obliquely reflects the particular context for writing—expressing a personal opinion and showing how to solve a problem. Alternatively, the teacher could look for readings whose content focuses on the type of issues he would like the students to see as potential topics for discussion in their own papers or that might serve to have them broaden and deepen their understanding of what institutional problems can look like in the first place. Having a specific writing goal would first motivate the selection of specific reading passages (in contrast to selecting a text for its presumed interest value) and then frame a purpose for the students reading the text—either to note how an author or authors approach the task and/or to learn more background information in preparation for writing. (Translation of the reading, for example, would no longer be a plausible agenda.)

Where the teacher has selected problem solution texts, the reading lesson in which the passage is reviewed can now be directed towards an examination of how such texts are structured rather than being the random collection of comprehension questions and test of recognition of superficial rhetorical properties that our opening sample lesson appeared to be. I am not suggesting that the reading be used as a "model," whose features must be closely identified and imitated. Rather, the text should be explored to see how the author shaped it to accomplish his or her goals. In our opening lesson, for example, our teacher looked for topic sentences to point out to the students or quizzed them on their ability to identify transition words, believing that he was conducting a lesson in rhetoric. But a teacher knowledgeable about reading would ask students to focus on how the text solves the rhetorical problems it sets up for itself, based on its own purpose for being. Finally, the writing to follow is no longer motivated by the content of the reading per se, but is motivated by content the student selects as it relates to his or her own school situation.

Reading Like a Writer

In order for the lesson described above to work, the first key concept that must be part of a teacher's knowledge base is what it means to read as a writer. Writing teachers need to understand how to train their students in reading a text rhetorically, because this is a process that promotes the integration of reading and writing: "[R]eaders are participants in a rhetorical situation in which communications have a purpose" (Flower, 1988, p. 539). Smith (1983) makes the strong claim that we "must read like a writer in order to learn to write like a writer" (p. 562). That is, one can read a text not only to "learn" its content but to "learn" choices that writers have made in producing it. While Smith claims that such "learning is unconscious, effortless, [and] incidental" (p. 561), I think we must at least initially ask our ESL students to engage in this kind of reading consciously in order to alert them to ways of reading that they might not otherwise engage in. Both reading and writing are acts of composing (Tierney and Pearson, 1983), and teachers need to bring this to the attention of students who are otherwise likely to believe that only writing is composing. Asking a student to stop after a certain point in the text and guess what will follow forces the student to articulate how he or she is processing an author's presentation; that is, the student is "composing" an individual reading. If the student guesses correctly, then he or she has shown an ability to "read like a writer" in deciding where the writer is going, an important skill for being able to compose a text for the readers of his or her future text. If the student guesses incorrectly, then he or she needs to return to the text to look for ways in which the author might have led him or her astray or to reevaluate his or her own synthesis of the text up to that point. In either case, again the student is reading like a writer, a valuable tool for later being able to write like a writer. Paying conscious awareness to how one processes a text as a reader helps a writer to better understand what readers will be doing with texts he or she writes.

Hairston (1986, p. 181) spells out a set of five guidelines to help teach students how to read from a writer's perspective. She suggests how teachers can focus student attention on such issues as authorial purpose in constructing text, audience considerations, and choices the writer has made in producing his or her text, concluding, "This set of guidelines . . . makes every discussion about reading a discussion about writing" (p. 182). A detailed step-by-step example of one way to approach a reading from a rhetorical perspective in the freshman composition writing class is provided by Gottschalk (1988, pp. 49–55), who uses a portion of a text by anthropologist Jacob Bronowski as an example of how to focus not only on the content but also on the structure of a passage. Dubin (1986, pp. 149–153) provides a detailed example of how to present a text to ESL students within a framework that promotes goals similar to Hairston's guidelines for using a rhetorical perspective, although she does not use the term. The writing teacher who lacks knowledge about this aspect of reading theory ultimately shortchanges his or her students. Rather than leaving the writing class with a range of ways to attend to a text, students retain "a naive, information-driven focus on content" (Flower, 1988, p.

545) that restricts rather than enlarges the ways in which they will approach future writing tasks, particularly those that involve reading.

Writing Like a Reader

Our hypothetical lesson ended at the point at which students were preparing a first draft of a paper; we have not followed this class long enough to see what the students have done (or have been asked to do) with their developing texts or how the teacher and/or other students have responded to these or subsequent drafts. However, we might assume our teacher follows a typical process approach of requiring multiple drafts and utilizing peer review. What is especially important for the students in terms of developing their mastery of writing is that they understand how the texts they produce are "readings" and how they can utilize their knowledge of the ways readers behave to help them learn to write better. Here is where writing teachers' horizons need to be expanded to include awareness of the reading side of writing and the second key concept that should form an integral part of their knowledge system, how to write like a reader. For it is only when a writer is able to cast himself or herself in the role of a reader of the text under preparation that he or she is able to anticipate the reader's needs by writing into the text what he or she expects or wants the reader to take out from the text.

Of course, the first reader of a text is the writer, and the ability to distance oneself from one's writing, examining it as a reading passage, facilitates revision and rewriting, essential components of most successful writing processes. If the student believes his or her task is completed when the draft first appears on the page, there will be no "reading," only writing. But simply reading over one's paper without attending to how readers actually behave may not be enough to prompt effective revision. Again, reading theory must be brought into the writing classroom. Beach & Liebman-Kleine (1986) provide a detailed analysis and specific lesson plans for how classroom teachers can enable their students "to imagine reader attributes and to use those attributes to assess their [own] writing" (p. 65). In this way, writers can revise and polish their rough drafts into final drafts that are shaped by an appreciation of the needs, knowledge, and beliefs of their intended audience, be it actual readers or readers that the writers must hypothesize (Ede & Lunsford, 1984). Rather than forgetting the reading texts that have been introduced in class, again a pattern of our sample opening lesson, students should be reminded to consider ways in which previous readings studied in class have addressed and resolved the very issues that they are grappling with.

Beyond self as reader, there is outside audience as reader, and many student writers have a great deal of difficulty producing texts that are appropriately decipherable by this "outside" audience. Coining a term to name a type of writing that fails to factor in the needs of a prospective reader, Flower (1979) discusses "writer-based prose," a type of writing whose meaning is clearly understood to the writer but not necessarily to a reader: "[T]he source [of this problem] can often be traced to the writer's underlying strategy for composing and to . . . failure to transform private thought into a public, reader-based expression" (p. 19). While learning theory in general points to the underlying complexity of the terms *expert* and *novice* (Carter, 1990), numerous studies of skilled (or professional) writers vs. unskilled (or novice) writers (reviewed by Raimes, 1985) show that less proficient writers, both in L1 and in L2, have difficulty in imagining an audience or completely overlook the factor of an audience for their work and thus tend to write prose that fails to meet the needs of the reader.[9] Skilled writers, on the other hand, consciously conjure up an audience and simultaneously attend to its needs.[10] The more that writing teachers understand what readers need and do as they read, the more they can help their students learn to construct papers that are reader-based.

CONCLUSION

Teaching students to write better and perhaps thereby to succeed better in meeting some of the academic demands of their college and university careers is a challenging and difficult enterprise. ("Pure") ESL teachers, like their ("pure") composition colleagues, often operate in an environment in which the courses they offer are viewed as either remedial in nature or as a service to the institution, rather than as an important component of the student's education (Benesch, 1988). While the academy demands professionalism of faculty engaged in teaching such diverse courses as mechanical engineering, economics, special education, business management, and even literature and foreign languages, it has not always been as demanding of those faculty engaged in teaching native or non-native speakers of English to write. It sees the teaching of the former group as complementary to engagement in ongoing research activities and the teaching of the latter group as isolated from research activities. The mixed message the institution conveys is that it wants its graduates to have mastered a certain level of literacy but that it does not encourage the professionalism of faculty working to help students attain that goal. And the quality of education is affected. According to Robinson, "Injustices are wrought upon the students in composition classes taught by teachers who do not know

---

[9]To help with promoting awareness of audience, Brookes & Grundy (1990), in a book targeted for ESL students, provide a series of exercises (pp. 114–119) designed to help writing students understand who their readers might be and how different readers' needs would necessitate a differential set of choices in the preparation of a text.

[10]Elbow (1987) offers an alternate view, claiming that there are occasions for writing in which the writer should *not* attend to the needs or existence of any audience aside from himself or herself alone.

their business. These teachers in turn are produced by English departments that do not hire...persons genuinely qualified in composition" (1991, p. 348). This philosophy allows programs and departments to staff writing classrooms with untrained or underprepared teachers rather than to staff those classrooms with people sufficiently trained in both research (theory) and pedagogy.[11] So even as we work to improve our teacher training programs for prospective teachers, we must work to have administrations recognize the value of literacy instruction in the education of our students and to insist that colleges and universities provide opportunities for current teachers to expand their knowledge base and also to become more fully aware of the value of uniting the teaching of reading and writing.

Those of us who serve in the trenches (i.e., the ESL and writing classrooms) know that "the line between theory and classroom practice has begun to be breached, the dichotomy between the two questioned" (Tinberg, 1991, p. 36), and we can be effective teachers only if we learn as much as we can about how to promote student mastery of *our* subject matter—writing. What I have tried to suggest in this chapter is that writing is integrally connected to reading in several important ways that must be part of our agenda for the writing classroom. And a critical part of the agenda for how we train ESL writing teachers is to include attention to reading theory. Teaching writing without teaching reading is not teaching writing at all.

---

[11]On the high school level, a study by Storms (1988) found that mean scores for students' writing assessments increased as the teacher's level of training increased, empirical evidence supporting the concerns of Robinson (1991) and Roy (1988) for staffing composition classrooms with professionally trained teachers.

REFERENCES

Barnett, M.A. (1989). *More than meets the eye: Foreign language reading: theory and practice.* Englewood Cliffs, NJ: Prentice Hall Regents.

Bartholomae, D. & Petrosky, A. (1986). *Facts, artifacts and counterfacts: Theory and method for a reading and writing course.* Upper Montclair, NJ: Boynton/Cook.

Beach, R. & Liebman-Kleine, J. (1986). The writing/reading relationship: Becoming one's own best reader. In B.T. Petersen (Ed.), *Convergences: Transactions in reading and writing* (pp. 64-81). Urbana, IL: NCTE.

Benesch, S. (Ed.). (1988). *Ending remediation: Linking ESL and content in higher education.* Washington, DC: TESOL.

Bishop, W. (1990). *Something old, something new: College writing teachers and classroom change.* Carbondale: Southern Illinois University Press.

Bogel, F.V., Carden, P., Cox, G.H., Davis, S., Freedman, D.P., Gottschalk, K.K., Hjortshoj, K., & Shaw, H.E. (1988). *Teaching prose: A guide for writing instructors.* New York: Norton.

Bowen, J.D., Madsen, H., & Hilferty, A. (1985). *TESOL techniques and procedures.* Cambridge, MA: Newbury House.

Bridgeman, B. & Carlson, S. (1983). *Survey of academic writing tasks required of graduate and undergraduate foreign students.* (TOEFL Research Report #15). Princeton, NJ: Educational Testing Service.

Bridges, C. (Ed.). (1986). *Training the new teacher of college composition.* Urbana, IL: NCTE.

Brookes, A. & Grundy, P. (1990). *Writing for study purposes: A teacher's guide to developing individual writing skills.* Cambridge: Cambridge University Press.

Carrell, P.L. & Eisterhold, J.C. (1983). Schema theory and ESL reading pedagogy. *TESOL Quarterly, 17,* 553-573.

Carter, M. (1990). The idea of expertise: An exploration of cognitive and social dimensions of writing. *College Composition and Communication, 41,* 265–286.

Celce-Murcia, M. (Ed.). (1991). *Teaching English as a second or foreign language,* 2nd edition. New York: Newbury House.

Chapman, D.W. & Tate, G. (1987). A survey of doctoral programs in rhetoric and composition. *Rhetoric Review, 5,* 124–186.

Chaudron, C. (1988). *Second language classrooms.* New York: Cambridge University Press.

Christison, M.A. & Krahnke, K.J. (1986). Student perceptions of academic language study. *TESOL Quarterly, 20,* 61–81.

Comley, N.R. (1986). The teaching seminar: Writing isn't just rhetoric. In C.W. Bridges (Ed.), *Training the new teacher of college composition* (pp. 47–57). Urbana, IL: NCTE.

Conference on College Composition and Communication. (1989). Statement of principles and standards for the postsecondary teaching of writing. *College Composition and Communication, 40,* 329–336.

Corbett, E.P.J. (1990). The writing teacher as historian. In D.A. Daiker and M. Morenberg (Eds.), *The writing teacher as researcher: Essays in the theory and practice of class-based research* (pp. 30–37). Portsmouth, NH: Boynton/Cook Heinemann.

Dubin, F. (1986). Dealing with texts. In F. Dubin, D.E. Eskey, & W. Grabe (Eds.), *Teaching second language reading for academic purposes* (pp. 127–158). Reading, MA: Addison-Wesley.

Ede, L. & Lunsford, A. (1984). Audience addressed/Audience invoked: The role of audience in composition theory and pedagogy. *College Composition and Communication, 35,* 155–171.

Elbow, P. (1987). Closing my eyes as I speak: An argument for ignoring audience. *College English, 49,* 50–69.

Ellis, R. (1990). *Instructed second language acquisition.* Oxford: Basil Blackwell.

Eskey, D. (1986). Theoretical foundations. In F. Dubin, D.E. Eskey & W. Grabe (Eds.), *Teaching second language reading for academic purposes* (pp. 3–23). Reading, MA: Addison-Wesley.

Flower, L. (1988). The construction of purpose in reading and writing. *College English, 50,* 528–550.

Flower, L. (1979). Writer-based prose: A cognitive basis for problems in writing. *College English, 41,* 19–37.

Flower, L., Stein, V., Ackerman, J., Kantz, M.J., McCormick, K., & Peck, W.C. (1990). *Reading-to-write: Exploring a cognitive and social process.* New York: Oxford University Press.

Foster, D. (1983). *A primer for writing teachers: Theories, theorists, issues, problems.* Upper Montclair, NJ: Boynton/Cook.

Frankenberg-Garcia, A. (1990). Do the similarities between L1 and L2 writing processes conceal important differences? *Edinburgh Working Papers in Applied Linguistics, 1,* 91–102.

Freeman, D. (1990, March). Learning to teach: "Interteaching" as evolution of pedagogical expertise. Paper presented at the 24th Annual TESOL Convention, San Francisco, CA.

Gantzer, J. (1991). Issues in ESL: Putting ESL in its place. *College ESL, 1* (2), 21–28.

Gefvert, C.J. (1980). Training teachers of basic writing. In L.N. Kasden & D.R. Hoeber (Eds.), *Basic writing: Essays for teachers, researchers, and administrators* (pp. 119-140). Urbana, IL: NCTE.

Gere, A.R. (1985). Teaching writing teachers. *College English, 47,* 58–65.

Gold, R.M. (1991). How the freshman essay anthology subverts the aims of the traditional composition course. *Teaching English in the Two-Year College, 18,* 261–265.

Gottschalk, K.K. (1988). Classroom activities. In F.V. Bogel, P. Carden, *et al.*(Eds.), *Teaching prose: A guide for writing instructors* (pp. 46–86). New York: Norton.

Graves, R.L. (Ed.). (1990). *Rhetoric and composition: A sourcebook for teachers and writers,* 3rd edition. Portsmouth, NH: Boynton/Cook Heinemann.

Grellet, F. (1981). *Developing reading skills: A practical guide to reading comprehension exercises.* Cambridge: Cambridge University Press.

Grosse, C.U. (1991). The TESOL methods course. *TESOL Quarterly, 25,* 29–49.

Hairston, M. (1986). Using nonfiction literature in the composition classroom. In B.T. Petersen (Ed.), *Convergences: Transactions in reading and writing* (pp. 179–188). Urbana, IL: NCTE.

Harmer, J. (1991). *The practice of English language teaching.* New edition. London: Longman.

Hashimoto, I.Y. (1991). *Thirteen weeks: A guide to teaching college writing.* Portsmouth, NH: Boynton/Cook Heinemann.

Hirsch, E.D., Jr. (1980). Research in writing: The issues. In L.N. Kasden & D.R. Hoeber (Eds.), *Basic writing: Essays for teachers, researchers, and administrators* (pp. 153–163). Urbana, IL: NCTE.

Hubbard P., Jones, H., Thornton, B., & Wheeler, R. (1983). *A training course for TEFL.* Oxford: Oxford University Press.

Johns, A.M. (1991, April). Insights into the reading–writing relationship. Paper presented at the 22nd Annual CATESOL Conference, Santa Clara, CA.

Jordan, R.R. (1989). English for academic purposes (EAP). *Language Teaching, 22,* 150–164.

Kantz, M. (1990). Helping students use textual sources persuasively. *College English, 52,* 74–91.

Krapels, A.R. (1990). An overview of second language writing process research. In B. Kroll (Ed.), *Second language writing: Research insights for the classroom* (pp. 37–56). New York: Cambridge University Press.

Kroll, B. (1991). Teaching writing in the ESL context. In M. Celce-Murcia (Ed.), *Teaching English as a second or foreign language,* 2nd edition (pp. 245–264). New York: Newbury House.

Kroll, B. (1988, March). Graduate preparation for future ESL writing teachers. Paper presented at the 22nd Annual TESOL Conference, Chicago, IL.

Lindemann, E. (1987). *A rhetoric for writing teachers,* 2nd edition. New York: Oxford University Press.

Long, M.H. & Richards, J. (Eds.). (1987). *Methodology in TESOL: A handbook of readings.* New York: Harper & Row.

Lunsford, A.A. (1978). What we know—and don't know—about remedial writing. *College Composition and Communication, 29,* 47–52.

Neel, J. (1984). Reading and writing: A survey of questions about texts. In M.G. Moran & R.F. Lunsford (Eds.), *Research in composition and rhetoric: A bibliographical sourcebook* (pp. 153–188). Westport, CT: Greenwood Press.

North, S.M. (1987). *The making of knowledge in composition: Portrait of an emerging field.* Upper Montclair, NJ: Boynton/Cook.

Peterson, A. (1989). The writing–reading connection: Taking off the handcuffs. In A.H. Dyson (Ed.), *Collaboration through writing and reading: Exploring possibilities* (pp. 249–253). Urbana, IL: NCTE.

Raimes, A. (1987). Language proficiency, writing ability, and composing strategies: A study of ESL college student writers. *Language Learning, 37,* 439–468.

Raimes, A. (1985). What unskilled ESL students do as they write: A classroom study of composing. *TESOL Quarterly, 19,* 229–258.

Reid, J.M. (In press.) *Teaching ESL composition.* New York: Prentice-Hall.

Reid, J.M. (1989). English as a second language composition in higher education: The expectations of the academic audience. In D.M. Johnson & D.H. Roen (Eds.), *Richness in writing: Empowering ESL students* (pp. 220–234). New York: Longman.

Richard-Amato, P. (1988). *Making it happen: Interaction in the second language classroom.* New York: Longman.

Robinson, W.S. (1991). The CCCC statement of principles and standards: A (partly) dissenting view. *College Composition and Communication, 42,* 345–349.

Roy, A. (1988). ESL concerns for writing program administrators: Problems and policies. *WPA: Writing Program Administration, 11,* 17–28.

Schlumberger, A. & Clymer, D. (1989). Teacher training through teacher collaboration. In D.M. Johnson & D.H. Roen (Eds.), *Richness in writing: Empowering ESL students* (pp. 146–159). New York: Longman.

Schuster, C.I. (1991). Theory and practice. In E. Lindemann & G. Tate (Eds.), *An introduction to composition studies* (pp. 33–48). New York: Oxford University Press.

Shaughnessy, M. (1977). *Errors and expectations.* New York: Oxford University Press.

Silva, T. (1991, March). Comparing composing processes: ESL and NES freshman writers. Paper presented at the 25th Annual TESOL Convention, New York.

Smith, F. (1983). Reading like a writer. *Language Arts, 60,* 558–567.

Spack, R. (1988). Initiating ESL students into the academic discourse community: How far should we go? *TESOL Quarterly, 22,* 29–51.

Spivey, N.N. (1990). Transforming texts: Constructive processes in reading and writing. *Written Communication, 7,* 256–287.

Spolsky, B. (1989). *Conditions for second language learning.* Oxford: Oxford University Press.

Storms, B.A. (1988). Teacher training in writing instruction and its relationship to student achievement, instructional practices, and teacher attitudes. Unpublished doctoral dissertation, Northern Arizona University.

Tarone, E. & Yule, G. (1989). *Focus on the language learner.* Oxford: Oxford University Press.

Tate, G. & Corbett, E.P.J. (Eds.). (1988). *The writing teacher's sourcebook,* 2nd edition. New York: Oxford University Press.

Tierney, R.J. & Pearson, P.D. (1983). Toward a composing model of reading. *Language Arts, 60,* 568–580.

Tinberg, H.B. (1991). "An enlargement of observation": More on theory building in the composition classroom. *College Composition and Communication, 42,* 36–44.

Trimmer, J.H. (1987). Basic skills, basic writing, basic research. *Journal of Basic Writing, 6,* 3–9.

Troyka, L.Q. (1986). Closeness to text: A delineation of reading processes as they affect composing. In T. Newkirk (Ed.), *Only connect: Uniting reading and writing* (pp. 187–197). Upper Montclair, NJ: Boynton/Cook.

Wiener, H.S. (1981). *The writing room: A resource book for teachers of English.* New York: Oxford University Press.

Williams, J.D. (1989). *Preparing to teach writing.* Belmont, CA: Wadsworth.

Zamel, V. (1991). Acquiring language, literacy, and academic discourse: Entering ever new conversations. *College ESL, 1*(1), 10–18.

SECTION II

COGNITIVE PERSPECTIVES

Section II focuses on the cognitive dimensions of reading in the composition classroom. The first two chapters provide the theoretical framework for the remaining chapters in this section, which offer research and pedagogical perspectives.

The theoretical frameworks outlined by Carson (Chapter 4) and Devine (Chapter 5) survey work in first language reading and writing on cognition and metacognition, and note the implications of this work for second language learners. What is apparent in these theoretical chapters is the relative absence of second language research that explores ways in which cognitive processes in reading and writing might be the same as or different from first language processes. However, second language research on L2 reading/writing cognitive processes is beginning, and Chapters 6 (Flahive & Bailey), 7 (Connor & Carrell), and 8 (Sarig) look at three of the crucial issues: the relationship between reading and writing abilities in second language learners, the effect of task representation on writers and readers of second language essays, and the transfer of reading/writing skills across languages. Chapters 9 (Spack) and 10 (Gajdusek & vanDommelen) suggest ways in which teachers can implement reading/writing connections in pedagogical practices that both build on and enhance cognitive processing in reading and writing.

CHAPTER 4

Reading for Writing: Cognitive Perspectives

Joan G. Carson
Georgia State University

Composition teachers who find ways to integrate reading into the writing curriculum usually do so with some specific pedagogical purpose in mind: to provide rhetorical models, for example, or as an impetus for topic generation and content development. But in addition to these specific purposes is the more general assumption teachers often make that any reading, in and of itself, is somehow "good" for writers. The most common formulation of this belief is the statement that writing competence results somehow from exposure to reading, and that good readers make good writers. As Krashen (1984) claims, "It is reading that gives the writer the 'feel' for the look and texture of reader-based prose" (p. 20). Intuition and experience tell us that this is probably so, but in fact the connections between reading and writing are much more complex—and interesting— than these statements would have us believe. Once we understand the many facets of this relationship, we can understand why the case for reading in the composition classroom is so compelling.

The phrase *reading for writing* can be understood as referring most specifically to the literacy event in which readers/writers use text(s) that they read, or have read, as a basis for text(s) that they write. This specific interpretation reflects the fact that this type of reading-to-write assignment is common in formal classroom contexts, both academic and non-academic. Reading for writing can also be understood as acknowledging that writing is often the resultant physical artifact of reading/writing encounters. However, these situation-specific interpretations of reading for writing should not obscure the fact that reading and writing are *equally* important processes of a literacy event in which the most significant product is not the writing per se, but the meaning that has been created by the reader/writer from both comprehending and composing text(s). According to Tierney & Leys (1986), our perspective on reading/writing relationships has been limited by the belief that reading and writing are related in some simple way. This single response answer seems to them to be incorrect. Rather, they say,

> We are convinced . . . that the study of reading-writing connections involves appreciating how reading and writing work together in myriad ways as tools for information storage and retrieval, discovery and logical thought, communication, and self-indulgence. (p. 26)

It is this more general and ultimately more useful perspective on reading for writing that is the focus of this chapter.

I must note at this point that much of what we know about the reading/writing relationship in general, and about reading for writing in particular, comes from first language research. What little second language research there is will be included in my discussion here, and the results seem to point to cognitive processes and effects similar to those found in the L1 studies. Nevertheless, we should be cautious about applying L1 findings to L2 situations. While there is undoubtedly much that is of value for second language teachers in the research on first language reading/writing relationships, there is also much that remains to be examined from the second language perspective. This chapter, in addition to exploring the cognitive dimensions of reading for writing, might also begin to suggest an agenda for researchers interested in this aspect of second language literacy.

APPROACHES TO READING/WRITING RELATIONSHIPS

Interest and research in reading/writing relationships have both emerged from and been drawn from many areas, including reading theory, cognitive psychology, linguistics, pragmatics, reader response theory, communication studies, literary theory, and rhetoric. (See Reid, this volume, for an overview of some of these influences.) This cross-disciplinary research has resulted in distinctly different approaches to investigating the reading/writing connection. In their comprehensive review of reading–writing relationships, Tierney & Shanahan (1991) suggest three general categories of inquiry that have been pursued by various researchers and theorists:

1. Reading and writing as shared knowledge and shared processing;
2. Reading and writing as transactions among readers, writers, and texts;
3. Reading and writing as collaborative events.

Using Tierney & Shanahan's categories, I will briefly review the research findings for categories one and two. I will then focus the remainder of the chapter on what we have learned about the third category, exploring the reading for writing issues, including the cognitive processes involved in and the cognitive effects claimed for this particular reading/writing relationship. Finally, I will discuss the implications of these perspectives in order to make the argument that the reading for writing perspective is the most valuable for composition classrooms.

Reading and Writing: Shared Knowledge and Shared Process

Tierney & Shanahan's first category comprises research that suggests that what reading and writing have in common are shared knowledge and shared processes. That is, what we know about reading is similar to what we know about writing, and the way that we comprehend text is similar to the way that we compose text. The shared knowledge/shared process perspective is an absolute view in which reading and writing are seen as separate from their social, communicative, or functional effectiveness and from each other (Shanahan & Tierney, 1990).

Evidence of **shared knowledge** has been summarized in Stotsky's (1983) and Belanger's (1987) extensive reviews of correlational studies of reading and writing performance. Their summaries of research findings yielded the following:

1. There are correlations between reading achievement and writing ability. Better writers tend to be better readers.
2. There are correlations between writing quality and reading experience as reported through questionnaires. Better writers read more than poorer writers.
3. There seem to be correlations between reading ability and measures of syntactic complexity in writing. Better readers tend to produce more syntactically mature writing than poorer readers.

The results of these studies showing correlations between better readers and better writers suggest that shared knowledge is available to readers/writers in both domains. In other words, whatever knowledge contributes to making someone a good reader may also be contributing to making that person a good writer as well.

Theorists of the **shared process** perspective, acknowledging a conceptual shift to reading as meaning making and to writing as process, have looked at the possibility that parallel cognitive processes underlie reading and writing. Bracewell, Frederiksen, & Frederiksen (1982), Squire (1983), Tierney & Pearson (1983), and Wittrock (1983) all claim that common generative cognitive processes are involved in meaning construction in both composing and comprehending text. Kucer (1987) proposes four potential key cognitive mechanisms for reading and writing: (1) both emphasize background knowledge, (2) both draw on a common data pool of written language, (3) both utilize similar transformation processes of background knowledge into text, and (4) both employ common processing patterns in text production as individuals read and write. It is from this common pool of cognitive and linguistic operations, Kucer claims, that readers and writers construct text world productions. These models all provide frameworks for acknowledging the shared processes that readers and writers draw on in comprehending and composing text. In other words, they assume that whatever processes a reader uses to make meaning of a text may also be the same processes that a writer uses to create meaning.

Transactions Between Readers and Writers

The second perspective that Tierney & Shanahan discuss is one emanating from reader response theory and communication studies. This view, which Sternglass (1986b) refers to as transactive, is concerned with how readers think about authors in constructing text meaning and how writers consider readers' needs. The reading/writing relationship is understood as negotiation, and competency is conditional, not absolute, dependent on readers' and writers' goals, intentions, and circumstances (Shanahan & Tierney, 1990). In the transactional model there is no ideal text, only "effective" text in which success equals effective communication relative to participants' goals. This perspective is clearly more social than cognitive in nature and will be covered more completely in Chapter 12 (Eskey, this volume). Nevertheless, because social and cognitive dimensions of literacy are in reality inseparable, I will briefly discuss this transactive view of reading/writing relationships.

The theoretical groundwork for the transactional perspective in literacy research comes from reader response criticism, which examines text structure and processes by which meaning results from writer-text-reader transactions. For Rosenblatt (1978), the meaningful experience of a text is in the transaction between the text and the reader. The text itself, she claims, is incomplete; it needs a reader's experience to make it understood. A literary work is what is read; it exists in the mind, not on the page, and meanings vary with different readers. The text itself checks excessive variations, although Fish (1980) says that agreement comes from an interpretive community that reaches consensus on meaning.

Bleich's subjective criticism (1975) attempts to make readers aware of how they arrive at the meaning of a text. His response heuristic is an approach to instruction, based on reader response theories, that asks writers to write (1) what is perceived in the text, (2) how the writer feels about it, and (3) what associations inform and follow from their perceptions. Petrosky (1982), arguing for the value of reader response, notes that comprehension is heavily subjective, a function of the reader's prior knowledge plus text plus context. Readers compose as they comprehend, and the interaction of reading, responding, and composing is what results in understanding.

A focus on the transactional nature of reading/writing encounters highlights readers' and writers' reciprocal roles, whether as a reader, critic, and supporter of one's own writing (Murray, 1982) or as a thoughtful reader of others' writing (Pearson & Tierney, 1984; Smith, 1983). In any case, as Tierney & LaZansky (1980) note, readers and writers have an obligation to consider each other when comprehending as well as composing. Research shows, however, that writers tend to be affected by readers' needs more than readers are affected by writers' intentions (Tierney & Shanahan, 1991).

Reading-to-Write/Composing from Sources

In addition to the views of the reading/writing relationship as the interaction of shared knowledge/shared process and as the transaction between readers and writers, a third perspective examines the cognitive dimensions of reading for writing. In this third perspective, which I will explore in the remainder of the chapter, the focus is on what happens when reading and writing are used together.

Discussions of reading for writing acknowledge that reading and writing are separate abilities, yet the collaborative nature of composing from sources strengthens the connection between them. "Because reading and writing processes blend and co-occur," Spivey (1990) says,

> it would be inaccurate to portray intentional acts of composing from sources as a linear, two-step procedure in which a person reads a source text simply for comprehension in a text-driven way before beginning the process of writing. Acts of composing from sources are hybrid acts of literacy in which writing influences reading and reading influences writing. (p. 259)

Researchers interested in the collaborative uses of reading/writing relationships have looked at two aspects of reading for writing. First, they have examined the cognitive *processes* involved in reading for writing. This research has centered on the specific reading-to-write activities of summarizing and synthesizing texts. Second, researchers have examined the cognitive *effects* claimed for reading-to-write. This research focuses on ways in which some combination of reading and writing promotes ongoing thinking and learning. In the following sections, I will examine each of these aspects (cognitive processes and cognitive effects) of the reading-for-writing collaboration. (See Devine, this volume, for a discussion of metacognition in ESL reading-for-writing tasks.)

Reading for Writing: Cognitive Processes

Summarizing Text

Summarizing is a common academic literacy task that entails both reading and writing abilities. Much of the research on cognitive processes in summarizing comes from cognitive psychology and schema theory, building in particular on Rumelhart's (1977) and Kintsch & van Dijk's (1978) work. According to Rumelhart, texts are defined by their constituent structure. Within the constituent structure, major constituents are those represented at the highest level of the text—the constituents, typically represented in summaries, that distinguish the important or critical parts of a story from its details. Summarizing, then, is the act of "trimming" the structural tree to leave only those major constituents at the level of generalization required of the summary.

While Rumelhart focuses on the importance of constituent text structure in his discussion of summarizing, Kintsch & van Dijk (1978) describe the mental operations underlying summary production. Their processing model specifies sets of operations by which the full text meaning can be condensed into its gist. To produce the gist of the text, macro-operators transform the text base by (a) deleting or (b) generalizing irrelevant or redundant propositions, and by (c) constructing new inferred propositions. Production of summaries is understood both as a process of reproducing information (the stored macrostructure of the text) as well as a process of construction (generation of plausible inferences).

Using Rumelhart's and Kintsch & van Dijk's claims for summary writing as both reproduction and construction, other researchers have borrowed and expanded on these models to look more closely at the processes involved in summarization, as well as at the way these processes develop over time. Brown & Day (1983), expanding on the Kintsch & van Dijk model, identified the following six summarization strategies:

1. **Delete** trivial material.
2. **Delete** redundant material.
   [Strategies 1 and 2 are Kintsch & van Dijk's "delete."]
3. Substitute a **superordinate** term for a list of items or actions.
4. Substitute a **superordinate** action for subcomponents of that action.
   [Strategies 3 and 4 are Kintsch & van Dijk's "generalize."]
5. **Select** a topic sentence from the text.
6. If no topic sentence, **invent** one.
   [Strategy 6 is Kintsch & van Dijk's "construct inferences."]

Brown & Day's analysis of the types of summarization strategies used by fifth graders, seventh graders, tenth graders, and college students yielded a developmental continuum of summarization strategies. Apparently, the first strategy to emerge is deletion (strategies 1 and 2), followed by superordination (strategies 3 and 4), and then by selection (strategy 5). Invention (strategy 6) is a late-developing strategy.

While the continuum of summarization strategies suggests the order in which summarization skills develop, it does not account for the fact that some summaries (and summarizers) are more successful than others. What accounts for the differences in summary quality and summarizing abilities? Winograd (1984) explored the connection between reading proficiency and summary writing ability. In a study of eighth graders' summarizing strategies, Winograd identified three areas in which reading proficiency and summary writing interact. First, he found that better readers were more sensitive to importance in the text and were able to identify important elements in the text, using both textual and contextual cues. Second, Winograd found that the ability to produce summaries was related to this sensitivity to importance. These first two results suggest that the ability to identify important elements in the text may be the skill underlying both summarizing and comprehending. Finally, Winograd found that poor readers were not able to use effectively the summarization transformations used by better readers. Poor readers have trouble integrating individual propositions into larger units.

Johns' study (1985) of summaries of underprepared and adept university students resulted in findings of patterns similar to those of Winograd's good and poor readers, as well as evidence of strategies supporting the developmental continuum proposed by Brown & Day. Johns found that adept students' writing summaries included more of the important ideas than did those of underprepared students. Also, underprepared students included more reproductions than combinations or macropropositions. She concluded that underprepared students did not seem to be using the summarization strategies required to produce summaries. Although Johns does not make the claim that underprepared students' inclusion of fewer important ideas is related to their reading proficiency, as Winograd does, this might, in fact, have been the case.

Hidi & Anderson's model (1986) recognizes the crucial effect on summarizing strategies of the reader/writer's sensitivity to important elements in the text. They agree with Winograd that summarizing involves higher level operations requiring evaluation of the relative importance of various elements of the text. In their review of research on the development of summary writing abilities, Hidi & Anderson outline developmental differences. Although the developmental continuum of summary skill development that they describe is essentially the same as Brown & Day's, they claim that the major difference between young children and adults, as Winograd has noted, is their sensitivity to important elements in the text. Adults and college students tend to include central ideas of topic sentences, whereas children's choices tend to be those ideas that they find interesting.

Thus there is evidence that reading proficiency may be a factor in summarization ability, insofar as it allows reader/writers to pick out important textual elements. In addition, though, Hidi & Anderson note that factors influencing task demands, such as characteristics of the target material and task procedures, can make the process more difficult and can result in differences in the quality of summaries, as well as in the ability to apply different summary strategies. A final significant factor is the type of summary that the writer must produce. Writer-based summaries (study summaries, for example), those written for the purposes and uses of the writer, are likely to entail the writer's processing smaller units at any one time during construction. Furthermore, there is likely to be little attention to form, because a writer-based summary need only satisfy the needs of the writer. Reader-based summaries, those written for the purposes of a reader other than the writer, are likely to involve the writer's rereading the whole text before constructing the summary, as opposed to the writer-based strategy of constructing the summary from smaller units. Space constraints of reader-based summaries might also entail higher levels of cognitive processing, with the summary requiring more condensation, transformation, and integration.

There has been little research on summary writing in a second language, involving either text or processes. Johns & Mayes (1990), examining high- and low-proficiency ESL writers' summaries, found evidence that language proficiency plays a role in summary writing. In their study, low-level students did more direct copying than did high-level students, and high-level students did more combining of idea units within a paragraph. While these differences were significant, Johns & Mayes did not find them as great as the differences that Johns (1985) found between under-prepared and adept native-speaking students.

Sarig (this volume) looks at the summary composing processes of a university student writing a study–summary (a writer-based summary) in his first and second language, and notes both similar processes and products across languages. Because so little has been done with summarization processes in second language research, we can only make the very tentative suggestion that proficiency in L2 summary writing is likely to be (a) a function of L2 language proficiency insofar as this proficiency affects L2 reading and writing abilities, as the Johns & Mayes study suggests, and (b) related to summarizing abilities in the L1, as the Sarig study suggests. A relationship between L1 and L2 summarizing abilities is plausible, since summaries typically follow the text being summarized and do not require the writer to generate a language-specific rhetorical form. As a result, the cognitive processes required in summarizing are likely to generate similar summary products across languages.

Synthesizing Texts

In addition to examining the cognitive processes involved in summarizing, researchers have also looked at the cognitive processes involved in synthesizing texts. Much of the work on summarizing has been done by reading researchers, because summaries give readers the major role: The summary is guided by the text that was read and by the reader's comprehension of it. However, research on text synthesis tends to be done by writing researchers, since with synthesis the writer has the principal role: It is the writer's text that controls the reading of source material as well as the use of that source material in the text that is being written.

The phrase *composing from sources* suggests somehow a process in which reading precedes and unilaterally affects writing. However, what is being written can also affect what is being read. As Spivey (1990) notes, readers who are reading to write attend *selectively* to content that may be relevant to written text, even though that content may not be what is emphasized in the text itself:

> When writers compose from sources, reading and writing processes blend, making it difficult, if not impossible, to distinguish what is being done for purposes of reading from what is being done for purposes of writing . . . . We often cannot say whether a writer performs a certain operation to make meaning of the text that is read or to make meaning for the text that is being written. (p. 258)

This interaction means that composing from sources makes complex demands on writers. According to Stein (1990), these demands include reading and understanding different materials on the topic, sorting out similarities and differences in the sources, determining how to apply prior knowledge, deciding what is important, choosing a format to suit the topic and materials, and, finally, attending to the usual demands that writing tasks make.

How do writers manage this complex task? Spivey argues that no text is original—most must be considered as composed from sources. The sources writers use are immediate source texts and long-term memory, although much of background knowledge comes from experiences with other texts. These two sources (source texts and background knowledge) affect each step of the text synthesizing process.

Spivey's model (1990) of composing from sources borrows three constructs from reading research—organization, selection, and connection of content—to show how textual meaning is shaped. The first of these constructs, organization, refers to the way reader/writers organize information from the text being read for the text being written. The writer's created text may be organized differently from the source text, Spivey says, since readers of source texts are often writing to construct different meanings, "with intentions to create their own new texts, to make their own contributions" (p. 265).

In addition to organizing content, reader/writers need some criteria for picking out the important elements in a source text. According to Spivey, writers use textual relevance as one criterion, but they also consider intertextual relevance, noticing the information that is common across texts. Additionally, writers give relevance to the emergent structure of their own text as they transform source material. That is, material in a source text can become relevant because it is functional to the specific structure of the text the writer is creating.

Spivey's third construct, the connection of content, focuses on the role of background knowledge in synthesizing texts. Writers composing from sources, she notes, interweave source texts with prior knowledge, but the extent of content generation varies. When synthesizing texts, if the writer does not possess relevant background knowledge, extensive generation of content may not be possible. In this case, writers *have to* rely on source material. Also, if source texts are sufficient, writers may not *need to* add much. Still, background knowledge, when necessary and possible, can help the reader/writer connect content in the text being written.

In Spivey's synthesizing model of organizing, selecting, and connecting content, the issues of task representation and background knowledge are the ones most likely to cause difficulty for writers composing from sources. Task representation can be problematic for writers composing from sources, because it is the writers' discourse goals that determine the way the text will be structured and also the relevance of content to that structure. In other words, the way writers represent the task determines the structure of their text. What makes task representation difficult is that a) students' representations do not always match the requirements of a particular task, and b) task representations are by their very nature continually under construction and thus unstable.

In a study of college freshmen reading to write, Flower (1990b) found that the way students represented the task to themselves varied considerably and resulted in a range of more and less successful writing. When students do not do the task, Flower claims, it is not necessarily that they do not have the ability or the knowledge, but that they have construed the task differently from what was actually intended.

The mismatch of task requirements and task representations is an important source of difficulty for writers composing from sources. Equally difficult, though, as Flower (1990b) has noted, is the instability of task representations throughout the composing process. Deep into a discussion of an interesting point, writers can find that the text being created has taken a different turn from the task as originally represented. Good writers can make adjustments—either by restructuring the task or by eliminating whatever has caused the text to become disjointed. Less able writers may have difficulty recognizing the conflict, or, having recognized it, may not be able to resolve it. In both cases, in the mismatch of task and task representation and in the instability of task representations, reader/writers can be faced with problems as they work to organize and select text—the texts that are read as well as the texts that are written.

The role of background knowledge, along with task representation, is the other major problem area for reader/ writers who are reading to write. The writing process, as Sternglass (1986a) notes, is constrained by what the reader/writer knows as well as by the source texts, and research seems to confirm the importance of background information for writers composing from sources.

Ackerman (1991) examined the synthesis essays of two groups of graduate students, one group that was familiar with the topic and one group that was not. He found that background knowledge did affect the quality of the essays. High-knowledge writers used more local and evaluative elaborations and were more aware of rhetorical contexts. Furthermore, they included more new information in the top levels of their essay structure. Ackerman concluded that writers do use topic knowledge as well as reading and writing experience when composing synthesis essays.

Johns (1991) studied the writing performance of an ESL student who wrote acceptably for content classes yet failed English competency writing exams. She concluded that it was the student's familiarity with content that allowed him to earn A's on content exams. He knew the vocabulary of the discipline, the types of knowledge claims he could make, and the appropriate rhetorical forms. Thus, background knowledge allowed him to perform competently in his content area, and lack of background knowledge when writing the English competency exam led to less effective writing.

Given Spivey's model of text synthesis (organizing, selecting, and connecting content), we have seen a) how task representation affects the cognitive processes of organizing and selecting text, and b) how background knowledge plays a crucial role in the process of connecting content. How do reader/ writers attend to these different components of the synthesizing process?

Not surprisingly, Spivey & King (1989) in their study of sixth, eighth, and tenth graders producing a synthesis essay of three texts, found developmental patterns in organizing, selecting, and connecting text. Older students' writing was more coherent and included more content and information that had intertextual importance (i.e., information that was included in all three texts). The researchers also found relationships between reading ability and the ability to produce synthesis essays. Better readers produced better syntheses by making more use of sources and by producing texts with better local and global coherence. Better readers also made more elaborate plans and spent more time on task.

In perhaps the most comprehensive reading-to-write study to date (Flower, et al., 1990), various analyses were done with freshmen writers composing from sources. As part of this study, Stein (1990) examined the way in which writers used various cognitive processes. She found that writers spent the most time (43%) elaborating, or comparing source text to their own knowledge (Spivey's connecting content). They spent 27% of their time monitoring, 19% planning, and 11% structuring information (Spivey's organizing and selecting text). These percentages were relatively the same, whatever the type of paper. However, Stein says, it is not enough to look only at the cognitive processes involved in composing from sources. Because reading-to-write constitutes a complex task environment,

> changing contexts and goals often leads to differences in the way people use basic processes, as well as in the kind of papers they write. Such a view suggests that as students perform this kind of task, they make choices about which cognitive processes to use and when to use them. (p. 125)

Thus, Stein claims, we need to look not only at the cognitive processes involved, but also at the way strategy use is related to goals, plans, and task representation.

As with other aspects of reading/writing relationships, little L2 research on reading for writing has been done. One relevant study, however, is Campbell's comparison (1990) of native speakers with more- and less-proficient non-native speakers in their uses of information from an article when writing an essay. She found differences between the native speakers' and non-native speakers' essays and concluded that language proficiency affected the way that writers used the source reading text in their writing.

The cognitive processes involved in synthesizing texts are complex, as these researchers are discovering. What seems to account for this complexity is the fact that synthesizing texts requires the interaction of processes and strategies. In order to write effective synthesis essays, writers must control far more than what is needed for summarization. For text synthesis, the complexities involved in organizing, selecting, and connecting content, as well as the problems entailed by the need to a) construct effective and appropriate task representations and b) utilize appropriate background knowledge, make composing from sources difficult for writers in general and, considering the language factor, for second language writers in particular.

Reading for Writing: Cognitive Effects

In addition to describing cognitive *processes* underlying the reading/writing connection in summarizing and synthesizing texts, theorists and researchers are also beginning to explore the cognitive *effects* of reading for writing. The impetus for much of this research has been the need to specify the role that reading and writing play in helping students develop what has been termed "critical literacy." Critical literacy, Flower (1990a) says, is different from receptive literacy, which emphasizes getting information. Rather, critical literacy "typically means not simply building on but going beyond reception and understanding" (p. 5). A critically literate person is a person who

> not only understands information but transforms it for a new purpose. He
> or she is able to turn facts into concepts, to turn concepts into a policy or
> a plan, and to see the issue and define the problem within a problematic
> situation. (p. 5)

Because reading to write requires reader/writers to produce a text of their own, they must a) transform information to their own purposes in reading and b) synthesize their own knowledge with that of another text in writing. This transformation and synthesis of knowledge is the ultimate goal of critical literacy.

Critical literacy is particularly important in school, where critical thinking is valued and fostered. This link between critical thinking and critical literacy can be seen in "writing across the curriculum" programs, in which students are required to write in content courses in order to enhance their thinking and learning in those content areas. Schooling typically encourages complex combinations of reading and writing in order to think and learn. Reading to write is "a tool used to learn, to test learning, and to push students to build beyond their sources" (Flower, 1990a, p. 4).

Reading-to-write activities allow students, as McGinley & Tierney (1989) say, "to avail themselves of . . . different perspectives and ways of thinking" (p. 245). Using Wittgenstein's metaphor of a "topical landscape," McGinley & Tierney claim that reading and writing work together in knowledge acquisition. In their formulation, content domain is understood as a landscape that may be explored and crossed from many directions and perspectives, and different forms of reading and writing are the different routes through which a domain may be explored. Writing and reading thus lead to learning or understanding that is better than that achieved by either reading or writing alone.

Several recent studies have explored the cognitive effects of using reading and writing together. Tierney et al., (1989) looked at various combinations of reading and writing (such as writing a letter to the editor, reading an editorial passage, or answering questions related to the topic) to see how they affected the learning of 137 undergraduate students. The results showed that students who wrote and read had the advantage. In addition, the reading/ writing group revised more, which, the authors suggest, indicates the ability/willingness to revise one's position, an indicator of critical thinking.

Newell & Winograd (1989) looked at the way analytic essays affect learning from text. In their study, eleventh-grade students read science and social science passages and did one of three things: (a) completed study questions, (b) took notes, or (c) wrote an essay. The results showed that analytic essay writing allowed students to recall the gist better than either responding to questions or taking notes. Newell & Winograd claim that essay writing seemed to provide the occasion for writers to represent relationships in the discourse which then became the basis for recall and comprehension. Because essay writing required more complex manipulation of themes, those thematic structures might be more easily recalled.

Marshall (1987) argues that writing can also help shape the understanding of literary texts. In his study, high school students responded in four different ways to literary texts: (a) no response, (b) restricted writing (short answers), (c) personal writing, and (d) formal writing. Marshall found that personal analytic and formal analytic writing had generally comparable effects and that each form had its own advantages and disadvantages.

The results of Marshall's study imply that in developing reading/writing interactions to foster critical thinking, we need to look beyond traditional school-sponsored reading-to-write tasks, such as formal writing. At the same time, as Marshall's study shows, we should not assume that *all* or any reading/writing interaction will result in enhanced thinking and learning. As Tierney (1990) warns, only some combinations of reading and writing seem to promote ongoing thinking and learning. Others seem to stifle learning or result in shallow understandings, paraphrase or plagiarism often being the result. He concludes that "reading and writing together are tools which may constrain or enhance creativity" (p. 140).

READING AND WRITING IN THE COMPOSITION CLASSROOM

Clearly, the gaps in the second language research show that there is much to be done before we fully understand the ways in which these first language findings on reading/writing relationships apply to second language learners. Still, each of the three perspectives offers broad conceptual parameters for second language teachers trying to define the role of reading in composition classrooms.

The perspective of reading and writing as shared knowledge/shared process assumes a) that what we know about reading is likely to be similar to what we know about writing, and b) that the way we construct meaning in reading is likely to be similar to the way we construct meaning in writing. This shared knowledge/shared process model tends to be strictly cognitive, with few contextual considerations. For this reason, it lends itself to the widest, perhaps even indiscriminate application in the classroom. If *knowledge* is shared in reading and writing, this finding can be interpreted as suggesting that all reading has effects on all writing, and conversely that all writing has effects on all reading. This interpretation justifies the use of any type and/or combination of reading and writing activities, since it is assumed that all reading and writing is "good for you" and that each activity has benefits in both domains. However, Tierney & Shanahan caution that correlations in the performance studies tended to be moderate. (See Carson *et al.*, 1990; and Flahive & Bailey, this volume, who found similar results with L2 readers and writers.) Tierney and Shanahan (1991) suggest that while it is likely that knowledge is shared, the relationship is neither simple nor complete. One possibility is that the knowledge may be instantiated differently in reading than it is in writing.

Additionally, while there is research evidence that confirms the view that reading and writing share general cognitive *processes,* cautions are in order here, too. Although reading and writing can be defined in terms of the same processes, differences may result from the way that students call on strategies. That is, different students may use different strategies, and the potential for difference may be even higher for second language readers and writers whose L1 strategies may conflict with either the learning or the application of successful L2 strategies. The experimental studies reviewed by Tierney & Shanahan (1991) show that writing did not always lead to improved reading, nor did reading always result in improved writing. Clearly, teachers must consider the complexity of the reading/writing relationship as well as individual differences among students before assuming that prescribed reading and writing activities will be mutually beneficial.

The transactional perspective, that readers and writers share mutual responsibility for creating meaning in text, is a particularly important one for second language writers. A writer's responsibility to the reader plays out as the issue of audience awareness in the composing process. But in the transactional model, readers also have responsibilities. Asking students to read like writers means asking them to try to understand writer intentions and to develop a sense that meaning is not just in the text, but also in the reader. However, the notion of reader responsibility is already a familiar and predominant perspective for some L2 learners (Hinds, 1987). Native Japanese speakers, for example, are socialized to value the ability of the reader to read between the lines (Carson, 1992), accepting primary responsibility for successful communication. ESL composition teachers need to be aware that the notion of reader responsibility, in these cases, may work against the need for writers to also learn to accept responsibility for clear communication by writing explicit and detailed prose.

Also related to the transactional perspective is the fact that in many composition classrooms, collaborative learning experiences are valued as a way of highlighting both readers' and writers' roles in the writing process. However, as Flower (1989) has noted, if we are aiming for instructional effectiveness, we need to consider the cognitive issues as well as the social ones:

> [I]t seems naive to assume that the cognitive processes we desire will naturally follow from the social situations we engineer. (p. 286)

In other words, it is not context alone that automatically generates specific cognitive processes, and it is not simply the carrying out of collaborative learning activities that will automatically lead to the development of the cognitive processes required of successful writers.

Although of some value, the indeterminacy of the first two perspectives on reading/writing relationships does not offer as much to the composition teacher as does the third perspective. Theory–practice connections are clearest from the perspective of reading and writing as collaborative events. As language teachers, we know that language is always used to do something; it is not meaningful in and of itself. Reading for writing is functional and meaningful because it creates a purpose for reading as well as a real-world text base for writing. Furthermore, reading-to-write also underscores the fact that most writing, particularly in academic contexts, depends to a large extent on reading input—either directly from source texts, or indirectly from background knowledge, which itself results from experience with texts.

The research on cognitive processing in summarizing and synthesizing tests offers specific directions for classroom practices. Known relationships between proficiency in specific reading skills and summarizing and synthesizing provide a blueprint, if not a mandate, for teaching the relevant reading and writing skills together. Findings of developmental continua provide teachers with a logical teaching order for the various skills involved in summarizing and text synthesizing. Evidence that language proficiency plays a role in reading to write for second language learners suggests that the developmental continua of summarizing and synthesizing abilities may interact with and depend on developing language skills, and this suggests a sequence of reading-to-write skills in relation to the language-learning syllabus.

Finally, reading and writing together allows students to develop critical literacy—the ability to transform information for their own purposes in reading and to synthesize their prior knowledge with another text in writing. As Gajdusek & vanDommelen (this volume) note, the claim that some combination of reading and writing enhances thinking and learning argues for the value of using reading and writing collaboratively in composition as well as in reading classrooms. Together, reading and writing facilitate the development of critical thinking and critical literacy that are not only essential for second language students in academic programs, but are also crucial for second language learners in any context.

REFERENCES

Ackerman, J.M. (1991). Reading, writing and knowing: The role of disciplinary knowledge in comprehension and composing. *Research in the Teaching of English, 25*, 133–176.

Belanger, J. (1987). Theory and research into reading and writing connections: A critical review. *Reading–Canada–Lecture, 5*, 10–18.

Bleich, D. (1975). *Readings and feelings: An introduction to subjective criticism.* Urbana, IL: NCTE.

Bracewell, R.J., Frederiksen, C.H., & Frederiksen, J.F. (1982). Cognitive processes in composing and comprehending discourse. *Educational Psychologist, 17*, 146–174.

Brown, A.L. & Day, J.D. (1983). Macrorules for summarizing texts: The development of expertise. *Journal of Verbal Learning and Verbal Behavior, 22*, 1–14.

Campbell, C. (1990). Writing with other's words: Using background reading text in academic compositions. In B. Kroll (ed.), *Second language writing: research insights for the classroom* (pp. 211–230). Cambridge: Cambridge University Press.

Carson, J.G. (1992). Becoming biliterate: First language influences. *Journal of Second Language Writing, 1*, 53–76.

Carson, J.E., Carrell, P.L., Silberstein, S., Kroll, B., & Kuehn, P.A. (1990). Reading–writing relationships in first and second language. *TESOL Quarterly, 24*, 245–266.

Fish, S. (1980). *Is there a text in this class?* Cambridge: Harvard University Press.

Flower, L. (1990a). Introduction: Studying cognition in context. In Flower, L., Stein, V., Ackerman, J., Kantz, M.J., McCormick, R., & Peck, W. *Reading–to–Write: Exploring a cognitive and social process* (pp. 3–32). Oxford: Oxford University Press.

Flower, L. (1990b). The role of task representation in reading–to–write. In Flower, L., Stein, V., Ackerman, J., Kantz, M.J., McCormick, R., & Peck, W. (1990). *Reading–to–Write: Exploring a cognitive and social process* (pp. 35–75). Oxford: Oxford University Press.

Flower, L. (1989). Cognition, context and theory building. *College Composition and Communication, 40*, 282–311.

Flower, L., Stein, V., Ackerman, J., Kantz, M.J., McCormick, R., & Peck, W. (1990). *Reading–to–Write: Exploring a cognitive and social process.* Oxford: Oxford University Press.

Hidi, S. & Anderson, V. (1986). Producing written summaries: Task demands, cognitive operations, and implications for instruction. *Review of Educational Research, 56,* 473–493.

Hinds, J. (1987). Reader versus writer responsibility: A new typology. In U. Connor & R. Kaplan (Eds.), *Writing across languages: Analysis of L2 text* (pp. 141–152). Reading, MA: Addison–Wesley.

Johns, A. (1991). The ESL student and the English competency exam: Issues in task representation. *Written Communication, 8,* 379–401.

Johns, A. (1985). Summary protocols of "underprepared" and "adept" university students: Replications and distortions of the original. *Language Learning, 35,* 495–517.

Johns, A. & Mayes, P. (1990). An analysis of summary protocols of university ESL students. *Applied Linguistics, 11,* 253–271.

Kintsch, W. & van Dijk, T.A. (1978). Toward a model of discourse comprehension and production. *Psychological Review, 85,* 363–394.

Krashen, S. (1984). *Writing: Research, theory and applications.* Oxford: Pergamon Institute of English.

Kucer, S. (1987). The cognitive base of reading and writing. In J.R. Squire (Ed.), *The dynamics of language learning* (pp. 27–51). Urbana, IL: ERIC Clearinghouse on Reading and Communication Skills

Marshall, J.D. (1987). The effects of writing on students' understanding of literary text. *Research in the Teaching of English, 21,* 31–63.

Murray, D. (1982). Teaching the other self: The writer's first reader. *College Composition and Communication, 33,* 140–147.

McGinley, W. & Tierney, R.J. (1989). Traversing the topical landscape: Reading and writing as ways of knowing. *Written Communication, 6,* 243–269.

Newell, G.E. & Winograd, P. (1989). The effects of writing on learning from expository text. *Written Communication, 6,* 196–217.

Pearson, P.D. & Tierney, R.J. (1984). On becoming a thoughtful reader: Learning to read like a writer. Reading Education Report #50. Urbana, IL: Center for the Study of Reading.

Petrosky, A. (1982). From story to essay: Reading and writing. *College Composition and Communication, 33,* 19–36.

Rosenblatt, L.M. (1978). *The reader, the text, the poem.* Carbondale, IL: Southern Illinois University Press.

Rumelhart, D.E. (1977). Understanding and summarizing brief stories. In D. LaBerge & S.J. Samuels (Eds.), *Basic processes in reading: Perception and comprehension* (pp. 265–303). Hillsdale, NJ: Erlbaum.

Shanahan, T. & Tierney, R.J. (1990). Reading–writing connections: The relations among three perspectives. In J. Zutell & S. McCormick, (Eds.), *Literacy theory and research: Analyses from multiple paradigms.* 39th Yearbook of the National Reading Council (pp. 13–34). Chicago, IL: National Reading Council.

Smith, F. (1983). Reading like a writer. *Language Arts, 60,* 558–567.

Spivey, N.N. (1990). Transforming texts: Constructive processes in reading and writing. *Written Communication, 7,* 256–287.

Spivey, N.N. & King, J.R. (1989). Readers as writers composing from sources. *Reading Research Quarterly, 24,* 7–26.

Squire, J.R. (1983). Composing and comprehending: Two sides of the same basic process. *Language Arts, 60,* 581–589.

Stein, V. (1990). Exploring the cognition of reading–to–write. In Flower, L., Stein, V., Ackerman, J., Kantz, M.J., McCormick, R., & Peck, W., *Reading–to–Write: Exploring a cognitive and social process* (pp. 119–143). Oxford: Oxford University Press.

Sternglass, M. (1986a). Introduction. In B.T. Petersen, (Ed.), *Convergences: Transactions in reading and writing* (pp. 1–11). Urbana, IL: NCTE.

Sternglass, M. (1986b). Writing based on reading. In B.T. Petersen, (Ed.), *Convergences: Transactions in reading and writing* (pp. 151–162). Urbana, IL: NCTE.

Stotsky, S. (1983). Research on reading/writing relationships: A synthesis and suggested directions. *Language Arts, 60,* 627–642.

Tierney, R.J. (1990). Learning to connect reading and writing: Critical thinking through transactions with one's own subjectivity. In T. Shanahan (Ed.), *Reading and writing together: New perspectives for the classroom* (pp. 131–143). Norwood, MA: Christopher–Gordon.

Tierney, R.J. & LaZansky, J. (1980). The rights and responsibilities of readers and writers: A contractual agreement. *Language Arts, 57,* 606–613.

Tierney, R.J. & Leys, M. (1986). What is the value of connecting reading and writing? In B.T. Petersen (Ed.), *Convergences: Transactions in reading and writing* (pp. 15–29). Urbana, IL: NCTE.

Tierney, R.J. & Pearson, P.D. (1983). Toward a composing model of reading. *Language Arts, 60,* 568–580.

Tierney, R.J. & Shanahan, T. (1991). Research on the reading–writing relationship: Interactions, transactions, and outcomes. In R. Barr, M.L. Kamil, P. Mosenthal, & P.D. Pearson (Eds.), *Handbook of reading research,* Volume II (pp. 246–280). New York: Longman.

Tierney, R.J., Soter, A., O'Flavahan, J.F., & McGinley, W. (1989). The effects of reading and writing upon thinking critically. *Reading Research Quarterly, XXIV,* 134–173.

Winograd, P.N. (1984). Strategic difficulties in summarizing texts. *Reading Research Quarterly, 19,* 404–425.

Wittrock, M.C. (1983). Writing and the teaching of reading. *Language Arts, 60,* 600–606.

CHAPTER 5

The Role of Metacognition in Second Language Reading and Writing

Joanne Devine
Skidmore College

I. INTRODUCTION

In the past two decades, research has greatly enhanced our understanding of cognitive process; we now have exciting insights into how humans reason, solve problems, remember, and, in the area of literacy, how we go about reading and writing. Research has also provided increasingly detailed pictures of how these abilities are acquired in the normal course of development and has suggested effective techniques for instruction in these areas. And most recently, researchers have begun to investigate the impact of the social context in which these cognitive operations take place. The emergence of metacognitive theory in the 1970s (see, for example, Flavell, 1971, 1976, 1979; and Brown, 1977) has further added to our understanding of complex cognitive phenomena by providing data on learners' awareness of and control over their cognitive activities.

The study of metacognitive processes involved in literacy (especially reading) has been particularly fruitful, yielding extensive insights into learners' conceptions of the demands of reading tasks and awareness of their own levels of text comprehension. As Garner notes, the richness of the application of metacognitive theory to reading is not surprising, given "recent insights about its [reading's] interactive, constructive nature [that] place a great deal of emphasis on an active learner who directs cognitive resources to complete the task" (1987, p. 28). Despite the richness of data emerging from metacognitive studies of reading behavior, it must be noted that for the most part, these insights apply to young native readers; only recently has there been a corresponding interest in metacognition in second language reading behavior. Furthermore, there has been relatively little study—first or second language—of the role of metacognition in the "other" literacy skill—writing.

This essay summarizes recent research on the role of metacognition in second language reading and writing and offers thoughts about the ways that this research can enhance our understanding of reading-to-write in a second language. Part II provides a general discussion of the dimensions of metacognition as they have been described and elaborated on by researchers. Part III reviews the research data on studies of metacognition in L2 reading; Part IV provides the same treatment for L2 writing (although, as noted above, far less explicit attention has been paid to the role of metacognition in writing). The essay concludes with a brief discussion of the metacognitive processes in reading-to-write in the L2 composition classroom.

II. METACOGNITION

Garner has observed that "[i]f cognition involves perceiving, understanding, remembering, and so forth, then metacognition involves thinking about one's own perceiving, understanding, and the rest" (1987, p. 16). Every act of cognition is directed towards a cognitive goal, "the tacit or explicit objectives that instigate and maintain the cognitive enterprise" (Flavell, 1981, p. 40); to achieve that goal, a learner employs cognitive actions or strategies. Metacognition can be thought of as thinking about these cognitive activities or, simply put, thinking about thinking. Flavell (1978) has elaborated on this basic notion, observing that metacognition is knowledge which focuses on or regulates any part of cognitive activity. He identifies two general dimensions of metacognition: knowledge and experiences. He observes that metacognitive knowledge and metacognitive experiences differ in content and function, but not in their basic nature, from other types of knowledge and experience.

Metacognitive Knowledge

Relatively stable and usually statable, metacognitive knowledge "refers to the part of one's acquired world knowledge that has to do with cognitive . . . matters" (Garner, 1987, p. 21); it can be subdivided into three distinct types: person variables, task variables, and strategy variables. In the first category is knowledge about the learner, including information about the self, i.e., what kinds of tasks the learner is good at; comparative knowledge about the self in relation to other learners, for example, that a friend is better at math than the learner; and universals of cognition, such as the fact that there are different types of understanding—problem solving, remembering, and so forth.

   The second category comprises knowledge about the tasks the learner undertakes, including information about the kinds of processing required and the information processing demands a task might place on the learner. Recognition of task variables has obvious implications for a learner's ability to successfully engage in cognitive endeavors. As Flavell notes, "[O]ne must take these demands [of the task] into account and act accordingly if the task goal is to be achieved" (1987, p. 23). In the final group is knowledge of strategies or procedures available for achieving various cognitive goals as well as knowledge about the relative effectiveness of available strategies for achieving specific cognitive goals. Paris, Lipson, & Wixson (1983) further refine the concept of strategy variable by suggesting that metacognitive knowledge about strategies is of three types: declarative, or knowledge about strategies; procedural, or knowledge about how strategies can be employed; and conditional, or knowledge about when it is appropriate to apply strategies.

As numerous researchers have noted (Flavell, 1985; Wellman, 1985, 1978; Wellman, Collins, & Glieberman, 1981) these three types of knowledge are highly interactive. Flavell (1985) argues that metacognitive knowledge, in addition to being highly interactive, is qualitatively similar to other types of knowledge. Like other types of knowledge, some of this knowledge is declarative, some procedural; its slow and gradual growth is dependent on years of experiences with cognitive activities; it can be, and often is, activated automatically; and, finally, it can be flawed—that is, learners can hold mistaken ideas about the nature and application of metacognitive knowledge.

Metacognitive Experiences

Garner (1987) observes that metacognitive knowledge functions as the basis for metacognitive experiences that have been variously described as "awarenesses, realizations, 'ahas' or . . . 'clicks and clunks'" (p. 19) of realized or expected successes or failures in cognitive enterprises. These experiences are conscious ideas or thoughts about the cognitive endeavor that has been undertaken. They often begin when there is a cognitive failure or a sense of confusion about the progress towards the cognitive goal, especially in circumstances that call for careful, conscious attention to thinking.

When there is a breakdown in the movement towards a cognitive goal, what the learner can do (or is willing to do) to eliminate confusion or repair the breakdown depends in large part on the metacognitive knowledge that the learner possesses. Information about personal cognitive abilities, task demands, and universal strategies that the learner possesses can prompt the use of strategies to redress possible cognitive failures. Of course, this flash of insight into cognition gone awry does not always occur; learners may be unaware that they are not successfully proceeding toward cognitive goals; they simply might not possess the relevant metacognitive knowledge needed to recognize stalled progress towards a cognitive goal. Nor do metacognitive experiences have to be explicitly conscious (Markman, 1981) for a learner to call forth appropriate cognitive and metacognitive strategies to remedy the situation. Thus learners may not recognize that something is amiss, or might not possess sufficient or task appropriate metacognitive knowledge that would aid in correcting the course of the cognitive endeavor. And some learners might automatically make adjustments in cognitive strategies thereby eliminating the problem.

Cognitive Monitoring and Strategy Use

Fischer & Mandl (1984) note that metacognitive knowledge and metacognitive experiences interact both with each other and with cognitive goals and actions (or strategies). For example, if a learner has a cognitive goal of wanting to know the sum of a column of numbers, a reasonable cognitive action or strategy would be to add the numbers up. In this case the relationship between goal and action is straightforward; in many cognitive endeavors, however, the goal is more difficult to define, and multiple strategies may be needed to achieve that goal. As the complexity of the relationship between goal and appropriate strategies increases, the interaction among metacognitive knowledge, metacognitive experiences, cognitive goals, and cognitive strategy use becomes more significant.

The possibilities for interaction among the elements discussed above are extensive. (See Fischer & Mandl [1984] for discussion.) The interaction between metacognitive knowledge, metacognitive experiences, cognitive goals, and cognitive actions (or strategies) is the basis for what Flavell (1978, 1981, 1985) refers to as cognitive monitoring and what Baker and Brown refer to as self-regulation or control over learning (also frequently discussed as "executive control"; see Yussen [1985] and Garner [1987]). In formulating his model of cognitive monitoring, Flavell distinguishes between cognitive strategies and cognitive monitoring, which he classifies as a metacognitive strategy:

> We develop cognitive actions or strategies for making cognitive progress, and we also develop cognitive actions or strategies for monitoring cognitive progress. The two might be thought of as cognitive strategies and metacognitive strategies respectively. The former can yield metacognitive experiences as well as cognitive outcomes. The latter will yield cognitive outcomes as well as metacognitive experiences. (1981, p. 53)

Cognitive strategies are employed to make cognitive progress toward the cognitive goal, whereas metacognitive strategies are used to monitor that progress. As Flavell (1981) observes, in solving the addition problem mentioned above, the cognitive strategy is to add the numbers up. Adding the figures a second time would serve to monitor the progress of the initial cognitive endeavor; checking your calculations would then be a metacognitive strategy, functioning to monitor the success of the cognitive strategy employed.

There is ample evidence that the ability to monitor cognitive activities clearly differentiates good learners from poor learners and younger, less developed learners from older, more experienced learners. In the area of first language reading, for example, research has consistently found that "younger children and poorer readers are unlikely to demonstrate that they notice major blocks to text understanding. They seem not to realize that they do not understand" (Garner & Reis, 1981, p. 571, quoted in Garner, 1987); in other words, they do not have metacognitive experiences—those flashes of awareness that cognitive efforts have gone awry. And while most often it is poor and immature readers who do not monitor their cognitive efforts at comprehending a text, faulty monitoring frequently occurs among readers at all ages and levels of proficiency (Brown, Armbruster, & Baker, 1986). For all readers then (and by extension, for all learners), cognitive monitoring behavior is variable, depending upon both knowledge base and situation.

Metacognitively speaking, the picture of a good learner (or good reader) that emerges from vast research is of one who has ample metacognitive knowledge about the self as learner, about the nature of the cognitive task at hand, and about appropriate strategies for achieving cognitive goals. Perhaps more importantly, a good learner engages in cognitive monitoring that evaluates the success of cognitive endeavors and strategically regulates progress towards cognitive goals (Baker, 1985) by checking outcomes of attempts to solve problems, planning subsequent moves, evaluating the effectiveness of cognitive strategies, revising inappropriate strategies, and remediating any difficulties by employing compensatory strategies (Baker and Brown, 1984b). In sum, good learners possess knowledge about strategies; they also know both *how* and *when* to apply this knowledge to help them achieve cognitive goals (Paris, Lipson, & Wixson, 1983).

The preceding discussion has very broadly outlined the dimensions of metacognition as they have been articulated and refined over the last few decades. It suggests a number of interrelated questions concerning the role of metacognition in second language reading and writing.

On metacognitive knowledge:
- What is the nature and content of the metacognitive knowledge of reading and writing possessed by second language learners?
- What impact does metacognitive knowledge have on L2 reading and writing performance?

On metacognitive experiences:
- Do L2 reader/writers recognize when their cognitive efforts break down?
- What is the relationship between metacognitive experiences and metacognitive knowledge for L2 reader/writers?

On cognitive monitoring and strategy use:
- To what extent and with what success do L2 learners monitor their efforts in reading and writing?

- How do L2 reader/writers go about monitoring their reading/writing efforts? (What strategies do they employ?)
- Can L2 reader/writers be taught to be strategic in their reading and writing?
- What is the relationship between metacognitive knowledge and cognitive monitoring for these reader/writers?
- What is the relationship between strategy use and successful reading/writing in a second language?

The consistency of L1 research findings that indicate metacognitive abilities are dependent upon age and level of cognitive development suggests answers to the above questions will depend in part on the level of L2 language proficiency of readers and writers. The perennial question of language transfer might also profitably be considered in terms of metacognitive abilities in L2 reading and writing. While research into second language reading/writing has yet to focus on many of these areas, a growing body of research has begun to provide preliminary answers to some of the questions listed above.

III. METACOGNITION AND L2 READING

Initial interest in the role of metacognition in L2 reading can be traced to the proliferation of metacognitive studies of early L1 reading. (See Garner, 1987; Brown, 1981, 1987; and Baker & Brown, 1984a for excellent reviews of this research.) Carrell (1989) has lamented that relative to our understanding of metacognition and L1 reading, "we know very little about metacognitive factors in second language reading" (p. 123). While this is certainly the case, recent research has generated a growing body of information about the role of metacognition in L2 reading in two broad areas: the nature and content of metacognitive knowledge and metacognitive strategies, or more specifically, cognitive monitoring strategies.

Metacognitive Knowledge and L2 Reading

There has been relatively little study in the area of metacognitive knowledge in second language reading. Devine (1984) examined readers' conceptions of the nature of the reading process (Flavell's task variables) and the impact of those conceptions on both reading performance and reading success. Through close analysis of subjects' responses to reading interview questions, Devine was able to classify readers into three broad groups: sound-, word-, or meaning-oriented. These orientations or models of reading were shown to have implications both for task performance and reading success. Miscue analysis of the oral reading of those subjects who regarded the reading task as primarily phonological recoding (sound oriented readers) showed them to be slow, laborious decoders, focused on correct pronunciation with little concern for making sense of the text. In a retelling task based on their oral reading, sound-centered readers were judged to have poor comprehension. In sharp contrast, analysis of the miscues of meaning-centered readers' oral reading performance suggested that these subjects were concerned with making sense of the text; their comprehension of the text ranged from good to excellent.

The results of studies that rely on oral reading and oral interview data must, of course, be interpreted cautiously (Wixson, 1979; Leu, 1982). Especially in the case of young or inexperienced readers, the reliability of self-reports about task performance is suspect (Garner, 1982, 1987; Phifer & Glover, 1982; Fleisher, 1988). The results of Devine's study, however, suggest that second language readers have and can articulate notions about the reading task and furthermore that, in a very broad sense, these conceptions have implications for task performance and the success of the endeavor. In addition, this research demonstrates that, as Flavell (1985) asserted, metacognitive knowledge can be flawed. The sound-centered readers appear to have misconstrued the nature of the reading task; their comprehension of the text suggests that their orientation towards reading is, at best, inefficient and counterproductive.

Other studies have broadly focused personal and strategy variables. In a study of foreign language reading, Barnett (1988) investigated mature readers' knowledge about strategies (i.e., which strategies they regarded as most productive); perceptions about their own strategy use; and the impact of this knowledge on reading performance. She found that readers who were able to identify effective strategies and who "use those strategies considered most productive actually do . . . understand more than those who do not think they use such strategies" (1988, p. 156). Or in terms of metacognitive knowledge, those readers for whom knowledge about appropriate strategies (Flavell's strategy variables) interacted with knowledge about their ability to use those strategies (Flavell's personal variable) evidenced better text understanding than those readers who did not appear to possess these types of knowledge. Pardon & Waxman (1988), in a study of elementary ESL readers, obtained results similar to Barnett's. Carrell (1989) notes a number of problems with the format of the questionnaire Barnett used in her research; nonetheless, this study provides useful and suggestive preliminary data about foreign language readers' knowledge of reading strategies, their performance on reading tasks, and the relationship of these variables to successful reading comprehension.

Carrell's own far-reaching study (1989) explores "the metacognitive awareness of second language readers about reading strategies in both their first and second language (Spanish and English), and the relationship between their metacognitive awareness and their comprehension in both first and second language reading" (p. 123). Using a metacognitive questionnaire and reading tasks in subject's L1 and L2, Carrell found that in the L1, the use of local reading strategies correlated negatively with reading performance. In the L2, for native English speakers with low Spanish language proficiency, the use of local reading strategies correlated positively with reading performance; on the other hand, for native Spanish speakers with high English language proficiency, the use of global strategies correlated positively with L2 reading performance. The study establishes, then, that metacognitive awareness of certain strategies, including knowledge of how and when to use these strategies (procedural and conditional knowledge of strategies in the scheme of Paris, Lipson, & Wixson) has an impact on reading performance. The varied nature of the strategies that correlate positively with enhanced reading performance as well as the interaction of those strategies with language proficiency suggest the need for further study along these lines.

Strategies in L2 Reading

Reader strategies, taken in a very general sense, have received far more research attention than metacognitive awareness in L2 reading research. Various researchers have compiled inventories of strategies used by L2 readers (Hosenfeld, 1977, 1984; Knight, Padron, & Waxman, 1985; Block, 1986; Sarig, 1987; Padron and Waxman, 1988; Kern, 1988; Barnett, 1989; and Anderson, 1991—see Barnett for a comprehensive summary of much of this work); we now have a fair amount of information about the various cognitive strategies that readers employ in their attempts to read in a second language. And while knowledge of strategies, including knowing when and how to apply the strategies, is generally part of metacognitive knowledge, to appreciate the role of metacognition in L2 reading, it is important to return to Flavell's distinction between cognitive and metacognitive strategies.

It may be recalled that Flavell (1981) distinguishes between cognitive strategies, which allow learners to make progress towards a cognitive goal, and cognitive monitoring, which involves the monitoring of the progress of cognitive strategies. Strategies that function to monitor or regulate cognitive strategies are thus *metacognitive* strategies. And strategies that are designed to move readers towards text comprehension (whether indeed they do or do not), such as skimming, scanning, paraphrasing, using semantic mapping, etc., are not metacognitive strategies, since they do not involve monitoring or regulating acts of cognition. It bears repeating that knowing about cognitive strategies—what they are, how to use them, when to use them—is a part of metacognitive knowledge. Hence, for example, skimming a text for key information involves using a cognitive strategy. Information about skimming—what it is, how it is done, when it would be appropriate to skim—would be part of a reader's metacognitive knowledge base, whereas assessing the effectiveness of skimming for gathering key textual information would be a metacognitive strategy.

Inventories of L2 reader strategies have sometimes blurred the distinction between cognitive and metacognitive strategies, making it difficult to assess the role of metacognition (as opposed to cognitive strategy use) in L2 reading and to evaluate the success of strategy based instruction. Hence, although we currently have an increasingly detailed picture of the range and types of strategies that L2 readers at varying proficiency levels use as well as a growing sense of the role of strategy use in text comprehension (see Anderson, 1991 for a recent example), our understanding of metacognitive strategy use and its implications for successful L2 reading is far less comprehensive.

In a strict sense, only cognitive monitoring activities qualify as metacognitive strategies. For reading, cognitive monitoring may be equated with comprehension monitoring, since the cognitive goal of reading is comprehension of the text (Baker & Brown, 1984b). Included in comprehension monitoring activities, then, are any behaviors that allow readers to assess their level of understanding, to plan remedies when comprehension fails, and to self-regulate those strategies used to remediate comprehension failures (Paris & Meyers, 1983). Observing that L1 reading research has clearly demonstrated the importance of comprehension monitoring abilities in successful reading (Golinkoff, 1975; Harste & Burke, 1977; Brown, Campione, & Day, 1981), Casanave (1988) calls comprehension monitoring a "neglected essential" in ESL reading and argues for both research and pedagogical agenda that place greater emphasis on this "essential."

Research that has explicitly investigated the comprehension-monitoring activities of second language readers suggests that good L2 readers behave metacognitively very much like good L1 readers: They are aware of and can use and adapt their monitoring skills in order to self-regulate their comprehension of texts, and they know how to repair breakdowns in that understanding.

Given the evidence that the ability to monitor comprehension plays a significant role in successful reading, researchers have quite naturally been interested in the impact of training in metacognitive strategies on the reading of less competent readers. Direct instruction in strategy use (including metacognitive strategies) in first language reading (Brown, Campione, & Day, 1981; Palincsar & Brown, 1984; Winograd & Hare, 1988) suggests that this training enhances the metacognitive knowledge base of readers and results in improved reading performance. To date, there have been relatively few studies of metacognitive strategy training in second language reading. Those that do address the impact of this training for L2 readers (notably Carrell, Pharis, & Liberto, 1989; and Kern, 1989) have generally affirmed the findings from L1 research.

To summarize broadly from the above: Although far from possessing a comprehensive picture of the role of metacognition in L2 reading, we are amassing information in a number of important areas, most notably those of metacognitive knowledge and metacognitive strategies. Of special interest will be further research that attempts to clarify the interaction among metacognitive knowledge and performance (or use of metacognitive strategies) and success in reading, among instruction and metacognitive awareness and strategy use, among language proficiency and metacognitive knowledge and metacognitive strategies, and between metacognitive knowledge and strategy use in the L1 and the L2. Further studies might also address an area that has yet to receive research attention: L2 reading and metacognitive experiences. Perhaps one of the largest problems facing readers in a second language is knowing when they don't know. While a number of researchers (Baker, 1985; Carrell, 1989; Block, 1992) have made the distinction between evaluation and regulation of comprehension—between recognizing when comprehension breaks down and being able to do something about it—there has been little mention in L2 metacognitive reading research of the detection of cognitive failures. More attention to the role of metacognitive experiences should provide yet a fuller picture of metacognition in L2 reading.

IV. METACOGNITION AND L2 WRITING

To date, there has been little research in L2 writing that explicitly addresses the role of metacognition; there is, however, a growing body of information about what L2 writers know, and need to know, as they compose. There is also a longstanding interest in cognitive processes or strategies involved in writing in a second language. It bears repeating, however, that most of the information available on metacognition in L2 writing comes either indirectly through studies with other primary focuses or from applying the finding of L1 writing research to an L2 context.

Metacognitive Knowledge and L2 Writing

Bereiter & Scardamalia have suggested that proficient writing critically depends upon writers possessing appropriate knowledge that is "coded in ways that make it accessible" and having the cognitive resources "for bringing this knowledge into use at the right times and in the proper relation to other resource demands of the task" (1982, p. 43). The first category broadly corresponds to Flavell's "metacognitive knowledge," and the second could be said to describe the activity of cognitive monitoring or of Brown's "executive control." Focusing on the first category, Bialystok & Ryan (1985) have further argued that writing demands higher levels of metacognitive knowledge than does reading. They explain (referring to the work of Bereiter & Scardamalia, 1982):

> The primary difference between the two activities is that writing depends on more detailed analyzed knowledge. The required degree of analyzed

knowledge about sound-spelling relationships is greater when expressive-
ly spelling words than when receptively recognizing them. Similarly,
vague notions of discourse structure may be adequate to interpret written
texts but are decidedly inadequate to produce it (p. 224–225).

Like readers, then, writers must possess a body of information—in
Flavell's term, metacognitive knowledge—in order to move towards a cognitive goal, in this case, that of creating a meaningful text.

At first glance, the role of metacognitive knowledge in successful
writing appears to be of little interest to L2 writing researchers. But at
least some of the debate about competing models of L2 writing—a topic of
considerable interest to these researchers—centers on the types and
extent of metacognitive knowledge needed to successfully engage in the
cognitive task demands of writing. Much of the controversy in current L2
(and L1) composition theory and pedagogy centers on competing
"approaches": process approaches versus interactive approaches versus a
social constructionist view (Johns, 1990); process orientation versus textual orientation (Leki, 1991); and focus on form, on writer, on content, and
on reader (Raimes, 1991). Despite these differing characterizations, it
could be argued that, in fact, most current research (and much current
pedagogical practice) falls into two very broad categories. In the first category is process approach writing, especially "cognitivist" process writing;
the second group comprises approaches that focus on aspects of the text,
including content, audience, and social context demands. These two general categories might profitably be examined as different conceptions
about the requisite content of metacognitive knowledge.

It may be recalled that Flavell divides metacognitive knowledge into
three types that interact during cognitive efforts: personal variables, task
variables, and strategy variables. While it would be too sweeping to argue
that process and textual approaches focus on the importance and impact
of one of these types of knowledge to the exclusion of the others, the
approaches can perhaps be regarded as placing different emphasis on the
role of these types of metacognitive knowledge in L2 writing. In the case
of cognitivist process writing, the emphasis would be on knowledge of
strategies and to a lesser extent on knowledge of self (as in "expressivist"
process writing). Approaches to writing that focus broadly on features of
text—content, audience considerations, and social context demands—
place emphasis on knowledge of task.

Process studies of L2 writing have typically focused on those dimensions of metacognitive knowledge referred to by Flavell and others as personal and strategy variables. "Expressivist" process approaches, with their
attention to "integrity, spontaneity, and originality" (Faigley, 1986, p.
529) have encouraged a view of writing as self-discovery (Johns, 1990).
Classroom activities such as journal writing, free writing, and personal
essays allow students to explore their interests, discover their personal
voice, and determine their strengths as writers, presumably with an eye to

improving their writing in a variety of domains. While expressivist process writing has not been the explicit subject of research in L2 composition (although see Spack & Sadow, 1983), it has had a substantial impact on L2 writing pedagogy.

The cognitivist process approach, on the other hand, has had a significant impact on both research and pedagogy in L2 writing. Johns (1990) has called this approach "writing as problem solving," observing that cognitivists are interested in both strategic thinking (problem solving) in a general sense and the specific strategies that underlie the writing process. While process writing necessarily involves attention to task variables, such as the rhetorical demands of writing, in a metacognitive sense this approach emphasizes the contribution of the students' cognitive resources, especially their strategic knowledge, to L2 writing. Silva (1990) has summarized a wealth of ESL composition pedagogy with his observation that in the classroom, cognitivist process writing is aimed at helping students "develop viable strategies for getting started . . ., for drafting . . ., for revising . . .; and for editing" (p. 15). (Also see Hughey et al., 1984; Krapels, 1990; Liebman-Kleine, 1986; Raimes, 1983; and Zamel, 1983 for treatments of the cognitivist process writing approach in the second language classroom.)

Research into L2 composing within a cognitivist process approach has also focused on strategy use. Krapels' recent review (1990) of a large body of process research emphasizes this interest in strategy knowledge and use (behaviors, in her term), and her comprehensive summary of the findings of writing process research (pp. 49–50) provides a wealth of information about the role of strategy use in L2 writing (and, by extension, of knowledge of strategy; see Baker & Brown, 1984b). We now have data suggesting (see Krapels, p. 49, for citations):

- the relatively greater importance of composing strategies over linguistic competence in successful L2 writing;
- the similarities between the composing strategies of unskilled L1 and L2 writers (reinforcing the notion of "composing proficiency" suggested by other studies);
- possible differences in L1 and L2 composing processes;
- first language writing strategies transfer to the L2;
- the common writing strategy of using the L1 when composing in L2 (1) varies in frequency; (2) differs widely among writers, with some writers focusing on vocabulary in L1, while for others the use of L1 is inventional, organizational, and/or stylistic; and (3) certain writing tasks seem to elicit more frequent L1 use in L2 writing.

While process approaches to L2 writing emphasize the role of strategy variables (and to a lesser extent personal variables) in writing, textual approaches place greater weight on a different type of metacognitive knowledge—that of task variables. This group of variables includes a wide range of what Carter (1990) calls "local knowledge" about the demands of the particular task. In the case of second language writing, this local knowledge might include information about features of texts, including possible rhetorical organization, appropriate academic content, the academic reader's expectations (and their implications for the form and content of compositions), and the range of "acceptable writing behaviors dictated by the academic [or other discourse] community" (Horowitz, 1986, p. 789).

There is a growing body of research on these types of information and their role in L2 writing. Extensive studies of constrastive rhetoric (see Leki, 1991 for an excellent review) have identified the forms and purposes of rhetorical patterns from a variety of cultures, suggesting the complex nature of the local information that a writer must possess (and employ). Other textual approaches, such as "English for academic purposes" (Horowitz, 1986; Spack, 1988; Santos, 1988) and those which focus on the social construction of texts (Johns, 1990), while they place emphasis on other types of local knowledge associated with the writing task, also stress the primacy of this type of knowledge.

As the above discussion suggests, approaches to L2 writing that are sometimes seen to be in opposition (both in research and in pedagogy), might from a metacognitive perspective be better understood as differing emphases on the role of types of metacognitive knowledge. As many writers have stressed, all types of metacognitive knowledge are highly interactive (see, for example, Raimes, 1991; Leki, 1991). Indeed, Carter (1990) has argued that expertise in writing can be understood only in terms of both general (or strategic) knowledge and local (or task) knowledge.

Cognitive Monitoring in L2 Writing

Just as writing requires more detailed analyzed knowledge than does reading, so too does it require more attention to monitoring (Bialystok & Ryan, 1985). But successful monitoring is possible only if there is an available knowledge base. One of the problems that L2 writers face in attempts to monitor their production is a limited metacognitive knowledge base. Especially in the area of knowledge of task variables, second language writers may simply not possess sufficient information to determine if they are making progress towards the goal of the writing task. For example, writers who are unfamiliar with rhetorical structures or content demands of academic tasks are hardly in a position to adequately determine the success of their composition efforts. Instruction that functions to help second language writers remediate deficiencies in their knowledge base of task variables suggests that with enhanced understanding of the task demands as well as explicit instruction in how that knowledge might be applied, L2 writers are better able to monitor their writing (Connor & Farmer, 1990; Weissberg, 1984).

L2 writers, like other writers in a classroom setting, may also have monitoring difficulties associated with a general failure to recognize the importance of this activity. In a classroom setting, the instructor quite often takes responsibility for detailed responses to students' writing. In anticipation of that feedback, many students simply fail to recognize that they themselves need to engage in regulation of their progress towards the cognitive goals associated with writing. L2 writers, then, may fail to recognize their responsibility for monitoring their own writing. Interest in the role of teacher comments on L2 writing (in effect, teacher monitoring) addresses, among other things, the issue of teacher versus writer monitoring in second language writing (Leki, 1990; Zamel, 1985; Radecki &Swales, 1988). Research with young native writers suggests explicit attention to the role of self-monitoring in writing results in greater use of self-monitoring strategies (Gordon, 1990); further research of this type with L2 readers is certainly in order.

Yet another issue in cognitive monitoring of L2 writing involves the actual setting of cognitive goals by the writer. It is, after all, the cognitive goal or purpose that is monitored. In reading, the cognitive goal is fairly straightforward: the comprehension of the text. Cognitive monitoring, then, may be (and often is) equated with comprehension monitoring (Baker & Brown, 1984b). In writing, however, the nature of the monitoring task is far more complex. To begin with, in order to monitor the progress towards the cognitive goal, a writer must have a clear sense of what that cognitive goal is. But unlike the reading task, the goals may not be entirely clear; indeed, writers may not have specific goals in mind. Or there may be multiple goals, all of which the writer must attempt to monitor. And often it is the case that second language writers in academic situations do not themselves set the goals for their writing. Rather, they are writing in response to a teacher-determined task and to a teacher-specific audience. These same teachers will later provide extensive feedback on the progress towards the writing goal. Hence for many L2 writers, it makes little sense to speak of monitoring the progress towards a cognitive goal, since often as they write in the L2, there is no real cognitive goal.

Because much of the above discussion is speculative, that is, it does not report on research specifically focusing on metacognition in L2 writing, it is difficult to draw conclusions. However, it might be fruitful to suggest a number of research themes that would build on the current trends in L2 writing research and at the same time provide explicit information about the role of metacognition in second language writing. First, since the ability to monitor any task depends in large part on the extent and appropriateness of the knowledge base, L2 writing researchers might direct more attention to that knowledge base, especially as it differs from the knowledge base that might be more typical of L1 writers. Second, in the area of cognitive monitoring, there is currently very little information about L2 writers' efforts to regulate and monitor their progress in writing;

introspective studies of L2 writers engaged in composing (see Cohen & Cavalcanti, 1990) would provide essential preliminary data on the extent and impact of L2 writers' self-monitoring behavior. Finally, as with studies of L2 reading, information about metacognitive experiences, those events that precipitate metacognitive action by the learner, would provide a fuller picture of L2 writing.

V. METACOGNITION AND READING-TO-WRITE IN THE L2 WRITING CLASSROOM

There is currently a growing interest in L1 (Flower *et al.*, 1990) and L2 (Campbell, 1990; Kirkland & Saunders, 1991) composition research in reading to write. While it is beyond the scope of this paper to review this body of literature, it might be useful to consider what the review of the literature on metacognition in L2 reading and L2 writing suggests about the role of metacognition in reading-to-write in a second language context.

Success in both reading and writing depends on having appropriate knowledge and on the learner's ability to monitor progress towards the cognitive goal. In a general sense, reading and writing may be regarded as depending on the same cognitive base. Bialystok & Ryan have, in fact, argued that "apart from different levels of analyzed knowledge and control that are required, reading and writing are essentially equivalent in their cognitive basis" (1985, p. 225). However slight these differences in knowledge and control might be when considered from the larger perspective of cognitive processing, it is these very differences that are critical when L2 (or L1) learners read to write.

In an obvious way, reading-to-write alters the reading process; as Sternglass has observed, "having to write about something (almost anything!) about . . . readings force[s] a level of engagement beyond any reading strategy or combination of reading strategies" (1988, p. 103). This enhanced level of engagement necessitates changes in the knowledge base (the metacognitive knowledge) and a reconsideration of the role of cognitive monitoring during reading. With respect to the metacognitive knowledge base, reading-to-write changes the focus and content of both task and strategy variables as well as their interaction in reading. Knowledge of task variables includes a recognition of the nature of information needed and the processing demands that a task places on a learner. While different types of texts clearly make different processing demands on readers (Carrell, 1984), reading-to-write involves a major shift in what Flower (1990) refers to as "task representation," or ways of conceiving of the cognitive problem that is to be solved. In part, the ways in which an instructor frames a reading-to-write writing assignment explicitly alter (or attempt to alter) the type of processing that a reader engages in. For example, in a summary task, an instructor might direct students to present the main points of a text; as they read that text, learners are thereby required to attend to the content in potentially different ways, especially regarding the need to apprehend and recall the main points.

However, even the most explicit attempts to reframe reading task representation for reading-to-write tasks are unlikely to be particularly helpful for L2 writers who may hold some very different assumptions about supposedly typical academic reading-to-write tasks. For readers coming from a different rhetorical background, with restricted under-standing of social and academic contexts of the required writing, and with limited reading experiences in the L2, task representation may be highly problematic.

Metacognitive knowledge of strategy variables, including knowledge about available strategies as well as how and when to employ those strategies, might be counted on to help readers successfully comprehend a variety of texts. These same strategies, however, may not serve the L2 reader well in a reading-to-write task. L2 reading strategy research indi-cates that readers are often unaware of efficient strategies or do not have sufficient information about how to employ them. However, as Carrell (1989) and Block (1992) have both noted, L2 readers may often fail to use appropriate reading comprehension strategies, not because they are unfa-miliar with those strategies, and perhaps not even because they do not know how to use those strategies, but rather because they do not know *when* to employ that knowledge. The strategy problems of L2 readers as they read-to-write might therefore arise from a number of sources. Some L2 readers may be unaware of the strategies that are needed for reading-to-write tasks; other second language readers may not possess sufficient knowledge about how to adapt familiar strategies to reading-to-write tasks. Still other L2 readers may not have sufficient knowledge of when to employ otherwise familiar strategies in the new context of reading-to-write. Even if L2 readers successfully negotiate the problems of task repre-sentations in reading-to-write tasks in a second language, they may not have the appropriate declarative, procedural, and conditional strategic knowledge needed to support completion of the task.

Cognitive monitoring of reading in reading-to-write tasks may also present special difficulties for the L2 reader. The equation of comprehen-sion monitoring with cognitive monitoring might adequately, if simplisti-cally, describe cognitive monitoring in reading. However, in reading-to-write tasks, not only must the learner monitor progress towards a different and probably vaguely defined goal, but that learner must also look ahead to the writing task, incorporating information from the text into part of the task representation for the writing task to follow. Such monitoring activities as judging the effectiveness of the cognitive strategies employed, revising inappropriate strategies, and remediating difficulties by employing compensatory strategies must be engaged in with an eye for not simply (or perhaps only) comprehending the text, but also for the extent to which they prepare the reader to become a writer, that is, to meet the cognitive goals of the writing task.

Flower has observed that reading-to-write "involves reading a situation and setting appropriate **goals**, having the **knowledge** and **strategies** to meet one's goals, and finally, having the metacognitive knowledge or **awareness** to reflect on both goals and strategies" (1990, p. 23). As researchers continue to explore the role of metacognition in L2 reading and writing, we may expect to gain fuller insights into the subtle interplay between metacognitive knowledge and cognitive monitoring. This understanding of the dimensions of metacognition should further enhance our understanding of reading-to-write tasks, which will increasingly come to be regarded as strategic, knowledge-based, cognitive activities subject to self-regulation and monitoring in complex ways that involve new conceptions of both the reading and the writing task.

REFERENCES

Anderson, N.J. (1991). Individual differences in second language reading strategies. Paper presented at TESOL Conference, March, New York.

Baker, L. (1985). How do we know when we don't understand? Standards for evaluating text comprehension. In D.L. Forrest-Pressley, G.E. MacKinnon, & T.G. Waller (Eds.), *Metacognition, cognition, and human performance* (Vol. 1, pp. 155–205). Orlando, FL: Academic Press.

Baker, L. & Brown, A.L. (1984a). Metacognitive skills and reading. In P.D. Pearson (Ed.), *Handbook of reading research.* (pp. 353–394). New York: Longman.

Baker, L. & Brown, A.L. (1984b). Cognitive monitoring in reading. In J. Flood (Ed.), *Understanding reading comprehension: Cognition, language, and the structure of prose* (pp. 21–44). Newark, DE: International Reading Association.

Barnett, M.A. (1989). *More than meets the eye.* New York: Prentice Hall Regents.

Barnett, M.A. (1988). Reading through context: How real and perceived strategy use affects L2 comprehension. *Modern Language Journal, 72,* pp 150–162.

Bereiter, C. & Scardamalia, M. (1982). From conversation to composition: The role of instruction in a developmental process. In R. Glaser (Ed.), *Advances in instructional psychology,* (Vol. 2) (pp. 1–64). Hillsdale, NJ: Erlbaum.

Bialystok, E. & Ryan, E. (1985). A metacognitive framework for the development of first and second language skills. In D.L. Forrest-Pressley, G.E. MacKinnon, & T.G. Waller (Eds.), *Metacognition, cognition, and human performance* (Vol. 1) (pp. 207–252). Orlando, FL: Academic Press.

Block, E. (1992). See how they read: Comprehension monitoring of L1 and L2 readers. *TESOL Quarterly, 26,* 319–343.

Block, E. (1986). The comprehension strategies of second language readers. *TESOL Quarterly, 20,* 463–494.

Brown, A. (1987). Metacognition, executive control, self-regulation and other more mysterious mechanisms. In E. Weinert & R.H. Kluwe (Eds.), *Metacognition, motivation, and understanding.* Hillsdale, NJ: Erlbaum.

Brown, A. (1981). Metacognition: The development of selective attention strategies for learning from texts. In M.L. Kamil (Ed.), *Directions in reading: Research and instruction* (pp. 21–43). Washington, DC: National Reading Conference.

Brown, A. (1977). Knowing when, where and how to remember: A problem of metacognition. (Tech. Rep. No. 47). Urbana: University of Illinois, Center for the Study of Reading.

Brown, A.L., Armbruster, B.B., & Baker, L. (1986). The role of metacognition in reading and studying. In J. Orasanu (Ed.), *Reading comprehension: From research to practice* (pp. 49–75). Hillsdale, NJ: Erlbaum.

Brown, A.L., Campione, J.C., & Day, J.D. (1981). Learning to learn: On training students to learn from text. *Educational Researcher, 10,* 14–21.

Campbell, C. (1990). Writing with others' words: Using background reading text in academic compositions. In B. Kroll (Ed.), *Second language writing* (pp. 211–230). New York: Cambridge University Press.

Carrell, P.L. (1989). Metacognitive awareness and second language reading. *Modern Language Journal, 73,* 121–133.

Carrell, P.L. (1984). The effects of rhetorical organization on ESL readers. *TESOL Quarterly, 18,* 441–469.

Carrell, P.L., Pharis, B., & Liberto, J. (1989). Metacognitive strategy training for ESL reading. *TESOL Quarterly, 17,* 553–573.

Carter, M. (1990). The idea of expertise: An exploration of cognitive and social dimensions of writing. *College Composition and Communication, 41,* No. 3, 265–285.

Casanave, C.P. (1988). Comprehension monitoring in ESL reading: A neglected essential. *TESOL Quarterly, 22,* 283–302.

Cohen, A.D. & Cavalcanti, M.C. (1990). Feedback on compositions: teacher and student verbal reports. In B. Kroll (Ed.), *Second language writing: Research insights for the classroom* (pp. 155–177). Cambridge: Cambridge University Press.

Connor, U. & Farmer, M. (1990). The teaching of topical structure analysis as a revision strategy for ESL writers. In B. Kroll (Ed.), *Second language writing: Research insights for the classroom* (pp. 126–139). Cambridge: Cambridge University Press.

Devine, J. (1984). ESL readers' internalized models of the reading process. In R.A. Handscombe & B.P. Taylor (Eds.), *On TESOL '83: The question of control* (pp. 95–108). Washington, DC: TESOL.

Faigley, L. (1986). Competing theories of process: A critique and a proposal. *College English, 48,* No. 6, 527–539.

Fischer, P.M. & Mandl, H. (1984). Learner text variables, and the control of text comprehension and recall. In H. Mandl, N.L. Stein, & T. Trabasso (Eds.), *Learning and comprehension of text*. Hillsdale, NJ: Erlbaum.

Flavell, J.H. (1987). Speculations about the nature and development of metacognition. In E. Weinert & R.H. Kluwe (Eds.), *Metacognition, motivation, and understanding* (pp. 21–30). Hillsdale, NJ: Erlbaum.

Flavell, J.H. (1985). *Cognitive development* (2nd ed.) Englewood Cliffs, NJ: Prentice-Hall.

Flavell, J.H. (1981). Cognitive monitoring. In W.P. Dickson (Ed.), *Children's oral communication skills* (pp. 35–60). New York: Academic Press.

Flavell, J.H. (1979). Metacognition and cognitive monitoring: A new area of cognitive–developmental inquiry. *American Psychologist, 34,* No. 10, 906–911.

Flavell, J.H. (1978). Metacognitive development. In J.M. Scandura, & C.J. Brainerd (Eds.), *Structural/process theories of complex human behavior* (pp. 213–245). Alphen a.d. Rijn, The Netherlands: Sijthoff & Noordhoff.

Flavell, J.H. (1976). Metacognitive aspects of problem solving. In L.B. Resnick (Ed.), *The nature of intelligence* (pp. 231–235). Hillsdale, NJ: Erlbaum.

Flavell, J.H. (1971). First discussant's comments: What is memory development the development of? *Human Development, 14,* 272–278.

Fleisher, B. (1988). Oral reading cue strategies of better and poorer readers. *Reading Research and Instruction, 27,* No. 3, 35–50.

Flower, L. (1990). Introduction: Studying cognition in context. In L. Flower, V. Stein, J. Ackerman, M.J. Kantz, K. McCormick, & W.C. Peck (Eds.), *Reading-to-write* (pp.1–32). New York: Oxford University Press.

Flower, L., Stein, V., Ackerman, J., Kantz, M.J., McCormick, K., & Peck, W.C. (Eds.) (1990). *Reading–to–write*. New York: Oxford University Press.

Garner, R. (1987). *Metacognition and reading comprehension*. Norwood, NJ: Ablex.

Garner, R. (1982). Verbal report data on reading. *Journal of Reading Behavior, 14,* 159–167.

Garner, R. & Reis, R. (1981). Monitoring and resolving comprehension obstacles: An investigation of spontaneous text lookbacks among upper–grade good and poor comprehenders. *Reading Research Quarterly, 16*, 569–582.

Golinkoff, R. (1975). A comparison of reading comprehension processes in good and poor comprehenders. *Reading Research Quarterly, 11*, 623–659.

Gordon, C. (1990). Changes in readers' and writers' metacognitive knowledge: Some observations. *Reading Research and Instruction, 30*(1), 1–14.

Harste, J. & Burke, C. (1977). A new hypothesis for reading teacher research: Both teaching and learning of reading are theoretically based. *Reading: Theory, research, and practice: Twenty–Sixth yearbook of the National Reading Conference.* Clemson, SC: The National Reading Conference.

Horowitz, D. (1986). Process not product: Less than meets the eye. *TESOL Quarterly, 20*, 141–144.

Hosenfeld, C. (1984). Case studies of ninth grade readers. In J.C. Alderson & A.H. Urquhart (Eds.), *Reading in a foreign language* (pp. 231-244). New York: Longman.

Hosenfeld, C. (1977). A preliminary investigation of the reading strategies of successful and nonsuccessful second language learners. *System, 5*(2), 110–123.

Hughey, J.B., Wormuth, D.R., Hartfield, V.F., & Jacobs, H.L. (1984). *Teaching ESL composition: Principles and techniques.* Rowley, MA: Newbury House.

Johns, A. M. (1990). L1 composition theories: Implications for developing theories of L2 composition. In B. Kroll, (Ed.), *Second language writing: Research insights for the classroom* (pp. 24–36). Cambridge: Cambridge University Press.

Kern, R.G. (1989). Second language reading strategy instruction: Its effects on comprehension and word inference ability. *Modern Language Journal, 73*, 135–149.

Kern, R.G. (1988). *The role of comprehension strategies in foreign language reading.* Unpublished dissertation, University of California, Berkeley.

Kirkland, M.R. & Saunders, M.A.P. (1991). Maximizing student performance in summary writing: Managing the cognitive load. *TESOL Quarterly, 25*, 123–144.

Knight, S.L., Pardon, Y.N., & Waxman, H.C. (1985). The cognitive reading strategies of ESL students. *TESOL Quarterly, 19*(4), 789–792.

Krapels, A.R. (1990). An overview of second language writing process research. In B. Kroll, (Ed.), *Second language writing: Research insights for the classroom* (pp. 37–56). Cambridge: Cambridge University Press.

Leibman–Kleine, J. (1986). Towards a contrastive new rhetoric: A rhetoric of process. (ERIC Document Reproduction Service No. ED 271 963)

Leki, I. (1991). Twenty–five years of contrastive rhetoric: Text analysis and writing pedagogies. *TESOL Quarterly, 25*, 1, 123–144.

Leki, I. (1990). Coaching from the margins: Issues in written response. In B. Kroll (Ed.), *Second language writing.* New York: Cambridge University Press.

Leu, D. (1982). Oral reading error analysis: A critical appraisal of research and application. *Reading Research Quarterly, 17*(3), 420–437.

Markman, E.M. (1981). Comprehension monitoring. In W.P. Dickson (Ed.), *Children's oral communication skills* (pp. 61–84). New York: Academic Press.

Padron, Y. & Waxman, H. (1988). The effect of ESL students' perceptions of their cognitive strategies on reading achievement, *TESOL Quarterly, 22*(1), 146–150.

Palincsar, A. & Brown, A. (1984). Reciprocal teaching of comprehension–fostering and comprehension–monitoring activities. *Cognition and Instruction, 1*(2), 117–175.

Paris, S. & Myers, M. (1983). Comprehension monitoring, memory, and study strategies of good and poor readers. *Journal of Reading Behavior, 13*(1), 1–22.

Paris, S.G., Lipson, M.Y., & Wixson, K.K. (1983). Becoming a strategic reader. *Contemporary Educational Psychology, 8*, 293–316.

Phifer, S.J. & Glover, J.A. (1982). Don't take students' word for what they do while reading. *Bulletin of the Psychonomic Society, 19*, 194–196.

Radecki, P.M., & Swales, J.M. (1988). ESL student reaction to written comments on their written work. *System, 16*, 355–365.

Raimes, A. (1991).Out of the woods: Emerging traditions in the teaching of writing. *TESOL Quarterly, 25*(3), 407–430.

Raimes, A. (1983). *Techniques in teaching writing.* Oxford: Oxford University Press.

Santos, T. (1988). Professors' reactions to the academic writing of nonnative–speaking students. *TESOL Quarterly, 22*, 69–90.

Sarig, G. (1987). High–level reading in the first and in the foreign language. Some comparative process data. In J. Devine, P.L. Carrell, &

D.E. Eskey (Eds.), *Research in reading in English as a second language* (pp. 107–120). Washington, DC: TESOL.

Silva, T. (1990). Second language composition instruction: Developments, issues, and directions. In B. Kroll (Ed.), *Second language writing* (pp. 11–23). New York: Cambridge University Press.

Spack, R. (1988). Initiating ESL students into the academic discourse community: How far should we go? *TESOL Quarterly, 22*(1), 29–51.

Spack, R. & Sadow, C. (1983). Student–teacher working in journals in ESL freshman competition. *TESOL Quarterly, 17*(4), 575–593.

Sternglass, M. (1988). *The presence of thought: Introspective accounts of reading and writing.* Norwood, NJ: Ablex.

Weissberg, R.C. (1984). Given and new: Paragraph development models for scientific English. *TESOL Quarterly, 18,* 485–500.

Wellman, H.M. (1985). The origins of metacognition. In D.L. Forrest-Pressley, G.E. MacKinnon, & T.G. Waller (Eds.), *Metacognition, cognition, and human performance* (Vol. 1) (pp. 1–31). New York: Academic Press.

Wellman, H.M. (1978). Knowledge of the interaction of memory variables: A developmental study of metamemory. *Developmental Psychology, 14,* 24–29.

Wellman, H.M., Collins, J. & Glieberman, J. (1981). Understanding the combination of memory variables: Developing conceptions of memory limitations. *Child Development, 52,* 1313–1317.

Winograd, P. & Hare, V.C. (1988). Direct instruction of reading comprehension strategies: The nature of teacher explanation. In C.E. Weinstein, E.T. Goetz, & P.A. Alexander (Eds.), *Learning and study strategies: Issues in assessment, instruction, and evaluation* (pp. 121–139). San Diego: Academic Press.

Wixson, K.L. (1979). Miscue analysis: A critical review. *Journal of Reading Behavior 11*(2), 163–175.

Yussen, S.R. (1985). The role of metacognition in comtemporary theories of cognitive development. In D.L. Forrest–Pressley, G.E. MacKinnon, & T.G. Waller (Eds.). *Metacognition, cognition, and human performance* (Vol. 1) (pp. 253–283). New York: Academic Press.

Zamel, V. (1985). Responding to student writing. *TESOL Quarterly, 19,* 79–101.

Zamel, V. (1983). In search of the key: Research and practice in composition. In J. Handscombe, R. Orem, & B. Taylor (Eds.), *On TESOL '83: The Question of Control* (pp. 195–207). Washington, D.C.: TESOL.

CHAPTER 6

Exploring Reading/Writing Relationships in Adult Second Language Learners

Douglas E. Flahive
Colorado State University

Nathalie H. Bailey
Lehman College/CUNY Graduate Center

INTRODUCTION

Over the past two decades, second language teachers and researchers considered the literacy skills of reading and writing as somewhat separate. Recent reviews by Grabe (1991) of L2 reading research and by Raimes (1991) of L2 writing research illustrate these separations. While a significant majority of reading research is derived from the theories and protocols of cognitive psychology, research and practice in writing is far more eclectic.

However, in recent years a growing number of texts designed for L2 learners purport to integrate the literacy skills of reading and writing (Smoke,1990; Spack, 1990; Withrow, Brookes, & Cummings, 1990). These texts differ from traditional rhetorical readers, which contain readings that are selected and edited to serve largely as models for various expository and argumentative modes. The newer, integrated reading/writing texts are also obviously different from the separate skills reading and writing texts that experienced significant growth and popularity during the 1970s and early 1980s. The older texts were developed to meet the needs of a teaching community that viewed literacy skills as essentially separate. Reading was viewed as a decoding skill, writing an encoding skill.

However, schema-theoretic based studies of reading comprehension, begun in the late 1970s, and process-oriented approaches to writing research and pedagogy, which had their beginnings at about the same time, have led to the notion that reading and writing processes are more related than previously hypothesized. Now many hypothesize that since each skill is directed toward the creation of meaning, a view previously limited to writing, a number of common processes are shared by both.

At a more concrete, practical level, there is a near axiomatic face validity to this belief. Consider the reading/writing interactions of a typical student. Assignments are read with the purpose of writing responses to test questions. Chapters of books and articles are read with the purpose of putting together a research paper. Consider the reading/writing interactions of the various scholars who have contributed to this volume. Most of their papers are sprinkled with citations of the writings of other researchers. While these citations serve somewhat different functions in the hands of different authors, they are, in general, an index of the works a writer has read prior to writing.

Although several theorists have offered descriptions of parallels between reading and writing (Meyer, 1982; Squire, 1983; Shanahan, 1988) and some teachers and materials developers feel that the literacy skills can be enhanced by their integration in the classroom, empirical researchers have provided a very limited data base upon which to develop theoretically motivated pedagogical practices.

Granted, the quantity of research into reading/writing relationships in L1 learners is relatively impressive. Stotsky's comprehensive, but now somewhat dated, survey (1983) of studies of reading/writing relationships is instructive not so much for the conclusions she draws, but for highlighting the eclecticism that has characterized research into reading/writing relationships. A sampling of this eclecticism can be gleaned by examining the titles of the 81 sources cited. As the titles indicate, reading/writing relationships have been studied in learners ranging from elementary to college students. Designs of studies range from correlational to experimental. Reading scores were used as predictor variables in some studies, as criterion variables in others, and as independent variables in yet others. In some studies, reading was measured by experience, based upon data gathered largely by means of questionnaires; in other studies, reading achievement was determined by some type of comprehension test. For measures of writing ability, assessment procedures ranging from "syntactic maturity" to holistic scores were used.

Given the range of variables described above, the various educational levels of subjects and the widely diverse settings in which experimental classroom studies were conducted, generalizations concerning these studies would have to be highly tentative. They suggest that better readers tended to be better writers, a generalization that should come as a surprise to relatively few. Better readers also tended to use a more complex prose style.

In this correlational study we wanted to determine if these generalizations hold for adult non-native speakers. We test three specific generalizations derived from L1 studies of reading/writing relationships:

A—Subjects who read more are better writers.
B— Subjects who are better readers are better writers.
C—Subjects who read more and with better "comprehension" write more complex, more grammatically correct prose.

(We realize the highly relative nature and the somewhat unscientific tone of terms such as "better" and "more," but as will be seen below, such is the nature of descriptive, correlational research.)

THEORY AND RESEARCH IN ADULT L2 READING/WRITING RELATIONSHIPS

When we designed and conducted this study in mid-1988, the number of studies of reading/writing relationships of L2 learners was very limited. One of the first to appear in the literature was Janopoulos (1986). His study was designed to determine whether there is a relationship between amount of pleasure reading in L2 or L1 and L2 writing proficiency in university-level L2 students. His findings show that "heavy" L2 pleasure readers, those reporting 5 or more hours of pleasure reading per week, were also good writers. Deal (1988) attempted to replicate the Janopoulos study with a similar group of subjects and failed to find a relationship between L2 pleasure reading and L2 writing.

Each study was an attempt to test Krashen's "reading input hypothesis" (1987). This hypothesis, a direct extension of his "comprehensible input" hypothesis, claims that large amounts of self-directed pleasure reading in the target language will not only result in gains in writing proficiency, but will also help to improve writing style and contribute to the development of grammatical accuracy.

The issue faced by Janopoulos, by Deal, by us, and by any other researcher attempting to test the reading input hypothesis in a setting other than a controlled experiment is how to operationally define the relevant variables. Consider the variable of pleasure reading. Both Janopoulos and Deal used the tried-but-who-knows-how-true questionnaire. They asked subjects to estimate the number of hours per week they spent pleasure reading in L1 and L2. Under the best of circumstances, the responses could only be an approximation. For the measurement of writing, Janopoulos used a placement test; Deal used a class writing assignment.

We can only speculate why their results were different. The fact that the subjects in the Janopoulos study were just beginning their academic term and had time for non-school-related reading and the subjects in the Deal study were approaching the end of their term may be one factor. The different conditions for the gathering of the writing samples is obviously another. The different methods of data analysis is a third. Janopoulos categorized his variables; Deal used continuous variables. In fact, if Deal had attempted to use the categories developed by Janopoulos of +5 for "heavy" readers, between 1-5 hours for moderate, and below 1 hour for low, not one of Deal's subjects would have met the criterion for "heavy" readers.

Our purpose is not to engage in a typical rhetorical gambit found in research papers and draw critical comparisons between these two previous studies and then offer a design that remedies their potential faults. What we have done is to augment their design through the addition of reading, writing, and grammatical variables. In addition to assessing the pleasure reading habits of L2 learners, we have added a multiple-choice test of reading comprehension. In addition to a holistic writing score, we have further analyzed our writing samples with more analytic measures. Finally, we have included in our study two measures of grammatical proficiency, a multiple choice test and an error detection/editing task.

Our aim is also to highlight several of the data gathering/data analysis issues that are inherent in attempts to test first the reading input/pleasure reading hypothesis, hypothesis A above, as well as other related hypotheses concerning relationships between reading and writing in adult second language learners.

SUBJECTS

In this study we tested 40 adult ESL learners. They were either enrolled in university level composition classes for foreign students at Colorado State University or in an ESL program for matriculated undergraduates at Lehman College, CUNY. Twelve language backgrounds are represented in the sample, the largest being Spanish (15 students), followed by Vietnamese (6), Mandarin Chinese (5), and speakers of nine other languages. Their length of formal study of English ranges from 14 years to less than a year. Some plan to return to their countries after completing their academic work; others have become or plan to become U.S. citizens. Over half of the subjects had obtained TOEFL scores of at least 525. The remaining subjects were not required to sit for the TOEFL as a condition of their college entrance. Briefly stated, the sample is very heterogeneous. Testing was conducted during the first two weeks of the academic terms.

VARIABLES

In this study we have three groups of variables: reading, writing, and grammar/writing style. Each is described below.

Reading

We have selected two types of reading variables. One attempts to measure reading experience in both L1 and L2; the other was selected to assess reading achievement. Our measure of reading experience both in L1 and L2 is a questionnaire modeled after those in the Janopoulos and the Deal studies. We asked subjects to estimate the number of hours per week that they spent on non-school related reading. We mentioned such materials as newspapers, magazines, and works of fiction as typical examples. As our measure of reading achievement, we selected a widely used test of reading comprehension, the McGraw-Hill Reading Skills Test. It has a reported reliability of .89 (Raygor, 1970) and has been normed with large numbers of native-speaking high school students. Its format is similar to the reading comprehension portions of the TOEFL and Michigan tests.

Writing

Subjects were asked to write an argumentative essay in their respective classes. The essay was presented as an in-class diagnostic task. Topics from which subjects were asked to choose ranged from social issues such as permitting single men or women to adopt children to economic issues such as their views of advertising campaigns urging U.S. citizens to "Buy American."

Essays were holistically evaluated by two experienced ESL teachers, one an author of several ESL writing textbooks and the other a coauthor of a basic ESL writing text. Essays were independently scored, using a 1–9 scale. On 27 of the 40 essays, there was perfect agreement. For 12 of the remaining 13 essays, one-half of a point separated the two, and on one essay, a point separated the ratings. For purposes of this analysis, all ratings were averaged.

Grammar

Two tests of grammatical ability were administered. The first was the CELT, a widely used test of L2 grammar. The second was an error detection/editing task developed by Bailey for purposes of this study. For this task, subjects were asked to detect errors embedded in paragraphs. Each of the sentences in the paragraphs had three underlined portions. Subjects were asked to identify the underlined portion that contained the error.

Two additional measures of grammar were derived from an analysis of the student essays. For each essay, t-unit length averages were computed as well as percentages of error-free t-units, following Larsen-Freeman (1978).

RESULTS

As mentioned above, three interrelated hypotheses are investigated in this study. In Table 1 we present first the descriptive data to test the "reading input" hypothesis as well as descriptive data that forms the basis of Hypothesis B. Correlations are presented in Table 2, followed by brief comments.

Hypothesis A: There is a significant relationship between L1 or L2 pleasure reading and writing ability.

TABLE 1 Pleasure reading quantity and holistic writing

	Mean	Range
L1 reading time	3 3/4 Hours	0–9 hours
L2 reading time	5 1/2 Hours	0–10 hours
	Mean	Standard Deviation
Holistic writing	4.4	1.5

TABLE 2 Correlations among L1/L2 pleasure reading time and L2 holistic writing

	L1 Read Time	L2 Read Time
L1 Read Time	1.00	.79*
L2 Read Time	.79*	1.00
L2 Holistic Writing	.05	.11

*For N=40 an obtained correlation of .26 is necessary for significance at the .05 level.

There is, for all practical purposes, no relationship between the quantity of reading the subjects claim to do and the quality of their writing. As the results indicate, the amount of pleasure reading students claim to do in L1 is reasonably consistent with their reading habits in L2. This carryover of literacy habits from L1 to L2 probably comes as no surprise to those familiar with the results of large-scale, international studies of literacy.

Hypothesis B: There is a relationship between reading achievement and holistic writing.

As we mentioned above, our measure of reading achievement was a score on a standardized test of reading comprehension. When we correlated reading comprehension scores with holistic writing scores, the obtained correlation was .35, $p < .05$. For the reading comprehension test, the mean score was 17.3 with a standard deviation of 14.1. The maximum score was 30.

As the results indicate, we obtained a significant but modest correlation between our measure of reading comprehension and our holistic writing scores. As the descriptive data resulting from our reading comprehension test indicate, the scores were not normally distributed. In fact, a rather flat curve would result from a plot of these data. One possible problem we experienced with this test is discussed in the final portion of this paper.

Hypothesis C: There is a relationship between pleasure reading, reading achievement, and grammatical development/writing style.

Table 3 contains the mean scores and standard deviation obtained on the grammar development/writing style variables which we tested.

TABLE 3 Grammar/writing style variables

	Mean	Standard Deviation
CELT Grammar	71.7	13.2
Editing	27.8	5.1
T-Unit Length	15.5	3.3
Percent of Error-Free T-Units	74.7	16.8

TABLE 4 Correlations among L1/L2 Pleasure, L2 Reading Achievement, and L2 Grammar/Writing Style Measures

	L1 Reading Time	L2 Reading Time
CELT Grammar	-.06	-.006
Editing	-.11	-.06
T-Unit Length	.03	-.06
Error-Free T-Units	.11	.008
L2 Reading Achievement	.47*	.49*

* $p < .05$

If nothing else, the correlations found in Table 4 are remarkably consistent. All correlations between L1 and L2 pleasure reading and the various grammar/writing style variables hover around the .00 mark and appear to suggest that pleasure reading, as operationalized in this study, does not lead to increased grammatical proficiency. It would be nice to think that such a thing would be true, and it may be for some people in some settings, but not for the adult ESL students in the settings that we have described. There are significant positive relationships between pleasure reading in both L1 and L2 and scores on a reading achievement test. Note we are not claiming that more reading leads to better reading comprehension scores. Rather, we suggest that controlled, experimental research similar to that reported in Elley and Mangubhai (1983) be conducted to determine this. However, it was informative to find that self-reports have some degree of predictive validity. As we reported above, those who claim to read a lot do well on reading comprehension tests.

In a correlational study in which eight variables were either measured directly or derived from other measures, there are many possible relationships that we could examine. In examining the pattern of relationships seen in Table 5, it is clear that the relationship between holistic writing and a traditional test of grammar, the CELT, is among the strongest in our study, .65. It is nearly as strong as the correlation between the Error-free T-Units and holistic writing, .57. This supports the findings found over a decade ago in Larsen-Freeman (1978) and replicated in Homburg (1984). As seen in Table 4, these various measures of grammar are unrelated to time spent reading for pleasure.

TABLE 5 Correlations not related to the three hypotheses of this study

	Error ID.	CELT	Writing	T-Unit L	EF-T-U
Error ID					
CELT	.67*				
Writing	.46*	.65*			
T-Unit L	-.23	-.23	-.15		
EF-T-U	.25	.40*	.57*	-.26	
Reading Achievement	.23	.42*	.35*	.06	.24

* $p < .05$

DISCUSSION

This discussion is divided into four sections. The first addresses issues related to the interpretation of the data we have presented above. The second discusses measurement issues. The third highlights problems presented by individual differences, and the fourth and final portion of this discussion focuses upon the role of theory in reading/writing research and teaching.

Data Interpretation

Because the purpose of our study was exploratory, we wanted to test several of the hypotheses that emerged from L1 studies and adapt them to the L2 adult setting. By adding the grammar/editing tests along with the microanalyses of the L2 writing samples, we found that in our sample of adult L2 learners, grammar, reading, and writing are statistically interrelated. We also found that reading achievement and self-reported pleasure reading are related. We found that the former was related to holistic writing but that the latter was not.

After examining both individual correlations as well as patterns among them, we caution readers that by simply squaring our obtained correlations they can determine the amount of variance overlap, that is, the variance in one set of scores accounted for by the other. For example, if we took our obtained correlation between holistic writing and reading achievement, which was .35, and squared it, we would get .12. So, in effect, this statistically significant correlation would appear to have limited practical usefulness. Of the variance between the two measures, 88% is not accounted for. Obviously, much more work needs to be done before generalizations can be made concerning what specific constructs the skills of reading and writing have in common and what constructs are unique to each skill.

Measurement Issues

A reader of this study might claim that those who evaluated the essays may have used grammatical accuracy as the major criterion in scoring them. In a subsequent reanalysis of the essays, we have found this not to be the case. The constructs of content, organization, and accuracy were closely related in a significant majority of the essays.

We also mentioned in an earlier portion of this paper a potential problem with the reading comprehension test. It was administered as a speed test, with 40 minutes allowed for its completion. It was clear from scoring the tests that some students were unable to complete the test in the time dictated by the developers. In some cases, these were some of the better students. Their percentage of correct scores was extremely high, but since several had completed only 70–80% of the test, their scores were in the average range. What we are suggesting is the strong possibility that our obtained correlation between reading achievement and holistic writing could have been higher had the test of reading been timed differently.

Perhaps even more important is the measurement instrument itself. It measures "comprehension" in a fairly traditional way. Other measures of comprehension, e.g., more open-ended types of questions or even a different type of task, such as recall, might have produced different results. For example, in a more recent study, we used two measures of reading, a main-idea identification task and a rhetorical reading protocol, and did not obtain significant correlations between the two tasks (Flahive & Bailey, 1990). In a recent study by Carrell & Connor (1991), multiple choice and reading-recall tasks resulted in differing patterns of correlations between and among writing tasks and different methods of writing evaluation.

Individual Differences

This is an issue that is better illustrated than discussed. The highest scorer on our reading achievement test scored a 28 out of a possible 30. This score would have placed him in the 96th percentile of the norming group of native-speaking freshmen and sophomores attending four-year colleges and universities. His holistic writing score was 6, slightly above the average score. This was one of the more dramatic differences, but there were many other asymmetries in reading performance and writing performance demonstrated by our subjects. In examining our data by means of a number of categorical variables similar to those used by Janopoulos, we found over one-third of our subjects demonstrated significant asymmetries between reading and writing skills. Obviously, more-sensitive research procedures will need to be employed to examine and perhaps account for these individual differences if a generalized claim of a strong relationship between reading and writing is to be sustained.

Theory and Reading/Writing Research and Teaching

The findings that we have presented above suggest that reading, writing, and grammar are related second language learner abilities. Within the limits of our research, an argument could be made for a unified language proficiency factor underlying reading comprehension, writing ability, and the various measures of grammatical ability, similar to the claim made by Oller (1979). From the perspective of theory building, this would suggest that a theory of second language reading/writing relationships would need to be integrated into a more generalized theory of language acquisition.

As we mentioned early on, the theoretical motivation for this paper was derived from Krashen's reading input theory, which is an extension of his comprehensible input hypothesis, a component, of course, of his Monitor Model. (McLaughlin [1987] presents an excellent critical discussion of the components of the Monitor Model.) Our attempt to transform reading input theory, which specifically recommends massive doses of pleasure reading for the improvement of writing and grammar, into a testable hypothesis resulted in a failure to find the relationships that the hypothesis predicts.

There are, however, many other measurement issues that could be discussed in attempts to operationalize the "reading input hypothesis." Perhaps too few of our subjects engaged in the minimum amount of pleasure reading that the theory predicts. Perhaps a writing-from-sources task would have been a more appropriate measure of writing ability. Like many components of the Monitor Theory, there are problems in translating theoretical notions into operational definitions, a fairly widespread observation concerning Monitor Theory.

Like many theories, Monitor Theory might be useful for a specific set of teachers, in a specific type of teaching/learning situations, with specific ages/types of students. While this theory might be a useful guide to structuring curricula designed for L1 children or certain L2 acquirers, extensive pleasure reading alone did not account for successful argumentative essay writing nor did pleasure reading account for grammatical perception/production skills. What we did find is that those who read more performed better on a measure of reading comprehension than did those who read less. This result suggests that reading abilities developed through pleasure reading transfer to more traditional academic reading tasks. It also provides a small measure of validation for the common L2 pedagogical practice of combining intensive and extensive reading activities within a single reading course.

In the absence of a testable theory of reading/writing relationships, it would seem that for teachers to adopt a predominantly reading-input approach to the teaching of second language literacy and grammar skills would be risky in the absence of confirming research. A more prudent and more theoretically defensible approach would be to place equal emphasis on the traditional skills of reading and writing.

The rather tentative nature of the above discussion is the consequence of failing to confirm the predictions of an existing theory and not being able to argue for an alternative theory. The fact is that there exists no alternative theory of reading/writing relationships for second language learners.

Perhaps this absence of an applicable theory of reading/writing relationships for adult second language learners would provide language teaching practitioners and second language researchers an opportunity to engage in an activity that many have pointed out the absence of but few have engaged in—collaborative classroom research.

This collaborative research between second language literacy teachers and L2 researchers would by its nature be longitudinal. The approach would be in marked contrast to the overwhelming majority of L2 reading and writing studies, which are cross-sectional snapshots of isolated performances. It would be collaborative with varieties of reading/writing tasks appropriate to the specific level of the learners' language ability. This approach might help to narrow the theory/practice–researcher/teacher gaps that many have recently pointed out. It would also be eclectic in that social and cognitive factors would be integrated with a genuine teaching/learning environment.

Such collaborative research would be "exploratory" in the sense that teachers, researchers, and learners would interact in an environment in which reading/writing tasks would be developed, their processes and products evaluated, and their impact on subsequent literacy tasks assessed. Out of such a process could emerge a variety of testable hypotheses which could then form the basis of a working model of reading/writing relationships.

REFERENCES

Carrell, P.L., & Connor, U. (1991). Reading and writing descriptive and persuasive texts. *Modern Language Journal 75*(3), 314–324.

Deal, R. (1988). The reading–writing connection: Does it hold between languages? M.A. professional paper, Colorado State University.

Elley, W. & Mangubhai, F. (1983). The impact of reading on second language learning. *Reading Research Quarterly 19*(1), 53–67.

Flahive, D.E. & Bailey, N. (1990). Rhetorical reading and summary writing strategies of L1 and L2 learners. Paper presented at the 24th Annual TESOL, San Francisco, March 1990.

Grabe, W. (1991). Current developments in second language reading research. *TESOL Quarterly 25*(3), 375–406.

Homburg, T.J. (1984). Holistic evaluation of compositions: Can it be validated objectively? *TESOL Quarterly 18*(1), 87–108.

Janopoulos, M. (1986). The relationship of pleasure reading and second language writing proficiency. *TESOL Quarterly 20*(4), 763–768.

Krashen, S. (1987). The power of reading. Paper presented at the 5th Rocky Mountain Regional TESOL Conference, Denver, November 1987.

Larsen–Freeman, D. (1978). An ESL index of development. *TESOL Quarterly 12*(4), 439–450.

McLaughlin, B. (1987). *Theories of second–language learning.* London: Edward Arnold.

Meyer, B.J.F. (1982). Reading research and the composition teacher: The importance of plans. *College Composition and Communication 33*(1), 37–49.

Oller, J. (1979). *Language tests at school: A pragmatic approach.* London: Longman.

Raimes, A. (1991). Out of the woods: Emerging traditions in the teaching of writing. *TESOL Quarterly 25*(3), 407–430.

Raygor, A. (1970). *McGraw Hill Basic Skills System Test Manual.* Monterey: McGraw Hill.

Shanahan, T. (1988). The reading–writing relationship: Seven instructional principles. *The Reading Teacher.* March, 636–647.

Smoke, T. (1990). *A writer's worlds.* New York: St. Martin's.

Spack, R. (1990). *Guidelines: A cross–cultural reading/writing text.* New York: St. Martin's.

Squire, J.R. (1983). Composing and comprehending: Two sides of the same basic process. *Language Arts 60*(5), 581–589.

Stotsky, S. (1983). Research on reading/writing relationships: A synthesis and suggested directions. *Language Arts 60*(5), 627–642.

Withrow, J., Brookes, G., & Cummings, M. (1990). *Changes: Reading for ESL writers.* New York: St. Martin's.

CHAPTER 7

The Interpretation of Tasks by Writers and Readers in Holistically Rated Direct Assessment of Writing

Ulla M. Connor
Indiana University at Indianapolis

Patricia L. Carrell
University of Akron

INTRODUCTION

Direct assessment of ESL writing using an essay task has gained popularity in the past few years. Since 1986, more than a million international students have written a 30-minute essay for the Test of Written English (TWE), administered by the Educational Testing Service's TOEFL division. More and more U.S. institutions of higher learning have started to require a TWE score as an admissions requirement in addition to a TOEFL score (Kroll, 1991).

The TWE is a holistically rated test. The essays are scored for "overall effectiveness of the communication" (Stansfield & Webster, 1986, p. 17). The holistic scoring guide has six levels and includes syntactic and rhetorical criteria. (For the development of the guide, see Stansfield, 1986.) For example, an essay in the highest category, according to the "Test of Written English (TWE) Scoring Guidelines" (1989),

- effectively addresses the writing task
- is well organized and well developed
- uses clearly appropriate details to support a thesis or illustrate ideas
- displays consistent facility in the use of language
- demonstrates syntactic variety and appropriate word choice.

Several researchers have questioned the use of holistically rated direct assessment because little is known about what factors influence the scores students receive (Huot, 1990; Charney, 1984). After reviewing research on rater judgments of writing quality, Huot concludes that although many research studies in the past twenty years have tried to discover relationships between holistic ratings and factors such as discourse mode or type of writing, rhetorical specifications of prompts, wording and structure of prompts, and textual features of essays, little agreement about the relationships has emerged. A fruitful area of investigation, according to Huot, is to focus on the raters themselves. In particular, with the current interest in the role of prior knowledge and expectations in the fluent reading process (Fish, 1980; Tierney & Pearson, 1983; Carrell, 1983a, 1983b), it is important to investigate how scoring procedures act as a controlling influence on the impact of personal experience, variation, and expectation of the raters.

Analogously, "there has been almost no work done on students' attitudes and approaches to writing assessment," writes Durst in an evaluation of composition research (1990, pp. 403–404). In ESL, only two studies have attempted to address this issue. Hamp-Lyons (1990) and Johns (1991) both conducted think-aloud studies of ESL students writing on essay prompts. Johns interviewed a student in sciences, attempting to compare the student's strategies of writing for ESL and writing for academic tasks. Hamp-Lyons conducted interviews and analyzed think-aloud protocols of three ESL students. Hamp-Lyons' findings indicate that successful ESL writers incorporate personal experience as evidence for arguments in writing for others. Neither study offers conclusive evidence about ESL writer strategies in test settings.

In this chapter we focus on the interpretation of the task in an essay writing situation by both student writers and teacher reader/raters. In the study reported here, we examine this unique writing/reading situation as a complex communicative/cognitive activity. We are particularly interested in an area that has not been addressed previously at all, namely the possible mismatch of interpretation of the task by writers and readers and its effect on the assessment of the writing.

WRITING AND READING AS COMPLEX COMMUNICATIVE/COGNITIVE ACTIVITIES

Writing is a complex phenomenon that obviously involves an interaction between writer and reader. It is recognized that in a genuinely communicative social interaction, a writer pays careful attention to the audience and its needs in order to make sure that the text is comprehensible, persuasive, or memorable—whatever the specific writing situation demands. Therefore, texts are not seen as overt, concretely describable entities. Rather, according to text linguist Enkvist (1990), "the interpretability [of texts] is the dependence of situational context and the knowledge of the world shared by the producer and the receptor of discourse" (p. 26). Many models of writing address this mutual dependence. For example, Kinneavy's widely accepted "theory of discourse" (1971) is based on four components: encoder, decoder, reality, and signal. Depending on the situation, the signal (language) emphasizes the encoder or the decoder, the reality to which the reference is made, or the product (text produced). Consequently, discourse can be "expressive" (focus on the encoder), "persuasive" (focus on the decoder), "informative" (focus on the reality), or "literary" (focus on the text).

Clearly, as an act of communication between reader and writer, writing is also a complex cognitive activity requiring a set of processes and strategies. In the past two decades, a great deal has been learned about these processes. Both L1 and L2 researchers have examined the mental states of writers, their problem-solving strategies, and decisions about focus, audience, language use, and composing processes. One of the most powerful models of composing is that developed by Flower & Hayes (1981), from their studies of think-aloud protocols collected from mature, college-level writers. Their cognitive-process model consists of four interactive components—task, environment, the writer's long-term memory, and the composing processes themselves (planning, translating, reviewing).

Writing an essay in a test situation is also a communicative/cognitive activity requiring an additional set of strategies and skills. The IEA Study of Composition, which examined the instruction and testing of writing in 14 different countries (Gorman, Purves, & Degenhart, 1988; Purves, 1988), provides important information about "school writing" in testing situations across cultures. The IEA data indicate that school writing in all the participating cultures makes varied cognitive demands on students as well as demands that they write for varied purposes and varied audiences. Writers in situations involving direct assessment react to a written prompt and typically write under a time constraint. They must make decisions about whether they are to address a specific audience, what the purpose of the writing is, what style and tone is expected, what length is expected, etc. Although student writers do not write to one specific audience, they need to learn to address their real audience, the teacher/raters. This activity involves a complex set of cognitive and composing processes and strategies.

Raters, the real readers of test essays in large-scale assessment situations, also perform complex communicative and cognitive activities when they read and score an essay. Raters' stimuli are the essays themselves, but at the same time raters need to be aware of the prompt and the scoring guidelines. Raters are not reading the essays for pleasure, to be persuaded, or to be informed. Their purpose for reading in this context is to produce fair and reliable scores. As reading research has shown (Anderson & Pearson, 1984; Rumelhart, 1985; Samuels & Kamil, 1984), reading is a complex psycholinguistic activity that is sensitive to the sociological situation. In a rating situation, raters bring multiple domains of knowledge to the task. Raters are often English teachers with several years of experience teaching and grading student essays. But a more important domain of knowledge in holistic rating sessions is the knowledge about the particular scoring guidelines.

Therefore, both student writers and teacher/raters have definite purposes in their writing and reading. Students strive to write a good essay and to impress the rater with their language and writing abilities. Teacher/raters attempt to be fair, fast, and reliable scorers. But what guarantees are there that student writers and teacher/raters are on the same track? Little is known about the commonalities between these two sets of individuals and tasks. Neither is much known about the effects of the context and the external stimuli in the situation: the access to the prompt for both writers and readers, and the scoring guideline, to which only raters have access. The scoring guideline contains criteria for evaluation concerning the importance of language and rhetorical components in writing. It is necessary to learn whether writers have a sense of the relative importance of components of writing quality in the same way that teacher/raters are trained to interpret the quality of this writing.

THE STUDY

Purpose

The purpose of the present study was to investigate how ESL writers perceive an essay task and write an essay, and how raters interpret the prompt as well as use the TWE scoring guide to read and rate the essay. This study sought to identify reactions of both writers and raters concerning three areas of the reader/writer relationship:

1. Role of organization, development, unity, language use, and syntactic variation in the quality of an essay and how raters and writers make decisions about the respective importance of each.
2. Interpretation and conceptualization of the prompt.
3. Envisioning the situation of reader and writer.

METHOD

Subjects

The student writers in this study were five graduate students at a large Midwestern university. They had volunteered to participate in the research project as a preparation for an essay test for the university's Office of Writing Review. The students' average TOEFL score was 589. Their language backgrounds were Greek (2), Chinese (2), and Turkish (1). All the students were science majors: math (3), computer science (1), and engineering (1). Figure 1 shows a summary student profile.

FIGURE 1 Characteristics of Sample Students

Subject	TOEFL Score	Native Country	Major Field	Essay Scores
1	577	Hong Kong	Mathematics	(4, 4, 4, 5, 5)
2	623	Greece	Computer Science	(5, 6, 5, 6, 6)
3	577	Turkey	Mathematics	(5, 5, 5, 3, 4)
4	547	China	Engineering	(3, 3, 4, 3, 3)
5	620	Greece	Mathematics	(5, 5, 6, 5, 5)

The five raters in this study were TOEFL-trained TWE readers with experience in actual TWE readings. One was a native speaker of Spanish with a native-like English proficiency; the others were native speakers of English. All had taught ESL for several years.

Testing Materials

The essay prompt in this study was a 1987 TWE prompt, used with the permission of the Educational Testing Service. The prompt read:

> It is generally agreed that society benefits from the work of its members. Compare the contributions of artists to society with the contributions of scientists. Which type of contribution do you think is valued by your society? Give specific reasons to support your answer.

The scoring scale used by the raters in the study was the *TWE Scoring Guidelines* (1989) (see Appendix A). The scoring guide and the "benchmark" training essays were used with the permission of the Educational Testing Service.

Procedures

The data collection for the writing was done at mid-term in the fall semester of 1990. The five student writers met with one of the researchers once for the following procedures:

1. An introduction to the project and to think-aloud composing.
2. A session during which the students composed aloud (audiotaped). Students were allowed 40 minutes to write and compose aloud, instead of the usual 30 minutes allowed for the TWE. A pilot testing had shown that the time allotment of 40 minutes was appropriate to accommodate the added time of thinking aloud.

The data collection for the reading/scoring part of the study was done at the beginning of the spring semester of 1991. After a pilot test with one TWE-trained rater, one of the researchers met with the raters for the following procedures:

1. An introduction to the project and to think-aloud while scoring.
2. A calibration, using three separate sets of benchmark essays and the scoring guide.
3. A session during which the raters thought aloud (audiotaped) while scoring the five essays, which had been rewritten by hand by one person.

To assess and compare the writing and rating processes of the subjects, we used protocol analysis, a methodology borrowed from cognitive psychology to generate verbal data from informants who perform a particular task. Protocol analysis has been used in ESL composition research to examine students' writing processes (Raimes, 1988; Cumming, 1989; Friedlander, 1990) and in a study on the rating processes of scorers (Cumming, 1990).

The protocol analysis used was a "concurrent" analysis, which revealed what writers or raters were concerned about as they wrote or rated. Both writers and raters in this study were asked to verbalize any thoughts they had while writing or rating. The training of both groups of subjects in this study was based on a general set of guidelines developed by Ericsson & Simon (1984, pp. 375–377) and employed by previous composition studies (e.g., Cumming, 1990; Huot, in press).

Data Analysis

All protocol sessions were recorded on cassette tapes. These tapes were transcribed by a typist experienced in transcribing. All verbalizations were transcribed. The protocols were segmented into separate *decision statements.*

The transcripts of the student think-aloud protocols were coded, using the coding scheme in Cumming (1989). The categories of the scheme represent five aspects of writing on which people focus while composing: language use, discourse organization, gist, intentions, and procedures for writing. Figure 2 contains the coding scheme and shows examples for each category. The figure also indicates that we added subcategories in the code for the special purpose of the present study: In "Language Use," we added "lexical" convention; in "Intentions," we added a subcategory of "audience awareness" (4.1); in "Procedures," we added subcategories of "referring to the prompt" (5.1) and "writing down text" (5.0). Cumming's coding scheme was used because it includes the aspects of essay writing in which this study was interested: task interpretation and decision-making about quality of writing (see "Procedures," such as referring to the prompt, and "Gist," such as formulating and reconsidering ideas), envisioning the situation of the reader (see "Intentions," which includes audience), and quality of text (see "Language Use" and "Discourse Organization").

FIGURE 2   Coding Scheme for Student Think-Alouds*

1. Language Use (statements referring to lexical, grammatical, punctuation, or orthographic conventions):

> "is flourish a better word?"
> "—my letters are awful—"
> "the next generation, the next generation's . . ."

2. Discourse Organization (statements referring to organization of discourse, interrelations of rhetorical units—e.g., paragraphs, introductions, conclusions, examples, points):

> "So we must have an outline here."
> "let's see, we can . . . let's put communication first."
> "Okay, so we talked about transportation and . . ."

3. Gist (statements focusing on writer's thoughts or ideas, including formulation, consideration, and reconsideration of ideas):

> ". . . but, but it's, it's more of a mental and a, it's not psychological, mental and psych—okay, but it doesn't affect . . ."
> "I'm not thinking!"
> "became, um, became away from asthetic—asthetic, how can we write this?"

4. Intentions (statements relating to personal goals or purposes of texts through writing; includes audience consideration):

> "If I had more time I would write better."
> "So do I talk about the people that really study these things?"
> "I think I have not responded very well to you specifically, this isn't what you're asking . . ."

5. Procedures (statements referring to a writer's procedures for doing something while writing—e.g., writing itself, making notes, checking something, reading written text, and referring to prompt as separate categories):

> "—just looking back—"
> "The development of each society is a function generally dependent on its members."
> "I have no idea what this 'compare the contributions of artists to the society with the contributions of scientists.'"

*Adapted from Cumming, 1989; examples from sample essays in the present study.

One rater coded all the transcriptions. Another rater coded 20% of the transcriptions. The inter-rater reliability between the two raters was high; their agreement rate was 94.7 percent.

The transcriptions of the rater think-aloud protocols were coded, using the coding scheme in Cumming (1990). The 28 strategies identified in Cumming's research were found to be appropriate descriptors of the utterances by the raters in the present study also. As in Cumming, the strategies deal with four kinds of focus: raters' self-control of their own reading or judgment processes (items 1, 2, and 8–13); content of the texts (items 3, 4, and 14–18); uses of language in the texts (items 5, 6, and 19–24); or rhetorical organization of the texts (items 7 and 25–28). Cumming's coding scheme was again considered appropriate because it addresses task interpretation and decision making about scores ("self-control" 1, 8–13), envisioning the writer ("self-control focus" 2), and quality of text ("language focus" and "organization focus").

Figure 3 contains the rater coding scheme. Two independent raters scored the protocols; the agreement rate between the raters was 88.4%. A sample of a rater protocol is shown in Figure 4.

FIGURE 3   Coding Scheme for Rater Decision Making*

Self-Control Focus	Content Focus	Language Focus	Organization Focus
Interpretation strategies			
1. Scan whole text to obtain initial impression	3. Interpret ambiguous phrases	5. Classify errors	7. Discern rhetorical structures
2. Envision situation of writing and writer	4. Summarize propositions	6. Edit phrases	
Judgment strategies			
8. Establish personal response to qualities of items	14. Count propositions to assess total output	19. Establish level of comprehensibility	25. Assess coherence
9. Define, assess, revise own criteria and strategies	15. Assess relevance	20. Establish error values	26. Identify unnecessary repetition
10. Read to assess criteria	16. Assess interest	21. Establish error frequency	27. Assess helpfulness
11. Compare compositions	17. Assess development of topics	22. Establish command of syntactic complexity	28. Rate overall organization
12. Distinguish interactions between categories	18. Rate content overall	23. Establish appropriateness of lexis	
13. Summarize judgments collectively		24. Rate overall language use	

*Adopted from Cumming, 1990

FIGURE 4   Sample Rater Think-Aloud Protocol*

---

36   Okay, here we go to #3. I hope this is recording. / "Scientist are"— *III. 5*

37   verb agreement. / "Scientists have produced harmful"—oh, *ideas.* Harmful *III. 23*

38   ideas? / "For example, like guns, rockets, or atom bombs." That's a fragment *III. 5*

39   there. / Plus, why do we need "for example" and "like" together? / This seems *III. 6* *IV. 7*

40   almost to be more stream-of-consciousness writing than sitting down and

41   organizing it well in an essay. / Another fragment—"Because even the simplest *III. 5*

42   illness could be dangerous or to grow anything in a farm was really hard." /

43   But this person is really fluent, too. / "Too much useful," / "work in the *III. 24* *III. 5* *I. 10*

44   offices which is designed for increasing the productivity and they eat fast

45   foods. So where is the beauty?" / *You* tell *me.* / "We live in a machie *I. 8* *III. 23*

46   world . . .?" Oh, I guess that's supposed to be "machine world?" ". . . where we

47   are supposed to behave and think as a robot." / Hmmm. Well, this *I. 2*

48   guy . . . / "scientists could be more useful in the old times but now they are *I. 10*

49   really too many . . ." / I would give this a 5, because of the development. / It's *II. 18* *IV. 28*

50   not nearly as organized as a 6 should be. / The subject/verb agreement keeps *III. 20*

51   tripping us up here and there. / But, really, the person is quite fluent. / He's *III. 24* *II. 17*

52   developed the topic and all of that. / So, it's a 5. *I. 13*

---

*Rater 2, Essay 3

Research Questions

There were basically three research questions addressed in this study:

1. Do writers and raters have similar understandings of what constitutes adequate content, rhetorical devices, and language use in essays, and how are these decisions reached?
2. Do writers and raters conceptualize and interpret the task in a similar manner?
3. Do writers and raters have a notion of each other's respective roles?

Results

We will examine and discuss the results of the data analyses pertaining to each of the three questions. For each question, rater responses are discussed as a group first. Second, writer responses will be explained as a group.

Do writers and raters have similar understandings of what consti-tutes adequate content, rhetorical devices, and language use in essays, and how are these decisions reached? Decision statements were counted for each rater, and percentages were calculated for each behavior category over the total number of statements by each rater. Percentages of behaviors were calculated for the rater group as a whole, as shown in Table 1.

TABLE 1   Percentages of Decision Statements by Behavior Category in Rater Think-Alouds

Self-Control Focus	Content Focus	Language Focus	Organization Focus
Interpretation strategies			
1. Scan whole text to obtain initial impression 7.4	3. Interpret ambiguous phrases .8	5. Classify errors 5.6	7. Discern rhetorical structures 1.4
2. Envision situation of writing and write 4.4	4. Summarize propositions 1.5	6. Edit phrases 1.3	
Judgment strategies			
8. Establish personal response to qualities of items 7.5	14. Count propositions to assess total output .7	19. Establish level of comprehensibility 6.3	25. Assess coherence 1.7
9. Define, assess, revise own criteria and strategies 3.9	15. Assess relevance 1.2	20. Establish error values 3.0	26. Identify unnecessary repetition .8
10. Read to assess criteria 14.6	16. Assess interest 1.7	21. Establish error frequency 2.7	27. Assess helpfulness 1.1
11. Compare compositions .4	17. Assess development of topics 4.6	22. Establish command of syntactic complexity 1.2	28. Rate overall organization 4.3
12. Distinguish interactions between categories .7	18. Rate content overall 2.2	23. Establish appropriateness of lexis 3.0	
13. Summarize judgments collectively 9.9		24. Rate overall language use 6.2	
48.8	**12.7**	**29.3**	**9.3**

Table 1 indicates that 48.8% of the combined rater statements dealt with the "self-control focus," 12.7% with "content," 29.3% with "language," and only 9.3% with "organization." The raters in the study behaved in a manner similar to the expert raters in Cumming's study (1990). They spent a great amount of effort in reaching decisions about the role of language, content, and other factors in a score ("self-control focus"). For example, the raters displayed self-reflexive behaviors by establishing personal response (7.5%), envisioning the writer's situation (4.4%), reading to assess own criteria (14.6%), and summarizing judgments collectively (9.9%). They also focused on assessing the development of topics (4.6%). Related to language use, the raters "classified" errors (5.6%) rather than "edited" phrases (1.3%). The latter strategy was preferred by Cumming's novice raters.

There was some individual variation, of course, in the decision statements of the raters in this study, as Table 2 shows. Raters 2 and 4 stand out as having the highest percentages of statements on "language use" and the lowest percentages on "self-control." Nevertheless, it should be noted that the previously observed general pattern persists: Statements on "organization" and "content" are the least frequent rater behaviors, while statements on "self-control focus" and "language" are the most frequent.

The results of the analyses of the student writers' data are shown in Table 3 as percentages of decision statements by student by category. The average percentage for "Language Use" is 7.1, 1.5 for "Discourse Organization," 42.4 for "Gist," 4.12 for "Intentions," and 44.7 for the combined "Procedures" (5, 5.0, and 5.1). The categories with the highest percentages are "Gist" and "Procedures." In "Procedures," the actual writing down of text (5.0) accounts for the largest number of statements. These two categories account for 87.1% of all student comments in the protocols.

The finding about the predominance of "Gist" statements in the student protocols accords with Cumming's 1989 findings: "[G]roup means indicate clearly that gist predominates as the aspect of writing to which all participants devoted the majority of their attention in their decisions in each task" (Cumming, p. 23).

TABLE 2 Percentages of Decision Statements by Rater in Rater Think-Alouds

	Self-Control	Content	Language	Organization
Rater 1	56.0	7.9	21.7	13.7
Rater 2	39.9	12.5	39.9	8.0
Rater 3	63.2	3.4	27.4	5.7
Rater 4	28.3	27.2	35.3	9.1
Rater 5	56.0	12.0	21.9	9.9

TABLE 3   Percentages of Decision Statements by Student and Behavior in Student Think-Alouds

	Student 1	Student 2	Student 3	Student 4	Student 5
Language					
Use	1.2	5.3	15.4	6.5	6.9
Discourse					
Organization	3.6	.7	.6	1.4	1.4
Gist	45.8	40.1	39.4	43.5	43.1
Intentions					
4	6.0	10.5	.6	.7	2.8
4.1	0	.7	0	0	0
Procedures					
5	4.8	2.6	8.6	5.8	2.8
5.0	37.3	35.5	34.3	41.3	40.3
5.1	1.2	4.6	1.1	.7	2.8

Unlike the raters, the writers were not concerned about commenting on "Language Use," with the exception of one student, Student 3, whose percentage on the language use category was 15.4. Throughout his think-aloud, Student 3 seemed concerned about language use, as the following examples demonstrate: "But—no but, second time but"; "produce/have produced"; "unnecessary—no, not unnecessary"; "which one really contributes more to the / which one is really contributing more."

Generally, the distribution of the statements seems consistent among the students. But there was some inconsistency. For example, three students—1, 2, and 5—made significant numbers of comments on "Intention." Examples of these statements are as follows: "so we have to start like what the society benefits from its members"; "okay, we must finish this now"; "so now I talk about the other side of the contribution of the scientist"; "But I've got to stop at some point and talk about the contribution of the artist."

As was the case with the raters, the students did not comment much on "Discourse Organization," with the exception of Student 5. Sample statements by Student 5 are as follows: "I think we have a—we can just use a historical review that most of the . . ."; "And then we have to refer to artists and scientists, so the artists helped more in the cultural development and the scientists the technological development"; "okay, now we compare the contributions of artists to society and the contributions of scientists"; "maybe another example would fit here."

To summarize the results related to the first research question, we note that both the raters and the writers spent a great deal of effort in making decisions about the importance of various aspects of text. The "self-control focus" for the raters and "procedures" for the writers were high. Further, both the raters and the writers considered content and development in the writing. Neither set of subjects, however, needed to mention the organization of the essay as important. Finally, the think-alouds revealed a greater emphasis on language use by the raters than by the writers.

Do writers and raters conceptualize and interpret the task in a similar manner? The analysis of the rater think-alouds shows that the raters did not comment on the organizational requirements of the prompt, e.g., the two tasks of comparing contributions and explaining the situation in [your society], during either reading the essay or while summarizing the final evaluation. This suggests that although the raters considered the text-internal organization and fluency important, they did not think it important for the writers to address the specific requirements of the prompt.

In examining the raters' statements about the essays, it is clear that no matter how well or how poorly the writers addressed the specific rhetorical requirements specified in the prompt, the raters' reading and evaluation of the essays were not affected. Instead, fluency of language, infrequency of language errors, and general development of ideas were consistently mentioned as criteria throughout the think-alouds and in final summative evaluations. To demonstrate this trend, the final summative statements of each rater commenting on Essay 2 are given in Figure 5.

The writers, likewise, were not concerned about addressing the specific demands of the prompt. At least, they did not verbalize their concern. To investigate further this research question, we analyzed the five essays—the finished products—to find out whether the writers addressed the tasks in the prompt. The prompt asked the writer to "compare the contributions of artists to society with the contributions of scientists." The writer was further asked "which type of contribution is valued by your society."

A content analysis of the essays reveals varying levels of addressing the task as specified in the prompt. Essay 1 contains neither a comparison of the contributions nor the specification of a society. Essays 3 and 4 attempt to compare the contributions; Essay 3 speaks of the need for scientists in the old days to cure illnesses and the need today for artists to make people feel better. Essay 4 provides little elaboration on its thesis: "Scientists who always contribute physical material to satisfy people. Artists who always contribute to satisfy people's brain to make people feel happy." Neither Essay 3 nor Essay 4 attempts to specify a society but instead talks generally of "our society." Two essays—2 and 5—compared extensively the contributions of artists and scientists as well as discussed at length the relative value placed on the two by the writers' society (Greek). The other students did not address both parts of the topic.

Do raters and writers have a notion of each other's respective roles? Do they try to envision each other's situation? The results show that the

FIGURE 5 Raters' Summative Comments on Student 2's Essay

Rater 1: "Hmm. Really good essay! I'm impressed by the content and by the strength of the persuasive side of it. I would give it a 6, even though it does have a few here and there grammar mistakes, but . . . boy, it's a good essay!"

Rater 2: "Yeah, 'the ancient Greek civilization of the 5th century"—this is a 6. It's got some grammatical problems, you know, with articles and minor things here and there. 'The futuristic poetry movement, which personally I view *it*'—with the added 'it' there in the relative clause and so on. But the overall fluency just makes up for that, with the level of the vocabulary and so on. And those are relatively minor problems with the language, so I go with the 6 for #2."

Rater 3: "It's a gorgeous content, it's either an extremely strong 5, or if you are trying to reward a student, maybe a low 6, but I think it's . . . okay, I'm reading the scoring guide. It has the characteristics of a 6, it's well organized, well developed, effectively addresses the writing task, certainly uses appropriate details, displays consistent facility in the use of language, demonstrates syntactic variety—oh, boy. That's a nasty one. I guess I could give it a . . . I don't know . . . it's a really a crap shoot on a 5 or a 6 here. There was a couple of spots where it just blew me away. I'll give it a very, very high 5."

Rater 4: ("My goodness, what a lot of writing! Distorted kind of writing. Interesting. My goodness, now he's going to the fifth century.") "Well, it doesn't end right, but it's still a 6. He certainly can express himself."

Rater 5: "Oh, this is a very, very strong piece. I would give it a 6. It did have one problem with a sentence where I struggled, but I think the facility of language use, the syntactic variety, and very, very strong use of examples, and the language just seems very obviously a person who's competent in—clearly demonstrates competence in writing. And so I'm comfortable with a 6 with that one."

raters did not try to envision the writer and his or her situation. The average number of decision statements in this category for all the raters was only 4.4% of the total number of statements. The individual percentages for the raters were 12.6, 2.7, 0, 4.5, and 2.1. The rater with the highest percentage of statements envisioning the writer (12.6) made comments about the handwriting of each writer, deciding whether the writer was male or female and which language background the writer came from, e.g., "Hmm—looks like the handwriting of a woman"; "but I think she must—she seems to be like an undergrad that can pick up a lot of language"; "This one talks about ethics"; "Huh! That's why he talked about philosophers"; "She—or he, I don't know, I can't tell by the handwriting this time."

Just as the raters did not envision the writers, neither did the writers try to envision the audience. Three students—1, 2, and 5—exhibited a fair percentage of statements in the "Intentions" category. And only one student, Student 2, made specific statements about an audience: "I think that I have not very well responded to you specifically, this isn't what you're asking."

CONCLUSION

This study was designed to explore similarities and differences between how ESL writers perceive a prompt and write an essay in response to that prompt and how raters interpret the prompt as well as read and rate the essay, using the TWE scoring guide. We sought to identify reactions of both writers and reader/raters concerning three areas of reader/writer relationships: (1) perceptions of text production (organization, content, development, and language use), (2) interpretation and conceptualization of the task required of the writers, and (3) envisioning of the situation of the writer and the reader.

Results showed that both the writers and the reader/raters spent considerable amounts of cognitive effort, as reflected in their think-alouds, in consideration of their specific tasks. In the case of the reader/raters, decisions related to giving a particular score, and in the case of the writers, procedures related to producing an essay. Yet both reader/raters and writers exhibited concern about language use, content, and development of the text, and little concern about the organization. Surprisingly little attention was paid by either writers or the reader/raters to addressing all the parts of the topic as specified in the prompt. Finally, neither group appeared to make an effort to envision each other. Only one writer mentioned a possible audience. It seems that, for the writers, the audience was the English teachers who are expected to read a school essay, and there did not seem to be a need to think of that audience further. The reader/raters' only envisionment of the writers consisted of occasional predictions about the sex, nationality, or language proficiency of the writer.

Thus, within the limitations and context of the study, writers and reader/raters apparently made similar and "efficient" assumptions about their respective tasks. The students in this study did not experience any apparent difficulty in knowing what was expected of them. Without any particular training in TWE test-taking skills, the students paid attention to the aspects of the task that the raters also found the most important. Given the context of an academic ESL program at an American university, both student/writers and teacher/raters focused on the same elements of writing—namely, content, development, and language (the latter somewhat more by the reader/raters than the writers)—and chose to ignore certain other aspects or elements of writing, namely, text organization, addressing all parts of the prompt and audience environment. One could say that this was indeed "efficient."

This consistency suggests to us that in educational contexts like those of the student/writers and teacher/reader/raters, namely academic ESL programs, there is apparently sufficient similarity in the assumptions by the writers and the raters about the purposes for writing tasks and their evaluation in direct assessment situations that there is little need for special pedagogy.

However, given a different context—e.g., ESL students writing in different pedagogical settings, for different potential reader/raters, or in non-pedagogical settings—there may be less consistency in the assumptions by ESL writers and reader/raters, and hence there may be a need for relevant pedagogy to make ESL writers aware of potential pitfalls resulting from their assumptions. If ESL writers write outside the context of ESL language classes (e.g., writing for content classes or for professional or employment purposes), a focus on language may be less important, for example, than completely addressing the writing prompt.

The consistent focus of our reader/raters also suggests a more positive state of affairs than some recent ESL literature would suggest regarding holistic assessment. We found that the raters in our study relied on a set of quite uniform principles to evaluate the compositions and that their comments followed the TWE scoring guidelines closely. This is in contrast to Vaughan's assertion (1991) that "raters are not adhering to a single, internalized method for judging essays" (p. 121). Vaughan found that the raters in her study, nine raters experienced in a specific university's holistic assessment system, varied greatly in their scores as well as the comments they made. Based on her findings, she suggests that holistic rating of essays is highly individualistic. She writes that "different raters focus on different essay elements and perhaps have individual approaches to reading essays" (p. 121). Since the selection, training, and calibrations for the raters in our study were clearly more rigorous than those described by Vaughan, we conclude that such factors are important considerations in arriving at consistent as well as reliable holistic assessments.

We see this research as among the first of its kind, and clearly more research of a similar kind is needed before any definite conclusions or implications can be drawn. Additional research is needed with larger groups of subjects, both writers and reader/raters, with writers at lower and higher proficiency levels of English, with writers and raters outside academic ESL settings in U.S. universities, and with different types of writing prompts.

APPENDIX A

Test of Written English (TWE) Scoring Guide

Revised 2/90

Readers will assign scores based on the following scoring guide. Though examinees are asked to write on a specific topic, parts of the topic may be treated by implication. Readers should focus on what the examinee does well.

SCORES

6 **Demonstrates clear competence in writing on both the rhetorical and syntactic levels, though it may have occasional errors.**
A paper in this category
- effectively addresses the writing task
- is well organized and well developed
- uses clearly appropriate details to support a thesis or illustrate ideas
- displays consistent facility in the use of language
- demonstrates syntactic variety and appropriate word choice

5 **Demonstrates competence in writing on both the rhetorical and syntactic levels, though it will probably have occasional errors.**
A paper in this category
- may address some parts of the task more effectively than others
- is generally well organized and developed
- uses details to support a thesis or illustrate an idea
- displays facility in the use of language
- demonstrates some syntactic variety and range of vocabulary

4 **Demonstrates minimal competence in writing on both the rhetorical and syntactic levels.**
A paper in this category
- addresses the topic adequately but may slight parts of the task
- is adequately organized and developed
- uses some details to support a thesis or illustrate an idea
- demonstrates adequate but possibly inconsistent facility with syntax and usage
- may contain some errors that occasionally obscure meaning

3 **Demonstrates some developing competence in writing, but it remains flawed on either the rhetorical or syntactic level, or both.**
A paper in this category may reveal one or more of the following weaknesses:
- inadequate organization or development
- inappropriate or insufficient details to support or illustrate generalizations
- a noticeably inappropriate choice of words or word forms
- an accumulation or errors in sentence structure and/or usage

2   Suggests incompetence in writing.
A paper in this category is seriously flawed by one or more of the following weaknesses:
- serious disorganization or underdevelopment
- little or no detail, or irrelevant specifics
- serious and frequent errors in sentence structure or usage
- serious problems with focus

1   Demonstrates incompetence in writing.
A paper in this category
- may be incoherent
- may be undeveloped
- may contain severe and persistent writing errors

Papers that reject the assignment or fail to address the question must be given to the Table Leader.

Papers that exhibit absolutely no response at all must also be given to the Table Leader.

REFERENCES

Anderson, R.C. & Pearson, P.D. (1984). A schema–theoretic view of basic processes in reading. In P.D. Pearson (Ed.), *Handbook of Reading Research* (pp. 255–291). New York: Longman.

Carrell, P.L. (1983a). Background knowledge in second language comprehension. *Language Learning and Communication, 2*, 25–34.

Carrell, P.L. (1983b). Some issues in studying the role of schemata, or background knowledge, in second language comprehension. *Reading in a Foreign Language, 1*, 81–92.

Charney, D. (1984). The validity of using holistic scoring to evaluate writing: A critical overview. *Research in the Teaching of English 18*(1), 65–81.

Cumming, A. (1990). Expertise in evaluating second language compositions. *Language Testing, 7*(1), 31–51.

Cumming, A. (1989). Writing expertise and second–language proficiency. *Language Learning, 39*(1), 81–141.

Durst, R.K. (1990). The mongoose and the rat in composition research: Insights from the RTE annotated bibliography. *College Composition and Communication, 41*(4), 393–408.

Enkvist, N.E. (1990). Seven problems in the study of coherence and interpretability. In U. Connor & A.M. Johns (Eds.), *Coherence in writing: Research and pedagogical perspectives* (pp. 9–28). Arlington, VA: TESOL.

Ericsson, K.A. & Simon, H.A. (1984). *Protocol analysis: Verbal reports as data.* Cambridge, MA: MIT Press.

Fish, S. (1980). *Is there a text in this class? The authority of interpretative communities.* Cambridge, MA: Harvard University Press.

Flower, L.S. & Hayes, J.R. (1981). A cognitive process theory of writing. *College Composition and Communication, 32*, 365–387.

Friedlander, A. (1990). Composing in English: Effects of a first language on writing in English as a second language. In B. Kroll (Ed.), *Second language writing* (pp. 109–125). New York: Cambridge University Press.

Gorman, T.P., Purves, A.C., & Degenhart, R.E. (Eds.). (1988). *The IEA study of written composition I: The international writing tasks and scoring scales.* New York: Pergamon.

Hamp–Lyons, L. (1990). *Essay test strategies and cultural diversity: Pragmatic failure, pragmatic accommodation and the definition of excellence*. Unpublished manuscript, University of Colorado, Department of English, Denver.

Huot, B. (in press). The validity of holistic scoring: A study of its influence upon the rating of student essays. In M.M. Williams & B. Huot (Eds.), *Holistic scoring: New theoretical foundations and validation research*. Norwood, NJ: Ablex.

Huot, B. (1990). The literature of direct writing assessment: Major concerns and prevailing trends. *Review of Educational Research, 60*(2), 237–263.

Johns, A.M. (1991). Interpreting an English competency examination: The frustrations of an ESL science student. *Written Communication, 8*(3), 379–401.

Kinneavy, J. (1971). *A theory of discourse*. Englewood, NJ: Prentice–Hall.

Kroll, B. (1990). Understanding TOEFL's test of written English. *RELC Journal, 22*(1), 20–33.

Purves, A.C. (Ed.). (1988). *Writing across languages and cultures*. Beverly Hills, CA: Sage.

Raimes, A. (1988). Language proficiency, writing ability, and composing strategies: A study of ESL college students. *Language Learning, 37*(3), 439–467.

Rumelhart, D.E. (1985). Toward an interactive model of reading. In H. Singer & R.B. Ruddell (Eds.), *Theoretical models and processes of reading* (pp. 722–750). Newark, DE: International Reading Association.

Samuels, S.J. & Kamil, M.L. (1984). Models of the reading process. In P.D. Pearson (Ed.), *Handbook of Reading Research* (pp. 185–224). New York: Longman.

Stansfield, C.W. (1986). A history of the test of written English: The developmental year. *Language Testing, 3*(2), 224–234.

Stansfield, C.W. & Webster, R. (1986). The new TOEFL writing test. *TESOL Newsletter, 10*, 17–18.

Test of Written English guide. (1989). Princeton, NJ: Educational Testing Service.

Tierney, R.J. & Pearson, P.D. (1983). Toward a composing model of reading. *Language Arts, 60*, 568–580.

Vaughan, C. (1991). Holistic assessment: What goes on in the rater's minds? In L. Hamp–Lyons (Ed.), *Assessing second language writing in academic contexts* (pp. 111–126). Norwood, NJ: Ablex.

CHAPTER 8

Composing a Study–Summary: A Reading/Writing Encounter[1]

Gissi Sarig

Kibbutzim State Teachers College

RATIONALE AND RESEARCH QUESTIONS

Summarizing tasks are junctions where reading and writing encounters take place and it is here that a complex composing process begins. First, summarizing brings about an author–learner encounter. In the course of this encounter learners produce inner speech (Vygotsky, 1962), private, self-addressed reductions of the source text. At this stage, what the learners have produced may be no more than writer-based, personal utterances (Flower & Hays, 1984; Olson, 1977). These utterances are often reader-insensitive and may therefore be meaningful only to the learners themselves. Moreover, these utterances will remain meaningful only for as long as the learners retain them in memory (Widdowson, 1983).

In certain cases, the learners will not stop here. They will become audience-aware revisors who transform the private, self-addressed summaries into reader-friendly, autonomous, literate, and reconceptualized target texts (Flower & Hays, 1984; Olson, 1977; Scardamalia & Bereiter, 1987; Widdowson, 1983). I would like to refer to the product of this conceptual transformation process as a "study–summary."

When do college students engage spontaneously in composing such a study–summary, apart from artificial teacher-induced situations? When do they feel it worth their while to put in the high mental investment necessary for the construction of a study–summary? For students to take the trouble to do this, they must first feel that the text they are reading may be of future use to them, even if at the time of reading they do not exactly know how. Secondly, they must realize that the text is too long and complex to fully comprehend and commit to memory without direct, intentional manipulation. It is then that college students will spontaneously engage in composing a study–summary. In this sense, the study–summary is a true literacy-act. It not only serves as a memory extender, but also as an epistemological tool; it "freezes" knowledge to be "thawed" later, at the user's convenience.

---

[1]This paper is an extended version of the one given in the colloquium on the interactive relationship of reading and writing, TESOL, March 6–11, 1989 Chicago.

For suspended knowledge to be fully effective and meaningful in the future, some offhand scribbling of spontaneous notes will not do. To attain this long-term objective, when composing the study–summary learners must recycle source material into a target text, which will be a tighter and a more coherent *reconceptualization* of the source text. Thus, in creating the study–summary, learners actually create knowledge. In the future, when the same study–summary is reused in new learning contexts, it will serve the learners as an agent in re-creating fresh knowledge yet again.

With this purpose in mind, college students compose L1 study–summaries for texts they read—whether the texts are in a first or in a foreign language. In EFL situations students do read texts in their first language. However, they must also read English texts: Johns (1988) points out that 80% of all published texts and many of the world's professional journals are written in English. No wonder, then, that college students need to become proficient summarizers from L1 and L2 texts alike.

What cognitive processes underlie the passage from source text to target text? Drawing mainly, but not only, from Kintsch & Van Dijk's text processing model (1978), past research into summarization processes has concentrated principally on source text and target text comparisons, using source and target text differences as a data base from which to infer cognitive operations (Garner & McCaleb, 1985; Hidi, 1984; Johns, 1985; Kuzminsky & Graetz, 1986; Winograd, 1984). In addition, other studies have opened a window on cognitive operations in the summarizing process (e.g., Kennedy, 1985; Taylor, 1986). However, summarizing behavior in these studies is treated too broadly, or from within a linear, non-integrative view of the learning process. Further, these studies focus on summarizing in L1.

The purpose of the present case study is thus twofold. First, it seems worthwhile to extend and deepen the efforts begun by Taylor and Kennedy and to embed them in a comprehensive theoretical framework. Second, since study–summarizing is often carried out in an EFL situation, it is interesting to compare processes and products of study–summaries written for L1 versus L2 texts.

With the purpose of focusing on the process of composing a study–summary, two research questions are at the heart of this case study:

1. What cognitive processes underlie the composing of a study–summary?
2. How do processes and products of summaries composed for L1 texts compare with those composed for L2 texts?

METHOD

The Subject

The subject, Amram, was a first-year philosophy of science student in the Open University in Israel. Amram was a suitable candidate for this study for two reasons. First, his English proficiency level was high. Second, he had a satisfactory background knowledge data base in the domain in which he read: philosophy of science, history, and the sciences. This combination, high linguistic proficiency and relevant prior knowledge, made him an ideal EFL reader. Thus, by analyzing Amram's process of composing a study–summary, it was hoped that it would be possible to learn about summarization processes as they took place in an optimal pedagogical situation. If Amram's performance was satisfactory, the data concerning it could be used as a basis against which to compare performances of less able students. If not, high-challenge aspects of summarization would be highlighted.

Materials and Corpus

Thirteen texts—five in Hebrew, eight in English—were selected for use in the study. All texts were authentic and, except for one, dealt with various issues related to science, technology, and culture. The texts varied in length, averaging 500 words. All texts were thematically self-contained. The corpus represented the type of texts a philosophy of science student encounters when reading to learn.

Procedures

Following recommendations for the production of reliable and valid verbal data (Cohen, 1987; Ericsson & Simon, 1980; Sarig, 1989), the subject was given a four-phase treatment in preparation for the study. First, he was given an explanation of the nature and value of verbal data. Next, he was given a demonstration of the production of think-aloud data while performing a problem-creating motor task—sewing on a button without looking. Then he was asked to perform the same task while verbalizing. His next training task was to verbalize while rationally sorting out a pile of 30 audiocassettes. Finally, he was given a verbalization-while-learning training task: He was asked to verbalize while performing a reading/writing synthesizing task, based on two short newspaper items.

This training session preceded the performance of the study: Summarizing in Hebrew thirteen EFL and Hebrew texts. The data-gathering sessions took place on days 2, 3, and 4 of the experiment, the first one beginning with a short warm-up stage. The subject first summarized five English texts. Then he summarized, in alternating order, eight more texts, five in Hebrew and three in English. In all, Amram read eight texts in English and five in Hebrew, producing thirteen study-summarizing protocols.

Type of Data Analyzed

Think-aloud protocols of the summary-composing process are expected to contain three types of discourse—read, spoken, and written: (1) *source text:* the original text the subject reads and rereads; (2) *intertext:* the learner-based, thought-regulating prose, produced in speaking while externally verbalizing self-addressed private speech; (3) *target text:* the final product—the written-out, literate study–summary.

For the purposes of this study, the intertext was analyzed for *process* information, and the target text for *product* evaluation. Actual physical reading and writing moves (such as reading, rereading, writing, rewriting) were excluded from the calculations. Thus, data analysis proceeded in three stages. First, the protocol was classified into *reading, speaking,* and *writing* moves. Next, the spoken discourse—the intertext—was analyzed using Sarig's model (1991, in press). Simultaneously, each move was classified as relating either to comprehending the *source text* or to creating the *target text*. Finally, the written products were evaluated using the product evaluation model presented below.

ANALYSIS

Product Data

Drawing mainly on Kintsch & Van Dijk's model of text processing (1978), the summaries were analyzed using a product evaluation model developed for this study. The model consists of the following categories: (1) *propositional comprehension:* the extent to which the summarizer displays distortion-free comprehension of source text, as it is reflected in retained summary information; (2) *language:* the extent to which the summarizer achieved communicative effectiveness in the final, written version; (3) *quantitative reduction:* the extent to which the summarizer has retained only and all non-trivial, non-redundant source text material; (4) *conceptual transformation:* the extent to which the summarizer used an appropriate macro-level rhetorical–conceptual framework to reformulate source-text propositional content and thus produce a tighter, more coherent, reader-based version of the source text. Each of these criteria was scored on a 0 to 6 scale, allowing for a maximal total score of 24.

Process Data

Initial analysis of the process data was carried out using the general framework of Sarig's recursive–interactive text processing model (1991, in press). This model consists of three major operations: planning, operating, and assessing. While planning, learners set goals and select strategies. Planning occurs at all times—prior to, following, and occasionally, even while assessing and operating. Planning products are monitored by the planning system and carried out by the operating system.

The assessing system evaluates content, linguistic, textual, and strategic resources, as well as processes and products. It is responsible for detecting and diagnosing errors in the resources the learners use, in the processes they undergo, and in the products they create. When errors are detected and diagnosed, the learners return to the planning system, which will produce revised goals and strategies, and then to the operating system, which will carry the plans out. If no errors are detected, the assessing system will give a green light for the next move. The learners will now turn to the planning system, to plan the next move.

As with planning and assessing, the operating system draws on the learner's linguistic, textual, and conceptual resources in order to perform the approved plans. It either performs corrective plans related to a former faulty product or produces a new one. Demonstration and further explanation of this process appears in the next section.

RESULTS AND DISCUSSION

First Research Question

The first research question was as follows: What operations are involved in the composing of a study–summary? To answer this question I will first present the qualitative data and then some quantitative data related to the major categories.

The Study–Summary Model—Qualitative Data

Figure 1 presents a static schematic view of the processes involved in composing a study–summary.

FIGURE 1   The Recursive–Corrective Processes of Composing a Study–Summary

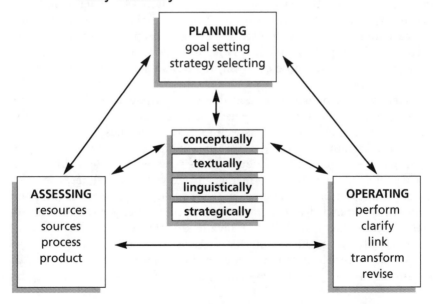

As the configuration shows, composing a study–summary is a highly interactive process, cyclic in nature. Amram employed a variety of strategies to move from planning to operating to assessing, from assessing to operating to planning, and from operating to assessing to planning. In planning, Amram set goals and selected strategies to attain them. Sometimes prior to and at other times after carrying his plans out, Amram assessed various aspects of his task performance. He assessed the relevancy of the prior knowledge he activated to make sense of the source text ("This is a paradigmatic shift. But he doesn't use this term here, so I won't write this"). He assessed his linguistic and strategic knowledge ("I'm not sure I can say what *cataclystic* means just from the sentence. I'll look it up"). Amram commented on the reliability, accuracy, and interest of the source texts ("Funny claim. I don't agree with him here"). He detected and diagnosed linguistic, textual, and conceptual errors ("I didn't say I'm enumerating the reasons here, so I'll add 'and these are the reasons why'" . . ."It sounds funny. I'll change it to . . ."; . . ."It's not fashion he's dealing with here. It's fashion *as an instance* of a cultural custom"). In doing so, Amram accepted or rejected goals and strategies, moving on or changing actions ("Aha. That's O.K"..."No. I'll first re-read this again..."). Comprehension or transformation products were also under constant monitoring ("I don't get this. What the heck does he say here?". . ."No. I can't give up this explanation. I'll add it").

Amram's operating system *performed, clarified, linked, transformed,* and *revised.* Once a miscomprehension or an error in comprehension was detected, Amram engaged in different types of substitution moves in order to clarify unknown words, concepts, ideas, or complex syntactic structures ("So . . . citizens are enslaved by the state . . . completely depend on it"). He linked propositional material both textually and conceptually, often transforming original material rhetorically and sometimes conceptually, by deleting, adding, collapsing, retaining, and reconceptualizing ("So first he criticizes and then he offers a plan for change . . ."; . . ."The sense of power manifests itself on two levels (a) . . . (b) . . ." etc.).

Finally, once products were evaluated as erroneous by the assessing system, Amram also set out to revise them. He engaged in linguistic, textual, and conceptual revisions, as well as in strategic ones.

Thus, Amram displayed the workings of a close-knit, interwoven processing system consisting of networks of schemata: content, linguistic, textual, and strategic. A strong metacognitive system coordinates the harmonious interaction among these networks. Drawing on sets of rules and networks of knowledge, the monitoring system selects goals and strategies to attain them, mobilizes relevant knowledge, and carries out its decisions, always on the lookout for erroneous decisions and products.

What cognitive operations underlie the reader/writer's reflective reasoning behavior? Figure 2 presents the full taxonomy of operations involved in composing a study–summary that resulted from the analysis of the protocols.

FIGURE 2   A Taxonomy of the Study–Summary Composing Processes

PLANNING

1. Goal Setting
2. Strategy Selecting

ASSESSING

1. Resources evaluation:
   a. Relevancy of knowledge of the world to text
   b. Quality of prior knowledge vis-a-vis the source text
2. Source:
   a. Text reliability: Is it reliable in terms of the facts it presents?
   b. Text interest: Do I find this text interesting?
   c. Text accuracy: Is the text accurate and specific enough in terms of my prior knowledge?
   d. Text contribution: Can I learn something new from this text?
   e. Text difficulty level: Do I find this text difficult?
3. Process evaluation:
   a. Goal
   b. Strategy realizing goal
4. Product evaluation and error diagnosis:
   a. Linguistic:
      i) Phonemic decoding: Have I decoded the word appropriately in terms of the immediate context?
      ii) Phrasing effectiveness: Have I phrased my ideas precisely as I understand them?
      iii) Logic of syntactic structure: Can the syntactic structure I used be taken as ambiguous?
   b. Textual:
      i) Phrasing, rephrasing: Does what I phrased/rephrased link well with what I wrote earlier?
      ii) Transformation: Is the textual transformation I performed appropriate/precise/logical in terms of my goal?
      iii) Revision: Is my revision effective in terms of the textual error diagnosed?
   c. Conceptual:
      i) Comprehension: Did I get this right?
      ii) Transformation: Let me try and get this better.
      iii) Guessed prediction: Is what I have guessed compatible with later sections in the text?

FIGURE 2   Continued

OPERATING

1. Perform
   a. Read, reread
   b. Write, rewrite
   c. Look up word
   d. Scan: detail, idea comment, lost example
   e. Skim
   f. Say repeatedly
   g. Copy
   h. Write out: Underline, mark
2. Clarify:
   a. Lexically: Decode denotations and conceptual meaning
   b. Conceptually: Clarify and pinpoint propositional content
3. Link:
   a. Textually: Relate discontinuous surface text materials by means of
      cohesion markers:
      i)   Relate anaphora to antecedent
      ii) Identify rhetorical linkage among textual segments using overt
           coherence cues
      iii) Predict text development on the basis of rhetorical conventions
      iv) Reproduce rhetorical text development
   b. Conceptually: Relate concepts using references and extratextual knowledge:
      i)   Relate topic to comment
      ii) Relate comment to commentator
      iii) Detect and resolve conceptual contradictions
      iv) Identify topic of discourse: Identify conceptual and textual
           redundancies—relate conceptually intersecting propositions
      v)   Predict text development and guess unknown content on the basis
           of logical expectations
      vi) Reproduce conceptual text development
      vii) Relate relevant knowledge of the world to the text
4. Transform: Produce a new version of the intertext relating to source and
   target text:
   a. Linguistically: Provide sequential substitutes for former intertext
      material, retaining original text organization
      i)   Lexically: Substitute present version with a lexically simpler, lower-
           register one
      ii) Syntactically: Substitute more complex present version with a
           syntactically simpler one
   b. Rhetorically illocutionally: Replace existing by a linear, sequential
      rhetorical intent paraphrase
   c. Conceptually: Change source text, intertext, and target text
      quantitatively and/or qualitatively.
      i)   Delete redundancies, trivia, supporting, elaborative qualifying material

FIGURE 2   Continued

    ii) Add and refine:
        (1) qualify; hedge
        (2) elaborate, specify
   iii) Collapse: Find a generic category to substitute included members
   iv) Reconceptualize:
        (1) qualitatively change the conceptual structure of the text: focus
            on conceptual distinction
        (2) use a similarity principle as a starting point for target text
            construction
        (3) re-arrange text by hidden topic of discourse
        (4) Re-arrange rhetorically using a rhetorical structure different
            from the one used in the text

5. Revise: Apply transformation to already performed processes and product, so as to correct a detected and at times diagnosed error:

  a. Linguistically:
    i)   Replace inappropriate lexical item
    ii) Change inappropriate register
   iii) Correct grammatical errors
   iv) Rephrase using a syntactic structure more appropriate than the former one

  b. Conceptually:
    i)   Delete:
        (1) redundancies unidentified earlier
        (2) trivia unidentified earlier
    ii) Add and refine:
        (1) qualify and hedge;
        (2) elaborate and specify;
        (3) restore erroneously deleted claim
        (4) textualize: write out mental intertext you thought you
            expressed, but actually did not
   iii) Collapse: correct former collapsing
   iv) Reconceptualize:
        (1) correct former transformation rhetorically
        (2) correct propositional focus of former transformation

  c. Strategically:
    i)   Replace an ineffective goal
    ii) Replace an ineffective strategy

    The taxonomy presented in Figure 2 is not a complete theoretical model in the sense that it does not describe or predict all potential summarization moves. It describes only those moves Amram realized in his process of composing a study–summary. Investigating summarization behavior of additional learners may enable the uncovering of additional subcategories at lower levels of the taxonomy. I would hypothesize, however, that the the first-, second-, and third-level categories may remain stable.

Quantitative Analysis of Qualitative Data

Table 1 presents frequencies of the main study–summary cognitive and metacognitive operations as they relate to source text and to target text, across texts and languages.

TABLE 1   a. Distribution of the Study–Summary Cognitive Operations Across Languages and Text-Types, and Across Languages and by Text-Types

| Category | Total | | Operations Related to | | | |
| | | | Source Text | | Target Text | |
	f	%	f	%	f	%
Plan	187	29	128	31	59	27
Assess	156	25	89	22	67	30
Transform	100	16	86	21	14	6
Revise	67	11	5	1	62	28
Link	65	11	54	13	11	5
Clarify	57	9	49	12	8	4
Total	632	100	411	100	221	100
% of Total	100		65		35	

TABLE 1   b. Bar Representation: Distribution of the Study–Summary Cognitive Operations Across Languages and Text-Types, and Across Languages and by Text-Types

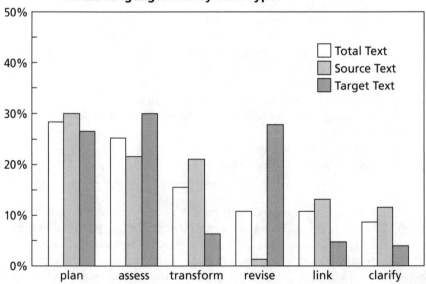

The data presented in Table 1 show that on the whole, activities related to the source text (411 moves, which are 65% of all moves) outweighed those related to the target text (221 moves, 35% of all moves). Metacognitive activities (29% planning, 25% assessing) account for over half of the overall cognitive activity (deducting the physical acts of reading, rereading, writing, rewriting, looking up a word, etc.). Next in relative weight were moves specifically related to source text reduction and reconceptualization: transforming (16%) and linking (11%), as well as revising (11%). Last in weight were clarifying moves, which constituted only 9% of total moves.

When classifying overall activity by source text and target text separately, differences arise with regard to the text Amram *read,* as opposed to the text he wrote. Metacognitive activity (i.e., planning and assessing operations) was still a predominant activity with regard to both source text (53%) and target text (57%)—planning and assessing combined. However, planning was the most important activity with regard to source text (31%), while assessing (30%) was most important with regard to target text activity. As for the other activities, transforming was a major category with regard to source text activities (21%), as compared to only 6% for target text activities, while revising was the second major category with regard to target text activities (28%), as compared with source text activities (1%). It appears then that for Amram, composing a study–summary is a highly metacognitively monitored activity, in the course of which goals and strategies get accepted, rejected, and replaced. Guided by these plans, Amram invested two-thirds of his efforts in activities related to the source text: He planned, assessed, transformed, clarified, and linked. A third of his efforts were invested in target text activities. Here he divided his efforts between assessing and planning on the one hand and—probably as a result—revising on the other. So as a summary composer, Amram is more of what traditionally would be considered a *reader* than a writer. This tendency manifests itself in the quality of his read or comprehended products, as opposed to his written products.

Table 2 presents product-evaluation scores. Each dimension is scored on a scale of 0 to 6, with a maximum score of 24.

The data in Table 2 show Amram to be a moderately successful study-summary composer (M = 17.5, i.e., 73% success). When one studies the scores of each evaluation dimension separately, the process data seem to be confirmed: These product evaluation data also show how Amram allocated two-thirds of his mental effort to source-text activities, and only a third to target-text activities. His scores on the dimension more related to the source-text end of the summarizing continuum—propositional comprehension (m = 6)—show him to be a proficient reader. He was also able to reduce the text quantitatively rather well (m = 5).

However, with regard to the operations more related to the target-text end of the summarizing continuum—reconceptualization—Amram did

TABLE 2 Summary Evaluation Scores

Text and language	Total score	Propositional comprehension	Linguistic realization	Quantitative reduction	Reconceptualization
# 1 E	20	6	4	6	4
# 2 E	17	5	4	6	2
# 3 E	16	6	4	4	2
# 4 E	18	6	6	4	2
# 5 E	13	5	4	4	0
# 7 E	17	5	6	4	2
# 9 E	18	6	4	6	2
# 11 E	23	6	6	6	5
Mean for the English Texts	18	6	5	5	2
# 6 H	18	5	4	6	3
# 8 H	15	6	4	4	1
# 10 H	17	6	6	4	1
# 12 H	17	6	4	6	1
# 13 H	19	6	6	4	3
Mean for the Hebrew Texts	17	6	5	5	2
Mean across languages	17.5	6	5	5	2

E = English   H = Hebrew   Maximal score: 24

less well. In reconceptualizing, learners create a novel, high-level conceptual structure from discrete source text materials. To do so, learners must be able "to get away" from the concrete, discrete, and specific manifestations of knowledge in the source text. They must create a tight conceptual representation of the underlying logical structure of these discrete idea units. Using this novel structure, they will be able to transform source text material into a new and independent coherent whole.

Amram's reconceptualization achievements leave a lot to be desired: His average score is only 2. Low-level process data[2] related to his transformation activities may support this result: These data show that while composing, only 81 moves (13% of the overall activity) were invested in

---

[2]The data referred to in this comment are third-level data in the taxonomy and are not presented here.

conceptual transformation (i.e., in reconceptualizing the source text). Of these, 54 (two-thirds of the overall reconceptualization moves) were related to the source text, rather than to the target text.

These results are in line with a growing number of studies of various operations involved in summarization. These studies show that while summarization deletion and selection (Kintsch & Van Dijk, 1978) operations are relatively easy to internalize and activate, construction (which necessitates some degree of reconceptualization) is the toughest nut to crack (Day, 1986; Garner, 1985; Hidi, 1984; Hidi & Anderson, 1986; Johnson, 1983; Johns, 1985).

What can we make of the fact that Amram, a learner high on linguistic proficiency and content schemata, functioned below his cognitive level when reconceptualization was concerned? This study did not set out to investigate this question. However, several possible explanations, separately and together, may be relevant here:[3] (1) a deficit in relevant procedural knowledge; and, consequently, (2) a faulty task representation; (3) a gap between process and product; (4) a developmental-acquisition gap; and (5) insufficient or inadequate explicit teaching. Let us look into each of these possibilities separately.

The first explanation is related to the quality of learners' theoretical knowledge regarding the desired specifications of the text they are aiming at. This aspect of literacy may explain why although Amram showed a most pronounced metacognitive planning and assessing behavior, his goals may not have been sufficiently focused on reconceptualization. Sarig's model (in press) highlights the relation between learners' procedural knowledge and their ability to use learning–promoting strategies effectively. The model predicts that learners will be able to assess the quality of their own texts efficiently only if their criteria for assessment are based on explicit theoretical knowledge regarding the standards for an adequate, effective text (e.g., "A good topic sentence is a generalization that can be fully specified within the limits of the paragraph"; "A considerate text must be explicit in terms of the background knowledge of its intended audience," etc.). It is only when the planning and assessing systems are "equipped" with such relevant sets of criteria with which to perform knowledgeable planning and assessing that effective processing can come about.

The Sarig & Folman (1990) study supports this model. This study shows how induced metacognitive awareness alone would not improve coherence production in the summaries of expert learners; it was only explicit instruction in what coherence is all about that improved coherence production. Similarly, revision research has shown how revisions will be effective only when carried out after careful and knowledgeable diagnosis (Flower, et al., 1986; MacCutchen, Hull & Smith, 1987). It is

---

[3]I am indebted to Joan Carson for her valuable comments in this respect.

thus possible that Amram's planning and assessing systems have not yet fully developed the explicit criteria that will enable him to diagnose a need for reconceptualization.

The second possible explanation for Amram's low level of reconceptualization is directly related to this deficit in theoretical knowledge. Recent research into writing-to-learn tasks shows that learners' lack of success in academic tasks can be related to an underdeveloped or inadequate *task representation*, i.e., how learners envision what it is they are actually supposed to do in carrying out a given learning task (Flower, 1987; Green, 1991; Prior, 1991). Like other immature learners, it is possible that Amram, too, did not yet finish constructing an adequate task representation for the study–summary task. He was not yet fully aware of the crucial role of reconceptualization in constructing a good study–summary.

The third possible explanation comes from recent research into the multisource discourse synthesis task (which is a complex study-summarizing task). These studies show that immature learners fail to fulfill their effective synthesizing plans. Thus there is a gap between intention, as it emerges in the "intertext," and the actual target text. (See Stein, 1989; Peck, 1989; Sarig 1991.) This gap may partially explain Amram's failure: It is possible that Amram did not transfer his reconceptualizations from his intertext to his target text.

The next two possible explanations for Amram's difficulty to reconceptualize are related to the literacy nature-versus-nurture controversy. On one hand, it is possible that reconceptualization ability does not come naturally to learners, even when they are otherwise successful. Within this view of literacy acquisition, it is possible that even learners with the right mental repertoire, such as Amram, need to be explicitly taught to internalize and activate first-rate literacy skills. However, it is possible to reject this explanation on the grounds that like other literacy skills, reconceptualization too can be acquired naturally, given time and exposure to high-quality models of performance. If this approach to the development of literacy is adopted, it is possible to hypothesize that the reconceptualization skill develops late in learners' academic lives and that, given time and a real need to "freeze" knowledge for yet unknown future use, Amram may overcome his difficulty.

In sum, the following factors may be related, separately or interactively, to Amram's low level of reconceptualization: (1) a deficit in relevant procedural knowledge; and, therefore, (2) a faulty task representation; (3) a gap between process and product; (4) a developmental gap; and (5) insufficient or inadequate explicit teaching.

In light of the summarizing–comprehending–writing controversy, another interesting question presents itself: Is reconceptualization a reading or a writing procedure? The findings of this study seem to suggest it is *both*. For Amram, however, conceptual transformation appeared to be more of a reading-related activity than a writing-related one. This is so, because as a study–summarizer, Amram was more of a reader than a writer. However, in principle, there is no theoretical justification for viewing conceptual transformations as chiefly a reading-related function.

To sum up the answer to the first research question, for the subject in this case study, composing a study–summary was an interactive writing endeavor with considerably more work done on comprehension than on writing. Both of these reading and writing activities were closely metacognitively monitored, as the composer planned and assessed his moves. When reading, apart from monitoring, *transforming* was the most important category, followed by moderate linking, revising, and clarifying. When writing, apart from monitoring, *revising* was the most important activity, followed by low-intensity transforming, linking, and clarifying. With regard to product quality, a truly literate, epistemological summary—one constructed on the basis of a reconceptualization of the source text—did not seem to come naturally, even to a gifted student such as Amram. It appeared that highly developed linguistic skills, coupled with sound background knowledge, could produce a study–summary of only mediocre quality. To achieve a high-quality summary, one that not only condenses the source text but also transforms the knowledge inherent in it so that it can effectively suspend knowledge for future use, having "the right qualifications" was not enough.

The Second Research Question

The second research question was as follows: How do study-summarizing processes and products in the first and in a foreign language compare? Table 3 presents data related to this question.

To achieve a Pearson Product Moment Correlation value, 12 percentile values of planning, assessing, clarifying, linking, transforming, and revising were used (with regard to source text and target text activities separately). The Pearson Product Moment Correlation value calculated on these data was $r = .74$, significant at the .001 level. This correlation shows that as far as a student with high linguistic ability is concerned, the processes of composing a study–summary from L1 and L2 texts were related to a considerable extent.

Did the relative weights of each of the cognitive categories in the summary-composing process vary cross-linguistically? When data from source text and target text activities were combined, metacognitive activities (planning and assessing) took the lead in composing from both English (56%) and Hebrew (52%) texts. The interlinguistic differences concerned the other categories. While linking (13%) and transforming (13%) were second in importance in composing from English texts, transforming (19%) and revising (15%) came second and third in composing from Hebrew texts. While linking was second in importance in English

TABLE 3 a. Distribution of Study–Summary Cognitive Operations: A Cross-Linguistic Comparison by and Across Text Types

| | Total | | | | Source Text | | | | Target Text | | | |
| | E | | H | | E | | H | | E | | H | |
Category	f	%	f	%	f	%	f	%	f	%	f	%
Plan	101	29	86	30	60	17	68	23	41	12	18	6
Assess	91	27	64	22	51	15	37	13	40	12	27	9
Clarify	37	11	21	7	28	8	21	7	8	2	0	0
Link	46	13	20	7	36	10	18	6	10	3	2	0
Transform	45	13	54	19	32	9	54	19	13	4	0	0
Revise	23	7	44	15	1	0	4	1	22	6	40	14
Total	343		289									

E = English   H = Hebrew
Pearson Product Moment correlation based on percentile values: r = .74   p < .001

TABLE 3 b. Bar Representation: Distribution of Study–Summary Cognitive Operations: A Cross-Linguistic Comparison by and Across Text-Types

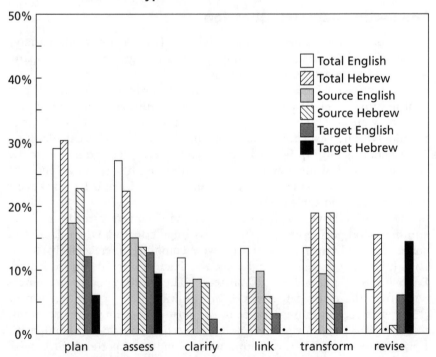

(13%), it was of considerably less importance in Hebrew (7%), after both transforming and revising.

When studying the data for source and target text activities separately, more differences became apparent. Concerning source text activities, the most important categories in composing from English texts were planning (17%) and assessing (15%), followed by linking (10%), transforming (9%), and clarifying (8%). In composing from Hebrew texts, the most important categories were planning (23%) and transforming (19%), followed by assessing (13%), clarifying (7%), and linking (6%). Revising was of minor or no importance in composing from both languages.

Differences become more pronounced when data related to target text activities were concerned. In composing from English texts, activities were observed in all categories. In composing from Hebrew texts, however, activities were noted only in revising, assessing, and planning.

Although these differences were not too dramatic, they should not be ignored. The differences ranging from a low 1% (source text revising) to a maximum of 10% (source text transforming) may be attributed to both slight cross-linguistic cognitive behavior variations and/or variations in text challenge level.

It is quite interesting and perhaps significant that the most dramatic difference appeared in the most problematic of all categories—transforming (9% as compared with 19%; see ST data). If not accidental, this difference may suggest that cognitive challenges became more demanding when the learner faced a text in a foreign language. A part of the process of composing from L1 was shown to differ from the process of composing from L2 texts; perhaps the cognitive load related to language problems blocked some of the learner's resources, which he otherwise would have invested in transforming. Another explanation, perhaps interacting with the first, may be that for cross-linguistic transfer of cognitive skills to take place, the learner must first achieve complete mastery of the skill to be transferred. As shown, this was not the case with regard to transforming in the L1.

How did summarizing achievement compare cross-linguistically? The data presented in Table 2 show that Amram's achievements, both total and along the separate evaluation dimensions, were almost identical when summarizing from English and Hebrew texts. His products resulting from Hebrew and English texts showed the same strengths and weaknesses, indicating a strong procedural transfer from L1 to L2.

To sum up the answer to the second research question, summarizing from L1 texts and L2 texts appeared to be related to a considerable extent. The .74 (p < .001) correlation between the processes involved in summarizing from L1 texts and L2 texts indicates a transfer of these skills from the first to the foreign language. The main difference, though minor in intensity, lay in transforming. This skill, which was problematic even in the L1, was applied even less in L2. As to product quality, there appeared to be an almost perfect parity between achievement in composing from L1 and L2 texts. These results are in line with Sarig's study (1987) showing transfer of reading skills and reading profile from L1 to L2, even when low- and medium-language-proficiency learners are concerned.

GENERALIZABILITY, FUTURE RESEARCH AND IMPLICATIONS

The case study reported here dealt with the processes that a good, though not expert, learner engaged in when summarizing texts in his domain of interest. In keeping with findings emphasizing inter-individual differences in high-level reading processes (Sarig, 1987), the results presented here should not be taken to represent the composing process of all highly qualified learners. More data concerning additional subjects should be collected in order to ascertain the parameters along which summarizers differ cognitively. It is recommended that the general outline of the taxonomy presented here be used for the diagnosis of other summarizing profiles. However, these differences are likely to emerge in the third- and fourth-level categories as opposed to the first- and second-level categories of the model. Inter-individual differences may also be related to the relative weight of each high-level category in the overall process.

Thus, the taxonomy offered here can be further applied to diagnose and compare summarizing profiles of learners varying in linguistic and domain–schemata proficiency, age, and motivation. Another line of research worth looking into is the relation between the relative weights of the cognitive categories and various textual properties.

Despite the limitations inherent in a case study such as this, one pedagogical implication is evident. It probably concerns most of the novice students in the EFL classroom, including those high in language proficiency. The data on Amram show how difficult it is, even for gifted learners, to reconceptualize source text material. Perhaps this is the result of years of instructing our learners that the essence of a good summary is lifting main ideas from the text. Learning to discard redundant and trivial material from source texts seems to have been a major goal in our classrooms. In most cases, this teaching goal seems to have been successfully achieved. We should now make *reconceptualization* our major "aggressive" teaching goal. Because explicit teaching in various aspects of text processing has been found to be successful (Ambruster, Anderson, & Ostertag, 1987; Berkowitz, 1986; Duffy, 1986; Fitzgerald & Teasley, 1986; Rahman & Bisanz, 1986; Raphael & Wonnacott, 1985; Reinhart, Stahl, & Erickson, 1986), and concentrating teaching efforts on this skill is recommended.

Learners' awareness of the goals and sets of criteria with which to evaluate performance has been found to be related to successful performances in text processing (Elliot-Faust & Pressley, 1986; Sarig & Folman,

1990). Summarization instruction therefore must start with explicit demonstration of what a good study–summary is and what part reconceptualization plays in making it good. Next, teachers can develop materials that first expose the learners to conceptual structures, and then offer raw materials to be transformed on the basis of these structures. Once the art of reconceptualization has been mastered, teachers should assign free, but explicit, reconceptualization tasks, starting with low-challenge texts and proceeding to challenging ones.

CONCLUSION

In sum, several conclusions about the nature of the study-summarizing composing process arise from this case study. First, it is a highly intricate process, combining metacognitive activity with *clarify, link, transform,* and *revise* activities. Next, reconceptualization appears to be a cognitive literacy challenge for even a highly qualified learner: Of all the operations involved in study–summarizing, reconceptualization alone did not come naturally to the learner and may need to be explicitly taught. Because reconceptualization did not come easily to Amran, it was therefore not an active part of the criteria that even a metacognitively active learner applies when planning and assessing summarizing behavior.

Finally, processes and products of summarization from L1 texts are closely related to those of summarization from L2 texts, at least when a highly proficient language learner is concerned. The main inter-lingual differences lie with conceptual transformation activities, which are still of a considerable challenge in L1 processing.

Thus it would seem worthwhile not only to turn conceptual transformation into a first-priority teaching goal, but also to invest explicit instruction efforts to achieve it. It is conceptual transformation that is the hard core of the summarizing activity as an epistemological literacy act. In directing resources to fostering it in our learners, we enable them to successfully "freeze" knowledge for future use.

REFERENCES

Ambruster, B.B., Anderson, T.H., & Ostertag, J. (1987). Does structure/ summarization instruction facilitate learning from expository text? *Reading Research Quarterly, 22,* 331–347.

Bereiter, K. & Scardamalia, M. (1987). *The Psychology of Written Composition.* Hillsdale, NJ: Erlbaum.

Berkowitz, S.J. (1986). Effects of instruction in text organization on sixth–grade students' memory for expository reading. *Reading Research Quarterly, 21,* 161–179.

Cohen, A.D. (1987). Mentalistic measures in reading strategy research: Some recent findings. *English for Specific Purposes, 5,* 131–145.

Day, J.D. (1986). Teaching summarization skills: Influences of student ability level and strategy difficulty. *Cognition & Instruction, 3,* 193, 210.

Duffy, G.G. (1986). The relationship between explicit verbal explanations during reading skill instruction and student awareness and achievement: A study of reading teacher effect. *Reading Research Quarterly, 21,* 237–255.

Elliot-Faust, D.J. & Pressley, M. (1986). How to teach comparison processing to increase children's short- and long-term listening comprehension monitoring. *Journal of Educational Psychology, 78,* 27-33.

Ericsson, K.H. & Simon, H.A. (1980). Verbal reports as data. *Psychological Review, 87,* 215–292.

Fitzgerald, J. & Teasley, A. (1986). Effects of instruction in narrative structure on children's writing. *Journal of Educational Psychology, 78,* 422–432.

Flower, L. (1987). The role of task representation in reading-to-write. Technical Report No. 6 (Reading-to-Write Report No. 2), Center for the Study of Writing at the University of California, Berkeley, and at Carnegie-Mellon University, Pittsburgh.

Flower, L. & Hayes. J.R. (1984). Images, Plans and Prose: The representation of meaning in writing. *Written Communication, 1,* 120–160.

Flower, L., Hayes, J.R., Carey, L., Schriver, K., & Stratman, J. (1986). Detection, diagnosis and strategies of revision. *College Communication and Composition, 37,* 16–56.

Garner, R. (1985). Text summarization deficiencies among older students: Awareness of production ability. *American Educational Research Journal, 22,* 549–560.

Garner, R. & McCaleb, J.L. (1985). Effects of text manipulations on the quality of written summaries. *Contemporary Educational Psychology, 10,* 139–149.

Green, S. (1991). Writing from sources: Authority in text and task. Technical Report, Center for the Study of Writing at the University of California, Berkeley, and at Carnegie-Mellon University, Pittsburgh.

Hidi, S. (1984). Summarization of complex texts (Occasional Paper #4). Toronto: Ontario Institute for Studies in Education, Center for Applied Cognitive Science.

Hidi, S. & Anderson, V. (1986). Producing written summaries: Task demands, cognitive operations and implications for instruction. *Review of Educational Research, 56,* 473–493.

Johns, A.M. (1988). He's illiterate! Paper presented at the colloquium on the interactive relationship of reading and writing. TESOL convention, March, Chicago.

Johns, A.M. (1985). Summary protocols of "underprepared" and "adept" university students: Replications and distortions of the original. *Language Learning, 35,* 495–517.

Johnson, N. (1983). What do you do if you can't tell the whole story? The development of summarization skills. In K.E. Nelson (Ed.), *Children's language,* Vol. 4 (pp. 315–383). Hillsdale, NJ: Erlbaum.

Kennedy, M.L. (1985). The composing process of college students writing from sources. *Written Communication, 2,* 434–455.

Kintsch, W. & Van Dijk, T.A. (1978). Toward a model of text comprehension and production. *Psychological Review, 85,* 363–394.

Kuzminsky, E. & Graetz, N. (1986). First versus second language comprehension. *Journal of Reading Research, 9,* 3–21.

MacCutchen, D., Hull, G.A., & Smith, W. (1987). Editing strategies and error correction in basic writing. *Written Communication, 4,* 139–154.

Olson, D. (1977). From utterance to text: The bias of language in speech and writing. *Harvard Educational Review, 476,* 257–281.

Peck, W. (1989). The effects of prompts upon revision: A glimpse of the gap between planning and performance. Technical Report No. 10, Technical Report No. 26 (Reading-to-Write Report No. 7). Center for the Study of Writing at the University of California, Berkeley, and at Carnegie-Mellon University, Pittsburgh.

Prior, P. (1991). Contextualizing writing and response in a graduate seminar. *Written Communication, 8,* 267–311.

Rahman, T. & Bisanz, G.L. (1986). Reading ability and the use of a story schema in recalling and reconstructing information. *Journal of Educational Psychology, 78,* 323–333.

Raphael, T.E. & Wonnacott, C.A. (1985). Heightening fourth-grade students' sensitivity to sources of information for answering comprehension questions. *Reading Research Quarterly, 20,* 282–296.

Reinhart, S.D., Stahl, S., & Erickson, L.G. (1986). Some effects of summarization training on reading and studying. *Reading Research Quarterly, 21,* 422–429.

Sarig, G. (In press). Comprehension-promoting strategies: The sum of the parts and the whole. *Communication & Cognition.*

Sarig, G. (1991). Learning-promoting strategies in composing a discourse synthesis. Paper read at the 1991 conference of CCC&C, March, Boston.

Sarig, G. (1989). The use of mentalistic measures for the application of individual principles in fostering high-level reading skills. *Education and Its Surrounding, 11,* 61–75 (in Hebrew).

Sarig, G. (1987). High-level reading tasks in the first and in a foreign language: Some comparative process data. In J. Devine, P. Carrell, & D. Eskey (Eds.), *Research in reading in a second language* (pp. 105–123). Washington, DC: TESOL.

Sarig, G. & Folman, S. (1990). Metacognitive awareness and theoretical knowledge in coherence production. In M. Spoelders (Ed.), *Literacy acquisition* (pp. 195–273). Lier, Belgium: J. Van In.

Stein, V. (1989). Elaborating: Using what you know. Technical Report No. 25 (Reading-to-Write Report No. 6). Center for the Study of Writing at the University of California, Berkeley, and at Carnegie-Mellon University, Pittsburgh.

Taylor, K.K. (1986). Summary writing by young children. *Reading Research Quarterly, 21,* 193–209.

Vygotsky, L. (1962). *Thought and language.* Cambridge, MA: MIT Press.

Widdowson, H. (1983). New starts and different kinds of failure. In A. Freedman & J. Yalden (Eds.), *Learning to write: First language/second language research* (pp. 34–47). New York: Longman.

Winograd, P. (1984). Strategic difficulties in summarizing text. *Reading Research Quarterly, 19,* 405–425.

CHAPTER 9

Student Meets Text, Text Meets Student: Finding a Way into Academic Discourse

Ruth Spack
Tufts University

Many composition instructors are faced with the challenge of teaching undergraduate second language students who are novices in the college setting and who are assigned to take one or two composition courses to fulfill graduation requirement. The instructors' goal is usually twofold: to guide students toward becoming fluent in written English and to introduce them to some of the rigors and conventions of academic writing.

Yet academic writing means different things to different people (Spack, 1988), and this phenomenon makes it difficult for composition instructors to determine what kinds of reading and writing tasks first-year college students should be assigned in their composition courses. The type of writing assigned can range from autobiographical essays to discipline-specific reports. Reading assignments also vary widely. Some composition text books offer no readings at all, while others include lengthy text book chapters and scholarly articles representing several fields across the curriculum.

These wide-ranging approaches to composition instruction grow out of differing views about how expertise in writing is achieved, with one end of the continuum emphasizing *general* knowledge and the other emphasizing *local* knowledge (Carter, 1990). At one end, students learn general strategies that can be applied to almost any composing process; at the other, they learn conventions that are shared by members of specific disciplines. Basing his argument on the findings of research on the role of knowledge, Carter challenges this dichotomy, pointing out that "performance is a complex interaction of general and local knowledge" (1990, p. 271). The continuum is developmental: The journey from novice to expert involves the acquisition of increasingly sophisticated frameworks of knowledge about composing. It is also recursive: "experts turn to relatively general strategies when they are faced with unusual problems in their field" (p. 270). Composition instruction, then, must first aid students in the acquisition of general knowledge about writing and then move them back and forth along the continuum to grow as writers as they build enough local knowledge to enable them to perform effectively. Students' writing ability will continue to mature as they are influenced by numerous classroom experiences within and outside of their declared majors. Mastery of the conventions of a specific discipline will come only through immersion in that field.

Yet some second language composition specialists argue that students whose native language is not English are special cases who need primarily local knowledge to succeed in an English-speaking environment. And these students, according to this view, must master discipline-specific formats and adopt the impersonal, detached stance of published scholars if they are to become accepted members of the academic discourse community. They are to be told that "the academic writer's task is not to create personal meaning, but to find, organize, and present data according to fairly explicit instructions" (Horowitz, 1986, p. 455). But this find–organize–present model is problematic and can be misleading, as demonstrated by the following actual classroom scene:

> Mark Dehaan is Dutch, but in crisp, correct—and somewhat indignant— English, [he] is complaining to his history teacher about an exam on Napoleon. "You want opinions!" Mark says. "We could give you all the facts and dates and battles you'd ever need, but you ask opinions!"
>
> History teacher Frank McGurk responds . . .: "You must make up your minds. Was Napoleon a hero or not? I'm going to judge you on how you *use* the information you've learned." (Mapes, 1990, p. 1)

As the above scene reveals, academic reading and writing do not necessarily demand only finding, organizing, and presenting information. More often, they are complex processes of actively engaging with and then revealing insight into course material, of learning and then *using* the information learned, of thinking things through. Students need general problem-solving strategies that allow them the flexibility to interpret content in relation to purpose if they are to succeed as academic writers (Rosebery *et al.*, 1989).

Discourse community theory is questionable, too, when proponents mistake "the pose of objectivity" in a text for "an absence of personal commitment in the creation of text" (Spellmeyer, 1989, p. 269). Spellmeyer argues that it is "both dishonest and disabling" to give students the impression that "writing, no matter how formal or abstract, is not created by persons" (p. 269). What is personal is that it is written by someone, a real person, out of that person's "lived experience." Lived experience, Spellmeyer reminds us, consists of the social, intellectual, historical, and institutional contexts that academic writers draw from to discuss issues, events, data, and texts.

Swales (1987) brought this phenomenon to the attention of second language specialists in a report on a sociological study of scientists who were participating in a laboratory study of potato protein. These scientists spent many months working in the lab, making rough notes and drafting and revising a paper. They were personally involved in their project, exhibiting an "early exuberance" that was later toned down to a "careful statement" of their work in a final, formal, publishable manuscript (p. 49).

The significant point to glean from this example is that if we limit our examination of academic writing to the products of professional academic writers, the "careful statement[s]," we limit our understanding of the essential nature of composing in the academy. Academic writing is not detached and impersonal, as some of its products suggest. Rather, it is an engaging and personal—sometimes exuberant—process of seeking knowledge and understanding. Academic writing presupposes concern, curiosity, commitment, a need to know, a need to tell.

ESTABLISHING MEDIATING LINKS BETWEEN STUDENTS AND THE ACADEMY

So where do we begin when deciding what to teach in composition courses for first-year undergraduate students? How do we prepare these students to become engaged readers and writers of various academic disciplines?

First, we need to begin at the beginning, the point of engagement, the point of "exuberance." We need to show students a *way into* academic prose, both as readers and as writers. Only then can they learn to think like the humanists, social scientists, scientists, and technologists they will become (see also Eskey, this volume, on Smith's notion of an invitation to literacy).

We should remember that first-year and even second-year students themselves are at the beginning, the beginning of an academic career. The reality is that few of our students move directly from first-year composition to become members of discipline-specific communities. Most students are simultaneously or subsequently part of a more general education; that is, they participate in core courses or introductory courses that *precede* field-specific learning (Anderson *et al.*, 1990). Susan Miller borrows Kenneth Burke's metaphor to remind us that "students in introductory classes are not yet personally invited to the 'party' at which ongoing conversations occur . . . in knowledge communities" (Anderson *et al.*, 1990, p. 29).

Our job as composition instructors of novice students is to establish mediating links to fill a gap between what students bring to the academic community and what the academic community will ultimately expect of them (Spack, 1988). Prince (1989) points out that this gap between actuality and expectation is essentially a problem of cultural literacy. Yet this is not a situation in which one group has culture and the other does not. Instead, this is a situation in which "two groups with different understandings of culture and knowledge need to be brought into contact"

(p. 735). Borrowing from David Hume, the eighteenth-century essayist and educational reformer, Prince uses the metaphor of the "ambassador" to explain the role of the teacher as a negotiator in this endeavor:

> [G]roups defined by different patterns of spoken and written interaction behave like citizens of different countries, even if they in fact occupy the same land. The metaphor [of the teacher as ambassador] implies . . . that the acquisition of . . . literacy for certain students may be tantamount to the experience of passing from one country to a very different one, and of constantly renegotiating the challenges of such border crossings. (p. 740)

This metaphor is particularly apt for ESL students, who are both literally and figuratively crossing cultural borders. Even for ESL students who are highly literate in their native language, the lack of L2 linguistic, rhetorical, and cultural knowledge can stand in the way of academic success (Spack, 1988).

In posing this metaphor of the ambassador, Prince parallels Spellmeyer's call to individual teachers to provide meaningful transitions to the most demanding varieties of academic writing by use of contexts familiar to students. As Prince says,

> Even if our eventual goal is to have students write the kinds of decontextualized, analytical essays required within most colleges, we might consider ways to invite students to reconceive such assignments as specialized transformations of more familiar modes . . . The value of such a sequence would depend upon teaching students to recognize similarities and dissimilarities between the contexts they have already mastered and those which seem more daunting. (p. 745)

Spellmeyer (1989) maintains that the essay assignment that allows students to write from their own perspectives as they examine the perspectives of others is "the common ground" between the individual and the academy. In writing such an essay, students make a "first step in . . . progress toward work that is more complex intellectually [and] more self-conscious stylistically" (p. 274). Prince, like Bartholomae & Petrosky (1986), advocates a syllabus that creates a sequence of assignments in which the instructor moves students from informal to more formal contexts, teaching the unfamiliar by way of the familiar, and fostering students' success stage by stage. Recursive as well as sequential, such a syllabus builds on and adds to students' uses of language.

DEVISING A SEQUENTIAL, RECURSIVE SYLLABUS BASED ON READING AND WRITING

One way we can help second language learners to become academic writers is by bringing them to the point at which they can write from and about written texts and gathered data. In writing from course readings or from researched sources, students draw on knowledge gained from numerous sources. They *think through* a subject as they read and reflect on the perspectives of authorities in a given field. By including references to these authorities, they reveal that they are aware of previous writing on the subject and that they are adding to that previous work. Their writing is building on a base of knowledge and thought on the subject.

The rest of this article will demonstrate the development of a sequence for an assignment in which students are asked to write from and about a written text.[1] For this assignment, which follows on the heels of an assignment to write a personal experience essay and precedes an assignment in which students analyze and synthesize material from several sources, students are to examine the relationship between ideas discussed in a course reading and what they know from experience. Students can show how the generalizations, theories, or experiences of a published writer compare with their own attitudes and experiences, or they can discuss how the writer's theories help them to make sense of their own worlds. In so doing, students are, in essence, illuminating, evaluating, or testing the truth or validity of what they have read.

Such an assignment asks students to incorporate key ideas and relevant facts from the course reading into their own essays. It also invites them to integrate their background knowledge into course material and to reinterpret their experience or the experiences represented in the text from a different perspective (Sternglass, 1986). From this unique point of view, they can bring original insights to the instructor even though the instructor is already familiar with the source (Sternglass, 1986).

To fulfill this assignment, students can choose from several essays and articles that have been read and discussed in class. The examples in the rest of this article are student responses to a research study titled "Intercultural Communication Stumbling Blocks" (Barna, 1990), the original version of which was published in the *Kentucky Speech Arts Journal*, a publication for professionals in the field of communication. In her study, Barna examines five barriers to successful cross-cultural communication: language, nonverbal signs, preconceptions and stereotypes, the tendency to evaluate, and high anxiety. She maintains that awareness of these stumbling blocks, knowledge of the values and attitudes of other cultures, and a nonjudgmental attitude can help to facilitate communication across cultures. Barna's research is based on previous writing on the subject as well as on observations of, interviews with, and the writings of non-native and native English-speaking college students in the United States. Her article includes excerpts from student writing.

---

[1]The sequence described here represents only one possible set of assignments. It is not intended to be prescriptive.

Many students need carefully structured support as they undertake tasks requiring increasingly complex analytic and critical thought. Space constraints preclude my explaining all of the reading/writing strategies students can use to prepare to write a formal essay about what they read. I will therefore briefly describe only a few strategies as examples of what can be done in the classroom to increase students' knowledge base by building on language resources students already have.

Writing Before Reading

We can aid students in approaching academic tasks by drawing on the wealth of language, culture, experience, and factual knowledge they bring with them into the classroom. One approach is to have students engage in a write-before-you-read activity (Spack, 1985), in which they write from their own experience and background knowledge about an experience or idea discussed in the work they are about to read. This can be approached as a freewriting exercise, in which students talk to themselves on paper or quickly write whatever comes into their minds about a topic. For example, the write-before-you-read activity given before students read Barna's "Intercultural Communication Stumbling Blocks" can be the following:

> Describe some difficulty you have had in making yourself understood in
> an unfamiliar culture or place, or in understanding someone or something
> from another culture or place.

Students can write in class for ten to fifteen minutes in response to this prompt and then share what they have written in small groups or with the whole class. In so doing, they informally generate much material about cross-cultural communication in preparation for reading about the subject in a formal article. This activity can stimulate interest in the reading. It also enables students to bring substantial background knowledge to the reading they are about to encounter. And this, in turn, may facilitate the reading process because "efficient comprehension requires the ability to relate the textual material to one's own knowledge" (Carrell & Eisterhold, 1983, pp. 556-557). Students can compare their own texts with the professional text and analyze similarities and differences in content and style. They can therefore develop a deeper understanding of how language can be used both to create and to comprehend a written text.

Annotating

Annotating a text is a highly individual process. Readers have different ways of summarizing and reacting to what they are reading. Some readers write notes about each paragraph; others do so about larger chunks of discourse. Some readers write a brief word or two; others write whole sentences. Some readers underline; some highlight; some circle. Some write in the margins; some write comments in a notebook. Some use a double-entry approach by separating, in left and right margins or columns, what the author is saying (summary) from what they think (reaction). Some write in English; some write in their native language. In class, students can share their varying strategies and become aware of the different possibilities. Whatever strategy they use, students should know that annotating can help them to focus on the reading task and to become actively involved in the reading, almost as if they were engaging in a dialogue with the author.

Keeping a Reading Journal

The purpose of keeping a reading journal is to allow students to explore their responses to the course readings. If they have annotated a text, they may reflect on, add to, or change their early impressions. They may write about experiences or ideas related to the reading, either those that support or those that contradict what the author has said. They may also discuss passages or specific examples from the reading that are notable—either because they like them or because they do not, or because they agree with them or do not—and they are invited to formulate questions about the reading to explore any confusion they may have. Informal journal writing thus gives students permission to question what they are reading and at the same time to question their reading of the reading. Being tentative about what they are learning is not only allowed but is encouraged.

Sometimes students write in a journal entry only that they couldn't get past the difficult vocabulary or couldn't grasp the complex concepts of the reading. For example,

> I couldn't quite understand the article on "Intercultural Communication Stumbling Blocks." The author used pretty deep vocabularies which I had some trouble to try to know the meaning. She also composed the essay very well. I think the author wrote this article intended for professors and students who has the same professing as him.

Such journal entries are instructive. Writing about reading, as Petrosky (1982) says, is one of the best ways to get students to "unravel their transactions so that we can see how they understand" (p. 24). If we see that they don't understand, we can intervene (see Leki, this volume). For some second language students, such as the writer of the above extract, vocabulary is such an overwhelming barrier that they do not allow themselves to read past the first few lines of a difficult text. They need extra help to develop strategies to overcome this block. One place to start is to assure them that even highly proficient or native language readers, including college professors, reread whole texts or parts of texts in order to understand them fully. Another recommendation is to encourage students to read first for overall meaning without trying to understand every single word.

Zamel (1992) has discovered that applying freewriting strategies to their reading (speeding up, moving forward without self-censorship) can contribute to students' development as readers.

Most students do read and grapple with even the most difficult readings, and many write lengthy responses. Here is an example of a journal in which a student reveals her struggle to understand and then her identification with the reading:

> When I read Barna's essay I found it very difficult. It is complicated and in the same simple. it is complicated since it has a lot of difficult words that make the foreign reader feels uncomfortable reading and picking up words out of the dictionary. It is easy because it discusses a subject that we (foreign students) are living each and every moment in the U.S. But, I liked the essay since it showed the true feelings and situations foreign student face in the U.S. It showed how much difficult for a foreign student to compete with American students in the university because of his/her broken English and slowliness in understanding and speaking in the same time. It showed how much embarrassment a foreign student can face if the teacher asks him a question that he/she will know, but can't find the words to express it, or to express it in a broken English that makes the class laugh at her.
>
> . . . In my last management class the professor divided the class to three groups with each a bunch of straws and a box of pins to create something with it. That project was going to be evaluated according to its strength, beauty and height. I had many ideas in my mind of what we should build, but unfortunately I did not find the words to express these ideas. At the end, I played my usual role of a watcher and agreed on what my group members choose to build. Isn't that unfair.

This student's identification with the text was so strong that she was willing and able to overcome the challenge of the vocabulary.

Agreement with the content of a text is not the only cause for students' engagement in the reading process. Sometimes students challenge or reject the author's approach or conclusions and then write journal entries arguing back. The journal assignment invites them to question what they are reading, and many students do so. For example:

> Firstly, my doubts or my uncertainty whether to accept these ideas [Barna's] as facts or fakes. She wrote, "The conversation may have confirmed his stereotype that Americans are insensitive and ethnocentric." Some examples of the Vietnamese and Japanese students' writings [reprinted in Barna's article] goes along with this idea. To tell the truth, I have never stereotyped Americans as insensitive and ethnocentric. It is only when I stepped down on this land and read some *American-written essays,* do I know this is a stereotype of Americans. But this process of knowing is not an assimilation and thus, by far, it is a stereotype (for me). What about the Japanese's or the Vietname's writings then? I assume

they don't know this as well too before they actually been here. Therefore, it is not fair to acquaint foreigners with this stereotype—as this appears to be, thru her flow of writing. She is stereotyping or making a judgement of foreigners! She is violating her own principles.

Because all these journal entries are brought to class and shared, students see that there are many possible responses to a given text. This awareness of varying interpretations provides them with "new frameworks with which to go back and read the text" (Zamel, 1992).

Summarizing the Reading

Students are asked to summarize the assigned reading, because the process of writing a summary helps them to explore their understanding of what they read. Because these summaries are brought to class and shared in small groups, students have the opportunity to discover that readers have different views of what the key ideas are. Together, they can begin to make sense of the text and discover that some details more than others are central to the meaning. Nevertheless, as the different groups compare the summaries that each group has decided upon, they again become aware that some readers attend more closely to some features in the text than others.

A summary can later be revised for inclusion in an essay about the text. This revised summary will take on two new purposes: to demonstrate the student's understanding of the reading and to establish the ideas that the essay will evaluate or analyze.

Discussing the Reading

Students bring journal entries to class, along with a summary of the reading, and discuss together in groups what they have read and their varied reactions to it. This sends them back into the text to reread and reflect on what they have learned and discovered. This process parallels the process most of us go through when we as professional academics confront new ideas or new formulations of ideas: We read, we relate what we read to what we already know, we question, we talk to colleagues. Academic discourse, as Harris (1989) has pointed out, is not limited to "the kinds of rarified talk and writing that go on at conferences and in journals"; it includes the "everyday struggles and mishaps of the talk in our classrooms and departments, with their mixings of sometimes conflicting and sometimes conjoining beliefs and purposes" (p. 20).

Analyzing the Essay Assignment and the Reading Audience

Up until this point, students have generated ideas to develop their own understanding of the subject. Now they must bring their thoughts into focus for a reader, to write an essay about the course reading in which they relate material from the reading to their own experience.

Sometimes the greatest problem students have in fulfilling assignments—in composition courses and in courses other than composition—is not a lack of knowledge of content or of language facility but a lack of understanding of the assignment and of the expectations of American academic audiences. Students can be taught to analyze the directions of the assignment and to consider both the essay's possibilities and its limitations. They can define the audience for a given assignment. Even when the audience is always the same instructor, students should consider what the instructor already knows about the topic, what the instructor wants to learn from the student, and what kind of evidence will be acceptable. Students need to learn how to make adjustments to accommodate the reader's [the instructor's] prior knowledge when they move, for example, from writing from their own experience (where they know more about the subject than the reader) to writing from course readings (where the reader knows more about the subject than the writer). They need to understand the rationale behind conventions of American academic writing such as summary, paraphrase, quotation, and citation—and they need to learn those conventions (Campbell, 1990). They also need to think about structuring their material to make it comprehensible to the reader.

Drafting the Essay

Having analyzed the writing assignment, students can then undergo a drafting process to create a paper to present for review by their classmates and instructor.

Most students write reasonably comprehensible drafts that fulfill the assignment. But as with almost anything else in teaching and composing, the aim and the result are not always an exact match. Sometimes this is fine, when students create essays so original in thought or style or format that they surpass expectations. But sometimes a student's interpretation of the assignment is not productive. This happens, for example, when a student assigned to write about a reading writes solely from experience and barely mentions the course reading or ignores it altogether. Some students may do this simply because they misunderstand the assignment. Others may do it because they are not yet ready to make the leap into more academic uses of prose. Whatever the reason, even if the personal experience essay the student produces is an effective one, it is—in the context of this sequenced syllabus—simply a repetition of the previous assignment (writing a personal essay solely from experience), and neither builds on what the student has already done nor increases the student's knowledge base. At this stage, the student needs to take a meaningful step from a personal world toward the world outside the self.

Students who do not adequately fulfill assignments may at first appear to be slow learners. But experience has shown that such students are "merely *behind,* not *slow*"; with meaningful and well-directed writing experiences, any student can develop as a writer (Nelson, 1991, p. 210). To give an example of this: In response to an assignment to examine the relationship between reading and experience, a student in a composition course I teach wrote a draft in which the only mention she made to a course reading was in her first sentence: "The Intercultural Communication Stumbling Blocks, which was written by Laray M. Barna, reminded me very much of myself when I first came to America." After that, her entire essay was a retelling of her own experiences. There was no summary, no paraphrase, no quotation from the reading, no discussion of the author's ideas. Her peer reviewers pointed out that she had not really fulfilled the assignment, and she recognized that; but she was unsure about how to proceed.

After a conference in which we scanned the reading, discussed its content, and discussed her reviewer's comments, she reread her own writing and wrote another draft. In this second draft, she began to integrate material from Barna's article into her own essay. However, her paper consisted mainly of two or three unexamined quotations or paraphrases from the reading matched by one or two examples from her own cross-cultural experiences. An excerpt from her paper, with material taken from the reading underlined, reveals the problem:

Excerpt from Pat's second draft

<u>The second problem was in the nonverbal area.</u> I remember seeing students kissing and hugging each other in public place. I was totally shocked because in my country these were the unpolite things to do. I also remember that my Algebra teacher winked at me once when he was telling a joke to his class. I became so stiffed. I did not realized he was just joking. Later, I found out that he winked at his students at least ten times a day.

This version, though a step in the right direction, did not reveal a deep understanding of the reading. Material from the reading is used simply as a way to introduce her own agenda. Once the reading is mentioned, it is ignored.

I therefore asked Pat to reread the article again and to write a third draft, using material from the reading to reinterpret her experience rather than just to introduce it. Here is an excerpt from that composition, with new sentences underlined:

Excerpt from Pat's third draft

The second problem that Barna mentions in the article is in the nonverbal area. <u>She wrote. "people from different cultures inhabit different nonverbal sensory worlds" (p. 82). A person interprets actions of other people from what he learns from his culture.</u> I remember seeing students kissing and hugging each other in the public place. I was totally shocked because in my country these were the impolite things to do. I also remember that my Algebra teacher winked at me once when he was telling a joke to his class. <u>According to my culture, his action would indicate that he wanted some kind of sexual thing with me.</u> I became stiffed. I did not realize he was just joking. Later, I found out that he winked at his students at least ten times a day. <u>This proves that Barna is so right when she says "it is possible to learn the meaning of these messages (once they are perceived)"</u> (pp. 82-83).

In this final version, Pat added fuller explanations, interpreting what the author meant and showing how the author's theories applied to her own experience and were therefore valid and true, from her perspective.

CONCLUSION

This student was offered and she accepted an invitation to find a way, through writing and discussion, to approach a complex academic reading and to come to an understanding of its personal relevance and larger implications. The process I have described, though not the only possible process, allowed her to be able to do this. Although this student may not be ready to master the conventions of a specific discipline, she has not been—and should not be—denied entry into the community of scholars.

To those who are concerned that she has not written abstract, impersonal prose or that she has not produced an essay that fits into any neat rhetorical form of discipline-specific category, I say: Don't focus on that. Focus instead on the fact that she has taken a giant step in her intellectual development and that she is ready to move on to even more complex activities. What she has done is to write an essay that reveals her ability to write from and about another text—to summarize it, to garner information from it, to clarify it, and to test its assertions against other experiences and values. This is academic writing, and we should validate it as such. Along with our colleagues in the content disciplines, we can determine what counts as knowledge in the academy. Our role as teacher-ambassadors, as Prince (1989) says, is not just to provide students access to academic culture, but also to make academic culture accessible to students and to create an academic environment that is responsive to their needs.

REFERENCES

Anderson, W., Best, C., Black, A., Hurst, J., Miller B., & Miller, S. (1990). Cross-curricular underlife: A collaborative report on ways with academic words. *College Composition and Communication, 41,* 11–36.

Barna, L.M. (1990). Intercultural communication stumbling blocks. In R. Spack, Guidelines: *A cross-cultural reading/writing text* (pp. 78–87). New York: St. Martin's.

Bartholomae, D. & Petrosky, A. (1986). *Facts, artifacts and counterfacts: Theory and method for a reading and writing course.* Upper Montclair, NJ: Boynton/Cook.

Campbell, C. (1990). Writing with others' words: Using background reading text in academic compositions. In B. Kroll (Ed.), *Second language writing: Research insights for the classroom* (pp. 211–230). Cambridge: Cambridge University Press.

Carrell, P.L. & Eisterhold, J.C. (1983). Schema theory and ESL reading pedagogy. *TESOL Quarterly, 17,* 553–573.

Carter, M. (1990). The idea of expertise: An exploration of cognitive and social dimensions of writing. *College Composition and Communication, 41,* 265–286.

Harris, J. (1989). The idea of community in the study of writing. *College Composition and Communication, 40,* 11–22.

Horowitz, D. (1986). What professors actually require: Academic tasks for the ESL classroom. *TESOL Quarterly, 20,* 445–462.

Mapes, G. (1990, March 6). Polyglot students are weaned early off mother tongue. *Wall Street Journal,* pp. 1, 6.

Nelson, M.W. (1991). *At the point of need: Teaching basic and ESL writers.* Portsmouth, NH: Boynton/Cook.

Petrosky, A. (1982). From story to essay: Reading and writing. *College Composition and Communication, 33,* 19–36.

Prince, M.B. (1989). Literacy and genre: Towards a pedagogy of mediation. *College English, 51,* 730–749.

Rosebery, A.S., Flower, L., Warren, B., Bowen, B., Bruce, B., Kantz, M., & Penrose, A.M. (1989). The problem-solving processes of writers and readers. In A.H. Dyson (Ed.), *Writing and reading: Exploring possibilities* (pp. 136–63). Urbana, IL: NCTE.

Spack, R. (1988). Initiating ESL students into the academic discourse community: How far should we go? *TESOL Quarterly, 22,* 29–51.

Spack, R. (1985). Literature, reading, writing, and ESL: Bridging the gaps. *TESOL Quarterly, 19,* 703–725.

Spellmeyer, K. (1989). A common ground: The essay in the academy. *College English, 51,* 262–276.

Sternglass, M. (1986). Writing based on reading. In B.T. Petersen (Ed.), *Convergences: Transactions in reading and writing* (pp. 151–162). Urbana, IL: NCTE.

Swales, J. (1987). Utilizing the literatures in teaching the research paper. *TESOL Quarterly, 21,* 41–68.

Zamel, V. (1992). Writing one's way into reading. *TESOL Quarterly, 26,* 463–485.

CHAPTER 10

Literature and Critical Thinking in the Composition Classroom

Linda Gajdusek and Deborah vanDommelen
San Francisco State University

It is the premise of this paper that the reading of literature—more precisely, interactive classroom work with a literary text—can provide the best solution to two important problems that we face as composition teachers: (1) finding genuinely engaging writing topics, and (2) introducing, modeling, and getting students to do the necessary thinking—the critical thinking—that is at the heart of the writing process.

FINDING TOPICS FOR STUDENT WRITING

Perhaps the primary challenge faced by a composition teacher is to find genuinely communicative (Savignon 1991, 1972) topics for students to address so that their writing is not just a meaningless exercise, but rather motivated by a purpose that seems "real" and therefore worth their effort. Providing such a topic is especially difficult given the often heterogeneous mixture of backgrounds and interests that we confront in an ESL classroom. Acknowledging the importance of having the student writer feel highly involved in the writing task, writing teachers have often turned to personal topics, attempting to exploit their students' knowledge of and involvement with their own life experiences. But there are several problems here. For one, in the case of ESL populations, such assignments often stress the experience of being foreign, "an outsider," just when these students need help establishing their identity within their new culture. More importantly, personal material is not easy for inexperienced writers to access for the very reason that it is personal. We forget that many personal topics—indeed, the very ones that might generate the level of involvement that we seek—are either taboo or at least highly uncomfortable subjects of discussion in other cultures. More importantly, we experience and store much personal history in a primarily nonverbal mode (Norman, 1982). Indeed, it is the achievement of experienced writers to be able to grasp and translate this nonverbal fabric of mental images, sensation, and emotion into the linguistic medium. But one must question the wisdom of asking inexperienced writers to begin with this challenge. Rather, might we not facilitate the transition from personal experience to written text by encouraging personal interaction in the classroom with a text? Because such interaction takes place in a linguistic mode to begin with, it provides student-writers with linguistic hooks or cues, that they can use to generate their own further written exploration of and response to the text.

Another major difficulty associated with personal writing topics is gaining the objectivity to write effective reader-based prose as opposed to writer-based prose (Flower, 1979). The term *writer-based* describes and explains the failure of inexperienced writers who do not present the background information, assumptions, connections, or transitions that a reader uninvolved in the writer's experience will need in order to follow the writer's argument. This failure to respond to the reader's needs occurs because the writer is "inside" the argument and thus unaware of the outside reader's perspective. Within this framework, the major task facing inexperienced writers is to learn to write reader-based prose, prose that succeeds because the writer is distanced enough to respond to the reader's need for sufficient information and recognizable (thus clear) transitions. The difficulty in gaining necessary distance and objectivity is compounded when inexperienced writers respond to personal writing topics.

To help students gain the needed distance and objectivity, composition teachers and textbooks have increasingly come to rely on reading to introduce objective content into the composition classroom (e.g., Raimes; 1987; Spack, 1990; Taylor & Kinsella, 1988; Withrow, Brookes, & Cummings, 1990). We see units presented in terms of several essays that have been grouped around a chosen topic, usually representing multiple approaches to or attitudes toward that topic. These essays perform the additional function of modeling the techniques of development and support that we encourage our student writers to internalize and use in their own writing. Certainly, such texts have an important place in a composition course.

However, in addition to essays and exemplary academic texts, interaction with imaginative literature should be an important part of the reading and classroom activity of composition courses for several reasons, reasons that will influence the way in which we structure the in-class interaction with literary texts.

First of all, a literary text allows us to create the level of emotional involvement that we have been seeking in more personal, subjective topics (Langer, 1990) without sacrificing the distance and objectivity that will encourage reader-based prose. But that involvement does not happen just because one is reading "literature." The experience and necessary involvement come *from* the process of exploration and discovery that literature *invites*, a process that we must exploit in the classroom.

Whereas an expository essay strives to construct an explicit argument with which readers may agree or disagree, a literary text is not so linear. Thus the reader's first task is to reconstruct the experience (Langer, 1990), the situation, or story that the text conveys. To do so, readers engage in what Widdowson (1982) calls "procedures for interpretation . . . making sense of the [text] by referring . . . to other parts of the [text]" (p. 210). Then they may turn to the underlying argument (the message or meaning) and, finally, formulate a personal attitude toward some aspect of what they have read. This view of reading is consistent with current descriptions of reading as a very active skill (Grabe, 1991). More significantly, we can take advantage of this active reader involvement to generate intensely personal yet objective writing tasks.

In addition, the classroom interaction with a text that will be described below and whose purpose is to discover ("construct") meaning, genuinely engages and empowers (see Brown, 1991) student-readers. They observe that there is not just one "right" meaning to be apprehended by the privileged few, but that their own experience *is* part of the meaning, which they, consequently, must assume responsibility for constructing. A writing task that extends this process can no longer be seen as an empty exercise; it becomes a meaningful act of personal exploration and discovery.

CRITICAL THINKING AND COMPOSING

Before we consider the relationship between critical thinking and exploring a literary text, we must establish the insufficiently acknowledged relationship between critical thinking and composing.

What, then, is critical thinking? The more recent and, for our purposes most useful, approaches to the topic begin by characterizing critical thinking as an active attitude toward received data—facts, theories, opinions. In the context of pedagogical theory, this attitude can easily come to be seen as the fundamental goal of the entire educational process. Basing their argument on the perception that as teachers we are "no longer essential as lecturers and information givers" (Meyers, 1986, p. 1), those who believe that education is essentially training in critical thinking argue that it is "increasingly important that students master the thinking and reasoning skills they will need to process the wealth of information readily at hand" (p. 1). This concern is shared by ESL professionals as well: In the April 1990 *TESOL Newsletter* we read, "Students need to learn critical thinking skills to cope with the constant flow of incoming information. Therefore, critical thinking skills should be among the most important contemporary academic skills for students to master. . . not as an educational option but as an indispensable part of education" (Stewart & Stoller, 1990, p. 4). Understanding surface meaning, remembering facts and theories—these are the lower order activities upon which the higher order processes and learning rest. It seems almost self-evident that to become a truly educated person, one must do more than merely collect information and understand surface meanings, even surface meanings of a highly technical or theoretical nature. While much traditional teaching focuses on, and tests for retention of, raw data (without requiring learners to ask how that data is significant with respect to the concerns of the discipline, much less to the broader concerns of the learner's life), advocates of education for critical thinking believe that becoming educated involves learning how to interact with information in a way that makes it useful or meaningful.

Certain mental activities or "thinking operations" (Raths *et al.*, 1986, p. 5) are what we actually "do" when we implement the attitude described as critical thinking. Common to all is the fact that each critical thinking operation involves some type of interaction between the learner/thinker and his or her materials. There is a constant cycling movement from concrete to abstract, "concrete experience first, then abstraction" (Meyers, 1986, p. 29). Typically mentioned critical thinking operations include (adapted from Raths *et al.*, 1986) compare, classify, observe, summarize, interpret, evaluate/criticize, draw and support inferences, look for assumptions, predict, analyze, and synthesize. In addition to key operations or processes, critical thought involves our ability to make "important distinctions" (Ruggiero, 1984, p. 63) between key concepts: truth vs. opinion, fact vs. knowledge, and fact vs. interpretation. Finally, critical thinking must include the ability to ask the questions of the data before us that will generate these meaning-producing operations and to recognize instances of their invalid or unjustified use.

Advocates of writing as process have long acknowledged the intimate and necessary relationship between writing and thinking. Flower & Hayes (1981) describe writing as a recursive "cognitive process"; Taylor (1981) calls it a "two-way street" in which meaning is not only expressed but discovered in the act of putting words on the page. It is, however, much more than thinking in this broad sense that relates critical thinking to the composition classroom. The fundamental (and circular) link between critical thinking and the kind of writing that is implied when we speak of "the composition classroom" becomes clear when we analyze the characteristics of the kind of texts that we encourage our students to produce. The basic model is exposition, whose clear delineation of logical relationships (development *from* a controlling thesis; use of *relevant* concrete supporting detail; clear use of cohesive and transition devices . . .) satisfies the reading expectations of members of the Western academically trained community. This same explicit delineation of logical relationships is, not surprisingly, the fundamental technique of critical thinking. Indeed, insofar as we accept that rhetorical patterns are shaped by culture (see Leki, 1991), we may say that patterns of critical thinking shape intellectual inquiry and presentation of thought in Western academic culture. So it is that in the composition classroom, we are engaged in the business of teaching the models of thought—the culturally appropriate ways of developing and presenting thought—that the critical thinking posture in general and the critical thinking operations in particular represent.

Both the underlying attitude toward education as well as the specific mental operations that critical thinking implies can become valuable tools for the developing ESL writer/thinker, tools that can be taught and learned (Collins, 1991). The operations associated with critical thinking not only facilitate active learning; they are the patterns that characterize Western academic thought. Thus critical thinking and the specific operations of critical thinking are simultaneously a device for learning, thinking, and exploring a topic while they also serve as model to guide the form of the writer's emerging text. As we help our students internalize these patterns of thought through an active—interactive—process of learning and discovery, these same patterns become more readily available to structure the form of their emerging written products.

The question then becomes how to model and have students participate in these operations. Analysis of well-structured (compared to not-so-well-structured) expository texts is one way. But this kind of teaching merely involves recognition, not active manipulation, of critical thinking relationships. It is the premise of this article that, if we can use the attitudes and techniques of critical thinking to solve the exciting "problems" of exploring a literary text in the ESL classroom, we can (1) produce genuine, student-centered interaction with the text, (2) model the techniques of critical thinking and (3) facilitate the transfer of those same techniques to the writing tasks of the composition classroom.

The claim is not that the literature itself will serve as a model for the kind of writing that we hope to teach; rather, that the classroom process of reading and interpreting a literary text genuinely involves student/readers while modeling the analytical patterns of thought that underlie expository writing. In support of this claim, this paper will work with a specific example, the modern American short story "A Summer's Reading" (Malamud, 1956), to demonstrate an approach to reading and working with literature in the composition classroom that models critical thinking procedures and thus encourages students to use them in their own writing.

WORKING WITH A LITERARY TEXT: "A SUMMER'S READING"

The goal of placing on the students maximum responsibility for finding meaning, a respect for schema theory (Carrell & Eisterhold, 1983), which reminds us that we must help students activate relevant background knowledge and then construct their own increasingly complex structures of knowledge about the text; as well as a commitment to teach in accord with the principles of critical thinking for genuine learning are all most fully realized if we adopt an "orderly sequence" for the exploration of any literary text that moves from concrete to increasingly abstract levels of interaction (adapted from Gajdusek, 1988):

I. PRE-READING
   A. To supply information vital to comprehension—key vocabulary
      and culture clues
   B. To activate schemata that will help students identify significant
      issues/meaning in the text—"write-before-you-read" (see Spack
      1985)

II. SURFACE LEVEL COMPREHENSION (to establish facts about the text)
   A. Who is telling the story (point of view)
   B. Who the story is about (characters: major, minor, background)
   C. When and where the story takes place (setting)
   D. What happens (situation and action)

III. DEEPER LEVELS OF EXPLORATION AND ANALYSIS
   A. Structure (organization)
   B. Characters' motives
   C. Image and metaphor (how used to establish meaning)
   D. Interpretation of meaning (theme)

IV. EXTENDING ACTIVITIES (writing based on the text)

Working with a literary text in the classroom, we can implement and model the movement from concrete to abstract that is basic to the critical thinking approach. The words of the text on the page are the concrete base. Teaching students to work with the text, to formulate and support opinion, interpretation, and inference with specific references to the text, we are establishing this most elementary concept of critical thinking.

Exploring the text through a sequence of problem-solving activities that involve and model critical thinking operations will focus attention on the specific and concrete—in this case, the text. In the context of teaching more effective composing, this focus is, itself, of value, demonstrating, as it cannot help but do, the importance of the concrete details in any text. As students begin to realize the tremendous amount of meaning carried in small details—facts that are keys to the puzzle–problems they are solving—they may realize the importance of developing their own writing with equally specific and relevant facts, of including concrete specific language in what *they* write. We can facilitate this transfer by explicitly discussing the way a particular detail helps us better understand a situation, character, or issue and then showing our students how to incorporate their concrete answers to study questions as support for their own (written) opinion or response. (See, for example, the activity described below, which explicitly relates an inference to the facts in the text and the general knowledge it rests on.)

The following discussion is not meant to equal a lesson plan. Rather, for each level of interaction with the text, possible activities that stimulate active involvement with the text and also actively engage principles of critical thinking will be described and linked to student writing strategies.

Bernard Malamud's story "A Summer's Reading" (1956) is a good choice for high intermediate or advanced ESL students, the level of students in many composition classrooms. The story is about the topic at hand—reading, but not just reading, instead how people feel about reading and how they feel about those who read and those who don't. The protagonist, George, is a young adult, a high school dropout who lives with his father and older sister in a lower-middle-class neighborhood of New York City. His life is repetitive and boring, lacking direction or promise of change in the future. We meet him one very hot summer, hanging around the house by day and aimlessly wandering the neighborhood streets at night. The story's complication begins when George finds himself lying to one of the old men of the neighborhood about his ambitious plans for summer reading.

In fact, the story is not just about reading, although the topic and cultural attitudes toward reading are central to the action. Also, and more significantly, it is a study of self-esteem, about the way one's self-esteem is dependent on the opinion of others and the way one's motivation and actions are dependent on one's self-esteem. The challenge in exploring the story in the classroom is to enable students to feel that they "know" the protagonist and finally to realize and articulate what they have learned from his story.

Level I: Pre-Reading

Respecting the principle of always moving from concrete to abstract, we would not begin work with this story in terms of anything as abstract as meaning or theme. In fact, before students even see the story for the first time, we need to anticipate obstacles to comprehension and provide minimal background information about key terms in the text that a culturally literate native speaker would recognize: the Bronx; the IRT; change maker; dough, a buck, two bits; the *News*, the *Mirror*, and the *Times*. This is not an occasion for elaborate discussion; the goal is to quickly ensure that *no one* in the class is handicapped by lack of necessary information.

On the other hand, the critical thinking operation of inferring meaning from context and then looking for support/confirmation in the text might encourage us to structure an inferencing activity around key vocabulary items that are significant to the meaning or interpretation of the story. Such an activity serves more than one purpose: It builds confidence in guessing, which, as Brown (1991) asserts, strengthens intrinsic motivation. It focuses student attention on *significant* clues in the context. It presents and models the critical thinking process of drawing inferences from what is given or known. Finally, it introduces students to certain concepts whose significance they may then more readily recognize in later analysis of the text.

Another type of pre-reading activity, "write-before-you-read" (Hamann *et al.*, 1991; Spack 1985), is especially appropriate for exploration of a literary text in the composition classroom. In this activity, students write for ten to fifteen minutes in response to a topic designed to raise issues that are central to the story that they *are going to* read next. The teacher can take advantage of this opportunity to target and prepare for a problem or important issue that students will encounter in the text. Ideally, the topic should elicit concrete personal experience without specific reference to the story. For example, one might decide to use the write-before-you-read activity to establish a clear sense of the social values that the story assumes, the cultural assumptions about the value of reading that must be made if one is to understand why people behave as they do in the story. The assumption is that people, even those who are not educated or who do not themselves read, respect those who do. When we ask students to write-before-you-read on the slightly ambiguous topic "What is the value of reading in your culture?," *their* responses, which we share and discuss in class, establish the necessary assumptions: Some talk about the way in which reading educates and enriches the one who reads, but others will talk directly about the response reading provokes in others, its cultural value:

> In our Chinese culture, scholars are often placed at the top of social strata. We respect them because they seem to have exceptional wisdom and knowledge.

> Reading is a good habit. Chinese people respect those people who like to read.

> Reading is an act to show others that you are intellectual. Reading is a respectful pastime.

> Reading in our culture is perceived almost the same way it is here in the United States. Most often when you see kids reading instead of doing foolish things or playing, you think that these kids will have a good future.

Indeed, the last writer even did the work of making the comparison between cultures explicit. If the discussion of student responses to the topic occurs after the class has read the story and as the first stage of discussion, then we are permitting students to (1) clarify assumptions, (2) compare relative cultural values, and (3) take responsibility for bringing the appropriate schema to bear on the story. Of course, the entire discussion rests on *written* responses to a topic—writing used to clarify meanings.

If, on the other hand, one wanted to use the write-before-you-read activity to prepare students to discover the deeper theme, the topic might be

Write about a time when you felt good about yourself *because of* some one else's response or praise.

1. Describe the situation.
2. Tell at least one thing you did because of the way you felt.

Write-before-you-read is consistent with the movement from concrete to abstract: personal experience (concrete) raises and prepares students to recognize an issue (abstract). Subsequently, the concept is more readily available (the schemata have been activated) for interpretation and analysis of the story. This writing also establishes a basis for personal connection with the situations and issues of the text, a connection that the student may later draw upon in a formal written response to the story. Thus a connection made for the apparent purpose of exploring the text has been established and will facilitate later written response.

Level II: Surface Level Comprehension (establishing "the facts")

In keeping with the central critical thinking goal of teaching students to take responsibility for asking the important, relevant questions, we take time before beginning work with the text to elicit questions—in writing—from the class (either as a homework assignment, or in class). The task is

Write two kinds of questions about this story.

1. Ask about things you did not understand—words or events.
2. Ask questions that we can discuss to understand more about the story.

When the first interaction we invite with the text is to ask questions, we convey to students our belief in the primary importance of questioning and we shift responsibility for interpretation to the students, who are thus allowed to set their own purpose for further reading (Gillespie, 1990) and exploration. Our principal task at this point is to put the student questions into a sequence that will permit the class to construct the answers to their own questions, through activities that maximize the critical thinking potential for interaction with the text.

The purpose of the sequence of activities that follows is to establish the facts of the story: what happened to whom, when, and where. We encourage students to take maximum responsibility for establishing these facts themselves and interacting with the text by assigning—before class discussion begins— study questions or charts that focus attention on important information in a way that will help significant patterns emerge. Students will find answers to the basic who-what-where-when questions either directly in the text or the answers can be directly inferred from what is given in the text. Throughout this phase of work, the teacher, having provided problem-solving materials that guide students, now strategically intervenes to help students recognize that they are working with concrete facts and how important these concrete facts are in establishing what the reader knows about the story. ("How did you figure that out? Can you give us proof—a line from the text?" "Now do you see why the writer mentioned that little detail—how would the meaning have been different if it had been X instead of Y?")

Point of View

Work with point of view is central to the mature, critical (i.e., objective) understanding of any text. By point of view we do not mean "attitude," but rather the perspective from which the story is told, the narrator—first- or third-person, limited or omniscient (see Gajdusek, 1988, pp. 239-240). One cannot read as a critical thinker, cannot look for the assumptions "that are implied or concealed in any situation" (Raths et al., 1986, p. 12), if one does not have information about the identity, values, and biases of the speaker/writer.

There is grammatical information in the text that allows us to identify the point of view and thereby know whether we can "trust" the facts because they come from an objective third-person narrator, or if, because we have a first person narrator, we must interpret the facts in terms of what they reveal about that character's values and bias. To identify point of view, we examine the pronouns that are *not included in direct quotes:* Are they third-person or first-person? In "A Summer's Reading" we only find third-person. All first- and second-person pronouns are included in direct quotes. So we have established a third-person narrator. Next we ask if that narrator is omniscient (we learn directly what all characters think/feel) or limited (we learn *directly* what only one character thinks/feels). In "A Summer's Reading," we can find lines in the text that directly describe George's thoughts ("He *thought* of the jobs") or feelings ("He *felt* embarrassed"), but we know only what Mr. Cattanzara or Sophie did or said. In fact, our knowledge of them is limited to what George knows about them. Therefore, we have established that the point of view is "limited."

More important than defining the point of view is discussing its implications for us as readers. Students must come to realize that since we have direct access to George's thoughts and motivations, we can establish these as facts with support from the text. But much of what we "know" about other characters comes from inference based on George's perceptions, and these may tell us more about George than about those characters.

Having helped student writers explore the significance of point of view in the interpretation of a literary text, we can ask the questions that will shift the discussion to the importance of point of view for readers of all texts, including their own, and the need to write reader-based prose that provides enough information for the reader to identify not only their position (thesis), but also what qualifies them to address their topic and what experience (personal, vicarious, academic) has shaped their position.

Character

We use the critical thinking operation of classifying (generating and applying a principle to relate many elements to one another) to elicit information about character in a way that forces readers to work critically with the facts. The task is not merely to list the characters, but to understand sufficiently how they relate to one another and to the story so that distinction of major, minor, and background characters can be made. In this as in many other activities, there will not be one "right" answer; rather, the quality of the argument—the relevance of facts brought to bear—is what counts.

Situation and Action

Here the focus is still on comprehension. We ask small groups to construct and compare time lines of the major events to ensure that everyone shares a basic understanding of what happened in the story. A more demanding and insufficiently taught activity (Hill, 1991; Kirkland & Saunders, 1991), one that requires more than surface-level comprehension, is summarizing.

Summarizing is a critical thinking operation that has an immediate, straightforward application to expository writing. Whether one is supporting a point by reference to another printed source or personal experience, one needs to summarize. Indeed, what is narrative but summary of experience? A selection of the relevant details—the "substance"—of a reality that is always more complex than any account of it. And, of course, the practice of selecting relevant and therefore effective detail teaches critical thinking:

> Methodologically speaking, summaries are great tools for teaching critical thinking, because they help students fix ideas in their minds, provide practice in identifying main issues and concepts, and offer opportunities for *prioritizing* [italics mine] information. (Corner, 1983, p. 75)

The question is at what point one wants to ask students to summarize a text. On the one hand, summarizing can be seen as a good device to check surface level comprehension. But if we consider the way a writer will use the technique of summarizing a source or event in the composing process, we realize that the writer's purpose is the criterion he or she will use to prioritize the information contained in the original source. This implies a need to teach summarizing with specific strategies for prioritizing and selecting the details that relate to the writer's purpose. Consequently, one might prefer to defer summarizing activities until the class has had a chance to work with the deeper levels of exploration and analysis, which will suggest a meaning or purpose for the summary to support.

Level III: Exploration and Analysis

Having established the "facts" (surface-level comprehension), the class is now prepared (they have built the necessary schemata) to do some serious analytical work with the piece, work that accomplishes several learning goals simultaneously. Even though the tasks are straightforward, a discussion of the multiple levels of teacher awareness that underlie the tasks runs the risk of seeming complicated. This is because at this level of analytical work with a literary text, we always have the potential to be accomplishing several goals simultaneously in any given activity. The first goal is to continue problem solving and interacting with the text, which can only result in deeper understanding of the themes, characters, and/or situations that are the content of the piece. Through this increasingly demanding interaction, students come to internalize and experience the literature so that they do, finally, have something that they truly feel and can express in subsequent written responses. Second, this level of work is the active analytical interaction with materials that is central to critical thinking. Third, while earlier analysis focused on meaning (the ideas or content conveyed by the text), this level of analysis shifts the focus from content to form: the textual and linguistic medium through which the meaning has been and is conveyed. Thus this level of analysis will invite explicit connections with the problems our students face in their own expository writing tasks. The following discussion will try to relate any given classroom activity to all three of these goals.

Structure

One of the major challenges we face as composition teachers is to convey to students what it means when we say that a well-written expository essay is organized and unified by a controlling sense of purpose. Our students understand the word *purpose,* but they still don't realize what this implies in terms of the form and content of their own writing. Experienced writers know how each part of their text relates to and serves that controlling purpose, and they often provide transition devices (words, phrases, whole sentences) that clarify these relationships for the reader. However, it is not the explicit transition devices, but rather the clear relationships signaled by them, that are the mark of the successfully developed essay. Some of the weakest student writing is produced by writers who apply transition devices to pieces of text that lack this underlying coherence. Recognizing this problem, we realize that before we can successfully teach cohesion and transition devices, we must address the more elusive issue of how to help students recognize the connections between and functions of the parts of any written text. If we can train students to identify the parts of a text—even (or especially) of a literary text that often lacks explicit transition devices—and to state how each part functions with respect to the whole (why the writer included it), then we have established a framework that students can use to analyze their own writing and discover parts that don't work—i.e., whose purpose or function the writer cannot identify or whose purpose, once identified, does not advance the purpose of the essay.

An analytical task that addresses this issue while seeming to merely extend understanding of the story is to have students divide the story into significant parts and to analyze the function of each. This task is challenging because it requires students both to generate and apply the criteria for each section. A less demanding task would be for the teacher to provide the criteria and ask the class to simply find the corresponding line references. In some stories one might ask the class to count and identify distinct scenes (marked by either a shift in location or a break in time or both). In this story, whose style varies between direct showing (a specific event is described) and less direct telling (information is provided about a period of time, but no one event is described), more subtle criteria will have to emerge.

Most students recognize that lines 1–74 (Malamud, 1956) constitute the "introduction" to "A Summer's Reading." But then we must ask those same students what they mean when they call this the introduction: What does Malamud *do* to introduce his story? What kind of information does he include? How does that information prepare the reader to understand the story? In short, *in this case* what does it mean to "introduce" the story? And by extension, in your *own* compositions, what kind of information will your reader need to understand what *you* are going to write about? Have you included adequate background for your reader in your introduction?

By breaking the story into sections, we also establish a meaningful way to divide up the story for group work at an in-depth level. (The psycholinguistic and pedagogical arguments for the effectiveness of small group work [see Long & Porter, 1985] are merely enhanced in this context.) Since the whole class has worked with and is therefore familiar with the entire text, each group can bring to their analysis of any one section information from the whole (a fact which suggests that, for more advanced learners, group work may be most effective at these more interpretative stages of interaction with the text). The particular focus of group analysis will vary from story to story, and we may want to include questions that class members formulated earlier (see above).

The task of defining and working with significant sections of the text also provides an opportunity for us to model the expository technique of introducing a paragraph with a topic sentence and also to suggest the way in which writers quite often add such sign-posting sentences as part of the *revision* process (i.e., after details of text have already been written). We can ask each group to conclude their analysis of the section they are working on by writing a topic sentence that Malamud could have used to *tell* his readers what the section was going to show them.

The movement is from concrete to abstract. These made-up "topic sentences" will be generalizations based on the concrete details of the section. For example, in the first 74 lines, we learn many facts: George had no job, no money to spend; his father was poor and worked in a fish market; his sister earned very little working in a cafeteria; the family lived in a flat above a butcher shop; the neighborhood sidewalks were thick and broken. From these concrete facts we infer what Malamud has not explicitly said, that this is a lower-middle-class family and neighborhood. Responding to these and additional facts about George's past, we can create a topic sentence: "George Stoyonovich was a young man from a lower-middle-class neighborhood who had low self-esteem because he had dropped out of high school and couldn't realize his dreams." Such a sentence would prepare us to learn more about the topics the sentence mentions (George's shame, modest hopes, family and neighborhood), which is just what Malamud has concretely presented in the first 74 lines of the story.

In subsequent class discussion, we evaluate each group's topic sentence for accuracy as well as to speculate about why Malamud, as a fiction writer, chose *not* to provide such explicit "topic sentences." The exercise is doubly valuable as it not only clarifies meaning but relates interaction with the text to writing concerns of the composition class. The discussion can further focus on the relationship between the abstract and the concrete in expository prose—stressing the need to support generalizations or assertions (including topic sentences) with solid, concrete detail (description, explanation, example).

Characters' Motivation

In order to clarify the characters' feelings, motives, and responses, we can prepare a task that involves the important critical thinking skill of making assumptions explicit. We can, additionally, structure this task so that it will clarify the relationship between facts and inferences and also increase critical awareness of the difference between interpretation based on personal (cultural) knowledge that we bring to the text and interpretation based on facts contained within the text itself. This is especially important in the context of ESL, where undetected cross-cultural interference may result in serious misunderstanding. We begin with quotes from the text that lead us to make assumptions significant to our understanding of characters and situations.

For example, when George had to tell Mr. Cattanzara that he wasn't doing anything with himself that summer, we read, "George felt *embarrassed.*" If we give this quote and ask "Why?," students will respond with the assumption—based on shared cultural knowledge—that people *should* be working at something, and it is therefore "bad" to admit that one is not. The reader already knows that George is not, and so this explains why he feels embarrassed. Students can then infer that George avoids Mr.

Cattanzara's question and lies in order to save face. Finally, they can find support for this inference just three lines later: "it shamed him to admit he wasn't working."

The task is best presented as a chart that will make the relationship between facts, assumptions, and inferences clear:

A	B	C	D
quote from the text	shared cultural/ personal knowledge relevant to A	what we infer from A & B about someone's feelings or motives	support for C
"George felt embarrassed." (Why?)	People *should* have a job; they don't want to admit they don't	George tries to save face, avoid embarrassment: he lies	"it shamed him to admit he wasn't working."

Finally, we can encourage the transition from exploration of facts to well-supported, writer-based prose by having students synthesize the information generated by this activity into short paragraphs.

Imagery and Metaphor

By imagery, we mean the concrete details in the text that we experience through the senses—things we (figuratively speaking) see, hear, feel (including temperature, texture, movement), taste, and smell. Although literal description may include a variety of sensory images, these images are often introduced through metaphor, which renders a more abstract concept in terms of—by implied comparison with—something more familiar and concrete. Lakoff (1987) designates these as the "target" and "source," respectively. For example, in order to give a sense of the uncomfortably intense summer heat against which the story takes place (the target), Malamud describes people as "wilted"; the image of a wilted drooping flower (the source) is familiar and concrete; it conveys the more abstract sense of human discomfort and response to extreme heat. Similarly, Mr. Cattanzara "mopped" his face with his handkerchief. Comparing the handkerchief to a mop and the act of wiping away sweat to mopping a floor, the metaphor makes us feel the excessive amount of sweat.

However, our goal in working with metaphor is far more than simply identifying metaphors in the text. As we analyze the comparison by which a metaphor achieves its meaning and effect, we may discover new levels of meaning in the text or find additional support for patterns we had already identified. The step-by-step process of analyzing a metaphor affords more sustained critical thinking practice than any of the activities we have considered so far. A metaphor implies a connection or similarity between two unlike things; the explication must state what the two things are, in what ways they are alike, and what the writer intends for us to realize from the comparison. Distinguishing the two sides or halves of a metaphor is all the more difficult because many metaphors "hide" or are implied in the verb.

For example, early in "A Summer's Reading," we are told that, after his late-evening walks, George "drifted back to his . . . neighborhood." The metaphor is in the verb *drift:* to be drawn along by a current. The metaphor compares George (the more abstract half of the metaphor, the "target") to a boat or raft (the more concrete "source") and implies that, like such a boat, his movement is not consciously controlled by his decision or will.

It is easier to discover what a metaphor means, if we "map" (Lakoff, 1987) the two sides or parts of the implied comparison onto each other in a question–answer process of constructing a two-column chart. It is important to note that we work back and forth from target to source and vice versa as we develop the chart. (The numbers on the chart below indicate the order in which the elements were added and correspond to the discussion that follows.)

"TARGET"	(is being compared to)	"SOURCE"
(1) George		(3) a boat/raft
(4) George's walking		(2) drifting
(5) George's goal/will		(6) the rudder
(8) George's daily routine		(7) the current

We begin with the elements given in the text, "George drifted." The target, what is being described, is (1) George. The metaphor is in the verb, the action of (2) drifting. So we must ask what it means to drift. Our experience (and the dictionary—always an excellent source at this point of analysis) tell us that *to drift* is to be carried along by a current. So we ask, "What drifts?" and understand that the metaphor compares (1) George to a (3) boat. Then we ask, "What action of George's is being compared to the drift of a boat?" Again we consult the text; the passage describes George's walking, so we know it is George's action of (4) walking that the metaphor describes. Our experience or sense of the word *drift* implies that George's movement is not consciously controlled by (5) a goal or conscious will. So we ask, "What is there in the source construct that accounts for this meaning?" The answer: that which provides control for the moving boat is (6) the rudder. In the image of the drifting boat the rudder is not engaged, just as George does not consciously control the direction of his evening walk. But we continue even further: The concept of "drift" includes the idea of (7) the current, that which draws the boat along. So we ask "What, in George's case, is being compared to the current?" As we seek an answer to that question, the process of explicating the metaphor produces further insight into George's situation: (8) the meaningless pattern of his days is the current in which George drifts.

Once the chart has been filled out, there is one more crucial step, to formulate a prose statement of *how* the metaphor works: This metaphor compares George to a boat in that he "drifts"—does not make decisions to consciously control his movements. Indeed, this analysis leads us to discover that George's aimless evening walks are, themselves, metaphors for George's life—drifting, controlled by the "current" of daily routine, not by George's decisions to take responsibility for his destiny. Finally, in a circular fashion, we use the context of the story as a whole to validate our interpretation, even as the act of interpreting the metaphor gives us a more powerful sense of meaning—in this case, of George's dilemma at the beginning of the story.

Extending Activities: Writing Based on the Text

Understanding the basic analogy that structures metaphors should help students more readily see the relationship between a particular story and its more abstract, general meaning—the story's theme(s). By the time a class has worked with a story analytically, the job of articulating the theme and finding evidence to support the interpretation (opinion) that a statement of theme represents should be easy. Certainly a perfect and challenging written response to the story would be to interpret the story's meaning or theme and to support that interpretation with coherently developed reference to and explanation of the text.

But there are so many other kinds of exploration that students are now ready to undertake. They can examine one character, his or her meaning, change, purpose in the story; they can study one aspect of the story, such as the use and effect of point of view or a particularly revealing metaphor. Some examples of writing topics that incorporate student-generated questions about the text (see above) include the following:

Discuss Mr. Cattanzara as a person *and* as an element in the story.

Questions to think about in relation to Mr. Cattanzara as a person:
— Why does he drink?
— Why does he read the paper every night?
— What happened to him when he was young?

Questions to think about in relation to Mr. Cattanzara as an element in the story:
— Did he intend to teach George a lesson? If so, when did he decide to do so, and why?
— What does it mean that his eyes "hurt if you looked at them too long"?
— Why did he hand George a nickel?

Discuss the topic of respect (self-respect and respect from others).
— How is self-respect related to respect from others in this story?
— How is self-respect related to motivation in this story?
— How does the author's view of these relationships differ from commonly held views?

Discuss the topic of lying as it is explored in this story.
— Lying to self vs. lying to others
— What is the gain from lying? the cost?

Discuss the ending of the story.
— Do you think George will/will not read "100" books?
— Why does George go to the library to start to read? (What truly makes him go?)
— What does the ending "mean"? What is the author trying to tell us with this ending?

Other possible assignments can invite exploration of personal experience that matches or opposes a situation in the text, or they can ask students to find meaningful connections between stories: to compare characters or points of view or attitudes toward ideas or topics that two pieces share in common.

The concept of audience requires careful consideration as we establish expectations for writing about literature, and, conversely, writing about literature helps students develop a sense of responsibility to their audience. While informal response to the text (e.g., entries in a journal or reading log) may assume the reader and writer share similar information about the text, requiring a formal essay to meet the needs of a reader unfamiliar with the text or with our classroom discussion is an effective way to help developing writers become aware of the distinction between reader- and writer-based prose (Flower, 1979). It also encourages the kind of explicit development and support that characterize effective expository prose in general and academic discourse in particular. In order to write reader-based prose, the writer will have to select, summarize, assert, support, and explain—in short, develop an argument based on the techniques of critical thinking that have driven the classroom exploration of the text.

CONCLUSION

Having critically worked with a literary text, students will have taken responsibility for discovering meanings—not only in the text but often ideas or concepts that they had not had occasion to consider before. They will have shared with and learned from one another. They will have formulated opinions that they care about and want to explore in a culminating and more deeply, thought-through response to the text—in writing. In short, they will be engaged in the writing task. Because they will have developed some strategies for formulating, refining, presenting, and supporting their ideas and opinions, they will be empowered, not daunted, by the writing task.

As the writing process begins, continued interaction between writer and readers (teacher and peers) that the process approach to writing encourages will facilitate the ongoing discovery of the text and the choice of the most effective composing strategies. The techniques of critical thinking that were used to explore the text will now provide the resources that student/writers need to feel confident and better meet the challenge.

REFERENCES

Brown, D. (1991). TESOL at twenty–five: What are the issues? *TESOL Quarterly, 25*(2), 245–260.

Carrell, P.L. & Eisterhold, J.C., (1983). Schema theory and ESL reading pedagogy. *TESOL Quarterly, 17*(4), 553–573.

Collins, C. (1991). Reading instruction that increases thinking abilities. *Journal of Reading, 34*(7), 510–517.

Corner, M. (1983). *Adaptable writing assignments: Summaries.* Mankato, MN: Valley Writing Project, Mankato State University.

Flower, L. (1979). Writer–based prose: A cognitive basis for problems in writing. *College English, 41,* 19–37.

Flower, L. & Hayes J.R., (1981). A cognitive process theory of writing. *College Composition and Communication, 32*(4), 365–387.

Gajdusek, L. (1988). Toward wider use of literature in ESL: Why and how. *TESOL Quarterly, 22*(2), 227–257.

Gillespie, C. (1990). Questions about student–generated questions. *Journal of Reading, 34*(4), 250–257.

Grabe, W. (1991). Current developments in second language reading research. *TESOL Quarterly, 25*(3), 375–406.

Hamann, L.S., Schultz, L., Smith, M.W., & White, B., (1991). Making connections: The power of autobiographical writing before reading. *Journal of Reading, 35,* 24–28.

Hill, M. (1991). Writing summaries promotes thinking and learning across the curriculum—but why are they so difficult to write? *Journal of Reading, 34*(7), 536–539.

Kirkland, M.R. & Saunders, M.A. (1991). Maximizing student performance in summary writing: Managing cognitive load. *TESOL Quarterly, 25,* 105–121.

Lakoff, G. (1987). *Women, fire and dangerous things: What categories reveal about the mind.* Chicago: The University of Chicago Press.

Langer, J. (1990). The process of understanding: Reading for literary and informative purposes. *Research in the Teaching of English, 24*(3), 229–267.

Leki, I. (1991). Twenty–five years of contrastive rhetoric: Text analysis and writing pedagogies. *TESOL Quarterly, 25,* 123–143.

Long, M. & Porter, P. (1985). Group work, interlanguage talk and second language acquisition. *TESOL Quarterly, 19*(2), 207–228.

Malamud, B. (1956). "A Summer's Reading." In B. Malamud, *The Magic Barrel.* New York: Farrar, Straus & Giroux.

Meyers, C. (1986). *Teaching students to think critically: A guide to faculty in all disciplines.* San Francisco: Josey–Bass.

Norman, D. (1982). *Learning and memory.* San Francisco: W.H. Freeman.

Raimes, A. (1987). *Exploring through writing: A process approach to ESL composition.* New York: St. Martin's.

Raths, L.E., Wassermann, S., Jonas, A. & Rothstein, A., (1986). *Teaching for thinking: Theory, strategies and activities for the classroom.* 2nd ed. New York: Teachers College, Columbia University.

Ruggiero, V.R. (1984). T*he art of thinking: A guide to critical and creative thought.* New York: Harper and Row.

Savignon, S. (1991). Communicative language teaching: State of the art. *TESOL Quarterly, 25(2),* 261–277.

Savignon, S. (1972). *Communicative competence: An experiment in foreign language teaching.* Philadelphia: Center for Curriculum Development.

Spack, R. (1990). *Guidelines: A cross–cultural reading/writing text.* New York: St. Martin's.

Spack, R. (1985). Literature, reading, writing and ESL: Bridging the gaps. *TESOL Quarterly, 19*(4), 703–725.

Stewart, C. & Stoller, F.L., (1990). Critical thinking through opposing viewpoints. *TESOL Newsletter, 24*(2), 4–5.

Taylor, B. (1981). Content and written form: A two–way street. *TESOL Quarterly, 15,* 5–13.

Taylor, B.P. & Kinsella, K.M. (1988). *What's your point: A collection of readings & activities for English 310.* San Francisco: San Francisco State University.

Widdowson, H. (1982). The use of literature. In M. Hines & W. Rutherford (Eds.), *On TESOL '81* (pp. 203–214). Washington, DC: TESOL.

Withrow, J., Brookes, G., & Cummings, M.C., (1990). *Changes: Readings for ESL writers.* New York: St. Martin's.

SECTION III

SOCIAL PERSPECTIVES

Section III explores the social dimensions of reading in the composition classroom. The initial theoretical discussion sets the framework for the pedagogical and research articles that follow in that order.

The reader will notice, however, that unlike Section II, the social dimensions of reading and writing emerge as pedagogical possibilities far more than as research results. The heavier emphasis given to pedagogy in this section on social perspectives is a reflection of the profession's research interests and traditions, which initially targeted cognitive dimensions of literacy and have only recently considered social domains. Thus, Eskey in Chapter 11 sets the theoretical framework for this section by calling for a *socio*linguistics of text worlds that L2 researchers are just beginning to probe.

In the meantime, the pedagogical instincts of ESL teachers have preceded research initiatives and drawn us to experiment with a variety of ways to combine reading and writing within the social settings of our classrooms. The pedagogically oriented articles of this section begin with three different classroom approaches for pre-academic and non-academic L2 student populations (Chapters 12, 13, and 14). Chapters 15 and 16 focus on ESP and graduate courses. Each of the courses considered here is shaped by a view of the learner within a particular sociocultural context.

But research questions on the social dimension of L2 literacy remain unanswered: How do our students construe L2 reading/writing tasks; what is the impact of their L1 literacies on their expanding L2 literacy; what do the communities of discourse look like that students are hoping to enter; what do those communities expect; how do non-native students construe and finally come to understand both those expectations and the communities' responses to their attempts to contribute to the ongoing textual conversations of the many disciplines of the academy? Chapter 17 addresses some of these issues and poses initial questions about ESL students' socially and culturally grounded academic literacy experiences.

CHAPTER 11

Reading and Writing as Both Cognitive Process and Social Behavior

David E. Eskey
University of Southern California

READING AND WRITING: FROM INFORMATION PROCESSING TO CREATION OF WORLDS

In a paper that should be required reading for anyone interested in reading and writing (now more often referred to as "literacy"[1]), Frank Smith (1983) has argued that the metaphors we use in characterizing these activities have a powerful effect on our attitudes toward them and toward the ways in which we go about teaching them. He is especially concerned that the tendency to think of reading and writing as varieties of "information processing" (a very popular metaphor these days, obviously related to the tremendous surge of interest in computers and artificial intelligence) has caused us to view reading and writing as something rather dull and mechanical, and to approach the teaching of these subjects in equally dull and mechanical ways. The truth is, he says, that reading and writing are *not* especially effective means for shuttling information around (machines can do that more efficiently) and that these very human activities can best be understood as what he now prefers to call "the creation of worlds."

In arguing for this change of metaphors, Smith takes the position that the interesting thing about human beings—perhaps the hallmark of the species—is not how we process information, but what we do with it in framing the pictures of the world that all of us carry around in our heads,

---

[1]This does tend to obscure the old common meaning (as applied to adults) of literate (having the ability to read and write) as simply the opposite of *il*literate (not having this ability) and might be dismissed as merely fashionable. However, as I try to demonstrate in this paper, there are some advantages to having a cover term for all the kinds of behavior associated with the uses a society makes of written language, including not only reading and writing as isolated "skills" but also the various ways in which the members of a discourse community interpret and compose—and talk about—texts for particular social purposes (critical or exploratory reading, for example, followed by writing in the same spirit, as opposed to simple indoctrination to a limited set of favored texts to be read for virtual memorization and, in written commentaries, to be applied prescriptively to all the problems of life). Literacy, in this larger sense, is not just something people have but something people do.

our visions of both the so-called "real world" and any number of other, possible worlds. As Chomsky (1965) has also noted, what makes human beings human in their use of language is the creative use of the systems they employ in turning ideas and feelings into words and sentences (Chomsky's interest) or, more precisely for the purposes of language educators, into meaningful discourse. Thus approaches to teaching that place less stress on basic information processing and much greater stress on the creative uses of language are more likely to result in our students' developing stronger literacy skills and, not incidentally, becoming more thoughtful and self-fulfilled people.

For those of us with strong humanistic biases, all of this is quite persuasive (who could quarrel with more imaginative teaching, or with more productive, happier students?), but my reaction to it is: right—but not so fast. As he readily admits, Smith himself has helped promote the notion of reading as information processing. It was in his widely read *Understanding Reading* (1971; 1978; 1982; 1988) that many of us first encountered such concepts as "noise" and "redundancy" in text processing, and the notion of information itself as simply "the reduction of uncertainty," best exemplified, perhaps, by his discussion of reading in relation to "signal detection theory" (1971, pp. 23-26) and the notion of striking a good balance among "hits, misses, and false alarms" in drawing meaning from a series of visual signals. What is more, we found these discussions very useful in developing a whole new understanding of the psycholinguistic processes a reader employs in comprehending a text. As teachers, we learned to see ourselves as informed facilitators of these processes, and to see the reading process as a whole as what Kenneth Goodman called, in a now-famous phrase, "a psycholinguistic guessing game" (1967). From this perspective, reading does not look like a simple reversal of the writing process—the reader working precisely back through the words as a means of taking out what the writer has put in— but as a process of predicting, sampling, and confirming as a means of *reconstructing* the meaning of the text, a process much more closely related to the other so-called "receptive" skill, listening, than to writing, which in turn looks more like speaking, the other so-called "productive" skill. As a total description of what reading is, this information-processing approach does, as Smith now suggests, obscure the creative dimension of the act, but it also provides us with invaluable insights into the psycholinguistics of reading, insights that I believe should be combined with, and not replaced by, those provided by the creation-of-worlds metaphor.

These metaphors are not, in fact, mutually exclusive, but complementary, the first focusing on process, the conversion of visual signals into meaning, the second on product, the new structures of meaning—in Smith's terms, the new worlds—so created. The net result is a more complete description of what reading comprehension is and how it happens. It could be argued that even now the combination of Smith's two metaphors constitutes a more informative description of reading and writing as cognitive acts than any of the currently popular models (e.g., "interactive" models of reading or "process" models of composing), all of which tend to emphasize the mere manipulation or restructuring of knowledge rather than the creation of new and largely unpredictable structures. This may be because so much research has been done on academic writing—and student academic writing at that—but even this kind of writing at its best may involve the creation of more original products than these models suggest.

THE READING/WRITING CONNECTION

One major virtue of the more comprehensive conception of reading that results from combining these metaphors is that it provides a conceptual basis for discussion of reading in relationship to writing. (By calling his newer metaphor a metaphor for *literacy,* Smith of course meant for it to cover both.) Viewed strictly as psycholinguistic processes, these two activities do not, as noted, look much alike, but when both are understood as the creation of a product—and the same kind of product—a different picture emerges. Just as the creation-of-worlds metaphor sheds new light on reading, without necessarily eclipsing the old, it can also shed new light on the reading–writing connection by illuminating the relationship between both of these activities and *texts,* those longer, more complex, and more permanent structures of linguistic meaning within which these worlds take on the kind of form that a language provides. This relationship is real and important. Text is in fact the link between reading and writing as the complementary halves of literacy, a cover term for the special uses of language (i.e., the comprehending of texts and the composing of texts) that our schools devote so much effort to teaching and that our society values so highly. Text is where reader and writer meet and interact.

Real texts, however, are always something more than the product of one writer's composing processes or one reader's comprehension processes. In the real world where readers and writers mingle, individual texts do not stand alone. They combine with other, similar texts to form what is sometimes called a *genre* or, to use the term most in use today (*genre* being somewhat static, too closely associated with poetry, and perhaps too hard to pronounce), the *discourse* of some particular group of readers and writers who read and write the same kinds of texts, that is, the discourse of everything from personal letters to linguistics or physics. (Swales, 1990 provides the best introduction to this issue in a second language context; there is also, of course, a substantial [and controversial] body of work [dating from Kaplan, 1966] on "contrastive rhetoric," comparing text or discourse types across cultures [see, for example, Connor &

Kaplan, 1987; Leki, 1991], which continues to intrigue half of those in the field and to annoy the other half). Since any particular discourse is composed of the work of the people who read and write its texts, it follows that discourse in general—and, by extension, literacy—has a *social* as well as a cognitive dimension, a dimension that plays a major role in shaping the literate behavior of readers and writers in any real-world context.

FROM LITERACY SKILLS TO LITERATE BEHAVIOR

For dealing with text as meaningful discourse—as information that the reader combines with his or her prior knowledge in creating new or expanded pictures of the world—the combination of Smith's two complementary metaphors is much more useful than either considered by itself. For dealing with questions of language, however, neither of these metaphors is very useful, the first lacking any means of distinguishing between human language processing and other kinds of information processing (that done by computers, for example), the second lacking any means of distinguishing between worlds made out of language and worlds made out of something else (like the worlds created by graphic artists or filmmakers). As systems for the creation of meaning, human languages themselves are social constructs, and like other social constructs, such languages involve sets of rules and conventions that can only be learned by participating in the kinds of social activities that the construct serves to facilitate. Ultimately, language is a form of behavior, but it is always rule-governed or, at least, rule-referenced behavior,[2] the rules of which must be learned in social settings.

---

[2]For an extended discussion of this important distinction between the differing functions of so-called "rules of usage" and so-called "rules of use" (i.e., communicative rules), see Widdowson, 1983. Linguists are fond of saying that language behavior is rule-governed behavior because they tend to equate such behavior with the formation of grammatical sentences. As Widdowson points out, however, the sentence is an artifact of linguistic analysis: It is by definition nonreferential, decontextualized, and without illocutionary force. (When discussing the *sentence* "The man killed the bear," for example, one cannot reasonably ask "what bear?" or "where and when?" or "why are you recounting this bloody event?") Real language behavior consists of *utterances* (organized into discourse), which are always referential and contextualized, and represent some intention of the speaker or writer. To the extent that any given utterance is grammatical, it is of course rule-governed, but communicative rules are of a different sort—general frameworks for organizing communicative events (such as conversing or writing a letter to a friend)—which the speaker or writer refers to but is not rigidly governed by (there are many possible ways of opening a conversation or a letter). To fully comprehend or to produce comprehensible written discourse, the reader or writer must, needless to say, employ many more rules than just those required for decoding or encoding well-formed sentences. Both kinds of rules—but especially rules of use—are best acquired by taking part in real, socially grounded communicative events like reading or writing for some authentic purpose or writing in a real genre for a real audience.

With respect to reading and writing, the key issue here is the crucial distinction (first discussed in Heath, 1985) between *literacy skills* and *literate behavior* or, in behavioral terms, between merely *having* literacy skills and actually *being* literate in a language. The former may be defined (although not acquired) in context-free ways (as test scores or grade-level performances, for example). The latter, however, clearly entails actually engaging in the reading and writing of texts of some kind for some meaningful purpose and in some real-world social context.

From this point of view, actually engaging in literate behavior is like belonging to a club, a club that has its rules for the formation of sentences and its conventions for relating sentences to context, which newcomers must learn by interacting with older, more experienced members while taking part in the club's activities. Since literacy conceived of in behavioral terms is just a special case of language use, it also makes sense to speak of a "literacy club," and this is the third of Smith's metaphors (1988), which contributes to a more comprehensive understanding of reading and writing as both process and product.

It should, however, be noted immediately that this metaphor derives not, like the other two, from essentially psycholinguistic concerns, but from a sociolinguistic perspective that deals with its human subjects as members of a group engaged in some kind of conventional behavior. Since real readers and writers are always both individuals, thus unique, and, simultaneously, members of a literacy club of some kind, thus bound by the same rules as all the other club members, both dimensions of the issue must be addressed, and each seems to call for its own kind of metaphor.[3]

The real value of the literacy club metaphor is that it serves as a social corrective to the notion that individual readers and writers process or create meaning out of thin air, when in fact they do so through the medium of language, a conventional system that must be learned in social contexts and that—and this is crucial for my purposes here—some people learn to use more successfully than others, psycholinguistic potential not withstanding. Given that during the past twenty years most of the major breakthroughs in reading research have been in our understanding of what individuals do when they read, and most of the major breakthroughs in writing research have been in our understanding of what individuals do when they compose, this social correction is certainly timely, perhaps

---

[3]One scholar whose ideas about language acquisition are based on similar principles is the Russian Lev Vygotsky, whose work of some sixty years ago has recently been revived by scholars concerned with the social dimension of human learning (Wertsch, 1987). Perhaps the best known of Vygotsky's metaphors is his "zone of proximal development," which is the distance between what a learner can do at a given moment and what he or she *could* do with the help of a more experienced tutor—a teacher or simply a more adept peer—and it is precisely this kind of help that the more skillful and experienced members would provide for new initiates in Smith's literacy club. (See Collignon, this volume, for further discussion of Vygotsky's analysis.)

even overdue. As the literary critic Northrop Frye has noted (1957), texts are made from other texts, not from raw experience, and those who read and write well are those who have mastered both the forms and the functions of the *language* of the kinds of texts they wish to read or compose.

It is now, I think, fairly common knowledge that researchers have established a causal link between extensive early reading (what Krashen calls "the flashlight under the blanket syndrome") and a later ability to write proficiently (Krashen, 1984), and the reason for this link should be obvious enough. Reading is the only means whereby anyone can become familiar with the worlds made out of language that writers create, and thus the only source of the knowledge of the language and structure of texts that a writer must have to compose successfully. Good writers must, by definition, be good readers, just as good painters must be keen observers of color and line. (See, however, Flahive & Bailey, this volume, for a discussion of exceptions.)

For the teaching of reading and writing skills, the study of the rules, conventions, and traditions of Smith's literacy club (and the study of who joins, who declines to join, and who is discouraged or prevented from joining) may thus provide us with the research breakthroughs of the future. In a recent review (1987) of the Commission on Reading's widely praised report *Becoming a Nation of Readers*, reading specialists Athey & Singer have argued that the Commission's optimistic belief that our new understanding of the reading process has set the stage for the possible golden age of reading suggested in the book's title fails to take into account the social problems of the schools, and of the larger community, which may be the real causes of so many of our students' failing to join the literacy club that we are trying so hard to recruit them for. Athey & Singer note that U.S. students, in comparison with others, do well enough in acquiring basic literacy skills but that by the upper elementary grades they have fallen behind their counterparts in other literate societies. They do learn to read, but as the years pass they do not read to learn. In terms of Smith's metaphor, they do *join* the club, but as the years pass they fail to take part in its activities and thus never become truly productive members of the club, for reasons having nothing to do with their basic linguistic processing skills and everything to do with social attitudes toward the value of becoming more fully literate.

Similarly, in the studies of Shirley Brice Heath, what emerges is not a simple black-and-white pattern of literate versus illiterate, but a kind of differential literacy. In her well-known *Ways with Words* (1983), the three groups of public-school students described all acquired some degree of literacy. But only one, the so-called "mainstream" group, produced a fair number of candidates for full-fledged membership in the literacy club that the schools promote, because only those students came from homes that embraced a view of literacy that correlated well with the values and behavior of that club.

To my mind, Heath's research, and that of others like her, takes us several steps beyond the uses Smith has made of his own metaphor and deeper into the world of *second* language literacy. Smith tends always to speak of *the* literacy club, as though there were only one, and to speak as though we know what its rules, conventions, and traditions are. Of course, we do know what club he is thinking of—the one that we promote in our schools—but as Heath's research suggests, and as those of us who work with second language students know, there are in fact many literacy clubs and we do not understand the differences between them.

First, we do not know much (and have made little effort to find out) about the theories and practices of literacy that our students bring to the task of acquiring the kind of literacy that we want them to acquire (which, in turn, we tend to equate with the concept of literacy itself: for most of us, the notion of many literacies is much harder to grasp than the notion of many languages). This holds just as true for the children of minority groups, whose preschool literacy experiences tend to differ from those of mainstream children, as it does for international students, who may have internalized literacy traditions markedly different from our own. Obviously, we cannot become experts on every kind of literacy, but we can become aware of the nature of the problem and of the need to make our own assumptions explicit.

Unfortunately, however, the second reason that we do not understand the differences between our kind of literacy club and others is that we do not fully understand the rules of this club we want our students to join, much less how to make them want to join such a club. Like the real rules of grammar or discourse structure, these are rules that are "understood" by competent native speakers at the intuitive level but normally not at the conscious level (we know good reading and writing when we see it but we can't define or explain it), and we are therefore far from sure how to teach these rules or, perhaps more realistically, how to create conditions within which our students will acquire these rules unconsciously, much as we did ourselves, and will enjoy the experience enough to want to go on reading and writing in English on their own, just as other club members do.

It seems to me, then, that now that we have explored, with some success, the psycholinguistics of reading and writing, we must turn at least some of our attention to the *sociolinguistics* of literacy in the context of second language learning and teaching. To better understand our students, we must find answers to such questions as: What do our students think reading is? What do they think writing is? What do they think is the purpose of these activities? What texts do they read and/or write or write about (in both their native languages and in English)? How? And for what purposes? Conversely, to better understand ourselves as teachers, we must also find answers to such questions as these: What is it that we want our students to do, or to be able to do, in their reading and writing?

How can we induce them to adopt and implement this particular approach to the value and uses of literacy? And why should they (or, for that matter, we or anyone) want to adopt this approach?

To ask why is to raise still another set of questions related to the *politics* of literacy. It may be true that literacy is power, but it is not always the learners who are empowered by it. Depending on the *way* that literacy is taught, it *may* serve as a means to empower learners or as a means for powerful elites to indoctrinate and to control other people, *or* as a little of both. A number of scholars, especially Freire (1985), Street (1984), Graff (1987), and, most recently, Gee (1990), have argued that literacy has to some extent been oversold as a means of turning learners into everything from qualitatively superior thinkers to well informed and responsible citizens. There is no doubt that literacy has considerable enabling *potential*, but much depends on the kinds of texts that learners are exposed to, the way they are encouraged to respond to those texts, and the kinds of texts they are expected to compose in particular discourse communities. The ethical and ideological questions that these issues entail may be the most important questions that language educators face in designing and promoting their literacy clubs. (For discussion, see Gee, 1990.)

Recent research on literacy has begun to provide at least the beginning of answers to questions generated by this new sociolinguistics of literacy and has also begun to shed some light on the complex relationship between the social and cognitive dimensions of specific literate practices. In current work, the old process-versus-product quarrel has largely given way to the recognition that literacy has both a cognitive and a social dimension, the former subsuming the processes whereby particular readers and writers engage in discourse tasks, that is, in the creation of products—texts—the nature of which is largely determined by the latter, the community that makes some use of these texts. Smith's notion of joining the literacy club is now generally characterized as being successfully acculturated to some particular *discourse community*. (See Swales, 1990 for extended discussion.) There are some clear advantages to the use of this term. It is obviously less metaphorical, more process oriented (discourse is clearly something people engage in), and because it is usually defined more precisely, the fact that there are many such communities follows naturally from these more detailed descriptions of them. On the other hand, there is at least one sense in which Smith's metaphor still seems to work better. Like so many concepts from cognitively oriented research, the concept of a discourse community tends to draw attention to expert as opposed to ordinary performance (models of the reading process, for example, are nearly always models of what *fluent* readers do, and discussions of writing within specific discourse communities tend to be discussions of what proficient writers—"insiders"—do) and to deflect attention from the issue of development. These models often obscure the problems of those who are just beginning to develop the kinds of discourse knowledge and skills that qualify people as practicing members of some particular discourse community. As Spack (pp. 183–184) notes,

> [A]pproaches to composition instruction grow out of differing views about how expertise in writing is achieved, with one end of the continuum emphasizing *general* knowledge and the other emphasizing *local* knowledge . . . . At one end, students learn general strategies that can be applied to almost any composing process; at the other, they learn conventions that are shared by members of specific disciplines. . . . Composition instruction, then, must first aid students in the acquisition of general knowledge about writing and then move them back and forth along the continuum to grow as writers as they build enough local knowledge to enable them to perform effectively. Students' writing ability will continue to mature as they are influenced by numerous classroom experiences within and outside of their declared majors. Mastery of the conventions of a specific discipline will come only through immersion in that field.

Smith makes a similar point in relation to the teaching of younger learners by observing that, in becoming a member of the literacy club,

> a child striving to read or write something is helped and encouraged, not given a low grade and a program of exercises. Members of the literacy club are people who read and write, even the beginners, and the fact that one is not very competent yet is no reason for exclusion or ridicule. A newcomer is the same kind of person as the most proficient club member, except that he or she hasn't yet had as much experience. (1988, p. 112)

The one discourse community that scholars have begun to explore in earnest is, not surprisingly, their own—U.S. and Canadian academia. In a first language context, a major example is the longitudinal study by Flower *et al.*, 1990, of U.S. college freshmen trying to make the transition from the kinds of reading and writing they learned to do in high school to the kind of reading-to-write (or writing-based-on-reading) that higher education demands. Overtly recognizing both the cognitive and social dimensions of this task (which she defines as a kind of "cognition in context" or "embedded cognition"), Flower in her introductory essay (pp. 4–7) characterizes the students' problem as moving from "receptive" literacy, "in which writing is merely a tool for testing recall" of the reading material assigned, to a more demanding "critical" literacy, which, in composing based on sources, calls for a creative synthesis of this material with what the reader has learned or experienced elsewhere, a transformation reminiscent of Smith's creation of new worlds.

In Flower's view, there is no need to posit a "deficit" model of these student writers as thinkers. They come to their university classes "with an impressive range of abilities that are fundamental to academic writing: the ability to summarize, to get the gist, to see key points and connections, and not least, to execute moves that make an essay seem coherent and on topic" (p. 221). They are also motivated: "The interviews and protocols show students who are also working and struggling with this assignment, wanting to appear smart, trying to say something 'interesting,' wanting the paper to show what they can do" (p. 221). They do, however, need help in specific areas, especially "task representation" (recognizing and articulating for oneself the real requirements for the task), acquiring the specific "specialized conventions and expectations" of the new discourse community, and developing some skill in "*integrating one's own ideas and knowledge* into the written conversation with one's sources" and "*interpreting sources for a purpose of one's own—applying or adapting knowledge to solve a problem or to reach one's own goals*" (p. 22). She also argues, however, that there is much more to becoming literate in this particular way than merely mastering some predetermined set of skills and conventions, and concludes that being an effective writer "means being able to read a situation, to weigh the costs and benefits of your own options, and to carry out the goals you set for yourself" (p. 23).

In a second language context, Basham, Ray, & Whalley (this volume) duplicated this study (on a smaller scale) for second language students and found some general similarities but specific differences among different national/cultural groups and between all the groups they studied and Flower *et al.*'s first language subjects. Combined with the work of scholars specializing in ESP (e.g., Johns, 1986, 1991, and this volume; Swales, 1990) and a scattering of others working in a "social constructivist" mode (e.g., Campbell, 1990), this kind of work points the way toward a new consciousness of the crucial role social variables play in successful adaptation to the literate behavior of particular discourse communities, especially when this adaptation involves moving from one major culture to another.

TEACHING READING AND WRITING AS BOTH COGNITIVE PROCESS AND SOCIAL BEHAVIOR

None of this, of course, is meant to suggest that in responding to such research, we should simply forget about what we have learned during the past twenty years about the reading and writing processes. We must continue to make use of all of Smith's metaphors, and of any other good ones, in attempting to develop better programs and courses for the teaching of second language reading and writing. It seems to me that as teachers of these subjects we have two major jobs—one more concerned with the products of literacy, with the kinds of texts that we read and compose and with the uses we make of these texts and why we do so, and the other more concerned with reading and writing as psycholinguistic processes. The first of these jobs, *motivating* our students to read and write English better in accordance with the rules of *our* literacy club (and its constituent discourse communities), depends on our understanding of and our skill in explaining—or, more importantly, in *demonstrating*—what it means to be literate in our society, and in introducing our students to the universe of texts in English, the products of a fruitful interaction between the language and the various communities that have used it. To motivate our students, we must find ways to make it clear what the value and uses of these texts are, and ways to make our students want to join the club in which texts of this kind are being read and being written.

The second of these jobs—*facilitating* our students' acquisition of the reading and writing skills—depends on our understanding of and our skill in helping our students to develop the basic processing skills of comprehending and composing, which, taken together, constitute the major means of acquiring most kinds of formal education.[4] To facilitate our students' acquisition of these skills, we must stimulate their creativity, but we must also find ways to help them solve problems at the nuts-and-bolts level of reading and writing, in such mundane areas as word and phrase recognition, reading rate development, grammatical sentence writing, and organizing discourse in accordance with the established conventions of some particular genre.

Thus the teacher of second language reading and/or writing must master two different, if complementary, approaches to the teaching of second-language literacy—one geared to the *sociolinguistics* of literacy as a form of cultural behavior, the other to the *psycholinguistic* skills required for successfully engaging in this kind of behavior. For the latter approach, the research base is substantial, if far from complete, and effective teaching methods and materials are currently widely available. For the former approach, however, we have hardly begun to lay the groundwork. If we want to help our students learn to read and write better, to comprehend texts in English and to compose texts in English more successfully, we will therefore have to develop, as a complement to our knowledge of the reading and writing processes, a more explicit understanding of what those texts—those products—are like, how they differ from the texts that our students have known, and what uses we typically make of them in our particular discourse communities.

---

[4]A good case could be made for the proposition that formal education can largely be reduced to the acquisition of literacy and numeracy skills in various domains, with literacy skills having by far the wider range of applications. Cultures are largely made out of language, and knowing a culture means, among others things, knowing the language of that culture. (It is therefore hardly surprising that many culture-bound tests of "intelligence" turn out to be mainly language tests.) In literate cultures, to a considerable extent, becoming literate and becoming educated are pretty much the same thing.

REFERENCES

Athey, I. & Singer, H. (1987). Review of On becoming a nation of readers. *Harvard Educational Review, 57,* 84-93.

Campbell, C. (1990). Writing with others' words: Using background reading text in academic composition. In B. Kroll (Ed.), *Second Language Writing* (pp. 211–230). New York: Cambridge University Press.

Chomsky, N. (1965). *Aspects of the theory of syntax.* Cambridge, MA: MIT Press.

Connor, U. & Kaplan, R.R. (1987). *Writing across languages: Analysis of L2 text.* Reading, MA: Addison-Wesley.

Flower, L., Stein, V., Ackerman, J., Kantz, M.J., McCormick, K., & Peck, W.C. (1990). *Reading-to-write: Exploring a cognitive and social process.* New York: Oxford University Press.

Freire, P. (1985). Reading the world and reading the word: An interview with Paolo Freire. *Language Arts, 62,* 15–21.

Frye, N. (1957). *Anatomy of criticism.* Princeton, NJ: Princeton University Press.

Gee, J. (1990). *Social linguistics and literacies.* Philadelphia: Falmer Press.

Goodman, K. (1967). Reading: A psycholinguistic guessing game. *Journal of the Reading Specialist, 6,* 126–135.

Graff, H. (1987). *The legacies of literacy.* Bloomington, IN: University of Indiana Press.

Heath, S. (1985). Being literate in America. In J. Niles and R. Lalik (Eds.), *Issues in literacy: A research perspective* (pp.1–18). Rochester, NY: National Reading Conference (34th yearbook).

Heath, S. (1983). *Ways with words.* Cambridge, MA: Cambridge University Press.

Johns, A.M. (1991). Interpreting an English competency examination: The frustrations of an ESL student. *Written Communication, 8*(3), 379–401.

Johns, A.M. (1986). Coherence and academic writing. *TESOL Quarterly, 20*(2), 247–264.

Kaplan, R.B. (1966). Cultural thought patterns in intercultural education. *Language Learning, 16,* 1–20.

Krashen, S. (1984). *Writing: Research, theory, and applications.* New York: Pergamon.

Leki, I. (1991). Twenty-five years of contrastive rhetoric: Text analysis and writing pedagogies. *TESOL Quarterly, 25*(1), 123–143.

Smith, F. (1988). *Joining the literacy club.* Princeton, NJ: Princeton University Press.

Smith, F. (1983). *Essays into literacy.* Portsmouth, NH: Heinemann.

Smith, F. (1971; 1978; 1982; 1988). *Understanding reading.* New York: Holt, Rinehart and Winston; Hillsdale, NJ: Erlbaum.

Street, B. (1984). *Literacy in theory and practice.* Cambridge: Cambridge University Press.

Swales, J.M. (1990). *Genre analysis.* New York: Cambridge University Press.

Wertsch, J. (1987). *Vygotsky and the social formation of mind.* Cambridge, MA: Harvard University Press.

Widdowson, H. (1983). *Learning purpose and language use.* New York: Oxford University Press.

CHAPTER 12

Reading as Performance: Reframing the Function of Reading

Linda Lonon Blanton

University of New Orleans

We never know what we've read until we are forced to perform as readers—as though we know what we've read—and we face all those occasions (lectures, tests, papers) with that sense of anxiety, that doubt whether we can pull it off, which is evidence that comprehension is not something we possess but something we perform. (p. 16, Bartholomae & Petrosky, 1986)

When I came across Bartholomae & Petrosky's work in 1987, I read it with a sizable amount of my own frustration perched in the background, a frustration resulting from years of thrashing about for satisfactory approaches to teaching ESL reading. I had tried different text-based approaches and found them lacking. I had practically given up on commercial ESL readers: Unrelated readings followed by comprehension questions and/or vocabulary and grammar exercises had not worked. (See Leki, this volume, for a discussion of the problem.) The assumption behind a text-based pedagogy seemed to me patently untrue: that working through enough texts, one by one, would eventually get students to the point where they could take off on their own, like building up enough speed to fly. I had ended each semester of advanced reading—the last reading course that my ESL students would take—with no confidence whatsoever that they would get off the ground when I was no longer there as their copilot.

Bartholomae & Petrosky's text allowed me to view my own experience as an ESL teacher from a different angle, to reframe it so that I could make better and more constructive sense of it. The change in my own point of view involved a shift in focus, a shift *from* the text—as the object of attention—*to* the reader. (See Reid, this volume, for a historical perspective on the focus on text versus reader.) The reader of the text became primary; the text, secondary. This simple yet profound change opened up possibilities for me in teaching ESL reading that I am still exploring.

Before I discuss ways that a reader-based pedagogy can shape materials and classroom activities, let me 1) profile the students that this approach works best with, 2) describe the reading behaviors that they bring to the classroom, and 3) explain the importance of students' interaction with texts.

PROFILE

At the urban university where I work, large numbers of refugees with uneven academic histories enroll as students. Some have spent considerable time in refugee camps where schooling was minimally provided or not provided at all; others moved around the States for a while before their families found work and a place to settle. Most of them entered American high schools that provided little in the way of ESL instruction and nothing in the way of sheltered English programs or ESL-through-content-area instruction. Consequently, their schooling was disrupted to the point that they were learning in neither their first nor their second language for substantial periods of time.

When these students get to the university—entering through open admissions—they speak English with relative ease, but they neither read nor write the language well. More than that, they don't like to read and write English, they say, and they don't consider themselves readers or writers—of English or their first language. They watch a lot of television; and they do not equate reading with pleasure.

They are at the university, they say, because their parents have impressed on them the value of an education; and they want to get good jobs and earn a lot of money. What it will take for them to succeed academically they seem to have little notion of, nor have they thought much about it. It hasn't occurred to them, it seems, that their command of English is less than adequate for college work. Some express surprise when they get the results of the placement test and find out that we are requiring them to take intensive ESL courses; they "know" English.

READING BEHAVIORS

The students profiled here act as if reading is passive and that they, as readers, have no role to play, no responsibility toward the text. I say this because of my experiences in text-based teaching, when time after time, text after text, students had no response. I experienced this silence, this passiveness, even after choosing texts on topics that they professed to be interested in—even after they chose the texts themselves.

The problem is not one of literacy, not in its most basic sense. Students can decode, and if new vocabulary is explained and confusing structures analyzed, they can be said to "understand" the text. That is, they can demonstrate that they know what the text says, if they are questioned in such a way that the questions correspond to the wording of the text and to the information contained therein. (See Eskey, this volume, for a discussion of *literate* and *literacy*.)

Students proceed, it seems, as if a text is self-contained, as if everything there is to know about a text lies on the page in black and white print. When they get to the last word on the last page, the text is "finished."

As readers, they act disconnected from the text, and it seems extremely difficult for them to believe that their perceptions, ideas, or reflections should have any connection to the printed page. In class discussion or written exercise, a query about the subject matter of the text sends them scurrying to find something from the text to copy, even if their responses do not fit the question.

When I asked a student why she thought the offer of "free coffee" might draw a person to an English lesson—this from a text about a Japanese coffeehouse that gives away coffee to students who drop by for English lessons—she looked down the page until she found something that caught her eye and responded that "students who study English never suffer from caffeine deprivation."

Since for these students the meaning of a text resides in the text, they read for information. When asked, they relay information. If they don't have the text in front of them, they then have to rely on memory. When they don't remember the writer's words, when their memories fail, they think they have failed as readers. They have forgotten, they say.

These behaviors are not surprising if students have come from backgrounds where they did no reading at all or have been in classes where the meaning of a text always resides in the text, where there are always "right" and "wrong" answers. If reading then becomes an exercise in trying to second-guess the right answer to questions about the text, then it is no wonder that students feel like failures—they have been denied opportunities to learn how to be readers.

According to Bartholomae & Petrosky (1986), a person learns to be a reader, learns the role of reader, when given opportunities to interact with a text. Through interaction, readers learn that reading is interaction and that they create the meaning of a text through the connection between the text and their own experience, their own ideas and reflections. Reading is not an attempt to guess at a meaning that belongs to someone else.

"Powerlessness" and lack of "authority," both terms used by Bartholomae & Petrosky (1986), Salvatori (1986), and Wall (1986), are the result of guessing at meanings that belong to someone else and describe my students' behavior as readers. It also explains their silence before a text. They don't know that power and authority come from having something individual to say about a text and are achieved through individualizing the text—through balancing their individual and personal words with the writer's words. They don't know that power and authority are not qualities that precede a reader's interaction with a text.

If power and authority are achieved through interaction with a text, through "displacing it—casting it into the reader's terms—turning it into a translation that can stand as a successful reading" (Bartholomae & Petrosky, 1986, p. 6), then my job as teacher is to help students create comprehension through interacting with texts. Hence, reading as performance—as what readers *do* with texts.

My focus is then on my students as readers. As a result, classroom activities become actions through which they create the meaning of a text. Between the time students first decode a text and return one final time to the actual print of the text, they have created a successful reading—if all has gone well.

RATIONALE FOR STUDENTS' INTERACTION WITH TEXTS

When students at the college level write down spoken language in response to academic assignments, write as if they were talking, we know that we are working with students who are inadequately prepared to begin college work. In the jargon of our trade, we talk about these students as not having been "socialized" into the "academic discourse community"; in other words, they don't write the way college students are supposed to—with that sort of detachment from speech that is characteristic of academic prose. And we can easily distinguish between the writing of a student who simply needs more English but has a solid academic background—one who can write academic prose, even if his or her English is limited—and one who needs English and practically everything else that we think necessary for academic success.

The latter lacks what Cummins (1984) calls cognitive/academic language proficiency (CALP)—the proficiency required to perform the conceptual, linguistic, and academic operations expected of college students. While oral fluency in English is necessary for anyone to function in an English-speaking environment, it in no way guarantees academic success. If it did, we would not have developmental/remedial classes in our schools full of fluent (native) speakers of English. We also know that it is not a matter of intelligence; again, we find students in developmental/remedial classes equally intelligent as those in non-developmental/non-remedial classes.

According to Cummins, it is cognitive/academic language proficiency (CALP) that is ultimately required for academic success. How do students acquire this proficiency? According to Cummins—and this gets me back to my earlier discussion about texts and reading—CALP is basically acquired through interacting with texts, and its acquisition occurs naturally in children who grow up reading and then writing about what they have read.

The students profiled here (who, for reasons of world politics as well as inferior American education, have not grown up reading and writing) are clearly in a double bind. They do not spend time reading and writing because they are not proficient readers and writers, and they have not acquired proficiency in reading and writing because they haven't spent time reading and writing. Even worse, they aren't writers because they aren't readers (Krashen, 1984); ultimately, they have no chance for academic success if they do not read and write well. Although orally fluent, they are not proficient, proficiency being defined in this context as the presence of a reader/writer persona. The students profiled here have not yet developed such a persona.

Where the research of Bartholomae & Petrosky, Cummins, Salvatori, Wall, and Krashen comes together is on the role of texts and the relationship of a reader to them. Even though these researchers work in different contexts and can even be said to work in different academic fields, all see a reader's facility in interacting with texts as the focal point of most everything on which deep literacy, learning, and academic success depend. More importantly for the discussion here, it is students' continual interaction with texts that transforms them into readers, writers, and academically/cognitively proficient people.

For Bartholomae & Petrosky, interaction between a would-be reader and a text is the only way to legitimize the role of reader, to show that the process of assigning significance to what the reader notices is a way of reading (p. 142). For Cummins, interaction with texts is how students acquire cognitive/academic language proficiency. For Salvatori, setting up a dialog with a text, questioning a text, is how a person learns to read (p. 146). For Wall, interacting with texts develops for students the authority to respond individually (p. 106), and maturity in responding to a text results from finding a balance between the demands of convention and individuality. For Krashen, interacting with texts is how everyone learns to write—as readers compose their responses to texts.

Comprehension then becomes a cognitive/intellectual interaction between the reader and the text; the deeper the involvement, the greater the comprehension. To take off on Wall's idea of maturity above, reading comprehension can be said to result from finding a participatory balance between the self (the reader) and the text.

If, for example, I read a text and find no way to connect it to myself, to my knowledge, to my own experience, then I have "understood" that text in only the most superficial way. I have decoded it, but I have not truly comprehended it; the text then means nothing to me, and I can walk away from it without its having made the slightest impact on me. As a consequence, my memory of the text would be short term and I would have gained nothing through the act of reading.

My observations of the reading behaviors of the students profiled here lead me to conclude that they do not comprehend what they read because they have no experience of connecting what they read to themselves. It seems not to occur to them that a connection is possible. Let me summarize the problem as follows: The students who fit this profile enter our ESL programs armed with oral fluency but not academic proficiency; their lack of academic proficiency is most clearly evidenced by their lack of comprehension when working with texts—that is, when reading.

Given the above discussion, students' lack of comprehension is both the cause and the effect of their lack of academic proficiency. Students have not developed proficiency because they have no background in comprehending texts; they do not comprehend texts (in fact, they are unaware that comprehension is possible) because they dwell outside of the world of texts. They are strangers to academia and to the roles of reader and writer; they are strangers to what readers and writers do with language.

Pedagogically, the only place I know to enter these students' sphere is by focusing on them as readers. Through a sequence of activities that require them to focus on themselves, I help them create a bridge between themselves and texts, between themselves and the language of the academy.

A READER-BASED PEDAGOGY

In a reader-based ESL reading course, the text forms the context within which readers listen and talk to each other and read and write. The text is not the focus; the readers are—what they think about a particular text, what they find significant in that text, what comes to their minds from their own backgrounds and experience when they read the text, and how they can intertwine the "story" of the text into their own "stories."

Class time is spent *doing* in a reader-based reading class. Readers spend time in small groups, sharing with their classmates their responses to a particular text; they read each other's responses to the text, their responses becoming new texts; they role-play the text, when it lends itself to role-play, putting themselves in the shoes of the individuals in the text; they write parallel texts; they write in response to the responses of their classmates to the text; they reexamine their own knowledge and experience in light of the text. (A list of sample activities is included in Appendix A at the end of this chapter; see also Spack and Collignon, this volume, for additional activities.)

To visualize the role of the text in a reader-based course, think of the text as the hub of a wagon wheel. Activities relating to the subject matter of the text spin off from the text as the spokes of the wheel. The readers collectively, but yet as individuals together, are represented by the circular frame, connecting to the text through the activities and yet creating a greater and richer text through the interaction and the varied backgrounds they bring to the original text.

The role of the teacher in a reader-based pedagogy is greatly reduced. He or she neither occupies center stage nor takes up much class time explaining. Basically, the teacher orchestrates the activities, serves as a resource, and stays out of the way.

What happens to students in a reader-based class is that they begin to "remember" what they know; they begin using the language of the texts to access their own reservoirs of knowledge and experience. As they do so, they expand their knowledge and find new ways to view their experience. In that way, they create a comprehension of the text.

Reading about animal communication, for example, causes one student to remember a dog that she had as a child; in her journal, she wrote about the ways in which that particular animal let her know when it was hungry, or happy to see her, or in sympathy with her when she was sad. Later, in an essay on animal communication, she wove her own story about her pet and the stories of her classmates into a new text that included references to the original text that the whole class had read. This is what academics do with language and with texts: They create new texts by weaving what is internal to the self to what is external—and creating new perspectives, new insights, as they go along.

What also happens to students in a reader-based class is that they begin to develop an awareness of themselves—an awareness of themselves as readers of others' discourse, as writers for others to read, as negotiators of meaning. Evidence of this awareness pops up in different places. Where it can be seen and heard first is in the increasing use of the first-person singular pronoun. For example, a student, in response to the same text on animal communication referred to above, writes in his journal that, "All pets understand people's simple commands but I don't think that they understand words. I think that they understand by tone of voice . . ." And this from a student who—several months earlier—would only report what a text said, if and only if the text were in front of him and the question were phrased to match the phrasing of the answer. (Other writing samples that I think illustrate an emerging sense of textual interaction are included in Appendix B at the end of this chapter.)

I remember vividly the moment when a student realized that she could understand one part of a particular text best because she was connecting it to her own experience. The thread that led to that revelation was my simple question of whether she liked the text she had just finished reading. Yes, she had liked the text, she said, but only one part of it. Then I followed up with a series of why-questions as she moved from observations about the text itself to a powerful perception about herself as a reader, a perception that both stunned and overjoyed her as she began to absorb its meaning. The student's moment of realization was powerful also for her classmates because they had hung in there with her through the dialogic process and her insight had created a new insight for them. It was also powerful for me because it gave me a new level of understanding of what it really means to comprehend a text.

Where does English—ESL—fit into a reader-based pedagogy? It fits everywhere indirectly and nowhere directly. Students read, discuss, converse, exchange information and ideas, write, read what their classmates have written, write some more, ask me questions, read some more—all within the context initially established by the text that begins each cycle of activities. I do not "teach" the vocabulary or grammatical structures of the text, although I answer questions about unfamiliar vocabulary or complex grammar if students ask. Or I ask them to explain to each other.

Although we do not have language lessons per se, I see in students' use of language—both oral and written—an increasing sophistication and accuracy as the semester continues. Because my students will either pass or fail a departmentally administered writing/reading test at the end of the semester, I give them periodic class tests, in which they write in response to a text and I grade their papers on content and form; these serve as trial runs for the final exam and give students a realistic sense of how close they are to meeting departmental standards. Students also write at least one formal essay within each cycle of activities; these I respond to but do not grade, since I want students to feel free to experiment without penalty. In their writing, I see increasing control over the language in ways that make a concern over verb tenses, for example, seem trivial. Grammar improves, to be sure, but grammatical accuracy improves as precision of thought improves, as verbal ability in maneuvering within a variety of perspectives increases.

Within a reader-based pedagogy, I now give students texts to read that I would never have given them when I was following a text-based approach. In fact, I found that when our focus was on the text itself, I kept watering down texts, because the energy level in the class sank lower and lower as we spent more and more time plowing through "difficult" texts.

Within a reader-based pedagogy, I keep upping the ante: My students now discuss and write about such complex issues as medical ethics, suicide, and the generational breakdown of family relationships—all initially introduced to the class through texts written for native speakers of English. Before, I would never have dared to use such linguistically complex texts; now, as long as students find the structures and vocabulary they need to keep up with the momentum generated by the activities of the class, why would I want to slow them down?

As I see students beginning to assume the stance of readers and writers and feel their way toward a balance between their own knowledge and experience and that of others, I am reassured of the value of a reader-based approach. I see the academic, intellectual, and linguistic socialization process at work. It affects every area—reading, writing, and thinking—on which students' academic success depends.

CONCLUSION

I was aware as I began this paper with Bartholomae & Petrosky's words—that we don't know what we've read until we begin to work with it by talking and writing about it—that I was about to model for myself what I attempt to do for and with my students.

As I went from the texts written by Bartholomae & Petrosky and others cited here, I connected their words with my experience and created meaning for myself. My meaning is not their meaning, but I created a transaction with their texts that allowed me to frame my own experience in such a way that I can gain insight from it.

I also didn't know exactly what I understood from each of their texts or how they all fit together or I with them until I began to write about them. In interacting with their texts, I created comprehension for myself. It is this experience that I want to help students create and recreate for themselves.

APPENDIX A

Sample Classroom Activities in a Reader-Based Pedagogy

1. After you and your classmates have all read the same text, choose a partner. You and your partner tell each other about the particulars in the text that "rang a bell." What meant something to you? After you and your partner have shared your responses to the text, compare the differences or similarities of your responses. Why might they be different or similar?

2. Write down your "story" (from #1 above) and write down your partner's "story." Then analyze how the two are similar or different.

3. You are an illustrator. Draw a picture or pictures to accompany the text that you have read. Describe your picture(s) to your partner. Explain your choice of images.

4. You are Mr./Ms. X (a person from the text). Tell the story from this person's point of view. Elaborate and personalize "your" role in the text.

5. Tell whether or not you would have "your" character (#4 above) play a different role, if you were the author of the text. Explain that role. Rewrite the text according to the changes you would make.

6. Write your own text parallel to the text that you've read.

7. Choose to be one of the people featured in the text that you've read. Write a script for your character; then role-play the character, with some of your classmates taking on the roles of the other characters.

8. Tell your partner about the text in such a way that he or she will be sure to want to read it. (In this case, different students have been assigned to read different texts.)

9. Draw a time line for the events in the text.

10. With your partner, create a new title for the text. Be prepared to explain to the class why your title is better than the original one. Analyze the differences.

11. Characterize the author's attitude toward the subject that she or he has written about. If you were writing about the same subject, what would your attitude be? How would your attitude change the text?

12. Choose one person, place, or object from the text. Describe her/him/it in full detail.

13. Write an advertisement for the text. Explain which group of readers you are targeting. Explain why your advertisement will appeal to them.

14.   Work with your partner to create a (different) subtitle for the text. Analyze your subtitle. What does it add to the title?

15.   Tell the class what the author of the text could have done to write a text that you would have liked better.

16.   Write that text (#15 above).

17.   State the thesis of the author of the text. Then discuss/write from your own experience. Does your experience lead you to the same conclusion? What is your own thesis? How does your own thesis compare to the author's?

18.   Take the subject of the text. Discuss with your partner your connection to this subject. What do you know about it? What experience have you had with it?

19.   Study the illustrations that accompany the text, if there are any. Tell your partner what comes to mind as you look at the illustrations.

20.   (variation on #19 above) Describe to your partner what illustration(s) should accompany the text. Explain in exact detail. Why would yours be better?

21.   Write a new text, in which you weave together your "story" with the "story" of the original text. (Your own life experience and knowledge of the subject of the original text constitute your story.) Include some of your classmates' stories, too. Before you are through, let those whose stories are woven into your new text read what you've written.

APPENDIX B

Sample Student Writing: Interaction with a Text

Samples 1 and 2

[Students were instructed, after reading a text on animal communication, to write about a pet and whether or not that pet could communicate, as the author of the text contended animals could do. Student work is freewritten and is included here unedited.]

"When I was a child, I had a dog. I thought this dog was very smart, it can understand what I said. If I said, "sit down," it sat down. Once I walk to school my dog taged along me, I got angry, and said " come back home," it felt very sad but finally my dog come back home alone. In my opinion, I think a dog can understand human language." (HT from Vietnam, 4/24/89)

"I think animals communicate with each other. For example, when a bird which sit on a tree is chirping, another bird comes from other place. They sit and chirp together. Sometimes, we can communicate with an animal too. One of my friends has a little puppy. She was so cute and follows us. If my friend says "sit" then the puppy sit, if my friend says "run" then the puppy runs. I think we can teach a language to animals." (K from Korea, 4/24/89)

Sample 3

[Students were asked to write parallel to the text they had read, a text in which the author related a series of tragic events and then reflected on them. The sample below is excerpted to include only part of the student's reflection.]

". . . I didn't tell the story of Maria just to give you an example of suicide; I told it because we should realized that most of the teenagers that take their lives come from parents that are divorced or from marriages that fight each other.

"We should take life more seriously and marriage too. We can marry just because we don't have any better thing to do; we should be more careful and more responsible for our actions, not only for us, but for our future children that will become parents like us." (NM from Nicaragua, 11/4/88)

REFERENCES

Bartholomae, D., & Petrosky, A. (1986). *Facts, artifacts and counterfacts.* Upper Montclair, NJ: Boynton/Cook.

Cummins, J. (1984). *Bilingualism and special education.* San Diego, CA: College Hill.

Krashen, S. (1984). *Writing, research, theory, and applications.* Oxford: Pergamon.

Salvatori, M. (1986). The dialogical nature of basic reading and writing. In D. Bartholomae & A. Petrosky (Eds.), *Facts, artifacts and counterfacts* (pp. 137–166). Upper Montclair, NJ: Boynton/Cook.

Wall, S.V. (1986). Writing, reading and authority: A case study. In D. Bartholomae & A. Petrosky (Eds.), *Facts, artifacts and counterfacts* (pp. 105–136). Upper Montclair, NJ: Boynton/Cook.

## CHAPTER 13

ESL Authors: Reading and Writing Critical Autobiographies

Sarah Benesch
College of Staten Island

The student-as-author approach, introduced by Graves (1983) in elementary schools and Atwell (1987) in junior high schools, calls on students to read authentic texts and to compose and publish their own. Extensive reading and writing are the hallmark of this approach, which has been adopted for ESL elementary school students (Hudelson 1989) and ESL college students (MacGowan-Gilhooly, 1991). As Graves (1983), Calkins (1983), Atwell (1987), and MacGowan-Gilhooly (1991) have shown, the full range of writing abilities is best developed when students read unabridged texts and write multi-chapter books, taking their work from initial ideas to final edited publication, to complete the "authoring cycle."

This chapter describes the student-as-author approach in an ESL college composition course in which students read and wrote an autobiography. The purpose of the course was to increase fluency, demystify the writing and publishing processes, and encourage students to think critically about their lives.

The rationale for assigning a semester-long project that connected reading and writing and for encouraging students to examine their lives critically is presented below. An outline of the reading and writing activities of this particular ESL class follows. Illustrations of the work of two students, one a permanent resident and the other a newcomer, are analyzed to show the influence of the assigned text on their writing, including the adoption of a critical stance and the development of writing abilities.

RATIONALE

Extensive Reading and Writing

L1 and L2 composition courses typically call on students to complete a series of unrelated assignments on topics derived from readings, students' journals, or composition textbooks. After receiving or selecting a topic, students write one or more drafts and then edit, repeating this process for each assignment. Once an assignment is completed, students move on to the next, with no opportunity to reconsider the ideas previously written about.

The need for sustained inquiry in composition classes has been addressed by Bartholomae & Petrosky (1986). To provide opportunities for greater intellectual penetration of a topic, they developed a semester-long basic reading/writing course, run as a seminar, in which freshmen read and wrote extensively about a single theme, such as "Work" or "Growth and Change in Adolescence." All reading and writing assignments were linked and focused on the single subject, allowing students to study the issue deeply. Ongoing dialogue and multiple opportunities to revise led to reexamination of previously held notions about the topic. One of the findings from studies of the Bartholomae/Petrosky program is that students who work extensively in a particular area of inquiry over a semester are more committed to revision than if the assignments are short term and unconnected:

> Revision for us [faculty] represents stages in the ongoing process of working out what we know and what we can say about the subject that engages us, a subject moreover, which may engage us for weeks, months or years. Student writers do not usually have the kind of long-term commitment to a project that keeps us going, reformulating our ideas as we recompose them. But a semester-long sequence of assignments on a topic of primary concern to them offers an approximation of the experience of sustained immersion in inquiry which gives our rewriting its meaning and its context. (Coles, 1986, p.168)

ESL faculty, aware of the gains made when students read and write extensively, have also structured their courses around semester-long assignments. MacGowan-Gilhooly (1991) reports on a program in which ESL college students read and responded to mysteries, biographies, science fiction, or romance novels, and then wrote their own multi-chapter texts in one of these genres. Students' gains in fluency, clarity, and correctness are described. MacGowan-Gilhooly advocates this approach as an example of whole language instruction that allows students to read and write authentic texts and to receive individualized feedback, be it nudges to continue, questions leading to revision, or comments about usage.

Critical Pedagogy

In addition to the above-mentioned features (extensive reading, reflection, discussion, and revision of whole texts), the course is also grounded in critical pedagogy. One goal of critical teaching is to locate student experience in its social context by making the course a study of themes in students' lives. Students consider in reading, writing, and speaking the social forces affecting them. As Auerbach (1990) explains, students become "the subjects of their own histories" (p. 47). For this they need "a critical distance on society in place of uncritical immersion in the status quo . . . " (Shor & Freire, 1987, p. 14).

Students' personal narratives are often the starting point of critical teaching. Through discussions of their daily lives, students reveal certain themes that the teacher "re-presents" to them for further inquiry:

> By identifying, abstracting and problematizing the most important themes of student experience, the teacher detaches students from their reality and then re-presents the material for their systematic scrutiny. (Shor, 1980, p. 99)

For ESL students, scrutiny of the themes of their lives validates their experience as newcomers or immigrants. Confusing or upsetting episodes become tools for learning about American culture. The problems of living in a new culture are seen as the result of social factors rather than of personal shortcomings. According to Wallerstein (1983), ESL students can gain inspiration from learning that there are social, political, and economic causes for their difficulties:

> By discussing their personal experiences, students can uncover the social pressures which affect them as members of an ethnic group. A critical view does not imply negative thinking. Critical thinking builds on the hopes that students have for a better life. Students have already experienced change in their lives by immigrating, and are searching for other changes in the U.S. Analyzing U.S. society enables students to adopt a positive stance toward the change they want in their personal lives or in the community. (p. 16)

The course described here used a critical approach in an ESL composition classroom to enable students to grasp the larger social context for the changes in their lives. This approach aimed to help them view their conditions with critical understanding of the options available to them.

A SEMESTER-LONG PROJECT

Reading and Keeping a Journal

Two Years in the Melting Pot, an unusually candid account by Chinese journalist Liu Zongren (1984) of two years he spent in Chicago, was the assigned reading for this course. It was chosen as a model of what the students were to write, an autobiographical account of life in the U.S. from the viewpoint of a non-native, written in clear prose and organized thematically into chapters. *Two Years* was also chosen as a model of careful observation and critical examination of life in an American city. The writing is analytic yet anchored in Zongren's experiences. He unflinchingly describes, for example, his own encounters with racism and tries to analyze the underlying social and economic causes. Zongren shares his negative and positive impressions of life in the United States, from the questionable spending practices of the government ("I wondered why the government didn't spend more money on children and less on prisoners," p. 87) to enlightened child rearing practices ("At the bookstand I later observed that children had just as much freedom in selecting books. The parents interfered with their children's choices only when a parent didn't want to pay for the selected volume," p. 189).

While reading *Two Years*, students kept double-entry notebooks whose contents were discussed in class and which I (the instructor) responded to in writing. After finishing the book, the students discussed its themes and structure. They were asked to speculate on the author's choices: How did he use the journal he had kept while in the U.S. to guide his writing once he got back to China? How did he decide which of his experiences to include in the book? What aspects of his past, present, and future did he include? How did he choose titles for the chapters? Why did he organize the chapters as he did? These questions demonstrated that writing is a matter of making choices and that autobiographical writing necessitates choosing from the vast array of one's experiences.

After extensive discussion of these questions, the class brainstormed possible topics for the chapters of their own autobiographies and came up with the following list from which eventually to choose: work, money, expectations of the U.S. before I came, shopping, my social life in the past and now, marriage, growing up, the way my parents raised me, immigration, trying to fit in, morality, homelessness, exercise, treatment of older people, treatment of women, my family's reputation in the U.S. and in my country, relationships between men and women, meeting people, being polite vs. being aggressive, returning home, college life, religion. Some of these topics came from their own concerns and experience; others came from *Two Years*, but all begged for a critical approach to the social context. Students recorded the list in their notebooks to use as a reference when working on their autobiographies.

Writing, Revising, and Editing

The bulk of the semester was devoted to writing the autobiographies. First, the students wrote essays introducing themselves to the class; these served as points of departure for their multi-chapter books. They were required to complete six to ten edited chapters, each of which went through several drafts based on peer and teacher feedback. To emphasize the importance of revising, 16 class periods (36 hours) were devoted to writing and revising. By comparison, only four class periods (eight hours) were devoted exclusively to editing.

To illustrate the connections between reading *Two Years* and writing autobiographies, as well as the impact of critical feedback, I will discuss the work of two students. The first, Evelyn, was a permanent resident; the second, Mei, was a newcomer. The difference in their resident statuses revealed itself both in their level of language and in their choices as writers.

BEYOND THE "BED TO BED" NARRATIVE

Evelyn was raised in Shanghai and since 1980 has been living in New York City, where she graduated from high school and community college before enrolling in senior college. While Evelyn wrote fluently and with great concentration, the ideas expressed in her initial essay of introduction were neither elaborated nor well-connected. She wrote what Graves (1983) calls the "bed to bed story," a series of chronological events recounted with little elaboration: "The report is thorough yet indiscriminate . . .. There are simple bonds to the chronology, each event following the other. The writer writes all that can be remembered" (p. 254). Each paragraph of the essay describes a different stage of Evelyn's life: departure from Shanghai, arrival in Hong Kong, arrival in New York, first language school, community college, and senior college. It is chronological and descriptive, leaving the reader with a desire for more analysis. The following excerpt from paragraph four of the initial essay shows that areas of experience are mentioned and left unexplored, including certain social problems:

> In Sept. of that year, I registered to be attended in W. I. High School where had a special English program for non-native students. I took an entercy tests. I was being arranged into a high level of science classes and the lowest level of English class. Amount of other students in my English class all come from other parts of the world, but we shared the common sensitive and spoke to each other with our undeveloped English. I wasn't feel so happy during the four years in high school. I got very good opportunity for learning English, but I failed for making friends.

Why was she unhappy? Why did she fail to make friends? What was the "common sensitive" shared by the non-native students? How did she get along in her non-ESL classes? These were some of the questions this paragraph essay provoked. There is a sense that the high school experience had both positive and negative aspects that deserved further exploration and that might be common among many non-native students in U.S. high schools. Evelyn may have viewed her difficulties as personal problems, shameful events from an unexplored past, when in fact they are common. Would the peer and teacher feedback help Evelyn gain some critical distance on her past experiences and allow her to see her life in the U.S. in a social context? Perhaps by seeing them as social problems faced by others, she could understand her past more clearly.

With the bulk of the semester ahead of her, Evelyn had time to explore in more depth each of the time periods, about which she had written one paragraph each. Using oral and written feedback, she expanded each paragraph into a chapter, analyzing the causes of the events rather than simply outlining them. She wrote more, and she wrote more critically about such issues as race relations in a New York City high school.

An excerpt from her chapter "High School" shows how she reflected on and expanded what she wrote about this topic. By continuing to write about the experience, she gave more evidence to show why she was not so happy in high school and why she did not make friends among her American counterparts. After describing her positive experiences in English and math classes, Evelyn goes on to tell about gym class and the tension between natives and non-natives:

> My perfect subjects were English and math. All students in my English class came from different countries around the world. Although some of us couldn't understand each other well, we all came here with one goal—to learn English. The English teachers had more experience dealing with foreign students than the teachers in the language training school [written about in previous chapter]. Basically the lessons were useful and helpful in my daily life. For instance, we separated the class in small groups . . . .
>
> Most of the teachers in my high school paid responsibilities to their job except one or two who lost their patience with students like me who couldn't speak English. I had one teacher in my gym class. Unfortunately, she got eight foreign students in her badminton class. Usually, she picked one of us as bad examples. She didn't care whether the American students hit the bird over the net or not. But if one of us made the same mistakes, then she would come over to us and ask, "Have you paid attention in the class? What did I just say?" The gym class was supposed to be fun, but I had no fun at all.
>
> The majority of students in my high school were American, 12% were Latin-American students, and 8% were Asian students. Most of the new immigrant students had a tough time with some of the American students. Because of the different culture, language, and background, most of us were not accepted. Many of us had experiences attacking by those students, but not too many of us would like to identify them because we were afraid that they would attack again after school. In order to protect ourselves for being attacked, we were gathering as a group. We tried to stay away from them because we didn't know who was good and who wasn't. As a result, we hadn't got a chance to speak English with American students. By the time I graduated from high school, I still couldn't handle a simple conversation. Overall, four years in high school were a sweet time and also were an unpleasant time for me.

These paragraphs clarify issues that are only touched upon in the original essay: non-native students had a common goal (learning English) but also a common problem (abuse by some teachers and students, and the apparent inaction of the school administration on this issue); the problem interfered with attainment of the goal of learning English. Evelyn's more complete explanation of her high school experience was due, I believe, to three factors. One is that revision was structured into the course, so there was enough time to elaborate, since there were no other assignments to distract from the semester-long project. Another is that her readers (peers and teacher) were giving extensive feedback toward revision, prompting further elaboration of the ideas and consideration of the social causes of her experiences. And the third is that in *Two Years*, the model of autobiography for the course, the author feels free to comment critically and socially. He does not downplay his negative impressions of American life, nor does he spare the reader some of his unpleasant experiences of racism or xenophobia. Perhaps Evelyn took courage from Zongren to write about all sides of her experience, sharing both the "sweet" and the "unpleasant."

REFLECTING ON A NEW LIFE

Mei, a young nurse from Taiwan, approached *Two Years* and the writing of her autobiography as a newcomer, still adjusting to life in New York, at an American college, and with her in-laws. Responding in her journal, she shares her fears, her hopes, and her ambivalence, filtered through some of the topics found in *Two Years:*

> I have the same feelings as Zongren's. I feel that I am a stranger too. I don't know how American treat other different people. Because I have heard about the racial conflict between the black and the white. I am not sure whether they treat the other people beside blacks good or unfair. Till now I feel uncomfort among people except some elder friend people. I don't be sure they have patient to understand what I have said, or they want to listen to my poor expression of English. Everybody here was hurried.
>
> When I was in my country, I made efforts to be a head nurse in one more year after graduating from college. I thought it was proud for me. I could charge a cardiovascular ward in easy, but I don't communicate with others well so I am nothing here. I don't know how to be more aggressive, and I don't know how to get the chance to speak with Americans.
>
> I also have some fear of being depend on my husband, I need the hand of his to do something when we are outdoors. Sometimes I feel I am too no use.
>
> I don't know whether I love America now. I need time to consider seriously about the problem because I don't assure what I will be in the future. If it worthly live here? A new life symbols a new beginning, even not knowing good or bad.

The rawness of Mei's response is moving; she is examining her new life, unsure how it will turn out. Unlike Evelyn, who had been living in the U.S. since 1980 and who wanted mainly to study those past years, Mei dealt with the immediacy of her present life. Yet she needed critical reflection to grasp the events at hand.

In her initial essay, Mei demonstrated great sensitivity to her new surroundings; she discussed the ways in which extremes in temperature, fast food in the cafeteria, Manhattan skyscrapers, and the wooden houses of Staten Island were affecting her. In writing her autobiography, she grouped these reactions into themes and then chapters, such as "Climate," "Food and Eating," "Buildings," expanding and refining her ideas, and gaining detachment from her immediate reactions. One tool that Mei used to gain critical distance on her reactions was to include academic information that she had acquired in her Taiwanese nursing studies and that was detached from the flow of events in her present American life. The inclusion of this information allowed her to study the changes taking place, through the lens of a health care professional. Her autobiography, titled *A New Idea of the U.S.*, is an interesting blend of personal narrative, critical observations of American life, comparisons between life in Taiwan and in the U.S., and medical information. This blend of elements can be seen in the chapter "Food and Eating," excerpted below. First, Mei describes her hunger resulting from a distaste for American food, then her observation of American eating habits, then comments about changing eating habits in Taiwan, next a discussion of the biochemistry of a high fat diet, and finally observations about dining out in the U.S. and Taiwan. She uses writing to make sense of her new life, to discover what to accept, to reject, and to question:

> When I go out of my home, I am usually coming home with much hunger. I can't understand how people eat hamburgers, steaks, French fried, and so on every day. How could people stand that? In the stores, many foods are sealed by cans, the broth, the fruits, and many many foods. It is strange enough. Why not people eat fresh foods or do something they like to eat? Are people very busy in America? Don't they have enough time to eat? cook? Although it takes much time to cook Chinese foods, I like it very much. Fortunately my mother-in-law can prepare three meals for us and she is a good cook. When I go to school I prepare sandwiches for myself . . . .
>
> In Taiwan fast foods having gradually become a tide. Young people accepted this quickly; I like it too. Because it is clean to eat, but it has its problem, not balanced in nutrition . . . .
>
> That's talk about nutrition in the food that people eat in America. Many heart diseases come from plenty of food, especially fat, animal oil and sea foods have eliminated much triglycerol and cholesterol in metabolic process. So people suffer more in cardiovascular diseases. That's

terrible, it is happened in Taiwan too. There has the highest mortality in people's death. Chinese foods have much salt and oil in them. How to get balanced foods has become the most important class today.

I shall admire eating behaviors of Americans. They usually have good and pretty environment around them when they are eating. Even in the restaurant, the atmosphere is so quiet and peaceful. In Chinese people pay friendship to others by pushing them to drink a lot. People are difficult to refuse this for their friends' kindness . . . .

Reaching this level of articulation was not easy for Mei. She was not as fluent a speaker and writer of English as Evelyn. For example, she had spent a two-hour class period writing one paragraph of her initial essay, relying heavily on her dictionary and reporting that she was afraid of making mistakes. However, with feedback and as she became proficient with the computer, she took more risks in her writing. In fact, she learned to use the cut and paste function more proficiently than other students, giving her great flexibility when revising.

The course allowed Mei to study the society she had been living in for less than a year. She began with visceral impressions, such as the feeling of wearing heavy clothes in winter and the first taste of yogurt, and expanded these into chapters that analyzed the changes taking place in her life. Taking cues from Zongren, she reported on her experiences like an anthropologist, a participant–observer whose reactions are mediated by experience of another culture and by a special body of knowledge, health and nutrition.

This method of critical reflection validated Mei and the other students as legitimate cultural commentators who contribute various types of knowledge to the challenge of learning English. The student is not treated as a cultural deficit who must be filled with culture and language.

CONCLUSION

Should students be invited to study their adopted society critically? One of my students, Lucia, an American citizen who had fled Cuba during the revolution, did not think so. "What right does he have to criticize?" she asked when we were discussing *Two Years* at the beginning of the semester. From Lucia's point of view, foreigners such as Zongren, or immigrants such as her fellow students, or even foreign-born citizens such as herself have no right to critique the country that has received them. In a critical classroom, a reaction such as Lucia's provides an opportunity to discuss openly the curriculum that is being co-developed by the teacher and students. The discussion that followed Lucia's question was rich; it included such topics as freedom of expression, the role of immigrants in the economic development of the United States, and the place of dissent in society.

Our students are affected by social conditions, and they have something to gain by analyzing social conditions as part of their linguistic and personal development. Through critical reflection, "society now reveals itself as something unfinished, not as something inexorably given; it has become a challenge rather than a hopeless limitation." (Freire, 1973, p. 13)

REFERENCES

Atwell, N. (1987). *In the middle: Writing, reading, and learning with adolescents.* Portsmouth, NH: Heinemann.

Auerbach, E. (1990). *Making meaning, making change.* Boston: University of Massachusetts, English Family Literacy Project.

Bartholomae, D. & Petrosky, A. (1986). *Facts, artifacts and counterfacts.* Upper Montclair, NJ: Boynton/Cook.

Calkins, L.M. (1983). *Lessons from a child.* Portsmouth, NH: Heinemann.

Coles, N. (1986). Empowering revision. In D. Bartholomae, & A. Petrosky (Eds.), *Facts, artifacts and counterfacts.* (pp. 167–198) Upper Montclair, NJ: Boynton/Cook.

Freire, P. (1973). *Education for critical consciousness.* New York: Continuum Books.

Graves, D. (1983). *Writing: Teachers and children at work.* Portsmouth, NH: Heinemann.

Hudelson, S. (1989). *Write on: Children writing in ESL.* Englewood Cliffs, NJ: Prentice Hall.

MacGowan-Gilhooly, A. (1991). Fluency first: Reversing the traditional ESL sequence. *Journal of Basic Writing, 10*(1), 73–87.

Shor, I. (1980). *Critical teaching and everyday life.* Chicago: University of Chicago Press.

Shor, I. & Freire, P. (1987). *A Pedagogy for liberation.* South Hadley, MA: Bergin & Garvey.

Wallerstein, N. (1983). *Language and culture in conflict.* Reading, MA: Addison–Wesley.

Zongren, L. (1984). *Two years in the melting pot.* San Francisco: China Books.

CHAPTER 14

Reading for Composing: Connecting Processes to Advancing ESL Literacies

Fran Filipek Collignon
International Institute of Rhode Island

"I have no words."

Ploua Lee Khang

Ploua Lee Khang says "I have no words" whenever it is time to write English. She and 23 other adult Southeast Asian refugees, employed as bilingual/bicultural workers in neighboring cities and towns in the Northeast, took Topics in Writing for the Helping Professions, a continuing education course at Rhode Island College in the summer of 1989. The demand for writing on the job brought Ploua and the other course participants to this in-service opportunity. They were experiencing a frustration shared by all too many non-native speakers of English—perhaps a majority of native speakers of English, as well—dissatisfaction with their own writing.

This chapter describes, from my perspective as the instructor and codesigner,[1] a course that took its direction primarily from the students' articulated learning needs. In designing the course, we took up a challenge to educators (Kazemek, 1988) to make some necessary changes, to explore new notions of literacy and practice informed by theory appropriate to adult learners. The design, therefore, frames the composition course in the context of adult literacy. Its underlying theoretical principles support interactions among participants that forge new awarenesses of the connections between reading and writing. Descriptions of part of the writing process of one participant, Ploua Lee Khang, highlight the significance of authentic reading to the composing process. The following narrative demonstrates how socially constructed learning supports adult learners, especially those minimally schooled, like Ploua, in owning their own processes of making and communicating meaning.

---

[1]Mary McGann was the codesigner of this course. She was the Director of the Writing Center at Rhode Island College and my academic advisor in advanced degree work there when "Topics in Writing for the Helping Professions" was offered in 1989. McGann facilitated the administration of the course, assisted me in its initial design, and engaged in reflections with me relative to its implementation before, during, and after the course.

HISTORY OF THE COURSE

The consequences of resettlement in a new country, especially the need to seek employment and pursue academic and professional credentialing, repeatedly confronted the refugees in Ploua's class with the inadequacies of their literacies. They experienced themselves as outside of what Frank Smith refers to as "the literacy club" (1985). (See Eskey, this volume, for further discussion of this issue.) These bilingual/bicultural workers had requested this writing class in a needs assessment that state officials had conducted ten months prior among service providers from the refugee communities. In response, a network of state, college, and agency representatives, as well as some prospective participants, collaborated in funding, designing, scheduling, and implementing the writing course.

THE PARTICIPANTS

The 24 men and women in Ploua's class ranged in age from 25 to 49 years old and represented three ethnicities: Cambodian, Laotian, and Hmong. Six months to ten years had elapsed since their forced departures from their homelands. The students' prior learning experiences varied as much as their accounts of escapes from war-torn countries. A few participants, like Ploua, had only a few years of formal education and no native language literacy until recently. Others were professionals in their countries of origin. In addition to their first languages, some were conversant in other languages (e.g., Lao, Thai, Hmong, Khmer, Chinese, and French) developed through the exigencies of survival or in academic settings. Changing discourse modes (cultural practices inherent in language use) in English now, too, became another challenge to them, as did their struggles to transfer known skills across very dissimilar languages.

Additionally, the multiple roles of parent, employee, student, and refugee presented these adults simultaneously with many new aspects of ESL literacy. Their input about writing needs from both their personal lives and their employment influenced the content of the class sessions. What their work supervisors originally had envisioned—a work-site class, introducing work-specific vocabulary—expanded in focus. The participants who sought assistance exclusively with work-related tasks, such as filling out client forms or writing business letters, were the exception. Instead, when asked what they needed to learn, most participants said "I need everything."

These adults reported variations of the frustration that Ploua experienced when trying to write English—"no words." Rather than needing "something to say," Ploua and her colleagues sought more strategies for getting started with writing and an expanded vocabulary for making sense in English. The demands for writing in the different roles of their adult lives were often interconnected. The students juggled languages and literacies. The course design took this reality into account. The syllabus was intended to advance literacies, instead of only to help with writing.

THEORETICAL ASSUMPTIONS

The theoretical principles of the Brazilian educator Paulo Freire and the Russian psychologist Lev S. Vygotsky appropriately frame a pedagogy focusing on how individuals, teacher(s) and students, progress as a community of learners. Freire and Vygotsky assign language a central role in transforming people's consciousnesses. Freire, in the literacy circles he convened in Brazil, and Vygotsky, in his research with collaborative problem solving in the Soviet Union, employ social interactionist frameworks to address problems; that is, they attribute changes in consciousness to the transforming power of personal interactions, Freire in the sociopolitical order and Vygotsky in the order of internal higher functions. These principles supported an interactionist approach for the proposed course, inasmuch as interactions around reading and writing in class sessions, facilitated by the teacher, a peer, or a visitor to the class, assisted learners in advancing their literacies.

Meaningful interactions within a community are a necessary context for advancement in communicative abilities, according to Vygotsky's analysis of human development (Cole *et al.*, 1978). In addition to insistence on meaningful interactions, Freirean social analysis posits that a more egalitarian approach to persons also increases communicative potential (1970). The assumptions of Vygotsky and Freire provide an effective theoretical basis for collaborative pedagogy. No one has all the answers or claims to. Power and responsibilities shift.

INTERRELATIONSHIPS

Freire and Vygotsky recognize that dialogical relationships between people foster experiences of co-learning. Educationally, Freire (1970) advocates co-intentional learning; participants and their worlds are subjects of each other's learning. For him, this perspective replaces the banking concept of education, a one-way transmission of information from teachers to students. Vygotsky also describes a dialogical process of development. In elaborating on a zone of proximal development, he describes this ZPD as a place between a child's "actual development level as determined by independent problem solving" and the higher level of "potential development as determined through problem solving under adult guidance or in collaboration with more capable peers" (Cole *et al.*, 1978, p. 67). The literacy class has the potential, in Freirean or Vygotskian terms, to function as such a developmental construct when teachers and multilevel groups of students exchange information and pass on successful processes.

In such an environment, the activities of the class are meant to empower participants, teachers and students alike, to discover and develop new interactive strategies around print. Both of these theorists advocate the use of dialectical concepts in order to transform people's consciousnesses so that they can use words in ways that constitute the new realities in their lives. Course participants were learning each other's languages and cultures. The functions that Freire and Vygotsky ascribe to literacy—a way of reading and writing the world (Freire & Macedo, 1987) and a tool of thinking (Vygotsky, 1986)—fit the expectations of the participants of the proposed course.

LITERACY

Selection of this theoretical framework for the course required shifts not only in the roles traditionally assigned to teachers and students, but also in educators' notions of literacy. Literacy practices in the class sessions included activities using speech and print; they took into account learners' current knowledge while simultaneously expanding it for the writing tasks they confronted in their jobs. An ideological view of literacy, as Street (1984) proposes it, moves understandings of literacy beyond those associated solely with the autonomous development of technical skills for reading and writing to the broader considerations of the necessity of these skills for communicating meaning and values for a variety of purposes. Nothing autonomous or disconnected from life would have assisted this course's participants. They already grappled with an economy of time and meaningful opportunities in which to address better ways of meeting the demands of their lives. An ideological view of literacy, as Street describes it, expresses and constitutes values for life. This view spoke to the concerns of the course participants.

Additionally, the use of "literacies" (Graff, 1987; Gee, 1989) instead of the narrower "literacy" linked the term as it was more broadly conceptualized to an underlying objective of the course. Participants desired culturally appropriate ways of using languages as well as differing discourse modes within one language. They recognized the need to discover processes to advance the uses of their literacies.

A multiplicity of writing needs was embedded in the authentic reading and writing tasks students brought to class. Responsive literacy practices of the class sessions attempted to move, for example, Ploua's "no words" along to her more confident use of a range of strategies for communicating the struggles, beliefs, and aspirations within her adult roles. Literacy in an interactionist approach became a developmental process as well as a term that identified using speech in the form of print.

Given the social dimensions of literacy, learning models that facilitate interactions among participants take advantage of the potential inherent in the multidimensional and multidirectional nature of people's literacies. Interactive processes that engender mutuality and trust among participants in classes capitalize on the social dimensions of literacy. Literacy is perceived as constitutive (Bruner, 1982). Participants' interactions do more than find words for their worlds; they create worlds (Smith, 1983). Collaborative learning in such a literacy setting becomes a dynamic process.

SYLLABUS

Cognizant that any group of non-native speakers of English, especially culturally diverse groups, come from and bring different sociocultural perspectives to tasks (Heath, 1982; 1983), as instructor I sought a shared context that would incorporate that diversity. My intention was to capitalize on the strengths of individual participants and also to bring their diversity to bear on the interactions around the authentic reading and writing in class. No prescribed, static syllabus could have predicted the direction the literacy practices among participants would take nor fully anticipate the range of goals of the students in the course. Of necessity, generating a dynamic syllabus collaboratively with students during the class sessions became an essential process during the course.

In class, we sought the discovery of needed strategies and processes. Often, a particular session focused on assisting learners in transferring skills and information they already grasped in another language (e.g., informal/formal greetings) or culturally appropriate ways of reporting information (e.g., acceptable clinical language). Chamot (1988), in presenting a cognitive academic language learning approach, advocates making strategies overt in order to increase participants' access to learning. Finding ways to make writing strategies more explicit became an overriding goal of the course.

Ploua, her colleagues, sometimes their supervisors, and the teacher sought the kind of strategies that Elsasser & John-Steiner (1977) suggest for enabling silent speakers to become potent writers. This search included explorations into the many forms of speech that could support the contextualization of thoughts students needed. Reading strategies were as vital as writing ones. When the participants could not read directions, extract meaning from the print they decoded, or interpret cultural nuances requisite for effective communication, they could not begin to write. The students' articulations of their own writing needs had initially given impetus to the course. The recognition of the ongoing nature of their writing needs continued to engage them in developing requisite strategies.

A process writing approach served as a point of entry from which to address a multiplicity of other literacy needs (e.g., the expansion of vocabulary, listening skills, comprehension, etc.). The writing processes that, for example, Graves (1983) and Calkins (1983) describe in their teacher research with children were adapted to fit the collaborative adult class. Introducing terms used in process writing (e.g., talking about drafts, revising, editing, etc.) and fidelity to the articulated need (writing) that brought these adults to the class also provided a link. The immediate composing tasks, specified by these refugees, expanded their supervisors' and teachers' understandings of the larger tasks incumbent on any refugee, those connected with "composing" self in a new culture.

CLASS

The following overview of the process within the class sessions demonstrates how using the interconnections around authentic reading and writing tasks in an interactive approach can be put to the service of the language development of any learners with a myriad of goals in literacy. Instead of attending primarily to learners' weaknesses (previously self-acknowledged to be their technical writing skills and inadequate English vocabulary), collaborative efforts to produce their requested reading/writing tasks shifted the focus to the class. A problem-posing approach, which Freire describes as a constant "unveiling of reality . . . which strives for the emergence of consciousness and critical intervention in reality" (1970, p. 68), engaged learners in reflection about their worlds. It tapped into the thinking, creating, and problem solving interests that Zamel (1987) recognizes as preferred activities characteristic of ESL learners who have progressed beyond their initial exposure to print.

The students in the course represented such a population considered somewhat orally fluent, employable, and assertive enough to take advantage of an optional in-service opportunity. They also exhibited enthusiasm regarding their thinking about, creating around, and problem solving from two lists of writing needs generated at the second session of the course: clinical descriptions of clients or patients, business letters, summaries of agency activities, record of patients' complaints, support letters, memoranda, reports, daily logs, cover letters, etc. The participants, 13 in one section of the course and 11 in another, met for two hours each week for 15 weeks to compose the listed writing products. The articulations in subsequent classes of additional writing needs came from students' work demands as they occurred (e.g., help with filling out data collection forms, preparing testimony for a legislative committee, preparing a commencement address, taking notes at committee meetings, and writing to immigration authorities). The requests included help with reading as often as with writing.

The preparation of each class session included selecting a codification (Freire, 1970). Beyond Freire's original use of the word to identify a picture that would codify the problem to be posed to a group, Wallerstein (1983) expands the concept of code to include any visual, transcribed dialogue or other representation that codifies a message of interest to learners. In this course, the use of codifications often meant eliciting from learners a consensus on which of the previously listed writing needs to address at the next class. Occasionally, a learner brought a code to class—a newspaper clipping, a form to be filled out, a street directory, an interoffice memo. Employing a code during the pre-writing time at each session centered students on a common task, raised consciousnesses through the ensuing dialogue, expanded the working vocabulary through the discussion, and provided the context out of which participants gained understanding about individuals' writing pieces.

Sometimes, pre-writing activities in class took the form of interviews, small group discussions, or other helpful formats. A first draft, written by each participant during each class session, would be read aloud in class. Oral reading was utilized as more than performance. It enabled the reader/writer to experience audience. The invited feedback from other participants often provided data for inclusion in the homework assignment, additional revising and editing of the draft. The writers who wished to would read their second drafts again aloud at the next class session. Each individual, after reading aloud and incorporating more feedback into the second draft, would then determine the next step for his or her draft. The options included decisions about whether to hand a composition in for feedback from the teacher, give it to another student for written comments, or keep it in order to revise and edit it oneself another time before submitting it in final draft form.

ROLE OF TEACHER/FACILITATOR

In the interrelationships within the class, the teacher emerged more as a facilitator than an instructor. The mutuality that Freire recommends in order to maximize the group's communicative potential is nurtured by the teacher's stance. Because of a sensitivity to nurturing reciprocal relationships, I attempted to create that environment by very explicit behaviors: (a) participating in every activity, not necessarily directing it; (b) sometimes selecting the codification and at other times encouraging another participant's initiative in supplying one; (c) engaging in the writing processes in class; (d) completing every homework assignment; and (e) exploring with students their suggested alternative strategies to the ones I proposed. For example, my partner in a class activity suggested that we write letters to each other weekly as an alternative to writing weekly in dialogue journals, the strategy I had suggested, used in most of the other dyads as an ongoing free-writing activity.

Decisions made and implemented by collaborating peers brought creativity and vitality to language development. Freirean and Vygotskian theories support what the interpersonal dynamics in the course demonstrated. As Freire insists that pedagogy must be "forged with, not for" people (1970, p. 33), Vygotsky, in his principles, advocates similar relationships. Commenting on Vygotsky's zone of proximal development, Wertsch (1985) refers to the ZPD as the sensitive region wherein an individual's development potentially occurs. In the collaborative pedagogy employed in this course, sometimes the teacher functioned as what Vygotsky calls a more capable peer (1986) working with the student. At other times, the students became informants to the teacher. They pointed out invisible cultural patterns (Erickson, 1990) that influence interethnic communication. All the participants, in the variety of interactions, contributed some significant expertise. The structure of class sessions evoked strengths rather than concentrating on deficits; it enlisted support for students, instead of exerting pressure on them. Such a design fostered the collaborations and productive dialogue within those collaborations (Erickson, 1989) that expanded literacies.

PLOUA

In such a learning environment, sophisticated, highly educated students did not necessarily have the edge on students like Ploua, minimally schooled and lacking prior experience in the workplace. The atmosphere of exchange, in fact, effectively addressed the professional development needs of especially those, like Ploua, needing insights about issues unimaginable to those who have never been in comparable circumstances.

Ploua, a 27-year-old Hmong[2] woman from Laos, came to class because she was newly employed in the helping professions and needed assistance with the writing involved in her job as a patient representative in a community-based health care facility. Her supervisor at work required very formidable tasks of her—the most challenging, that she document in English the conversations that she had with patients of the same ethnicity in their native language. For these tasks, Ploua felt ill-equipped.

---

[2]The Hmong are a hill tribe of Southeast Asia. They engaged in subsistence farming, moving from mountain to mountain as their slash-and-burn farming methods dictated. As a result of their involvement in the Vietnam War, almost a hundred thousand Hmong from Laos have been resettled in the United States. Their assistance to the CIA as a secret army during the war necessitated their flight from retaliation by the Vietcong victors at the war's end. Approximately 1,500 Hmong people live in Providence, Rhode Island now. Traditionally, the Hmong are said to have had no written language of their own. Only with Western domination of the areas they inhabited during the fifties and sixties did their language get recorded in the Roman Alphabet.

Having studied in school for only three years as a child in Laos, her country of origin, Ploua learned and became literate there in her second language, Lao, in order to assist her parents in the market they seasonally set up in the city. Of Hmong ethnicity, Ploua had used only her first language, Hmong, during the rest of her youth in her Hmong village. With a limited proficiency in Thai from her refugee camp stay and her grasp of English, Ploua was becoming increasingly multilingual. She had managed to become conversant in English and to read and write it minimally only since her arrival in the United States in March of 1980. The intake form from 1980 in the files of a local community-based refugee program reflects that, at that time, she could not even respond to questions about her country of origin. Besides her beginning Lao literacy as a child, Ploua had encountered print only one other time before her arrival in the United States—when she had studied Hmong literacy for a month in a refugee camp in Thailand, from a young Hmong woman who had been schooled in a Laotian city.

Ploua's current employment, therefore, faced her with very sophisticated needs: making multiple transformations of speech that second language (in Ploua's case, fourth language) learners require to contextualize verbal thinking into writing (John-Steiner, 1985). She used both her Hmong and English literacies daily at work and, sometimes even her Lao literacy (with a Laotian coworker). The above-mentioned minimal schooling in Laos, the month's tutorial experience in Hmong literacy, and sporadic study in adult refugee programs left Ploua with a very fragmented history of formal language learning. She registered for the course out of her determination to function well in her new position at work.

SESSIONS FIVE AND SIX

Tracing Ploua's speech in two class sessions provided me with an opportunity to appreciate how the various interactions around writing, especially reading, conducted Ploua through many transformations of speech and ultimately advanced her literacies. After Ploua and the other students in her class had reviewed at session four their previously listed writing needs, they chose a writing topic for session five—the need for a short answer in response to the repeated questions Americans ask: "Where do you come from?" or "Why are you here?" I responded to their requests with a slide presentation as the codification for the fifth class session. Five slides that I had taken four years earlier in Southeast Asia[3] became

---

[3]During the months of November and December of 1985, I accompanied a colleague in refugee work, Rev. William Tanguay, to Southeast Asia. In our visits to refugee camps and Hmong villages in Thailand near the Laotian and Burmese borders, he introduced me to perspectives on Hmong language and culture which supplemented the vestiges of Hmong life I had experienced in the United States.

the shared context from which we composed answers to the designated questions. Recognizing that the search for answers to the same questions learners report Americans frequently ask had motivated my own trip to Southeast Asia in 1985, I chose the slides as a way of entering into Vygotsky's zone of proximal development and what Freire would consider a dialogue among equals from which generative words and ideas flow.

No narration accompanied the slides I showed at session five. I introduced them only by stating those familiar American questions that had drawn me to Southeast Asia: Where do Southeast Asian refugees come from? Why are they here? The five slides projected on the screen depicted a large map of all of Southeast Asia, a close-up of a portion of the map (showing only Vietnam, Laos, Cambodia, and Thailand), a picture of myself in a crowd of Hmong people against a background of the mountains of Laos, a picture of myself gazing reflectively at the Mekong River, and people streaming into an airplane at the Bangkok airport.

Sighs and gasps accompanied the learners' first glimpses of the slides upon their recognition of maps of their homelands and the spectacular panoramas of the Mekong River snaking through the mountains. During the viewing of the slides, some learners remained quietly meditative on them; others conversed in their first languages. The pitch of excited conversations mounted during the viewing. When I asked the participants if they were ready to write yet, an unequivocal "no" came from the group. They were requesting additional discussion time in their respective first languages: Hmong, Cambodian, and Lao.

With this description of the context of the fifth class session, I frame the following responses of Ploua to the slides of Southeast Asian scenes and the reading and writing connections that ensued from the participatory session. When the majority of participants appeared ready to write, I slowly advanced each slide into view on the screen one more time. Ploua, again, as she initially did upon seeing the slides, proclaimed in Hmong "mi, mi, mi, mi, mi . . ." (the adjective for "small" in Hmong, repeated for intensity) upon reading Laos on such a small segment of the map on the first slide of all of Southeast Asia. Becoming aware of non-Hmong listeners, she translated, "Laos . . . small." She then told everybody, "My country's small. I don't know that," sounding surprised and disappointed at the same time.

Ploua's conversation with the colleague sitting beside her accounted for her reactions. She explained to the Laotian woman that she had never seen Laos on a map before. She then translated from Lao to English for me what she had said to this woman. Ploua did not know where to begin or how to describe the "new" Laos she saw on the map. When the other participants, as directed, began free-writes about their own countries, Ploua told me, as she usually did when it was time to write in English, that she had "no words for that." I suggested that she begin to write in Hmong first or that she get help from someone.

Ploua walked over to two other Hmong students who had begun to write. She asked if she could read their writing. They agreed. She stood over them, reading each one's writing from the papers on the table in front of them. After she finished, she told me that she had been reading their "words." She completed a short free-write. It read, "Laos is small country I think. My country is war." She asked the Laotian colleague sitting beside her to read her writing while she waited for everyone else to finish writing lengthier accounts. The woman assented, read her writing, and assured Ploua that she understood.

Reading the writing of her Hmong classmates accomplished several objectives for Ploua. In subsequent interviews with Ploua about the interactions of the class, she verified that she needed to be sure she understood the assignment. She needed to find new words from others and boost her own self-confidence in their encouragement to her to write what she could.

When I invited each person to read his or her free-write aloud at the end of the class, Ploua volunteered to go first. She warned her listeners that her contribution was "short, but O.K." After reading her two sentences aloud, she carefully listened to the other free-writes or rough first drafts as each participant volunteered, in turn, to read aloud. She copied down some words she heard. She brought her copy over again to one of the Hmong men she had originally consulted. He had since then read aloud his own very lengthy description of Laos and the plight of Hmong people. He and Ploua conversed in Hmong. Ploua brought her first draft home, rather than handing it over to me or another student for feedback.

When Ploua returned to class the next week, she had lengthened her original two-thought composition. She asked to read her composition aloud. She used *peddler* in her story. After her oral reading, other learners questioned her word choice. *Peddler* did not sound like her. Ploua described having accessed her American supervisor at work as her audience for her second draft and having gotten the word from her.

Ploua subsequently incorporated, in yet another draft, many suggestions that other participants made during these class discussions about her need to contextualize her ideas further (e.g., "Explain that you were looking at a map." Another piece of advice to her was "Give Americans something to compare with their own country."). In response, in her final draft, Ploua explained that her descriptions of Laos came from looking at a map. She created for American readers a basis of comparison, mentioning snow existing in the United States and not in Laos. Her final draft, expanded from its original two thoughts, demonstrates how a collaborative pedagogy has enabled her refrain of "no words" to progress through the multiple drafts she offered to read aloud in class and to audiences elsewhere.

Laos

In laos I'm not sure how big is it but I look on the
    map it looks like a small country.
   It has mountains and alot of bamboos
in laos it is very hot it doesn't had snow like the
United state it has rain on July for seven days
and seven nights. Our's country is beautiful.
   Some of the American people asked me
why I'm here, Then I said to them because our
country was war we couldn't stay in our
country when the communist came to our country
We didn't have enough food and clothes
everythings were expensive during that
time in 1975 and they killed many of the
Peddlers are walked from village to village
   Then I was so afraid that's why
I have to escape from place to place untill I
got here.

                           Ploua Lee Khang

Ploua's interactions around authentic reading and writing, recon-
structed from my field notes about the class, etched in my memory, and
verified by her in reflective cross-cultural interviewing (Spindler, 1987)
after the sessions, moved her literacy. Evidence of her expanded writing
process, culminating in her composition about Laos, only hint at the significance of what happened to most of the participants during the processes of the entire course. Descriptions of these two sessions provide only a
glimpse of the countless strategies that moved literacies.

As did the other participants, Ploua discovered that looking for help
could take many forms. In the fifth session, when she approached two
other men of her ethnicity before beginning to compose, admittedly she
sought support as much as technical assistance. She did, however, copy
words from them that she had not seen in print before. When she offered
to read her two thoughts aloud, she intended to test an audience. Their
suggestions for her continuation and additions to her story about Laos
became the core of her search for "words." Especially their questions
about a word, *peddler*, not seeming to be of her voice, caused her to question its use before eventually deciding to retain it in her text. Besides input
from her American supervisor at work, Ploua accessed classmates outside
of class time as well as during class. She and her two colleagues at the
community health center read their drafts to each other at coffee breaks.

Ploua no longer resorted to her refrain "no words," once she adopted
strategies from the participants in the course and developed her own
strategies for finding "words." She listened to, spoke, and read silently or

aloud Hmong, Lao, and English in her struggles to convey sense in her writing. Beyond the receptive posture of attaining "comprehensible input," which Krashen (1985) posited as central to second language acquisition, Ploua learned from the personal interactions that Vygotsky (1986) says begin all internalizations of meaning.

Ploua's thoughts spiraled through the generative circles that Freire (1970) describes; he images concentric circles representing the enlarging and contracting parameters of individuals' understandings as their consciousnesses focus on their changing inner and outer worlds. Ploua's Laos demonstrates this movement. Laos, previously imagined by her as the immense whole world, was dwarfed by its neighbors on the map of Southeast Asia when she saw it for the first time in the fifth class session. However, Laos expanded for her once again when she recognized its significance through the discussion in class of the worldwide presence of refugees needing resettlement.

An ideological view of literacy manifests itself in the discussions of the class about their war-torn lands. One of Ploua's Cambodian classmates poetically recounted her own country as having been "caught like a walnut in the jaws of its neighbors." In the interactions around describing the participants' countries of origin and in the mediation of print they read (even the print that labeled *Laos* on the map), Ploua and the other class participants experienced advances in their thinking and writing.

Many of the participants had minimal or sporadic schooling and, in addition to needing instruction in discrete skills, needed information about how and where to access the information they had never learned about grammar, syntax, punctuation, and diction. They also recognized the need for what Vygotsky (1986) refers to as scaffolding. Bruner (1987), elaborating on Vygotsky's concept, describes scaffolding as the use of an "aiding peer . . . until such a time as the learner is able to master his own action through his own consciousness and control" (p. 24). Reading silently or listening to other more experienced writers read their writing aloud provided such scaffolding for people like Ploua. With little exposure to English at home or in her social community, Ploua gained from the reading in class as a supplement to her only other opportunity for reading English—at work.

Connecting reading and writing in class sessions, through processes that are simple and replicable in numerous contexts, models for learners avenues for advancing their literacies. Social constructs that initiate the search for strategies engage learners in what Vygotsky considers "the discovery of the changeable nature of word meanings and their development" (1986, p. 249). While Vygotsky probes the internal transformations of speech and its effects on consciousness, Freire points up the societal ramifications of consciousnesses moved by the power of words: "[N]o one can say a true word alone—nor can he say it for another, in a prescriptive act which robs others of their words." (1970, pp. 76–77)

CONCLUSION

Finding words for their worlds preoccupies the learners in "Topics in Writing for the Helping Professions." Ploua and her colleagues struggle to convey meaning with words that Elsasser and John-Steiner (1977) call "fragile bridges," given the variables of users' backgrounds and experiences. Efforts that facilitate learners' searches for words through powerful and empowering strategies demonstrate not only the significance of personal interactions, but also of connecting those interactions with print, be it reading or writing. Forging these connections expands consciousnesses while advancing literacies. Socially constructed pedagogies, while supporting learners' expanding consciousnesses of their worlds, also enable teachers to develop more global understandings with which to assist learners. Connecting processes for and around the use of print strengthens the fragile bridges that words are for people trying to span worlds.

REFERENCES

Bruner, J. (1987). Prologue to the English edition. Vygotsky, L.S. Problems of general psychology, Vol. I. In R.W. Rieber & A.S. Carton (Eds.), *The collected works of L.S. Vygotsky* (pp. 1–16). New York: Plenem.

Bruner, J. (1984). Language, mind, and reading. In H. Goelman, A. Oberg, & F. Smith (Eds.), *Awakening to literacy* (pp. 193–200). Portsmouth, NH: Heinemann.

Calkins, L. (1983). *Lessons from a child.* Exeter, NH: Heinemann.

Chamot, A.U. (1988). Cognitive academic language learning, an approach for transitional students. Presentation at New England Multifunctional Resource Center Conference: Reflections on literacy. Portland, ME.

Cole, M., John-Steiner, V., Scribner, S., & Souberman, E. (Eds.). (1978). *Mind in society.* Cambridge: Harvard University Press.

Elsasser, N. & John-Steiner, V.P. (1977). An interactionist approach to advancing literacy. *Harvard Educational Review, 47,* 355–369.

Erickson, F. (1990). Collaboration in practice. Presentation at Multifunctional Resource Center Conference: Literacy, collaboration, and practice. Boston, MA.

Erickson, F. (1989). Research currents: Learning and collaboration in teaching. *Language Arts, 66,* 4.

Freire, P. (1970). *Pedagogy of the oppressed* (M.B. Ramos, Trans.). New York: Continuum.

Freire, P. & Macedo, D. (1987). *Literacy: Reading the word and the world.* South Hadley, MA: Bergin & Garvey.

Gee, J. (1989). What is literacy? *Journal of Education, 171*(1), 18–25.

Graff, H.J. (1987). *The legacies of literacy: Continuities and contradictions in western culture and society.* Bloomington, IN: Indiana University Press.

Graves, D.H. (1983). *Writing: Teachers and children at work.* Exeter, NH: Heinemann.

Heath, S.B. (1983). *Ways with words: Language, life and work in communities and classrooms.* New York: Cambridge University Press.

Heath, S.B. (1982). What no bedtime story means: Narrative skills at home and school. *Language in Society, II,* 49–76.

John-Steiner, V.P. (1985). The road to competence in an alien land: A

Vygotskian perspective on bilingualism. In J.V. Wertsch (Ed.), *Culture, communication and cognition: Vygotskian perspectives.* Cambridge: Harvard University Press.

Kazemek, F.E. (1988). Necessary changes: Professional involvement in adult literacy programs. *Harvard Educational Review, 58*(4), 464–486.

Krashen, S.D. (1985). *The input hypothesis: Issues and implications.* New York: Longman.

Smith, F. (1985). *Joining the literacy club.* Portsmouth, NH: Heinemann.

Smith, F. (1983). *Essays into literacy.* Portsmouth, NH: Heinemann.

Spindler, G. (Ed.). (1987). *Education and cultural process: Anthropological approaches* (2nd ed.). Prospect Heights, IL: Waveland Press.

Street, B. (1984). *Literacy in theory and practice.* New York: Cambridge University Press.

Vygotsky, L.S. (1986). *Thought and language.* (A. Kozulin, Trans.& Ed.) Cambridge: MIT Press. (Originally published in 1962).

Wallerstein, N. (1983). *Language and culture in conflict: Problem-posing in the ESL classroom.* Reading, MA: Addison-Wesley.

Wertsch, J.V. (1985). *Vygotsky and the social formation of mind.* Cambridge: Harvard University Press.

Zamel, V. (1987). Recent research on writing pedagogy. *TESOL Quarterly 21*(4), 697–712.

CHAPTER 15

Reading and Writing Tasks in English for Academic Purposes Classes: Products, Processes, and Resources

Ann M. Johns
San Diego State University

English for Academic Purposes (EAP) courses are designed to prepare ESL/EFL and native-speaking students for the literacy demands at the secondary or college/university level. Hundreds of EAP classes exist in many parts of the world, at language institutes, in university English departments, in learning skills centers, and sometimes in "home content" departments such as engineering or business. No matter where they are, these classes have engendered questions and debate about skills integration, class structure, and syllabus type.

Some of the skills debate has subsided, as indicated by recent research and the chapters in this volume. For example, it is now agreed that at least two of the academic skills, reading and writing, cannot be separated, either in terms of research or practice (Flower, *et al.*, 1990; Eisterhold, 1990; Johns, in press, a). Almost every writing assignment in the disciplines requires reading; many reading assignments and examinations require writing (Horowitz, 1986a). In addition, there is growing evidence for the relationship between effective reading and effective writing processes (Flower, *et al.*, 1990). Thus the papers in this volume are designed to encourage research, curriculum, and classroom activities that enhance the relationship between these two skills, which combined provide the basis for academic literacy.

A second, more controversial issue centers around class structure, specifically the relationship between an EAP class and the "outside," i.e., the academic classes (Brinton, Snow, & Wesche, 1989; McCormick, 1990; Swales, 1990). Some experts advocate a free-standing EAP class in which the principal aims are to encourage the writing process and increase student confidence (Spack, 1988). Members of this group often contend that literature may be the appropriate vehicle for achieving student understanding of the reading and writing processes, the English-language culture, and themselves (Spack, 1985; and Horowitz's response, 1990). Others design classes that are more self-consciously allied to academic content and context (Connor & Johns, 1989; Swales, 1987). For upper-division and graduate students in both English medium and EFL environments, the second choice seems to be the appropriate one. However, the debate about class structure and aims for those students whose academic and professional goals are not yet determined indicates that basic disagreements about these classes continue (Zamel *et al.*, 1991).

A third EAP issue is syllabus type; and here the debate can be seen as parallel to both the putative split between writing process and product (Goldstein, this volume; Coe, 1987; Silva, 1990) and the more obvious division between the self-contained and the outward-looking class structures. For the process advocates, who generally teach self-contained classes, it is the students' development and understanding of their own reading and writing processes that are central to the class syllabus. For the product-oriented, outward-looking faculty, or "social constructionists," the syllabus must begin with the written product and the disciplinary context for which it is produced.

In this paper, I will argue that in an EAP class in which reading and writing must be central, we cannot slavishly follow either process or product theories.[1] Instead, we should provide for our students the best possible opportunities to achieve academic success by developing a comprehensive, task-based syllabus founded upon all of the essential elements of academic literacy: the academic context, the learners and their processes, and the resources available. First, I explore some of the confusing array of definitions for *task*. Then, employing a broad definition of academic task (Doyle, 1983), including three components, *products, operations (also called processes or strategies), and resources*, I suggest questions that must be answered in the development of an EAP course. In responding to these questions with possible answers, I often use my own experiences with an EAP adjunct class, the class structure that I consider optimal for acquiring academic literacy.[2]

TASK DEFINITION

A confusing array of definitions for *task* exists in the literature. It is sometimes defined as "every human activity" (Crookes, 1986; Long, 1985). If we are to think of "every human activity" as directly related to learner-centered curricula, a variety of definitional possibilities still exist, including "a thinking process" (Moore *et al.*, 1986), "a strategy" (Chamot & O'Malley, 1986, 1987; Richards & Hurley, 1990), and "a learning behavior or action" (Nunan, 1988). However, if an academic curriculum is designed to take into consideration the situation in which a "human activity" must

---

[1]Raimes(1991) makes the same general argument; however, the practices she advocates are quite different from mine.

[2]My own social constructionist bent is evident here and throughout the text.

be performed, tasks can be seen as products or "real academic assign-ments" (Horowitz, 1986a) situated in a disciplinary context (Swales, 1990).

Fortunately, a number of experts have constructed comprehensive definitions of *task*, including both the learner-centered issues, which Mohan & Oszust (in press) call *learning tasks,* and the demands of the context, i.e., *target tasks,* since both task aspects appear to be necessary for promoting literacy goals (Flower, 1990; Ackerman, 1990). I have modi-fied one of these inclusive task definitions, by Doyle (1983), to establish the basis for this paper. Doyle breaks *task* down into components that represent the learning and the target issues discussed above:

> The term "task" focusses attention on three aspects of students' work: a) the products students are to formulate, such as an original essay or answers to a set of test questions (i.e., target tasks), b) the operations (or processes) that are necessary to produce these products, such as memoriz-ing and classifying (i.e., learner tasks), and c) the givens, the resources available to students while they are generating the product, such as a model essay. Academic tasks in other words, are defined by the answers students are required to produce and the routes that can be used to obtain these answers. (1983, p. 162)

Thus in Doyle's definition, there is a natural integration of process and product, obviating the necessity to separate the two, as is sometimes artificially done in the literature (Coe, 1987). The definition also provides accessible terminology for students, faculty, and administrators, and it can lead to authentic reading and writing activities and evaluation.

An integrated EAP syllabus will include all three of the components Doyle mentions, *products, operations, and resources.* Initially, I will sepa-rate them here, in order to pose—and attempt to answer—questions about each component. Readers will find that even in this artificial separation, there is an integration of the various elements.

MAJOR EAP CATEGORIES AND QUESTIONS

In the sections that follow, each of Doyle's major categories, products, operations (strategies), and resources (1983) will be discussed in turn, and methods for answering the questions posed for each category will be sug-gested. No integrated, finalized set of answers is proposed; instead, a vari-ety of possible answers are suggested, one or more of which may be of use to EAP practitioners.

Products: Genuine Academic Tasks

Question: *What methods can be employed to identify, collect, and ana-lyze genuine target tasks from academic environments?* Product identification and academic task analysis have long histories, for the issue of authenticity of texts and tasks is one that is central to EAP interests (Johns & Davies, 1981; Swales, 1987). The English for Specific Purposes experience, of which EAP is a major element, outlines a number of procedures for obtaining information about genuine written texts from real contexts and genuine tasks students must accomplish (Johns & Dudley-Evans, 1991; Robinson, 1991). Two of these methods will be examined here: surveys of faculty and student ethnographies.

Faculty Surveys

There are a number of important reasons for EAP teachers to survey faculty about the various products in academic contexts that students will exploit for reading and writing. The first reason, of course, is to provide authentic texts and tasks that will motivate students to read and write. The second is to make contact with faculty throughout a campus, thereby joining in conversations with experts (Carson, this volume; Swales, 1990). The best-known faculty surveys have been of writing demands, principally because proof of writing ability is central to advancement at many universities. A widely cited survey was conducted by Bridgeman & Carlson (1984) when preparing the TOEFL writing examination, the Test of Written English (TWE). Other, less comprehensive surveys have been employed on college campuses as well (Johns, 1981; Kroll, 1979; Ostler, 1980). Horowitz's work (1986a) is the most relevant to this discussion, for he studied academic literacy tasks for the purpose of developing a general EAP syllabus that would generalize from tasks in a number of disciplines. In his study, he surveyed university faculty from all disciplines and then collected their writing assignments. From this information, Horowitz compiled a list of common academic tasks (1986a, pp. 449–452): summary of/reaction to the data, report on a specified participatory experience, connection of theory and data, synthesis of multiple sources, and a "research project."[3] Not surprisingly, all of the tasks identified require the interaction of reading and writing. Though summary is the prototype of a reading-into-writing task, synthesis of multiple sources and research projects also require extensive reading before and during writing. In fact, from this list one could argue that it is impossible to assign academic writing tasks that don't require preliminary reading.

Though reading is necessary to the assignments discussed in the writing surveys, little if any research has been completed on the reading products in academic classes, or, more importantly, on the required interaction among literacy skills (i.e., reading, writing, listening, and speaking). However, a promising approach to assessing complex literacy demands has been instituted by Carson, Chase, & Gibson (in press), who

---

[3]Braine (1989) discovered many of the same types of assignments when surveying science and technology disciplines, heavily enrolled by ESL students.

investigated the interaction of reading, writing, listening, and speaking in a number of "identical" general education classes.

Student Ethnography

Another avenue for determining genuine literacy tasks in the disciplines is the student-as-ethnographer approach (Johns, 1990a; Swales, 1990). In an advanced EAP class, students can be assigned to collect, read, and discuss in writing the artifacts of their university courses and to record thick descriptions of lectures. At my university, San Diego State, cohorts of freshman students enrolled in adjunct reading and writing classes are also enrolled in a single general education class, e.g., introductory history or anthropology. One of the regular assignments for the adjunct classes is the collection of genuine reading and writing tasks and texts from their general education classes. From these data, and from their descriptions and experiences, we analyze and practice the literacy demands of their academic classrooms.

Question: *How can EAP faculty make the connection between pedagogy and the identified target tasks?* A more complex question relates to the connection between academic context and tasks and EAP classroom instruction, since genuine academic texts and tasks are socially constructed by and for disciplinary contexts (Ackerman, 1990; Prior, in press; see also Spack, 1988).

In my experience, the optimal answer for EAP classes may be found in the adjunct class structure, existing at my university and elsewhere (Brinton, Snow, & Wesche, 1989), in which an entire class of reading/writing students is enrolled in the same academic class. A "package" structure such as this is highly motivating, in that it permits the use of the genuine texts and literacy tasks from the academic class for all reading into writing assignments in the adjunct class. Thus students can read and summarize sections in their academic textbooks; they can read their notes and other texts in order to study for essay examinations; they can use the library purposefully to complete a research paper. Other alternatives for EAP classes, e.g., sheltered and theme-based, are more removed from the academic contexts. However, task surveys are available (e.g., Horowitz, 1986a), so instructors in other EAP class types can ensure a variety of reading/writing experiences, and students can practice necessary operations in these classes as well.

Operations or Strategies

So far, I have discussed issues of *product*, i.e., how we can identify and integrate real academic products into our EAP classes. Next, I will move to more learner-centered issues: what Doyle suggests as "operations" (1983) but what are often called "strategies" or "processes" in the literature. Although there are differences between strategies and processes, both fall under the "operations" rubric; therefore, for the purposes of this discussion, the three terms will be used interchangeably.

The first question under this category is the following: *What kinds of operations, processes, or strategies are useful to accomplish the required target tasks, and how can these operations be identified and employed in an EAP classroom?* The literature on strategies and operations is quite broad, overlapping, and complex. In order to focus this discussion, I have selected two approaches to researching operations or strategies, task representation and reading-into-writing, and one taxonomy of strategies, CALLA, assuming that readers will find among the three possibilities one useful approach for their EAP situations.

Task Representation

The first approach to researching strategies or operations to be discussed here is found under the task representation rubric (Flower, 1990). Native-speaking reading and writing literature is now expanding to include a number of studies to determine how students cognitively represent literacy tasks and the operations required for successful task completion. Some studies involve reading and writing task representation for English language writing classes or writing assessment. Connor & Carrell (this volume), for example, examined how writers and raters of a timed writing test represented the task. (See also Basham, Ray, & Whalley, this volume.)

In a study more directly related to EAP classrooms, Flower (1990) found that students and faculty in academic (i.e., content) contexts often represent reading/writing tasks differently, resulting in a student product that is unsatisfactory to the instructor who grades it. She also discovered that there are other factors influencing products as well, e.g., students' inability to carry out the plans they make for reading and writing due to lack of language proficiency or experience with a particular genre. Thus Flower concluded that students *do* have plans and goals for reading and writing tasks in content classes; however, written products sometimes do not reveal the successful completion of these plans—nor do they result in a high grade from faculty. When I conducted a study of faculty perceptions of students' literacy capabilities, focusing in particular on freshmen of diverse ethnic and linguistic backgrounds, I also found that novice students' plans for reading and writing sometimes did not serve them well:

> Comments from faculty about how students perform when they are asked to approach texts during classes indicate that ESL students read in very short phrases and tend to remember bits and pieces of what they read, rather than obtaining a more global view of the text. They stop at the most inappropriate moments to look up words, many of which are unimportant to the essence of the text. Their reading patterns are often inefficient and self-defeating, as we can discover if we ask them to summarize paragraphs or sections of text. (Johns, 1991a, pp. 169–170)

The success of task representation and planning may be dependent upon a student's prior experience with that type of task. Thus faculty ask students to perform tasks that they cannot conceptualize well because they have never performed them before. To explore this hypothesis, I juxtaposed an Asian student's interpretation of a reading-into-writing competency task with the task demands in his major, biology, in order to determine why a student with a high GPA continued to fail the writing competency examination administered by an English department (Johns, 1991b). I found that, among other things, the student had difficulty with the readings required for the writing competency task, since unlike readings in his science classes, the reading collections in his writing class had no disciplinary foundation and were based upon liberal values with which he was unfamiliar. Had the task been embedded in an adjunct situation, many of the problems that this student faced in task interpretation might have been solved.[4]

Though the work on task representation is recent, it provides avenues for determining the differences between expert and novice readers and writers and for identifying the operations and goals that appear to be more valuable to successful academic literacy in a number of contexts.

Reading-Into-Writing

A second, related possibility for research into strategies is found in the reading-into-writing literature. We are now beginning to ask questions about how students use readings in their writings, and the types of sequenceable activities necessary for teaching these skills. In her study of students completing research projects, Campbell found that university ESL students generally copy material; therefore, they "need to be given ample opportunity to practice this type of (i.e., research) writing in order to train themselves to edit out instances of copying. They also need to be trained in the various methods of documenting sources" (1990, p. 225). Although Campbell and others have identified the nature of some of the necessary operations in integrating reading sources into writing, much more needs to be done in this area, particularly on researching those specific operations in reading-into-writing that are difficult for the ESL student.

Cognitive Academic Language Learning Approach (CALLA): A Typology of Operations/Strategies

A third response to questions about operations or strategies can be found in the work of Chamot & O'Malley (1986, 1987), who are best known for their curricular contributions to secondary schools. Because of their success with their approach, called CALLA, I will employ two of

---

[4]This student's frustrations, which I find in many of my science and engineering majors, reveal the dangers in isolating reading/writing students from the "real world."

their three CALLA categories, "metacognitive strategies" and "cognitive strategies,"[5] for a final discussion of the nature of operations.

Metacognitive Strategies

One of the CALLA categories is "metacognitive strategies": "those that involve executive processes for learning, monitoring one's comprehension and production, and evaluating how well one has achieved a learning objective" (1987, p. 17).

Developing metacognitive strategies is one of the principal aims of the EAP adjunct program in which I teach. In this program, we use a variety of classroom techniques to assist students in using writing and reading to "learn, monitor, and assess" their progress. These are a few of the activities we find to be productive:

1. Summary and paraphrase, "executive processes": Campbell (1990) suggests that students should be able to summarize texts for a variety of purposes.[6] Because many ESL students do not have long experience with summarizing or with English texts, I have found that optimal methods for summary teaching involve providing students with an organizational scaffolding, based upon text type, that establishes the basis for their selection and arrangement of content. For argumentation texts, I use Toulmin's scheme (Connor & Johns, 1989); for problem/solution text types, I use Hoey's (See Johns, 1988); for most scientific texts, I rely upon the Johns & Davies categories (1981).

One example may suffice to explain this technique. Many texts in a variety of disciplines are of the problem/solution text type. Thus rather than asking students to summarize by using the textbook rules, which they find opaque (e.g., A summary should be one-fifth the length of the original; it should include only the main points, etc.), I ask students to first discover and list the *problem* identified in the text. Then I ask them to situate the problem within the context described. This is followed by the listing of the author's stated or implied *causes* for the problem, the suggested *solutions*, and, if present, the author's *evaluation* of these solutions.[7]

To monitor and evaluate their summaries, students meet in peer groups, use the problem/solution structure to compare their summaries, and juxtapose them with the text.

2. A second "executive process" necessary for my students' academic success is production of essay examination responses (Horowitz, 1986b). My adjunct class students and I spend long hours integrating lecture, reading,

---

[5]The third strategy mentioned by Chamot & O'Malley is "socio-affective": "The learner either interacts with another person in order to assist learning, as in cooperation or asking questions for clarification, or uses some kind of affective control to assist learning" (1987, p. 242).

[6]An excellent discussion of this variety appears in Ratteray (1985).

[7]For a thorough discussion of problem/solution structure in summarizing, see Johns, 1988.

and discussion from their academic class in preparation for writing possible essay examination questions. After we have prepared and evaluated several such prompts, I administer them under timed test conditions.

For monitoring and evaluation, I type up part or all of a variety of student responses, and we evaluate them together. In this evaluation, we are particularly concerned with two features of the responses: how they begin and whether they identify the concepts and terms essential to the core of the course. At first, students have great difficulty deciding which student responses are the best ones. However, as they continue in their content course and they begin to understand the core values, concepts, and questions in the discipline, they become more adept at writing examination responses that begin well (i.e., that pre-reveal the organization and topic of the essay, as determined by the prompt) and that reflect the values and concepts of the discipline. Therefore, with practice they are able to equate what they are beginning to understand about the discipline and the course to their essay responses.

Cognitive Strategies

The second strategy category mentioned by Chamot & O'Malley in the CALLA taxonomy is "cognitive: in which the learner interacts with the material to be learned by manipulating it mentally or physically" (Chamot & O'Malley, 1987, p. 229). In my classes, students combine mental and physical manipulation in order to achieve an overview of the course, thereby placing reading and writing demands within that overview. One important aspect of this overview is the concept web we develop. As we encounter new examples that reflect the concepts, we build a chart for the course, an intellectual scaffolding, if you will, that provides for students a place to record information from the reading for later use in the writing.[8]

This discussion has focused upon the operations or strategies that are essential to successful reading and writing in college. It can only touch upon what Flower tells us is a very complex, overlapping set of task representations and processes:

> Learning to write in college appears to be a mixture of questioning assumptions and building new task representations; of applying to school writing certain broad cognitive and rhetorical capabilities already possessed; and finally of learning certain new conventions, strategies and habits of mind. The teaching problem in helping students through this transition is inferring the appropriate balance—knowing when one needs to challenge the student with a classroom context that calls for those broad capabilities, when one needs to challenge the assumptions and prior images of the task

---

[8]In my chapter in the Murray volume (in press-b), I discuss how one student successfully uses this technique in a freshman general education class.

that may confound a student's effort, and when one needs to teach new strategies for thinking, [reading] and writing. (1990, p. 22)

Certainly, there is much in Flower's comment to consider.

Use of Resources

So far, I have posed questions—and suggested a few answers—relating to two of Doyle's components for academic task development (1983), *products* and *operations or strategies.* We will now move to the third and final component, *use of resources,* and some questions that might be raised about how the resources available through products research can be exploited in the classroom.

The first question in this section is the following: *How should model texts from the academic environment be employed in the EAP classroom?* As can be seen in the discussion above, I believe that linking EAP classes closely with content classes leads to student motivation and success. Thus answers to questions about resources are closely connected to this argument. One of the most important aspects of an EAP reading/writing class (or any ESL/EFL class) is the development of transfer of learning. In our classes, it involves performance of pedagogic tasks and exposure to genuine texts that lead students into application of the same operations when they really count, i.e., in the "outside world." The choice of models and their use is central to this transfer.

How are models used? I will make only a few suggestions; those who are interested in an extensive discussion should consult Swales (1990). Initially, we need to know what the text products are called by experts within the target discipline, i.e., whether they have different names, depending upon the discipline. For example, a number of faculty require what Horowitz (1986a) calls "the participatory experience." In some disciplines, this assignment may fall under the "lab report" rubric; in others, it may be called "an ethnographic interview or observation." Students need to understand that although the terms may be different, the texts themselves will share a number of features, such as acquisition and use of data, methodologies for data analysis, and arguments in the conclusions.

Second, we need to give students several models of what the discipline upon which they are focusing considers to be a genre (e.g., lab report) for purposes of comparison. In my students' anthropology class, for example, they were assigned to interview a new immigrant and to analyze the "adjustment strategies" that the immigrants used when confronting American culture. After they had finished collecting their data, I provided several models of successful, completed papers. Using Chamot & O'Malley's last category of strategies (1987), "socio-affective," we worked together to understand the models. First, we studied their major sections and the moves within these sections (Swales, 1990). In this case, we classified the larger sections as "justification," "purpose," "analysis," and "conclusion." Then we divided the sections into "moves" and studied the language characteristic of each move. From this activity, we established criteria for good papers of the type assigned: following the sections and moves, using academic language, successful classification, and insightful conclusions.

As the students study models and become more familiar with the academic class in which they are enrolled, they become more sophisticated about critiquing each other's work. Peer review leads to discussions of academic vocabulary and of the importance of certain features of academic style, e.g., hedging (see Berkenkotter, Huckin, & Ackerman, 1988). Elbow (1991) argues that there are certain general features of academic language,[9] and these should be discussed in class. However, style also varies considerably depending upon disciplines (see, e.g., Gross, 1991) and genre (Swales, 1990) and it is essential that students become sensitive to these differences early in their academic careers.

Students are also encouraged—in fact they are required—to talk to the instructor of their academic class about their work. We practice methods for question asking (not "What do you want?" but "I don't understand why this isn't correct.") and politeness strategies in academic contexts in order to increase feedback potential from faculty.[10]

Question: *How can students use their network of informants to juxtapose their ways of approaching tasks to the ways of experts?* Finally, the students need to be aware of the network of informants within the academic community who can be useful to them. In our EAP classes, they form study groups, groups that often continue throughout their academic careers. These groups serve a number of socio-affective purposes, one of which is to find out about which classes to take, and, once enrolled, to discover as a group successful approaches to these classes.

In addition, we discussed other possibilities for obtaining accurate information: Faculty and peer advisors are available for consultation; student groups based upon interest or ethnicity are also good sources. However, the best source for any single class is its instructor. Thus we focused on methods for obtaining important information and guidance from faculty who are often unaware of the implicit nature of their assignments and assumptions.

---

[9]In this useful article, Elbow (1991) points out a number of characteristics of academic language that reflect Western thinking. It is "detached and formal, explicit and factual, 'rubber-gloved' in terms of voice and register, governed by a set of social and authority relations, cautious and sensitive to genre" (p. 142).

[10]For a discussion of question-posing skills within lectures, another important strategy for academic success, see McKenna (1987).

CONCLUSION

In this chapter, I discussed some of the central issues in the planning of EAP curricula. Then I presented a number of definitions for pedagogic tasks, settling upon a comprehensive one, by Doyle (1983). Using this definition, I discussed questions relating to the three components mentioned for a full understanding of task: products, operations/processes and strategies, and resources. In order to elaborate, I have drawn from the growing literature on academic reading and writing and from my own experiences with adjunct classes, the class type I consider optimal for most academic environments.

Though I espouse a social constructionist approach to EAP theory and practice (Johns, 1990b; Swales, 1990), I have attempted to consider also the concerns of those who prefer other approaches. The result is a potpourri, from which EAP instructors can select what suits their classroom environment. Through this eclecticism, I hope that I have raised some questions—and provided some answers—for our English for Academic Purposes classrooms.

REFERENCES

Ackerman, J. (1990). Translating context into action. In L. Flower, V. Stein, J. Ackerman, M.M. Kantz, K. McCormick & W.C. Peck. (Eds.), *Reading-to-write: Exploring a cognitive and social process* (pp. 173-93). New York: Oxford University Press.

Berkenkotter, C., Huckin, T.N., & Ackerman, J. (1988). Conventions, conversations and the writer: A case study of a student in a rhetoric Ph.D. program. *Research in the Teaching of English, 22,* 9–44.

Braine, G. (1989). Writing in science and technology: An analysis of assignments from ten undergraduate courses. *English for Specific Purposes, 8,* 3–16.

Bridgeman, B. & Carlson, S.B. (1984). Survey of academic writing tasks. *Written Communication, 1,* 247–280.

Brinton, D.M., Snow, M.A., & Wesche, M. B. (1989). *Content-based second language instruction.* New York: Newbury House.

Campbell, C. (1990). Writing with others' words: Using background reading texts in academic compositions. In B. Kroll (Ed.), *Second language writing: Research insights for the classroom* (pp. 211–230). New York: Cambridge University Press.

Carson, J.G., Chase, N.D., & Gibson, S.U, (in press). Literacy demands of the undergraduate curriculum. *Reading, Research and Instruction.*

Chamot, A. U. & O'Malley, J. M. (1987). The cognitive academic language learning approach: A bridge to the mainstream. *TESOL Quarterly, 21,* 227–250.

Chamot, A.U. & O'Malley J.M. (1986). *A cognitive academic language learning approach: An ESL content-based curriculum.* Rosslyn, VA: National Clearinghouse for Bilingual Education.

Coe, R.M. (1987). An apology for form; or, who took the form out of process? *College English, 49,* 13–28.

Connor, U. & Johns, A.M. (1989 March). Argumentation in the disciplines: There is a difference. Paper presented at the Annual TESOL Conference, San Antonio.

Crookes, G. (1986). *Task classification: A cross-disciplinary review.* Manoa, HA: Center for Second Language Classroom Research: University of Hawaii. (Technical Report #4).

Doyle, W. (1983) Academic work. *Review of Educational Research 52,* 159–199.

Eisterhold, J.C. (1990). Reading–writing connections: Toward a description for second language learners. In B. Kroll (Ed.), *Second language writing* (pp. 88–101). New York: Cambridge University Press.

Elbow, P. (1991). Reflections on academic discourse. *College English, 53,* 135–155.

Flower, L. (1990). The role of task representation in reading–to–write. In L. Flower, V. Stein, J. Ackerman, M. Kantz, K. McCormick, & W.C. Peck (Eds.), *Reading-to-Write: Exploring a cognitive and social process* (pp. 35–75). New York: Oxford University Press.

Flower, L., Stein, V., Ackerman, J., Kantz, M., McCormick, K., & Peck, W.C. (1990). *Reading-to-write: Exploring a cognitive and social process.* New York: Oxford University Press.

Gross, A.G. (1991) Does rhetoric of science matter? The case of floppy-eared rabbits. *College English, 53,* 933–943.

Horowitz, D. (1990). Fiction and non-fiction in the ESL/EFL classroom: Does the difference make a difference? *English for Specific Purposes, 9,* 161–168.

Horowitz, D. (1986a). What professors actually require: Academic tasks for the ESL classroom. *TESOL Quarterly, 20,* 445–462.

Horowitz, D. (1986b). Essay examination prompts and the teaching of academic writing. *English for Specific Purposes, 5,* 107–120.

Johns, A.M. (in press, a). The reading–writing relationship: A review of the literature. In M. Hashemipour, D. Barrutia, R. Maldonada and M. van Naerssen (Eds.), *Tracy Terrell festschrift.* New York: McGraw Hill.

Johns, A.M. (in press, b). Toward developing a cultural repertoire: The case study of a Lao college freshman. In D.E. Murray (Ed.), *Diversity as a resource: Redefining cultural literacy.* Arlington, VA: TESOL.

Johns, A. M. (1991a). Faculty assessment of student literacy skills: Implications for writing assessment. In L. Hamp-Lyons (Ed.), *Assessing second language writing in academic contexts* (pp. 167–179). Norwood, NJ: Ablex.

Johns, A. M. (1991b). Interpreting an English competency examination: The frustrations of an ESL science student. *Written Communication, 8,* 379–401.

Johns, A.M. (1990a). Coherence as a cultural phenomenon: Employing ethnographic principles in the academic milieu. In U. Connor & A.M. Johns (Eds.), *Coherence in writing: Research and pedagogical perspectives* (pp. 209–226). Alexandria, VA: TESOL.

Johns, A.M. (1990b). L1 composition theories: Implications for developing theories of L2 composition. In B. Kroll (Ed.), *Second language writing* (pp. 24–36). New York: Cambridge University Press.

Johns, A.M. (1988). Reading for summarizing: An approach to text orientation and processing. *Reading in a Foreign Language, 4*, 79–90.

Johns, A.M. (1981). Necessary English: An academic survey. *TESOL Quarterly, 15*, 51–57.

Johns, A.M. & Dudley-Evans, T. (1991). English for specific purposes: International in scope, specific in purpose. *TESOL Quarterly, 25*, 297–314.

Johns, T. & Davies, F. (1981). Text as a vehicle for information. *Reading in a Foreign Language, 1*, 1–19.

Kroll, B. (1979). A survey of the writing needs of foreign and American college freshmen. *English Language Teaching Journal, 33*, 219–227.

Long, M.H. (1985). A role for instruction in second language acquisition. In K. Hyltenstam & M. Pienemann (Eds.) *Modelling and assessing second language acquisition* (pp. 77–99). London: Multilingual Matters.

McCormick, K. (1990). The cultural imperatives underlying cognitive acts. In L. Flower, V. Stein, J. Ackerman, M. Katz, K. McCormick, & W.C. Peck (Eds.), *Reading–to–Write: Exploring a cognitive and social process* (pp. 194–220). New York: Oxford University Press.

McKenna, E. (1987). Preparing foreign students to enter discourse communities in the U.S. *English for Specific Purposes, 6*, 187–202.

Mohan, B. & Oszust, V. (in press). Learning tasks as language socialization: A knowledge structure analysis of business case decision making by L2 learners. *English for Specific Purposes.*

Moore, D.W., Moore, S.A., Cunningham, P.M. & Cunningham, J. (1986). *Developing readers and writers in the content areas, K–12.* New York: Longman.

Nunan, D. (1988). *The learner-centred curriculum.* New York: Cambridge University Press.

Ostler, S.W. (1980). A survey of academic needs for advanced ESL. *TESOL Quarterly, 14*, 489–502.

Prior, P. (in press). Redefining the task: An ethnographic examination of writing and response in six graduate seminars. In D. Belcher & G. Braine (Eds.), *Academic writing in a second language: Essays on research and pedagogy.* New York: Ablex.

Raimes, A. (1991). Out of the woods: Emerging traditions in the teaching of writing. *TESOL Quarterly, 25,* 407–430.

Ratteray, O.M.T. (1985). Expanding roles for summarized information. *Written Communication, 2,* 457–472.

Richards, J.C. & Hurley, D. (1990). Language and content: Approaches to curriculum alignment. In J.C. Richards (Ed.), *The language teaching matrix* (pp. 144–152). New York: Cambridge University Press.

Robinson, P. (1991). *ESP today: A practitioner's guide.* New York: Prentice-Hall International.

Silva, T. (1990). Second language composition instruction: Developments, issues, and directions in ESL. In B. Kroll (Ed.), *Second language writing* (pp. 11–23). New York: Cambridge University Press.

Spack, R. (1988). Initiating ESL students into the academic discourse community: How far should we go? *TESOL Quarterly, 22,* 29–52.

Spack, R. (1985). Literature, reading, writing and ESL: Bridging the gap. *TESOL Quarterly, 19,* 703–725.

Swales, J.M. (1990). *Genre analysis: English in academic and research settings.* New York: Cambridge University Press.

Swales, J.M. (1987). Utilizing the literatures in teaching the research paper. *TESOL Quarterly, 21,* 41–67.

Zamel, V., Raimes, A., Brookes, G., Johns, A., Land, R., Spack, R., & Taylor, B. (1991, March). In the writing classroom: An interactive colloquium. Presented at the 25th Annual TESOL Convention, New York.

CHAPTER 16

Becoming a Member of the "Teaching Foreign Languages" Community: Integrating Reading and Writing Through an Adjunct/Content Course

Lynn M. Goldstein
Monterey Institute of International Studies

ESL students who matriculate as undergraduate or graduate students at American universities face a complex task. At the same time that they are dealing with unfamiliar content in their academic courses, they are often still in the process of acquiring the language skills that they need to succeed in these courses. Traditionally, such students take ESL reading and writing courses separate from their content courses, and these reading and writing courses are often even separate from each other.

The above approach has many inherent drawbacks. First, in many ESL reading and writing courses, students read and write "general" academic texts in which the discourse is often unrelated to the discourse of the actual texts they encounter in their academic courses. In such cases, students usually do not see the connection among texts they read in their ESL reading classes and those they write in their ESL writing classes and those they read and write in their academic classes (Shih 1986). Students feel that they are not quite "real" students, an attitude that undermines their motivation in their ESL classes and their confidence in their ability to succeed in their academic classes. In addition, they are left not as prepared as they need to be for the reading and writing tasks they are undertaking in their content courses.

Current theory in second language acquisition and in composition studies also argues against ESL reading and writing courses separate from each other and separate from the content students are studying. Language acquisition is fostered by engaging in real tasks (see, for example, Brinton, Snow, & Wesche, 1989), and writing and reading about the content students are studying enables students both to learn the content and to improve their reading and writing skills (see, for example, Mayher, Lester, & Pradl, 1983). Furthermore, when students read and examine the actual texts of their field of study, they learn to be better readers of these texts and they learn the rhetorical concerns of that field (Shih, 1986).

Some programs are now moving away from separate ESL reading and writing classes and towards either sheltered content classes (i.e., classes in subject matter areas designed and taught for ESL students) or adjunct classes (ESL classes that are paired with subject matter classes and are designed to help ESL students with the work of the subject matter class). This paper will address justifications for integrating reading and writing together in an adjunct model so that reading and writing skills improve while students learn the content of their academic courses. The paper will illustrate this integration with an example of a content course and its adjunct course being taught at a small graduate school. The adjunct course, designed for non-native speakers in an M.A. teaching of foreign languages program, is adjuncted to introduction to second language acquisition (SLA).

THE EARLY WRITING COURSE

The motivation to offer the paired adjunct and content course came from our dissatisfaction with a regular ESL writing course we offered in 1986 to a number of foreign-language teachers who had applied for our M.A. program. While they showed promise, they did not yet have the required level of writing proficiency needed to succeed in this program. On the whole, these students had TOEFL scores below 600, had been out of school for a long period of time, did not have American B.A.s, and had weak writing skills. The decision was made to offer a special writing course to help these students acquire the writing skills they would need in the M.A. program prior to entering the program. This writing course was first offered in the spring of 1987.

In the process of teaching this course, it became apparent that the students had many academic "problems" that went beyond writing, particularly with reading and understanding texts, generalizing, inferring and synthesizing ideas, and understanding and completing assignments appropriately. In addition, they exhibited low motivation. In discussions with the teacher, these students expressed that this low motivation stemmed from two primary sources: 1) writing was the content of the course instead of content about foreign language teaching and/or acquisition; and 2) the course was sheltered, making them feel inferior to and separate from other students in the M.A. program. The decision was made at that time to offer an introduction to second language acquisition (SLA) course to these students to which a writing course would be adjuncted. These students were required to take both the content and the adjunct course, but we decided not to shelter the content course, allowing any student in the M.A. program to take the SLA course as an elective.

The remainder of the paper will describe the content and the adjunct course, first in a general sense and then in a more specific way, showing how the work of reading and writing flows back and forth between the two classes.

THE ADJUNCT WRITING COURSE

Each course meets once a week for two hours. In SLA, students read the actual texts they will encounter in their field and in the course of the M.A. program. Currently, they read *Principles of Language Learning and Teaching* (Brown, 1987) and approximately 10–12 self-selected articles from professional journals or edited volumes on topics discussed in class or in the text.

Class time is spent in a number of ways. Primarily, the class is a seminar in which students discuss the content they are reading as well as any additional content the teacher or students bring up. Students are encouraged to make connections to what they have experienced as language teachers and as language learners. Through this process, students not only learn about second language acquisition, but also learn to sift through information, synthesizing what they are learning with what they already know. In addition, students are encouraged to critically examine and discuss what they read in light of their own experiences and intuitions and to critically examine long-held notions in light of their newly acquired knowledge. Thus, instead of engaging in skill building activities, the students actually engage in the processes of inferring, generalizing, relating, evaluating, and synthesizing about real and meaningful content.

In addition, the teacher can intervene at those moments when there are breakdowns in these skills and teach students to use these processes more effectively. For example, if a student is having difficulty in class discussing the differences between two authors' points of view, the teacher can ask questions to elicit whether the difficulty is in reading comprehension, or in seeing similarities and differences among different points of view. The teacher can then confer with the student about ways to solve this type of a problem, and the student gets an opportunity to put into practice in subsequent reading and class discussion what he or she has learned from the teacher's intervention. Unlike skill-building activities, this process allows teachers to identify more clearly sources of reading difficulty and offers students opportunities to use what they have learned from the teacher's intervention in a real context.

The students are also encouraged to bring to class for discussion questions about the content or concerns about reading difficulties they have. They can do this through entries in a journal they keep or through time set aside for this at the beginning of each class. Students have raised many different issues, such as how to read more quickly, how to budget time, how to find sources in the library, or what a particular word or line in a text means. These questions allow the teacher to go beyond discrete skill building exercises in helping students master the reading demands of their field.

Most of the writing assignments for the adjunct course come from the content course and are designed to help students become proficient in a number of genres they will need in the M.A. program. These assignments demand the same skills as do the discussions and readings: comparing and contrasting, inferring, generalizing, evaluating, and synthesizing. The reading and discussion of the content course also provide the content for these writing assignments as well as a jumping-off place for student choices about what content they want to follow up on through further readings they do for an oral presentation and a literature review.

The adjunct course takes as its content the readings from the SLA course as well as the writing assignments from the SLA course and a few additional writing assignments. In the adjunct course, the teacher begins the process of integrating reading and writing by having students examine the texts they are dealing with in the SLA class. Here they discover what types of issues are being written about, what kinds of audiences are being addressed, and what kinds of purposes writers have in this discourse community. These discussions of what they are reading include the notions of audience and purpose from the perspective of both the reader and the writer. We discuss questions such as who the audience is and what the writer's purpose and main points are. Here the teacher can intervene in the reading process if students have difficulty answering these questions. The students then move on to questions about the choices the writers have made to meet their audience's needs and to achieve their purposes. Such discussions begin to lead students to an understanding of the rhetorical devices needed to achieve their purposes and fulfill their audience's needs in their own writing. These are ongoing discussions that take place as students grapple with new reading assignments in their content course and as they work on the different writing assignments. Time is also spent in discussion of the types of assignments they are doing and can expect to get in the M.A. program, how to decipher these assignments, and effective means of completing these assignments.

The adjunct course also focuses more generally on process writing, and assignments are set up to encourage students to engage in effective processes. Assignments allow several weeks for completion and allow opportunities for students to engage in heuristics for discovering, generating, planning, and revising as well as opportunities for drafting and revision, peer editing, and conferencing with the teacher. Students also keep a journal for both classes in which they can discuss content, reading, writing, and assignments, as well as anything about which they have concerns. This journal gives students another avenue for learning and writing, and it gives teachers another place where they can encourage, motivate, and intervene when needed.

The work students do on the writing assignments also informs the reading they do in the content course. For example, as they learn to write a summary and then later a literature review, they learn to read carefully for the writer's intent so that they can use the information from the reading accurately and appropriately in their summary or literature review. In addition, if they have difficulty understanding a text when they read, it becomes apparent in their writing. Again, the teacher can intervene and help the student examine both his or her reading processes and the content itself.

How specifically do reading and writing become integrated in and across these two classes? Students spend the first four sessions of the SLA course reading about and discussing psychological and cognitive factors in language learning. Meanwhile, the first four classes of the adjunct course focus on process writing, heuristics and ways in, writing first drafts, rhetorical concerns of audience, purpose, unity, support, and organization. At first glance, it may appear that this sounds like a typical writing course. What makes it different, however, is that writing is not the sole content of the adjunct course *and* the content being written about comes from an academic content course (SLA). Thus, they are not using "pretend" content at the service of their writing, but using writing to learn and explore the content of the SLA course. In addition, as the class discusses general rhetorical concerns these first four weeks, all the examples of text and all exercises come from published articles about SLA. Thus, for example, as we discuss the notion of sufficient and appropriate support, we examine journal articles discussing what types of support were used, where they were used in the text, and why they were used in light of who the audience is and what the author's purpose is.

Throughout these first four classes students are also writing their first paper about the role of error correction in SLA. This topic is examined because error correction is a very important and controversial issue in their workplace. The content comes from the reading done in the SLA class as well as self-selected articles and from personal experience as language teachers and learners. In effect, this paper becomes the concrete means by which the students integrate what they are learning from their reading in the content course with what they are learning about writing in the adjunct course. The paper allows the students to simultaneously discover what they know and what they still need to learn about error correction and language acquisition, how they feel about the issue of error correction, and how effectively they can communicate their point of view in writing to a peer audience. Hence this process is very different from what occurs in traditional reading and writing courses. Students here are using the content (i.e., the reading) for real purposes, and they are writing for real purposes and audiences rather than imagined ones.

In the next part of the SLA course, we address social factors in language learning, such as attitudes, acculturation, and identification. As we move through the next three SLA classes, students begin to do oral and written summaries of a self-selected journal article. Thus the adjunct class takes up the topic of summary writing—again using articles from SLA as the content for the summaries. This serves two purposes: It prepares the students for their SLA assignment, and it begins to lay the groundwork for the literature review students will write later on. Importantly, as students discuss summary writing they are also focusing on their reading skills, since in order to summarize, the reader must first understand the writer's purpose and main points (see Carson, this volume, and Sarig, this volume, for a discussion of summary writing). Here, again, reading and writing become integrated.

During the first seven weeks of the course students have also been working on a research project. For this project they collect data about the language learning strategies, attitudes, and motivations of four foreign language learners. They use this data to write a paper in which they discuss the role these strategies, attitudes, and motivations have played in their subjects' language learning success. In addition, they compare their findings to those they have read about in the literature and account for the differences and similarities. This paper is discussed in both classes: the content issues in SLA, the writing issues in the adjunct course. These discussions are, however, not so neatly divided. In both classes students are encouraged to discuss whatever they feel they need help with. These discussions include understanding and evaluating what they are reading, tabulating and synthesizing the data they are collecting, making generalizations and conclusions about the reading and about their own data, comparing and contrasting the literature with their findings, and determining effective means of conveying their findings in writing. Here reading and writing cannot be separated from each other—they build on and reinforce each other in a cyclical fashion as students discover what they want to say.

The third section of the SLA class focuses on interlanguage: first language influences, cognitive factors, universal factors, communication strategies, and input and interaction. The adjunct course moves into discussions of literature reviews. The reading from the SLA course now provides the motivation for the literature review as well as models of literature reviews. Students are far enough along now in the SLA course that they have some strong interests that they would like to pursue. The literature review paper allows them to do this, and so the reading in the SLA course serves as motivation for writing the literature review. This works particularly well because instead of writing a literature review to display knowledge to an informed audience, students are writing a literature review to truly explore and learn about an area of interest they have developed through reading. In turn, as they write their literature review and also when they finish this paper, they share it with a somewhat uninformed and real audience, i.e., their classmates.

The final three classes of the SLA and the adjunct course are designed to pull together all that has been happening in and across both classes. In the SLA course students discuss issues of theory and practice. They are encouraged to reflect on and evaluate all the reading they have done and to reach personal conclusions about the processes and factors involved in language learning and teaching. The adjunct course provides the means for students to bring together this process of reflection. Here they work on the position paper assigned in the SLA class, which asked them to articulate what factors they believe influence language learning and how these beliefs inform language teaching. They write and conference on multiple drafts of this paper, and as they go back and forth between drafts and between classes once again they discover ideas, make connections, learn from and about reading, and learn from and about their writing. This paper is read by both teachers and evaluated by both if the adjunct class and the SLA class are taught by different instructors.

What have we learned from these classes over the past four years? First, a few caveats. Ideally, the same teacher should teach the content course and the adjunct course. The class works "seamlessly" that way—content, reading, and writing flow effortlessly across the two classes. It is, however, possible to have two different teachers as long as they continually coordinate, keeping track of the students' needs, concerns, and difficulties. If there are two teachers, it is imperative that the writing teacher know the content of the academic course. We found that when this was not the case, the writing teacher could not tell when content was misunderstood, misapplied, or misused in the writing assignments.

We have chosen not to shelter the content course; that is, we allow any student in the M.A. program, including those who do not need to work on their reading and writing skills, to take the content course as an elective without taking the adjunct course. Students who are required to take the adjunct course as well are motivated because their content course is a real one, in other words, a credit-bearing elective in the M.A. program. However, native speakers or more advanced non-native students in the content course can sometimes intimidate the students who need to work on their reading and writing skills. We have decided to require the instructor's permission to take the SLA course and to limit the number of proficient writers and readers.

In addition, we are currently considering adding extra class hours. Presently, the content and writing courses each meet two hours per week. This, however, has not been sufficient time to address the many questions and concerns that arise in the course of class discussions, including the fact that some do not know how to use a library, some do not know how to budget time, some do not how or when to indicate that they do not understand, and some have never typed a paper or used a computer. We are working towards adding an additional hour to address these concerns.

The ways in which reading and writing flow back and forth between the two classes as the students work with real texts and real tasks has been very exciting. They read texts exhibiting the discourse of their own academic and professional community and can therefore see the connections between the texts they are reading and those they are writing. Through this process, students not only develop the skills they need to succeed in their content courses, but they also enter into and become members of a real discourse community. They are highly motivated because they are writing for real purposes for the actual audiences they will continue to write for throughout the M.A. program and professionally, as well. The reading of the content course benefits the writing done in the adjunct course since it provides models of writing as well as content for writing. The content course has the added value of allowing students to grapple with content in a way that helps them to determine what they do and do not understand. Writing benefits reading, since writing about the content also allows students to see what they do and do not understand. In addition, as students write, they see how texts are put together and they see what the rhetorical concerns of the writer are for the needs of the reader. They bring that knowledge back to their reading as they interact with and comprehend texts. Finally, as they read and write across these two courses, they engage in the real behaviors of readers and writers. Instead of building skills discretely and delaying the writing and reading of complete texts particular to their field, students build the skills they need through learning the content they both need and want. They enter the M.A. program the following semester with the confidence of practiced and practicing members of the teaching foreign languages discourse community.

REFERENCES

Brinton, D.M., Snow, M., & Wesche, M. (1989). *Content-based second language instruction.* New York: Newbury House.

Brown, H.D. (1987). *Principles of language learning and teaching.* Englewood Cliffs, NJ: Prentice Hall.

Mayher, J.S., Lester, N.B., & Pradl, G.M. (1983). *Learning to write/writing to learn.* Upper Montclair, NJ: Boynton/Cook.

Shih, M. (1986). Content-based approaches to teaching academic writing. *TESOL Quarterly, 20*(4), 617–648.

## CHAPTER 17

Cross-Cultural Perspectives on Task Representation in Reading to Write

Charlotte Basham
University of Alaska Fairbanks

Ruth Ray
Wayne State University

Elizabeth Whalley
San Francisco State University

When composition teachers ask students to read a text and then to respond in writing, whether to summarize, criticize, or comment, they do so with certain underlying assumptions about the nature of texts, of literate practices in general, and more specifically, about what constitutes "academic discourse." The fact that these underlying assumptions are often left implicit can cause problems for students, particularly those second language learners who come to the university with very different expectations about discourse in general and academic discourse in particular. For example, Asian students may incorporate whole phrases from a known text into their own writing (Matalene, 1985; Scollon & Scollon, 1991). This practice does not easily translate into the Western academic context, where copying from source texts without appropriate citation constitutes plagiarism. Problems can also occur when students' culturally determined rules for spoken discourse affect their writing. Within the cultural experience of most Alaska Native groups, for example, there are limits to the authority a speaker may claim on a topic, depending on his or her personal knowledge and experience. The resulting circumspection of assertion is in direct variance with the demands of academic writing (Kwachka & Basham, 1990).

Learning to shape one's writing according to the conventions of academic discourse is clearly a process of socialization for all students (Bartholomae, 1985), but some students find themselves more alienated than others (Bizzell, 1986). This chapter discusses specific ways in which the expectations and strategies of three groups of "culturally different" college students diverge from the norms underlying traditional academic discourse. Using data gathered from Latino students in Detroit, Asian students in San Francisco, and Alaska Native students in Fairbanks, we present linguistic evidence of students' strategies for approaching a "reading-to-write" task and discuss ways in which these strategies reflect cultural orientations.

CULTURAL EXPECTATIONS OF READER/WRITERS: RELATED RESEARCH

Research on reading in English as a second language has focused attention on how this process differs from reading in one's first language. One approach to ESL reading research, derived from research in L1, is to take into account the background knowledge, or schema, a reader brings to the text. Differences in schemata are typically tested by summarization or recall tasks; the additions, substitutions, or omissions readers make in representing a text are taken as evidence that their culturally conditioned expectations and experiences influence the reading process. Carrell (1987) discusses the role of both content and formal schemata in relation to second language reading. She concludes that both previous knowledge relating to the topic and knowledge of discourse structure influence reading comprehension.

Cultural influences on the writing process in a second language have also been investigated. Kaplan (1966; 1987) has consistently argued that research in contrastive rhetoric can provide insight into why writers from a certain language background will organize their writing in English in fairly predictable, non-English patterns. Schecter & Harklau's comprehensive bibliography of writing in a non-native language (1991) provides a great deal of evidence for the effect of L1 culture on students' writing in L2. Achiba & Kuromiya (1983) and Ricento (1987) show a transference of rhetorical style from Japanese to English. Hu, Brown, & Brown (1982) found that cultural differences between Chinese and Australian students affect the content, voice, and mood of their writing. Culture was also found to influence writing for Arabic students (Atari, 1984), Navajo students (Frestedt & Sanchez, 1980), and Spanish students (Galvan, 1985).

Other studies have concluded a lack of cultural influence. Connor & McCagg (1987), for example, found no culture-specific patterns of organization in a summarizing task. Liebman-Klein (1986) argues that texts that apparently show cultural background may actually be a result of previous training in L1 writing. This claim supports the Mohan & Lo (1985) findings that Chinese students attributed their difficulties in organizing compositions to a need for training rather than transfer of text features from Chinese.

We suggest that one way to resolve the discrepancy in these findings, as well as to link L2 reading and writing research, is to posit a definition of "culture" that includes those expectations that readers/writers bring to any act of literacy. Those expectations are certainly influenced by schooling, but as Basham (1986) demonstrates for Alaska Native students, socially constructed discourse rules apply as well.

Our present work focuses on the processes by which readers construct and negotiate meanings in their interaction with texts. An important influence on this research has been the work of Flower , et al. (1990), who examined L1 college students' interactions with texts they were reading in order to write. Arguing that this function of reading is distinct from other functions, such as reading to learn or reading to do something, Flower et al. claim that the reading-to-write process is directly related to the development of critical literacy,

> because (at least in theory) it brings these two processes into strong inter-
> action. The reading process is guided by the need to produce a text of
> one's own. The reader is expected to manipulate and transform it to his
> or her own purposes. And the writing process is complicated by the need
> to shape one's own goals in response to the ideas or even the purposes of
> another writer. Without a critical, questioning response, the writer is
> simply replicating his sources. Without the ability to transform knowl-
> edge he cannot synthesize his own knowledge and goals with that of
> another text. (p. 6)

Using think-aloud protocols, interviews, and self-analyses of fresh-men writers at Carnegie Mellon University, Flower et al. conclude that their students' images of the reading-to-write task were "rooted in the students' histories, the context of schooling, and cultural assumptions about writing they brought to college" (p. vi). Specifically, they found that students' representations of the reading-to-write task showed their negotiation of "the socially weighted decision to take or relinquish authority over their sources," their ability and willingness to "think with and through written text," and their willingness to "test and transform" a text for their own purposes (pp. 3–5). Flower et al. assert that some of the "cultural and institutional factors that are silently but powerfully influencing [students'] reading and writing behavior" can be inferred from discussions with students and analysis of their texts (p. 195). They define "cultural and institutional factors" very generally in terms of the larger society in which students have been taught to read and write; the schooling students have had that inculcates the habits and assumptions that help sustain the expectations of the larger society; the academic discourse communities with which students come in contact; the preferred linguistic and rhetorical practices within those discourse communities that students have been taught; the classrooms in which students have participated; the previous reading occasions and writing assignments students have completed; and students' unique intellectual histories (pp. 179–180).

The student population described in Flower et al. appears to be a fairly homogeneous group of native English speakers educated in predominantly white, middle-class American schools. In this chapter, we present the results of a study addressing the question of how bilingual/bicultural students orient themselves to a reading-to-write task, that is, how as readers from a particular sociocultural background, they determine meaning and negotiate their own authority to make or find it. Specifically, we demonstrate that Asian, Latino, and Alaska Native students orient themselves differently to the "same" task, and we offer explanations for the roles their cultural backgrounds might play in these orientations.

DESCRIPTION OF THE STUDY

In the fall of 1989 data were gathered from writing courses in three universities. At San Francisco State University, participants in the study were 16 Asian students, 13 of whom were native speakers of Chinese, whose average length of stay in the U.S. was eight years. At the time of the study the students were enrolled in an ESL process writing course that met a university writing requirement. At the University of Alaska Fairbanks, participants were Alaska Native students in a course designed to prepare them for freshman English. Among the students were nine Eskimos[1] and five Athabaskan Indians. While seven of the Eskimos reported themselves to be bilingual, the other students claimed not to speak their ancestral languages. At Wayne State University in Detroit, participants were students in a basic writing class designed to prepare Latino students for freshman English. Of the 11 students represented in the study, most were second-generation Mexican Americans who spoke Spanish as their first language.

These three groups of students were of interest because their cultural and linguistic backgrounds had placed them outside mainstream composition classes (they were all enrolled in courses specifically designed for "culturally different" students), yet since most of them had attended high school in the United States, their situations and abilities were quite different from those of the newly arrived international students who form the primary audience for ESL materials. Students in all three groups were relatively proficient speakers of English but were perceived as needing special treatment to develop their academic/written registers.

The study was designed to examine three questions:

1. What do bilingual/bicultural students do when they read a text for the purpose of writing about it? That is, how do they represent the task to themselves and how do they plan for writing?

---

[1]Unlike researchers in Canada, where the term *Eskimo* is regarded negatively, Alaskan researchers continue to use the term as a group designator because the alternate term *Inuit* does not include the groups living only in Alaska.

2. What are the similarities and differences among the groups in terms of their representations?
3. Is what they do different from what mainstream students do (as reported in Flower *et al.*)? If so, to what extent can the differences be attributed to the students' cultural backgrounds?

Students in each class were given the same verbal instructions for the reading protocol: Read two short passages, select one, and talk about it on tape in terms of how they planned to write about it. They were also given written instructions for the essays, which were to be written after completing the protocol. In all three groups, the researchers modeled a think-aloud protocol, and the students were given tapes to produce their own protocols at home. For the essays, students were instructed to "first state the main idea of the reading passage and then discuss that idea, referring to your own knowledge of current examples, observations, and experience." One of the passages, by Margaret Mead, dealt with the topic of superstition. The second passage, by Caroline Bird, was titled "College Is a Waste of Time and Money." Since only a few students responded to the passage about superstition, we have chosen to focus exclusively on examples from the second passage, which is reproduced below:

Reading Passage A

A great majority of our nine million college students are not in school because they want to be or because they want to learn. They are there because it has become the thing to do or because college is a pleasant place to be; because it's the only way they can get parents or taxpayers to support them without working at a job they don't like; because Mother wanted them to go, or some other reason entirely irrelevant to the course of studies for which college is supposedly organized.

As I crisscross the United States lecturing on college campuses, I am dismayed to find that professors and administrators, when pressed for a candid opinion, estimate that no more than 25 percent of their students are turned on by classwork. For the rest, college is at best a social center or aging vat, and at worst a young folks' home or even a prison that keeps them out of the mainstream of economic life for a few more years.
—from "College Is a Waste of Time and Money," by Caroline Bird (pp. 3–4)

As an additional task, students were asked to transcribe their own taped protocols. It should also be noted that in the Alaska Native group two of the protocols were produced collaboratively; i.e., two students taped their conversation about the task and the topic and then wrote individual essays. This also occurred with one pair in the Latino group. The students also completed an information sheet about their language and educational backgrounds.

DISCUSSION OF FINDINGS

To investigate what students do when they read in order to write, we closely examined the transcripts of the think-aloud protocols, and in selected cases, we also listened to the tapes. We then compared the protocols to the written essays. Analysis of linguistic and rhetorical features in the transcripts and the essays revealed three general patterns. The first pattern is a dominant orientation to the text, reflected linguistically in references to the author, the title, or specific phrases of the source text, and by deictic expressions such as "this text" or "this word." The second pattern is an orientation to the task. Linguistic evidence for this pattern includes explicit reference to the written instructions or questions, such as "What do we have to do here?" The third pattern is an orientation to topic. While all students spoke and wrote about the topics suggested by the readings, some students did so to the exclusion of any reference to the source text or the written instructions; the transcripts and essays of these students dealt entirely with their own ideas on the topic. Though some students' protocols included evidence of all three orientations, general patterns did emerge within the language groups. In the next section we briefly discuss each type of orientation and then discuss them in relation to the language groups.

Orientation Toward Text

Teachers' expectations underlying a reading-to-write task certainly include orientation toward the reading passage; that is, teachers assume that in writing, the students will explicitly refer to the text and summarize the main ideas. However, the writing is expected to be more than a summary; it is expected to demonstrate a student's thinking through and with the text.[2] Writing that focuses primarily on summary is what Flower et al. refer to as "early comprehension" writing; it represents the "opening moves" by which students represent the task by determining what the reading is about and what the assignment asks of them. Most American college-level reading-to-write tasks require that students move beyond summarization to what Flower et al. refer to as "translation," whereby students use their notes and summaries to "transform" the reading, developing an individual purpose and plan for their writing and negotiating their roles as readers and writers. Flower et al. suggest that students who do not move into the "translation" stage of a reading-to-write task are probably relying on strategies learned in schools modeled on a traditional

---

[2]The authors' comments about teachers' expectations are derived from our own experience teaching college writing courses. As additional support, we note that several recent textbooks in composition, both for L1 and L2 instruction, explicitly refer to guidelines for summarization that are similar to our own (e.g., Spack, 1990).

"culture of recitation." Although these strategies may have served students well in high school, they work against the development of critical literacy in college because they diminish the student's role as agent, with the opportunity to effect change within a community of knowledgeable readers by limiting the development of new ideas and alternative approaches to a writing task (p. 184).

In our data, of those students who oriented themselves to the text, the degree of interaction ranged from a token gesture of mentioning the author or title of the reading passage to a high level of interaction with the text, where there is evidence of the writers questioning, disagreeing, and developing their own viewpoints on the topic.

Example (1) is the opening sentence of an Asian student's essay, which is presented as a "successful" summary statement (i.e., one which meets teacher expectations).

(1) The main idea of this passage by Caroline Bird is that college is a waste of time and money because only a portion of students in college really want to learn. (SF3e)[3]

This statement refers to the text, the author, and the gist of the passage. In the think-aloud protocol, there is evidence of her developing a critical stance, moving beyond the summary:

(2) To me...it's only true for those who go to school not for learning. Then college would be a waste for them time and money...but for those who really are anxious to learn, it would be an opportunity where they can get knowledge from...and hmmm, which they don't already know. (SF3p)[4]

The student who produced these examples had been in the U.S. for eleven years and had attended school in this country. Not all students were as adept at meeting the teacher's expectations. Yet the other transcripts and essays are more interesting to us as teachers and researchers, precisely because they do not meet the expectations and therefore provide insight into the processes second language learners follow when reading and composing texts in English for academic purposes.

For example, the following excerpt from a student's protocol is replete with references to the text, but the writer never develops her own thoughts on the topic.

---

[3]The code following each example is read as follows: *UA, WS,* or *SF* refer, respectively, to the University of Alaska, Wayne State University, and San Francisco State University; the number is for reference within the data set; and *p* or *e* refers to protocol or essay.

[4]Examples from student protocols and essays are presented essentially unedited, except that most pause fillers, such as "hmmm" in the transcripts were omitted for ease of reading.

> (3) [Student reads task] [reads passage A] [rereads part of passage A].
> MMM. I still don't understand. So this passage mean...tells us college is
> waste of money and time. So, um, there are not, okay, let me write this
> down, not in school, not in school because they want to learn, because
> they want to learn. [pause] So, but, but they they are in college because it
> has become a thing to do or college is a pleasant place to be. How come
> it's a pleasant place to be, but they don't like to go to school. [pause]
> [rereads passage] So, ummm, I am CONFUSED here. (SF13p)

This example suggests that, for this student and for many other Asian students who went over the text again and again, reading-to-write entails a
struggle for comprehension of what exists on the page. The issue confusing the student in (3) arises from her reading of the first sentence ("A great
majority of our nine million college students are not in school because
they want to be or because they want to learn."). With the inclusion of
the negative in the main clause, the sentence makes a claim that conflicts
with the student's expectation that students do go to college because they
want to learn.[5]

The student in (3) works particularly hard to resolve the conflict by
rereading, even though this strategy further confuses and frustrates her.
Another Asian student who had difficulty with the same sentence solved
the problem by changing the text:

> (4) I mean the passage contradict with each other. I mean it is contradict
> between, within the passage. But the, the question asks us to state the
> main idea of the reading passage and then discuss that idea, referring to
> your own knowledge. Maybe we can say, well, I think there's some print-
> ing error in the first sentence. Maybe I can cross out the "not," say a great
> majority of our 9 million college students are in school because they
> want to be or because they want to learn. That makes much more sense,
> right? Yea! Then it can kind of like, connect, hook to the passage. So the
> first thing, I gonna cross out the "not" in the passage. Hopefully I'm
> correct. . . . (SF9p)

Note that in crossing out *not* in the first sentence, the student solves
the sentence-level problem, but creates a larger, discourse-level problem;
it is now inconsistent with the negative tone of the passage and renders
the title of the work from which the passage is taken ("College Is a Waste
of Time and Money") essentially meaningless. It becomes clear from comparing this student's protocol and essay that he has some difficulty deal-

---

[5]Grammatically speaking, the placement of the negative is indeed confusing. Ron
Scollon (personal communication) suggests that for Chinese students, at least, there are
two additional problems with this sentence, one deriving from differences between
Chinese and English construction of causative sequences; the other is the students'
knowledge of English grammar, which might cause them to question the placement of
not in the sentence.

ing with negative scope, as the following excerpt from the written essay illustrates:

(5) The author Caroline Bird wants to address to the readers that there are so many college students in this country but not all of them *know the real purpose of going to college.(SF9e) [At the * the student inserted *do not.*]

By examining both the protocol and the essay we can see more clearly how this student's thinking evolves and how he transforms the text to fit his needs. If we were to read only the essay, we would not know the extensive process involved in arriving at the decision to edit the first sentence.

Similarly, for the Alaska Native students the transcripts reveal struggles for meaning in the reading that do not show up in the essays. The student in (6) below, for example, admits to herself that she does not understand what she has just read:

(6) The reading passage is talking about two things in both paragraphs. The first is talking about nine million college students who aren't in school because they want to be or because they want to learn. I don't really understand the first sentence in the first paragraph. (UA2p)

In contrast to the Asian student in (3), however, there is no evidence from the transcript that this Alaska Native student returned to the text for rereading; nor did she develop a strategy for resolving the problem, as did the student in (5).

Examples (7)–(9) demonstrate a different kind of orientation toward the text, one involving more interaction:

(7) I can write about this. Maybe I have to read again. [reads part of passage A] Huh . . . What does that mean, "turned on" here? [reads] Huh. Maybe I have to check what "candid opinion" mean. Huh. Maybe this is just a excerpt from an entire essay. This is just two paragraphs. It has not so much to do with the title, "College Is a Waste of Time and Money" as she stated. Maybe that's right for most of students but there are some, maybe 25% or less students who is really studying. I think so. I don't totally agree to say, saying that college is a waste of money. I don't like it. It depends on people. It is difficult to generalize. Huh. Right. (SF9p)

(8) [reads] "college is a pleasant place to be." Yes. Why is it pleasant? Yes. Why? Why? Yes. Why is it? Oh yeah. It is pleasant, but why? why? Is it because we don't have to work? We can find pleasure in working. Maybe we can study what we want to study. Yes. That's one of the reasons. (SF6p)

(9) I don't know if I agree with her or not, but I do feel that some students do go to college to learn and some just go to do something or get away from home. Maybe she was trying to say that most students are not

in school because they want to be or because they want to learn. That may be true, but most of the students that I know, are people who want to go college to learn and become someone. Its just the people that I know in my area, but she's probably saying that its the whole United States . . . . Most students who I have have known that have gone to college are people who want to learn and their trying hard to finish their education. College may be a waste of time and money, but I do feel that its helping most people I know and Im happy that college is something available to help us better our education. People have different thoughts and feelings and what are we to do about it? (UA9e)

In Example (7), the student reads, thinks about the connections between what the text suggests and his own experience, questions the meanings of words and phrases, and then determines that he disagrees with the text. Excerpt (8) shows the student focusing on a sentence from the text and questioning its meaning, as well as the author's claim that college students go to school to avoid forms of work. The student ultimately answers his questions by referring to his own experience. Example (9) illustrates both a high level of interaction and a circumspection of assertion that is characteristic of Alaska Native student writing. The writer clearly disagrees with the author's statement that college is a waste of time, but she carefully modifies her statements with an overabundance of qualifying phrases and modal auxiliaries, e.g., "That may be true, but most of the students I know . . . . [6] The writer acknowledges that what the author says may apply to some people, but in her own personal experience, with the people she knows, it does not. The final sentence exemplifies a characteristic reluctance to support a generalized viewpoint to the exclusion of others.

Asian students tended to be more straightforward in their disagreement. In one case, an Asian student's orientation toward the text took the form of questioning its authority, as in (10):

(10 I disagree with it because college is not a waste of time and money and what he wrote here is just his personal opinion. This is not a fact that there is no statistic support [for], there is no statistic supports. (SF15p)

We can assume that this student brings to the reading an expectation that claims must be supported by quantitative data.

In all of these examples of orientation toward text, the students are working directly with the reading passage—questioning words, structure, and author's intentions. We can conclude that for these students, reading-to-write involves accounting for some meaning that was intended by the author.

---

[6]This feature of Alaska Native student writing and its pragmatic applications is described in Basham & Kwachka (1991).

In general, the protocols and essays of students in the Latino and the Alaska Native groups demonstrated less evidence of orientation to the text than did the Asian students. In addition, the protocols of Asian students demonstrated a variety of text-based strategies, such as rereading, looking up the meanings of words, and asking grammatical questions. The Alaska Native students, on the other hand, were less likely to return to the text over and over until it became familiar; rather, they either abandoned the question or returned to the instructions to see if they were "doing it right." The Latino students spent little or no time either deliberating about the meaning of the text or becoming familiar with it.

ORIENTATION TOWARD TASK

In this category are examples of repeated references to the instructions, as well as evidence of students' struggles to figure out what they were expected to do. Not surprisingly, all of the examples of this orientation came from the transcripts, as in examples (11)–(14) below:

(11) Let me look at the title first. [reads task] State the main idea. OK. . . . "and then discuss that idea, referring to your own knowledge or current examples, observations and experiences." Discuss. Let me look at the book. It has the definition of discuss. (SF12p)

(12) Write the main idea . . . I have to quote, quote this sentence and I agree or disagree of it . . . [later] I agree. Oh God, oh I don't quite get it how to do this . . . I can't get it. I stated the main idea, so right now, what I have to do is to discuss the main idea, to discuss, so if stated the main idea, do I have to say from which article? I think I should say according to Caroline Bird, and she say this. (SF13p)

(13) A: I think this is what we're suppose to do I'm not sure if we're doing this right.

(14) [reads "referring to your own knowledge of current examples" . . . . [pause] okay. I'm pretty sure on the first one I just sort of talked about it already. (UA12p)

The student in (11) raises questions relevant to the task and even consults a reference book for a definition of *discuss*. In (12), the writer assumes that the task is to quote from the reading passage; it is quite likely that this assumption is related to a traditional Chinese view of literacy, which places a high value on exact quotation. In (13), two students discuss what it is they're supposed to do, orienting themselves to the task. The writer in (14) very carefully checks what she is doing against the written instructions. In some cases, students who demonstrate a strong task orientation spend much of their time figuring out what they are expected to do and how they are supposed to do it, and comparatively little time interacting with the reading passage or discussing the topic.

Orientation Toward Topic

As stated earlier, the tendency for students to talk or write about their own ideas to the exclusion of any explicit reference to the reading passage was categorized as an orientation towards topic. While there were students in each group who exhibited this tendency, it was the dominant characteristic of the Latino group. The majority of Latino students, however, spent little time negotiating the meaning of either the text or the task. In their protocols they were mainly concerned with "talking up" the topic, using the text as a "jumping-off point" for their own thinking, as Examples (15)–(16) illustrate:

> (15) OK, well, uh, in thinking about passage A, I think that this, uh, what this woman Caroline Bird writes is very true, no? A lot of these college students are not there, uh, because they want it or they like it, no? They just get pushed by their parents and by school, by society, by TV, by magazines, by teachers, by everyone, that you have to go to college in order to make it. You are not going to be able to survive. Which is not true, I mean, uh, not all the people, not all the successful people out there, uh, have a college degree, no? Umm, there's a lot of rich people out there who didn't finish grade school or something, no? They are the few, no? But, I mean, still, ah, with a college degree you still have your stupid McDonald's jobs, no? I mean, college people still get those junky jobs, so what's the use of spending four years or more in your college and still work for, ja! crap, no? . . . (WS4p)

> (16) [Initially done in Spanish and translated by the student when transcribing] I am not agree with passage A because I don't think that nobody is forced to go to school. This passage reminds me of my uncle because I just got here (in U.S.) three years ago and I finished high school and now I go to college and his sons are here since 1976 and the guys none of them finished high school. They are working on construction and because I go to college I think he's a little jealous . . . . (WS11p)

Examples (15)–(16), taken from the beginnings of two students' protocols, show that these students see their task to be a response to the general topic of the reading passage. Some of the Latino students, such as the one in example (15), produced lengthy protocols in which they offered a series of personal experiences in response to a single phrase or sentence from the text. The Latino students' protocols show few specific references to the text after the first reading of it. For these students, the text was not a particularly important aspect of their meaning-making; instead, they saw the reading-to-write task as essentially a brainstorming technique—

something to jar their memories and elicit an opinion. Their essays also clearly reflect this orientation. Aside from an initial reference to the author and title of the text in their first paragraphs (a requirement of the assignment reiterated many times in class by the teacher), the Latino essays focused on the students' own examples and experiences and rarely referred back to the reading passage through paraphrase, summary, or quotation.

CONCLUSIONS

Categorizing the data according to these three orientations, while admittedly very general, allows us to see differences among the groups that point the way to further investigation. Well aware of the dangers of making statements about cultural groups as a whole based on a small sample, we nonetheless feel comfortable in drawing the following generalizations from the students' protocols: Latino students tended to orient themselves more toward the topic, while Asian and Alaskan students oriented themselves more toward the text and the task, though with different levels of personal authority and conviction.

These results differ from those of Flower *et al.*, who found that the L1 students oriented themselves primarily toward the text. While the stronger writers in their study moved from an initial text orientation (evidenced by an emphasis on summary early in the protocols) to a "transformation" of the text that accounted for their own ideas and experiences in rhetorically persuasive essays, the weaker writers remained text-oriented, producing essays that were essentially detailed summaries of the source text. There is little evidence in Flower *et al.*'s study with L1 writers of primary orientations toward either task or topic. Although some of the students in their study were unsure of what was expected of them in the reading-to-write task, they tended to solve the dilemma of task representation by spending more time summarizing. Flower *et al.* attribute this strategy to the effects of American schooling.

We suggest that successful performance on an academic reading-to-write task requires more than "critical thinking," a cognitive strategy; it also requires an understanding of the sociocultural framework within which this literacy act takes place. One aspect of this framework is the relationship of the student writer to the reading passage and hence to its author. When that author comes from a very different cultural background and perhaps presents a viewpoint that is in conflict with that of the reader, the task of re-presenting the text (summarizing) becomes more difficult. A second sociocultural factor is the relationship of the student writer to the reader (in most cases, a teacher). For students who have been socialized to demonstrate to a parent or teacher what they know, regardless of how well they know it, the task of writing about reading will no doubt be seen in light of those expectations. However, students who have been socialized (whether at home or at school) to wait until knowledge is personal (i.e., until it can be claimed as one's own) before demonstrating it will have more difficulty discerning the appropriate rules for performing the task.

We feel that an understanding of cultural differences in attitudes toward literacy and literate practices such as reading-to-write can enhance our effectiveness in teaching both reading and composition to students for whom English is a second language. For Asian students, who are traditionally oriented toward the text, more emphasis might be placed on developing and expressing their own ideas in relation to the topic. For the Latino and Alaska Native students, more emphasis might be needed on demonstrating their interaction with the text and reporting the ideas of others.

Further, as a pedagogical issue, we suggest that think-aloud protocols such as the ones produced for this study can provide insights into the connections between reading and writing processes for ESL students. For example, for the Asian students it seemed that producing the transcript was a far more difficult task than writing the essay; there was evidence in most of the protocols of a fairly high level of interaction with the reading passage that did not translate into writing. It is clear from this study that ESL students need more explicit instruction in how to write essays that demonstrate an understanding of a reading passage through periodic references to the passage and that reflect their own thinking in relation to the topic.

This research was supported in part by a grant from the President's Research and Development Fund, San Francisco State University.

REFERENCES

Achiba, M. & Kuromiya, Y. (1983). Rhetorical patterns extant in the English composition of Japanese students. *JALT Journal, 5*, 1–13.

Atari, O. (1984). Oral style strategies in EFL written discourse: Implications for teaching college composition. Paper presented at Third Annual Linguistics Conference, Irbid, Jordan (ED 271–006).

Bartholomae, D. (1985). Inventing the university. In M. Rose (Ed.), *When a writer can't write* (pp. 134–175). New York: Guilford Press.

Basham, C. (1986). Summary writing: A study in textual and contextual constraints. Doctoral dissertation, The University of Michigan.

Basham, C. & Kwachka, P. (1991). Reading the world differently: A cross–cultural approach to writing assessment. In L. Hamp–Lyons (Ed.), *Assessing ESL writing* (pp. 55–75). Norwood, NJ: Ablex.

Bird, C. (1985). College is a waste of time and money. In C. Bird, *The case against college* (H. Mandelbaum, Ed.). New York: D. McKay.

Bizzell, P. (1986). What happens when basic writers come to college? *College Composition and Communication, 37*, 294–301.

Carrell, P. (1987). Content and formal schemata in ESL reading. *TESOL Quarterly, 21*, 461–481.

Connor, U. & McCagg, P. (1987). A contrastive study of English expository prose paraphrases. In U. Connor & R. Kaplan (Eds.), *Writing across languages: Analysis of L2 texts* (pp. 73–86). Reading, MA: Addison-Wesley.

Flower, L., Stein, V., Ackerman, J., Kantz, M.J., McCormick, K., & Peck, W.C. (1990). *Reading to write: Exploring a cognitive and social process.* New York: Oxford University Press.

Frestedt, M. & Sanchez, M. (1980). Navajo world view harmony in directives for English texts. Paper presented at the Annual Meeting of the University of Wisconsin–Milwaukee Linguistics Symposium, Milwaukee, WI (ED 193–661).

Galvan, M. (1985). The writing processes of Spanish–speaking bilingual/bicultural graduate students: An ethnographic perspective. Doctoral dissertation, Hofstra University (ED 870–0449).

Hu, Z., Brown, D.F., & Brown, L.B. (1982). Some linguistic differences in the written English of Chinese and Australian students. *Language Learning and Communication, 1*, 39–49.

Kaplan, R. (1987). Cultural thought patterns revisited. In U. Connor & R. Kaplan (Eds.), *Writing across languages: Analysis of second language text* (pp. 9–21). Rowley, MA: Newbury House.

Kaplan, R. (1966). Cultural thought patterns in intercultural education. *Language Learning, 16,* 1–20.

Kwachka, P. & Basham, C. (1990). Literacy acts and cultural artifacts: Extensions of English modals. *Journal of Pragmatics, 14,* 413–429.

Liebman–Klein, J. (1986, March) Toward a contrastive rhetoric: A rhetoric of process. Paper presented at the annual meeting of TESOL, Anaheim, CA (ED 271 963).

Matalene, C. (1985). Contrastive rhetoric: An American writing teacher in China. *College English, 47*(8), 789–808.

Mohan, B. & Lo, W.A. (1985). Academic writing and Chinese students: Transfer and development factors. *TESOL Quarterly, 19*(3), 515–534.

Ricento, T.K. (1987). Aspects of coherence in English and Japanese expository prose. Doctoral dissertation, University of California.

Schecter, S. & Harklau, L. (1991). *Writing in a non–native language: An annotated bibliography.* Technical Report No. 51. U.C./Berkeley: National Center for the Study of Writing and Literacy.

Scollon, R. & Scollon, S. (1991). Eight legs and one elbow: Stance and structure in Chinese English compositions. In R. Scollon & S. Scollon, *Launching the literacy decade: Awareness into action.* Second North American Conference on Adult and Adolescent Literacy Conference Report (pp. 46–62). International Reading Association.

Spack, R. (1990). *Guidelines: A cross-cultural reading–writing text.* New York: St. Martin's.

CHAPTER 18

EPILOGUE

Reading and Writing: Integrating Cognitive and Social Dimensions

Gayle Nelson
Georgia State University

Many of us trained in the teaching of ESL were taught to separate language into four skill areas: reading, writing, speaking, and listening. On closer inspection, we realized that these four "separate skills" are intertwined and interrelated in many ways, some obvious and some about which we are just beginning to learn. This volume integrates reading and writing, providing a holistic approach to that relationship and examining many of its complexities. Eskey (this volume) refers to reading and writing as "complementary halves of the literacy skills." Recognizing the relationship between reading and writing is a first step; understanding the nature of the relationship requires many more.

The organization of this volume into the cognitive and social dimensions of reading and writing, in part represents the historical evolution of reading and writing research and theory from a focus on the cognitive dimension to an emerging awareness of the social dimension. This emerging social dimension recognizes, for example, that in academic discourse communities, students read to write, that these two processes are not practiced in isolation from each other. In addition, the organization suggests that although the processes of reading and writing occur in a sociocultural context, we need not abandon strictly cognitive inquiry. Both cognitive and social inquiry have their own place (Flower, 1990).

In this concluding chapter, I illustrate the inseparable connection between the cognitive and social dimensions of literacy, suggesting that both literacy itself and the way we perceive literacy are embedded in context. First, I discuss the cognitive dimension of literacy, focusing on the sociocultural factors contributing to an individualistic view of reading and writing. Next, I discuss the social dimension of literacy: the multilayered dimension of context. Finally, the interaction between the cognitive and social dimensions of literacy is illustrated by selected chapters from this volume.

COGNITIVE DIMENSION: FOCUS ON THE INDIVIDUAL

Until recently, cognitive reading and writing researchers have tended to focus on the psycholinguistic processes of the individual, investigating the cognitive interaction between the individual and a text and asking, What cognitive processes occur when an individual reads and writes?

This individualistic, "solo-performer view" of literacy (Gere, 1987, p. 75), more common in the writing literature but equally applicable to reading (Miller, 1987), developed from several interrelated directions, including psychology, linguistics, and English/composition. Gere suggests that psychology's contribution to the solo-performer view can be traced to the work of Jean Piaget. She states:

> In his description of maturation, Piaget emphasizes the individual's transition from egocentrism (which puts the self at the center) to a more decentered perspective (which enables one to see from others' viewpoints). Although Piaget's theory assumes that the process of development is aided by socialization, it assigns an asocial genesis to egocentric speech. In other words, encounters with others help individuals develop decentered language, but egocentric speech originates within the individual, not from social interaction. (p. 77)

Gere further suggests that Piagetian theory developed from a Cartesian epistemology. Both emphasize the separation of the individual from society and focus on the nature of individual thought.

During the last three decades, the field of linguistics, dominated by Chomsky's distinction between competence and performance, has also encouraged a writer-as-solo-performer tradition (Bleich, 1989). It was thought that "if we could understand a single person's 'competence,' we would then understand the language competence of all people" (p. 16). Performance or language in use is not of particular interest to Chomsky; it merely represents different manifestations of competence. Within Chomsky's paradigm, social interaction (input) is necessary to trigger the acquisition of language, but beyond this initiating function, social context is of little or no interest.

The view of writing as a solitary act also has deep roots in the traditions of English literature, exemplified by authors such as Virginia Woolf writing in a room of her own. This romantic image of "the solitary writer, lost in a private war with words" (Ackerman, 1990, p. 173) has been perpetuated by countless English teachers and by writers themselves. More recently, composition theorists and researchers have contributed to the individualistic view of writing with the research on the composing processes of individuals. As Gere (1987) points out, Janet Emig (1971), one of the first researchers to investigate the composing process of native speakers of English, asked individual students to compose aloud. In presenting her findings in *The Composing Process of Twelfth Graders*, Emig focused on the students' individual thoughts. Gere notes that although Emig's students comment about their peers and demonstrate their peers' contributions to their understanding of themselves as writers, Emig chooses to mention them only in passing, thus fostering an "author-centered view of writing" (p. 79).

Johns (1990), elaborating on the work of Faigley (1986), suggests yet another group that contributed to the notion of the individualistic nature of writing—the expressivists. The expressivists view writing as an expression of self and include Donald Murray, Ken Macrorie, and Peter Elbow. For the expressivists, writing is an individual act. Competent writers establish purpose, meaning, and form, and create an audience that conforms to their texts and purposes (Nystrand, 1986). Teachers espousing expressivism encourage students to write for themselves and to find their own voice. Elbow (1981) best characterizes the individualistic nature of expressivism when he suggests that the goal of writing should be to move toward a condition in which one doesn't need an audience in order to write and speak well.

This individualistic view of literacy exists as part of a sociocultural context that has fostered a particular perspective. Although this individualistic perspective does not pay much credence to the larger social community, it was in fact created and sustained by the sociocultural forces discussed above.

SOCIAL DIMENSION: FOCUS ON CONTEXT

Interest in and research on the social dimension of reading and writing was not an abrupt departure from cognitive research. In fact, research on the reading and writing processes of individual students in part led to an awareness that cognition is embedded in context, that reading and writing have a multilayered social dimension (Applebee, 1984; Flower, 1990). Neither students nor teachers walk into class as blank slates. They bring numerous assumptions and expectations about literacy, about the teaching and learning of literacy, about education, and about the ways individuals relate to each other in the classroom. They also bring the values, attitudes, and behaviors of their home cultures and subcultures. All of these factors and more make up the social dimension of reading and writing.

The complexity of the social dimension is illustrated by Ackerman (1990). In his discussion of American university students, Ackerman specifies seven social contexts for native speakers of English: 1) reading and writing in society, 2) schooling, 3) discourse communities, 4) linguistic and rhetorical practice in communities, 5) classrooms, 6) assignments, and 7) a student's own intellectual history. When considering non-native speakers of English, these seven contexts are compounded to include their home cultures as well.

Ackerman states that reading and writing "are learned technologies that reflect the cultural needs of a society" (p. 179). These needs tend to become the purposes for which individuals learn to read and write. A major study investigating the role, functions, and cognitive effects of literacy in society was conducted by Scribner & Cole (1981) who studied the Vai in Liberia. The Vai invented a writing system that consists of two hundred characters with a core of twenty to forty characters. The Vai also have two other literacies, English and Arabic. English is learned in government or mission schools and is primarily used for government matters, such as maintaining court records and corresponding with political administrators, and Arabic is frequently learned in "schools" around a fire where students memorize and recite verses from the Qur'an. Arabic is primarily used for religious practices although it is occasionally used for correspondence, personal notes, and trade records. Individuals in the Vai community do not necessarily know all three scripts. Some Vai are illiterate, others are literate in one script, and still others in two or three scripts.

In understanding the context of reading and writing in society, Scribner & Cole's study is helpful in that it provides an example of literacy that is not school-related. Vai is learned with the help of a friend. Their study also illustrates the importance of the purposes for which reading and writing are learned. Scribner & Cole suggest that "Literacy is not simply learning how to read and write a particular script, but applying this knowledge for specific purposes in specific contexts of use" (p. 236). Individuals learn Vai for the purposes of keeping personal journals and records (to preserve information over time) and writing personal letters (to transmit information over space).

The Vai practice of learning to read and write from a friend, however, is not the way in which reading and writing are usually transmitted. Reading and writing are more frequently learned in school. Society and school are in many ways reflections of each other in that the reading and writing instruction students receive in school reflects the purposes for which a society needs literacy. In school, students also learn the ways or styles of writing that are valued in their culture. Liebman (1992), for instance, in a study of Japanese and Arabic writing instruction, found that in Japanese schools, writing instruction emphasizes the expressive function of writing, whereas in Arabic schools, instruction tends to emphasize the transactional function of writing. In addition, studies in contrastive rhetoric (see Connor & Kaplan, 1987; Purves, 1988) demonstrate the existence of cultural differences in preferred styles of writing. These preferred discourse styles are generally taught in schools.

The complexity of context increases as we consider the existence of the innumerable discourse communities both within and outside of schools. In discussing discourse communities, it is helpful to consider Frank Smith's metaphor of a literacy club (Eskey, this volume). The literacy club metaphor suggests the existence and participation of other members, and of rules, conventions, traditions, and membership criteria. To become a member of a literacy club or a discourse community, individuals participate in the particular literacy of that community.

Discourse communities include not only the individuals who participate, but also the linguistic and rhetorical practices that occur in particular communities. Ackerman (1990) argues that a community's "preferred forms and uses of reading and writing . . . are the boundary markers for a literate context in that reading and writing are visible and permanent indices of social interaction" (pp. 179-180). In other words, the existence of shared discourse features is evidence of a social context, of the "social foundation behind a discipline, a discourse community, or a classroom" (p. 180). Bartholomae (1988) writes of the linguistic and rhetorical practices within universities. A student, he notes, "has to learn to speak our language, to speak as we do, to try on the peculiar ways of knowing, selecting, evaluating, reporting, concluding, and arguing that define the discourse of our community"; as a student moves from course to course, from an English class to a psychology class, the discourse changes, and the student writes "as a literary critic one day and an experimental psychologist the next" (p. 273).

The context that may be of most interest to language teachers is the classroom. The classroom context includes the space in which students and teacher interact, but more importantly, it includes a host of other factors, such as interactions between student and student, expected roles of teachers and students, classroom management, appropriate classroom behaviors, teaching styles, and communication styles. It is in classrooms that the linguistic and rhetorical conventions and rules for particular discourse communities are learned. The classroom, however, is also its own subculture, and "students must learn the highly patterned ways of thinking and behaving appropriate to it" (Furey, 1986, p. 16).

Within classrooms, the immediate context that usually cues the reader/writer to action is the reading or writing assignment or task. The particular type of assignment relates to the other contexts: to literacy in society, in school, in discourse communities, and in the classroom. In learning Arabic, for example, the Vai are assigned Qur'anic verses to read and memorize. This assignment relates to the primary purpose of Arabic in Vai society, to recite Qur'anic verses during religious practices.

Although these spiraling dimensions of context may be similar for readers and writers within a particular subculture, each reader and writer also has his or her own personal interpretation, perspective, or point of view based on personal background and experience. This personal history is part of the context of reading and writing and affects readers' interpretations of texts and writers' interpretations of tasks. It also affects the content, organization, and style of writers' texts.

In addition to Ackerman's perspectives on context, the social dimension of writing also involves the relationship between the writer and the reader. Most texts are written to be read. Writers draw on their knowledge of writing and other knowledge of the world and attempt to compose a text to be interpreted by a reader. Stein (1990) describes this composing process:

> [W]riters generate a number of representations that may grow in purpose, fullness, and coherence as ideas develop . . . [T]he creation of such representations involves the selection, organization, and connection of ideas. That is to say, the text [a writer] produces must not only reflect her understanding of the topic and the world, it must also be shaped so that the reader can draw on shared knowledge to get the author's point as she intends it. These two goals—to say what is meant and to make that meaning accessible—and the processes that support them—invention and audience adaptation—shape the representation of meaning. (p. 147)

In her representation of the writing process, Stein highlights the important function of audience as shaper of the writers' words. It is the readers' responses to written texts that let writers know if they (writers) have said "what they meant" and if that meaning is accessible to the readers. It is here, at the juncture among writer, text, and reader that the social dimension of writing becomes clear. The writer draws on shared (social) knowledge and experience to create a text that is read by readers (social).

INTERACTION OF THE COGNITIVE AND SOCIAL DIMENSIONS OF READING AND WRITING

How does this complex, multilayered social dimension relate to the reading–writing process, that process described as a cognitive interaction between an individual and a text? As Flower (1989) points out, we "have little precise understanding of how these different processes feed on one another" (p. 282). Flower goes on, however, to suggest that as we move away from the view of writer as solo performer, "we see the ways other people, the past, and the social present contribute to the production of a text, through cultural norms, available language, intertextuality, and through the more directly social acts of assignment giving, collaboration, and so on" (p. 287). In other words, Flower suggests that although we don't understand exactly how the social dimensions or context of reading and writing affect cognition and vice versa, we know most certainly that the two dimensions interact in some way.

Flower suggests three possible principles or relationships between context and cognition. One relationship is that cognition mediates context. As Flower notes, "Context is a powerful force. However, it does not produce a text through immaculate conception" (p. 289). Context is mediated by the cognition of the reader/writer; cognition is the agent. The research findings of Flower *et al.* (1990) support the power of cognition to interpret and modify context. Their findings suggest that students from similar backgrounds interpret a shared writing assignment in different ways. Students in the study set different goals in creating their writing tasks, used different criteria in monitoring and evaluating their tasks, and called on different strategies for implementing their writing goals. These results indicate that cognition interprets context. The directionality of this relationship is

context ◄─────── cognition

Another possible relationship is that context shapes cognition. This view suggests that cognitive action "is often initiated in response to a cue from the environment" (Flower, 1989, p. 287); context determines or prompts the reader/writer's thinking. Context cues cognition in multiple ways. It affects us in the form of past experience and related assumptions and expectations. It affects how we think and what we see. Context functions as a cue to action; it triggers specific cognitive processes. The direction of the relationship is

context ───────► cognition

The third relationship is interactive and recognizes "both the mediating power of cognition and the directive cues of context" (p. 291). This interaction suggests that context influences but does not control cognition; the cognition of the reader/writer interprets and makes sense of context. Flower acknowledges the enormous role context plays in our thinking, reading, and writing, but also acknowledges that "within this looming landscape of internalized forces we do not control," human agency and intention assert themselves (p. 292). This relationship can be represented as

context ◄───────► cognition

This third relationship suggests that although cognition is shaped and affected by the context of an individual's culture, past experiences, schooling, and current situation, it is not a passive recipient; it does not merely react to external forces. Once cognition is created, it acts. The cognition of individual readers and writers perceives and interprets contexts differently, and by doing so—by perceiving differently and interpreting—it changes the context. Neither cognition nor context is static; they continually react to and change the other.

The following descriptions of reading and writing tasks illustrate the inextricable and reflexive relationship between cognition and context. Two specific examples illustrate this interaction, one for reading and another for writing: 1) A teacher assigns a reading text (context); students process the words on the pages (cognition), interpreting the meaning of the text (cognition) based on past experience (context) and possibly past schooling (context). The processing of the reading text (cognition) is also influenced by the reader's purpose (context) in reading. 2) A teacher assigns students a writing task (context); students interpret the writing task (cognition); students' interpretations of the writing task are influenced by past schooling and past experiences (context); students think about ideas and begin to write, organize, evaluate, rewrite, reorganize, and edit (cognition). The decisions they make on what to write about, how to write, and how to organize are based on past schooling and past experiences (context). The point here is that cognition always occurs in context. Therefore, although Flower's three relationships are theoretically interesting, they are not all possible. The relationship between cognition and context must be

context ◄————————► cognition

Many of the chapters in this volume focus on one part of this relationship, either on cognition or social context. In some chapters, the second part of the relationship is implicit; in other chapters it is explicit. What follows is a discussion of selected chapters that illustrate the continual interplay between the cognitive and social dimensions of reading and writing. The component of context that may be most salient to ESL teachers is the social context of the classroom. It is the classroom that we can, to use Flower's term, "socially engineer." The following discussion will also address a question of interest to ESL teachers: How can we orchestrate the social dimension of the classroom in such a way to facilitate students' development as readers and writers?

Chapters Focusing on the Cognitive Dimension

Two chapters (Connor & Carrell, Sarig) in this volume focus on the reading and writing processes of individual students. Each describes a study that in some way investigates cognition's ability to interpret and modify context, in particular, students' processing of specific tasks. Although the context/cognition relationship is interactive, the directionality that is of primary interest to these researchers is

context ◄———————— cognition

Two other chapters (Gadjusek & vanDommelen, Spack) focus on students' cognitive development as readers and writers.

Connor and Carrell's study focuses on the cognitive processes of individual students who interpret an essay prompt and write an essay, and on reader/raters who interpret the essay prompt and rate the essay. Although Connor & Carrell investigate cognitive processes by asking individual students to think aloud, social context is implicit in their study. The essay task (context) functions as a cue from the environment that initiates cognition. In addition, the choices students make as writers are conditioned by their past histories as writers (context) and the choices the reader/raters make as evaluators of written texts are influenced by their history as writers, readers of student writing, and raters trained in a specific method of evaluating student texts (context).

Their findings indicate that both the students and raters spent time considering specific tasks—to produce an essay and to give a particular score—and were more concerned about language use, content, and development of ideas than about organization. Raters thought that text-internal organization (e.g., coherence), fluency, and the general development of ideas were more important than organization and attention to task prompt. Raters' concerns with language use and text-internal organization are illustrated by the following rater comments, "but still there are a lot of grammar mistakes" and "I tended to lose some of the coherence."

Although their study addresses the cognitive half of the cognition/context relationship, the findings have implications for the social context of the ESL classroom. If the criteria used in this study are typical of American faculty who evaluate the writing of non-native speakers, then ESL instructors need to be aware of the evaluation criteria. Raters in this study were relatively unconcerned with the overall rhetorical structure of the essay. The question of concern to classroom teachers who are preparing ESL students to enter the larger university community is this: Should we be focusing more on text-internal organization and fluency and less on overall rhetorical structure?

Also using think-aloud protocols, Sarig investigates the cognitive processes of one second language (L2) student while he is performing a reading-to-write task: composing a summary by synthesizing two newspaper articles. The social context is implicit. The task of composing a summary by synthesizing two newspaper articles is a component of the social context and affects the kind of cognitive activity that occurs (e.g., synthesis? evaluation?). The student's past history as a reader/writer also affects his interpretation and implementation of the task. Sarig's findings indicate that composing a summary is a recursive, interactive process in which the individual moves back and forth between reading/rereading and writing/rewriting and from planning to operating to assessing, from assessing to operating to planning, and from operating to assessing to planning. Specifically, the cognitive activities involved are performing (e.g., reading, writing), clarifying (e.g., understanding previously unknown words or concepts), linking (e.g., using cohesion markers), transforming (e.g., producing a new text by deleting, adding, refining, or reconceptualizing), and revising (e.g., replacing a lexical item).

Sarig's findings as well as other considerations related to summary writing have implications for the social context of the classroom. First,

Sarig's findings indicate that at least one cognitive operation needs to be explicitly taught: reconceptualization (e.g., rearrangement of text by hidden topic of discourse or use of different rhetorical structure from the one used in the text). Students' difficulties in reconceptualization may be a result of past schooling where students learned that summary writing is paraphrasing the main idea of a text. Second, summarizing texts is a common writing task assigned by American university faculty (Horowitz, 1986). Thus, ESL students entering American academic discourse communities need to know summarizing skills. Finally, it is probable that summary writing varies from culture to culture. For example, American students tend to reframe a text, to demonstrate their own point of view in writing a summary, whereas Chinese students tend to closely adhere to original texts (Basham, Ray, & Whalley, this volume).

Spack argues for an ESL undergraduate writing program that begins with what individual students bring with them and moves to what their academic literacy communities will ultimately expect of them. She suggests that students need to understand academic articles through their personal experience, and describes the cognitive activities of students who read course texts and articles, think through their topics as they read, and make connections between prior and new knowledge. Spack presents pedagogical techniques that support and develop the kind of cognitive connections she's describing. For example, she suggests a write-before-you-read activity in which students write about an experience they've had that is related to the text they are going to read. Students then share their writing in small groups or with the whole class and eventually write about the academic article in terms of their own experiences.

Gadjusek and vanDommelen suggest that interaction with a literary text contributes to the critical thinking that is at the core of the writing process. They further suggest that specific classroom practices encourage this critical, analytical process of thinking. Although Gadjusek and vanDommelen begin their argument with the cognitive benefits, they move to the social arena of the classroom as the place where such critical thinking takes place. Merely reading literature does not necessarily result in critical thinking. It is the teacher's orchestration, the teaching, if you will, that guides students from concrete to abstract thinking and helps them develop specific critical thinking operations such as formulating and supporting opinions. In other words, teachers help students develop the thinking and writing skills to become members of American academic discourse communities.

Chapters Focusing on the Social Dimension

As suggested earlier, the social dimension or context of L2 reading and writing is multilayered and includes students' L1 and L2 cultures and languages. These contexts affect the ways in which students think, the ways in which they cognitively process reading and writing tasks. The directionality of the context/cognition relationship that these chapters address is:

context ──────────▶ cognition

As ESL teachers, the contexts that are likely to concern us are aspects of students' L1 cultures as they relate to reading and writing, and our own ESL reading/writing classrooms. For instance, we might ask: a) How do students' L1 cultures affect L2 reading and writing? b) How can ESL teachers create classroom conditions that facilitate students' development as readers and writers of English?

It appears that what students learn about reading and writing in their first languages transfers to reading and writing in their second languages. For example, the findings of Basham, Ray, & Whalley (this volume) suggest that students' native cultures affect how they interpret and perform reading-to-write tasks. Their findings suggest that Asian students demonstrate a strong orientation toward text, using passages from the reading text in their written responses. This text orientation probably derives from their L1 literacy, which emphasizes reading a text until it is familiar. Alaska Native students, on the other hand, demonstrate a more personal orientation toward the text and Latino students use the reading text as a "jumping-off point" for their own ideas. These differences in orientations to texts are most likely related to differences in students' L1 reading/writing orientations. This study illustrates but one example of how notions of reading and writing in students' first languages affect reading and writing in a second language. Research in contrastive rhetoric (see Leki, 1991 for a review) suggests that students also use L1 rhetorical patterns when writing in an L2.

The second, and possibly most important, context for ESL teachers is the social context of the classroom. Although we know little about how our classroom social engineering affects cognitive processing, we can make informed decisions based on current research and theory. We can structure our classes so that, to the best of our knowledge, the social environment contributes to our students' becoming better readers and writers.

Various ways of designing courses that contribute to students' development as readers and writers are illustrated by chapters in this volume (Collignon, Goldstein, Johns). One type of course design focuses on students' discourse communities. Examples include adjunct or sheltered ESL courses that focus on academic discourse communities and ESL classes designed for specific job-related discourse communities. Teachers can, for example, design a task-based syllabus that focuses on the tasks students need to perform as participants of a particular literacy club. The literacy club may be the club of academe (Goldstein, Johns) or the club of work (Collignon). In adjunct or sheltered ESL courses, students read and write texts (e.g., lab reports, research papers) related to their academic disciplines and courses. In work-related ESL courses, students read and write texts (e.g., business letters, memoranda, daily logs) that are identical or similar to the reading and writing tasks they perform at work. In both, students are reading and writing authentic texts and are reading and writing about common themes (e.g., their academic disciplines, their jobs).

By creating courses in which students read and write texts related to tasks they need to perform, ESL instructors are contributing to students' cognitive development as readers and writers in at least three ways. First, when reading and writing for purposes that they perceive as authentic and useful, students tend to be more motivated (Goldstein). Second, when reading and writing on a central theme (e.g., reading and writing for engineering, reading and writing in the helping professions), students develop a body of knowledge that should lead to increased reading comprehension and improved writing (Spivey, 1990). Third, in using authentic reading and writing tasks, teachers are helping students in an area that is likely to cause problems in reading-to-write tasks: task representation (Spivey, 1990). Collignon, for example, addresses the issue of task representation by asking students to identify their own writing needs (i.e., their writing tasks at work) and bring work-related discourse to class (e.g., inter-office memos), thus providing authentic representations of task.

Other types of ESL courses also contribute to students becoming better readers and writers. It appears that an increasing number of ESL reading and writing classes include opportunities for students to interact with their peers in ways that facilitate the cognitive processes of reading and writing. One use of peer interaction in a reading class is illustrated by Blanton (this volume), who describes a reader-based pedagogy that focuses on ESL students' responses and interpretations to reading texts. Her emphasis is on students connecting to texts by intertwining the "story" of the text into their own "stories." In such a class, students read texts, share their responses to texts with their peers, write responses to texts, and read these responses, creating an in-class social environment of students talking to each other about their interpretations of texts. By personally connecting with texts, students are using cognitive processes that go deeper than merely a superficial understanding of a reading text; they are connecting the reading text to their own knowledge (Carrell, 1983a; 1983b).

Connecting textual material to one's background knowledge is also important in the process of writing (Spivey, 1990). In addition, the reader-based pedagogy as described by Blanton contributes to students' development as writers in two additional ways. As students write responses to texts, read each other's responses, and write parallel texts, they are 1) functioning as an audience for other student writers, and 2) engaging in the cognitive processes of exploring, forming, clarifying, and reforming ideas (Zamel, 1983).

One use of peer interaction in an L2 writing course is described by Benesch (this volume). She proposes a reading-to-write course in which students first read an autobiography such as *Two Years in the Melting Pot*, by Liu Zongren, a Chinese journalist's account of his two years in Chicago, and then write their own autobiographies. During the weeks in which students are writing, other students and the teacher serve as an audience, reading chapters of the autobiographies and providing extensive feedback. Benesch has selected an autobiography about which her students have prior knowledge: a non-native speaker's impressions of the United States. She has, therefore, chosen a text that is likely to result in efficient reading comprehension. She has also designed a course that is likely to facilitate students' development as writers. Students in Benesch's class, working with other students and the instructor, participate in the cognitive activities of setting and resetting goals, generating ideas for chapters, elaborating on ideas, writing, and revising. In fact, 16 class sessions (36 hours) are scheduled for revision, and students review what they have previously written and answer their peers' and teachers' questions by adding new information. Zamel (1983) found that good writers revise frequently. Benesch's course allows time for students to reform their ideas and not merely make surface changes in the revision process.

CONCLUSION

As human beings we exist not only as individuals but as members of cultures and subcultures, and the acts in which we participate exist in the context of these cultures. It is impossible for an act or event to exist without social context or to be culture-free. Languages are social constructs and as such belong to the larger culture, which is learned, shared, and passed on through interaction with others. What general patterns emerge from the recognition of the social dimension of reading and writing?

First, the chapters in this volume suggest that, just as there is no single "correct" way to read or write, there is also no one "best" method to teach reading and writing. However, although this volume offers no final answers, it suggests important emerging patterns in the teaching of reading and writing that recognize the sociocultural dimensions of literacy. One pattern relates to ESL instructors' using authentic reading texts and writing tasks from students' L2 discourse communities. One means of accomplishing this is through adjunct or sheltered ESL courses. Another means is by acquiring authentic reading and writing texts or assignments from academic programs, work sites, or other situations in which students read and write. A related issue for students entering academic discourse communities is the need to learn typical academic rhetorical structures, an academic style of writing, and common academic tasks such as summarizing and synthesizing. If students are reading and writing to become full-fledged members of discourse communities, they are reading and writing for an authentic purpose; they are reading for content and meaning.

Second, these chapters suggest that specific classroom practices can make the social nature of writing more explicit and can contribute to students' understanding of the reading/writing relationship. For instance, in a writing class, the use of peer response groups in which students respond to their peers' texts-in-progress contributes to students' understanding that writing produces a text that is read by someone other than the writer. This in-class dynamic of students' writing texts, reading other students' texts, and rewriting texts can heighten students' awareness of the connection between reading and writing. Kroll (this volume) emphasizes the importance of this awareness and stresses that a student needs to read like a writer to learn to write like a writer, and to write like a reader, to be aware of oneself as "a writer producing reading, not a writer producing writing."

The final pattern relates to connections between the literacy task and students' experiences and backgrounds. This connection takes at least two forms. One is the personal experiences of students. For example, Benesch uses students' experiences of adjusting to the United States by asking them to read and write an autobiography about their adjustments. She suggests that such a connection leads to more efficient reading and improved writing. The second connection is between the task and students' L1 discourse communities and cultures. What students have learned in their home cultures affects their understanding of the task and their notions of "good" written texts, "good" group interaction, proper student/teacher relationships, correct classroom behaviors and activities, and effective communication styles.

This volume, however, represents more than practical applications for the ESL classroom. It calls for a new way of *thinking about* the reading/writing relationship. This new way of thinking recognizes that reading and writing are inextricably and reflexively connected, that a written text is a reading text, that we read to write and write to be read, and that reading and writing are similar processes of meaning making. It also recognizes that we use reading and writing within a specific context and that this context gives a purpose and a form to what we do. To paraphrase Geertz (1983), expert writers become experts by attaining the local knowledge that enables them to write as members of a discourse community. In other words, no one can universally be an expert writer; the notion of "expert writer" must be grounded in a specific sociocultural context.

REFERENCES

Ackerman, J. (1990). Translating context into action. In L. Flower, V. Stein, J. Ackerman, M.J. Kantz, K. McCormick, & W. Peck (Eds.), *Reading-to-write: Exploring a cognitive and social process* (pp. 173–193). New York: Oxford University Press.

Applebee, A.N. (1984). *Contexts for learning to write.* Norwood, NJ: Ablex.

Bartholomae, D. (1988). Inventing the university. In E.R. Kintgen, B.M. Kroll, & M. Rose (Eds.), *Perspectives on literacy* (pp. 273–285). Carbondale, IL: Southern Illinois University Press.

Bleich, D. (1989). Reconceiving literacy: Language use and social relations. In C.M. Anson (Ed.), *Writing and response: Theory, practice, and research* (pp. 15–36). Urbana, IL: NCTE.

Carrell, P.L. (1983a). Background knowledge in second language comprehension. *Language Learning and Communication, 2*, 25–34.

Carrell, P. L. (1983b). Some issues in studying the role of schemata, or background knowledge, in second language comprehension. *Reading in a Foreign Language, 1*, 81–92.

Connor, U. & Kaplan, R. (Eds.). (1987). *Writing across languages: Analysis of L2 texts.* Reading, MA: Addison-Wesley.

Elbow, P. (1981). *Writing with power: Techniques for mastering the writing process.* New York: Oxford University Press.

Emig, J. (1971). *The composing process of twelfth graders.* Urbana, IL: NCTE.

Faigley, L. (1986). Competing theories of process: A critique and a proposal. *College English, 48*, 527–542.

Flower, L. (1990). Introduction: Studying cognition in context. In L. Flower, V. Stein, J. Ackerman, M.J. Kantz, K. McCormick, & W. Peck (Eds.), *Reading-to-write: Exploring a cognitive and social process* (pp. 3–32). New York: Oxford University Press.

Flower, L. (1989). Cognition, context, and theory building. *College Composition and Communication, 40*, pp. 282–311.

Flower, L., Stein, V., Ackerman, J., Kantz, M.J., McCormick, K., & Peck, W. (Eds.). (1990). *Reading-to-write: Exploring a cognitive and social process.* New York: Oxford University Press.

Furey, P.R. (1986). A framework for cross-cultural analysis of teaching methods. In P. Byrd (Ed.), *Teaching across cultures in the university*

ESL program (pp. 15–28). Washington, DC: National Association of Foreign Student Affairs (NAFSA).

Geertz, C. (1983). *Local knowledge.* New York: Basic Books.

Gere, A.R. (1987). *Writing groups: History, theory, and implications.* Carbondale, IL: Southern Illinois University Press.

Horowitz, D.M. (1986). What professors actually require: Academic tasks for the ESL classroom. *TESOL Quarterly, 20,* 445–462.

Johns, A.M. (1990). L1 composition theories: Implications for developing theories of L2 composition. In B. Kroll (Ed.), *Second language writing: Research insights for the classroom* (pp. 24–36). Cambridge: Cambridge University Press.

Leki, I. (1991). Twenty-five years of contrastive rhetoric: Text analysis and writing pedagogies. *TESOL Quarterly, 25,* 123–143.

Liebman, J. (1992). Toward a new contrastive rhetoric: Differences between Arabic and Japanese rhetorical instruction. *Journal of Second Language Writing, 1*(2), 141–166.

Miller, J.H. (1987). *The ethics of reading: Kant, deMan, Eliot, Trollope, James, and Benjamin.* New York: Columbia University Press.

Nystrand, M. (1986). *The structure of written communication: Studies in reciprocity between writers and readers.* New York: Academic Press.

Purves, A. (Ed.). (1988). *Writing across languages and cultures: Issues in contrastive rhetoric.* Beverly Hills, CA: Sage Publications.

Scribner, S. & Cole, M. (1981). *The psychology of literacy.* Cambridge: Harvard University Press, 1981.

Spivey, N.N. (1990). Transforming texts: Constructive processes in reading and writing. *Written Communication, 7,* 256–287.

Stein, V. (1990). Elaboration: Using what you want to know. In L. Flower, V. Stein, J. Ackerman, M.J. Kantz, K. McCormick, & W. Peck (Eds.), *Reading-to-write: Exploring a cognitive and social process* (pp. 144–155). New York: Oxford University Press.

Zamel, V. (1983). The composing process of advanced ESL students: Six case studies. *TESOL Quarterly, 17,* 165–187.

AUTHOR INDEX

SUBJECT INDEX